MYSTICAL
CHRISTIANITY

MYSTICAL CHRISTIANITY

A Psychological Commentary on the Gospel of John

John Sanford

CROSSROAD • NEW YORK

1995

The Crossroad Publishing Company
370 Lexington Avenue, New York, NY 10017

Printed in the United States of America

Library of Congress Cataloging-in-Publication Data
Sanford, John A.
    Mystical Christianity : a psychological commentary on the Gospel
of John / John Sanford.
        p.   cm.
    Includes bibliographical references.
    ISBN 0-8245-1230-8; 0-8245-1412-2 (pbk.)
    1. Bible. N.T. John—Commentaries.   2. Mysticism.   I. Bible.
N.T. John English.   1993.   II. Title.
BS2615.3.S193   1993
226.5'07—dc20   92-35577
                                                                  CIP

This is not to say that Christianity is finished. I am, on the contrary, convinced that it is not Christianity, but our conception and interpretation of it that has become antiquated in the face of the present world situation. The Christian symbol is a living thing that carries in itself the seeds of further development. It can go on developing; it only depends on us, whether we can make up our minds to meditate again, and more thoroughly, on the Christian premise.

—C. G. Jung, *The Undiscovered Self*

Contents

INTRODUCTION TO
THE FOURTH GOSPEL

The Symbolic Method of Bible Interpretation

The Fourth Gospel can be likened to a kaleidoscope. If you turn a kaleidoscope now this way and now that way you will see it differently as various forms emerge, yet it is always one and the same kaleidoscope. So with the Fourth Gospel, if you view it now one way and now another you will see it differently, yet it is always one and the same Gospel.

Various commentators, in kaleidoscopic fashion, view the Gospel from different angles and so they see different things. Some commentators see in the Gospel a narrative that reflects the situation of the church at the time in which it was written. Others see in it a narrative that reflects the life and beliefs of a special segment of the church that they call the Johannine community. Still others see in the Gospel the result of a long line of historical development, and these commentators try to trace the major ideas of the Gospel back to historical sources. Pastors, on the other hand, may look to the Gospel for its ethical and pastoral teachings.

This present commentary, while not disparaging the above-mentioned viewpoints, will look at the Gospel as an expression of the mystical side of Christianity. By mystical I mean to refer to the Gospel's interior, psychological, and esoteric sense. My thesis will be that viewed from this perspective the Gospel proves to be *a treasure-house of psychological and spiritual insight.*

In looking for the interior or psychological meaning in John's Gospel I am not inventing a new hermeneutic (method of biblical interpretation) but am standing in an ancient hermeneutical tradition that goes back to the earliest Christian times. In ancient

Alexandria, for instance, which was at one time the most important center of Christian teaching, Origen and others of his school
of thought regarded the Scripture as having both a literal (*historia*
is the Greek word) and a spiritual sense (*theoria*).

The literal, or historical, sense of Scripture was its recounting of
actual events. The spiritual tradition, however, sought to arrive at
an understanding of the deeper meaning of Scripture, which was
often hidden in the text and could be grasped only by understanding the symbolic as well as literal meaning of Scriptural passages.
This method of interpreting Scripture, which was well developed in Alexandria, later found its most complete expression in
Antioch, where in the fourth century it was quite widespread,
especially among those churches influenced by Greek thought
and tradition. Here it found important adherents in the so-called
Cappadocian Fathers, especially Gregory of Nyssa, whose *Life of
Moses* and many other writings show the importance of finding an
inner meaning to Scripture as well as a historical and ethical one.[1]

The reason ancient biblical interpreters were open to the psychological or mystical method of Bible interpretation while most
modern commentators are not lies in the difference between
the ancient worldview and the modern worldview. Our present
Western consciousness is generally rationalistic, materialistic, and
extraverted in its attitude; therefore by and large we no longer
believe in the reality of an unseen spiritual world. In spite of the
insights of modern physicists who have exploded the old idea of
material reality as something solid and firm, most of us are still
encased in a materialistic way of thinking that believes that only
that which is perceivable by the senses, which lies outside of us,
and which can be made rational, exists or, at the least, is worth
taking seriously. In contrast, the worldview of the early church
led the early Christians to a more introverted attitude that directed their gaze into the world of the soul, which for them was a
living reality. This in turn enabled them to see the profound and
meaningful but irrational ways God worked throughout history,

---

1. This early hermeneutic was represented not only by Origen and Gregory of Nyssa,
but also by Irenaeus, Clement of Alexandria, Tertullian, Hippolytus, Methodius, Augustine, and many others. It remained prominent in Christian tradition until the twelfth
century and found some representatives even beyond that time. Its later adherents included Gregory the Great, Bernard of Clairvaux, John Scotus Erigena, Albertus Magnus,
Thomas Aquinas, and Joachim of Flora. It also seems to have influenced to a certain degree
the translators of the King James Version of the Bible, which lends itself more readily to
mystical and psychological interpretation than most modern translations.

in life, and in the soul itself to bring about the divine plan. For this reason the early Christian commentators were natural depth psychologists. They saw the soul as a battleground of archetypal forces and powers; for the most part they believed in dreams and visions as a way in which spiritual reality broke into human consciousness; indeed, some of them wrote treatises on dream interpretation. They also believed that God was working out the divine purpose in the whole sweep of history and also in the human soul itself.

Accordingly, as we have seen, early Christian Bible interpreters saw three dimensions to Bible interpretation: its historical or literal meaning, its moral or ethical meaning, and its spiritual or esoteric meaning. Early Christian biblical interpreters such as Gregory of Nyssa would have been adamantly opposed to both the fundamentalistic or exclusively literalistic point of view and also to the idea that the major ideas of the Bible are to be understood only in terms of their historical antecedents. For them a Bible passage was not completely understood until its symbolic or spiritual meaning had been comprehended. Only in this way could one relate to the Spirit who moved throughout the biblical narrative. An example is the way in which the early commentators dealt with numbers in the Bible. For them each number in the Bible had both a numerical and a symbolic meaning. Augustine was one of the many prominent representatives of this view. He once noted, "There is no one so foolish or absurd as to contend that [numbers] are so put in Scripture for no purpose at all, and that there are no mystical reasons why those numbers are there mentioned."[2] So important, in fact, was early Christian numerology, or number symbolism, that we will find ourselves referring to it quite often.

The basic difference between most ancient and most modern biblical interpretation, however, has to do with the different worldview that we have mentioned. From the ancient point of view, the world of the unseen, what we would call today "the

---

2. Augustine, *On the Trinity* 4.6. Number symbolism was almost universally used in the early church. All quotations from the writings of the Fathers are from *The Ante-Nicene Fathers: Translations of the Writings of the Fathers down to A.D. 325*, ed. Alexander Roberts and James Donaldson (Edinburgh, 1866–72, 10 vols.; reprint ed. Grand Rapids, Mich.: Eerdmans, 1981) or from *The Nicene and Post-Nicene Fathers of the Christian Church*, ed. Philip Schaff and Henry Wace (Buffalo and New York, 1886–90; first series of 14 vols., second series of 14 vols.; reprint ed. Grand Rapids, Mich.: Eerdmans, 1983).

unconscious" in the psychologies of Carl Jung and Fritz Kunkel, is as real, even more real than the world we apprehend through the senses of the body. For them the meaning that lies hidden within the literal meaning is an introduction to spiritual reality itself. As Thomas Merton once wrote: "What is hidden beneath the literal meaning is not merely another and more hidden meaning, it is also a new and totally different reality.... It is the divine life itself."[3]

The main emphasis of this commentary is to bring out the esoteric or psychological meaning of John's Gospel, hence the title "Mystical Christianity." However, modern scholars, while not always helpful with regard to the psychological content of Scripture, are quite helpful in many other ways, and I will often refer to helpful insights from the scholars, finding particularly useful the scholarly footnotes found in the Jerusalem Bible. Many serious students of the Fourth Gospel may wish to supplement the present commentary with the reading of other commentaries. Most of the remarks that complete this introduction are drawn from the hard work and skilled insights of contemporary Bible interpreters about the historical background of the Gospel, its authorship, and its structure.

The Historical Background to the Fourth Gospel

Historically the Fourth Gospel got off to a late start, most scholars reckoning that it was the last of the Gospels to be written. According to scholar E. R. Dodds, some Roman churchmen rejected the Gospel entirely, but by the time of Constantine the Great (early fourth century) it was regarded in the church as the most highly esteemed Gospel of them all.[4] Augustine tells us that even many of the Platonists were impressed by the Gospel of John. Part of its popularity lay in the fact that it appealed to intellectuals such as Neoplatonic philosophers and still retained its popularity with the common people, perhaps because of its many stories involving real people.

Of the four Gospels, Matthew, Mark, and Luke are so simi-

---

3. Thomas Merton, *Bread in the Wilderness* (Collegeville, Minn.: Liturgical Press, 1986), 166, quoted from Reinbert Herbert, "The Way of Angels," *Parabola* (Summer 1989): 86.

4. E. R. Dodds, *Pagan and Christian in an Age of Anxiety* (Cambridge: Cambridge University Press, 1965), 104.

lar they are called the "synoptic Gospels," meaning that they see things through "one eye." The synoptic Gospels share most of their stories in common. The Greek is also similar; expressions such as "the kingdom of God/heaven" occur in all of them; they have the same chronology of Jesus' life, and the Jesus they present is a Galilean who tells intriguing parables and utters his wisdom in relatively brief, pithy statements. However, when we come to the Fourth Gospel the atmosphere, and often also the facts, are markedly different. In John's Gospel we find fewer stories than in the synoptics, but much more use is made of each story for the purpose of teaching. Typically, a Johannine story is followed by a long discourse by Jesus on a theme the story introduces, a technique not found in the synoptics. The Jesus of the Fourth Gospel has a different personality from the Jesus of the synoptics; he is more the divine Christ than the human Jesus, and his statements are lofty and sometimes seem abstruse. The Greek of John's Gospel is also different; although the ideas in his Gospel are complex, the Greek is relatively simple. A beginner in New Testament Greek will want to translate John's Gospel first because it has the simplest sentence structure and the most basic vocabulary of any book in the New Testament except the three Epistles of John, which it closely resembles in language. The important expressions of the Fourth Gospel also differ from those of the synoptics; for instance, instead of the kingdom of God/heaven, we hear a lot about eternal life. Then there is the matter of the chronology and geographical setting. In the synoptics the stage is primarily Galilee; in John's Gospel most of the action takes place in Jerusalem. In the synoptics, Jesus goes to Jerusalem only once; in John's Gospel he goes three times. In the synoptics the Last Supper takes place on Passover Day; in John's Gospel Jesus is crucified on Passover Day.

There is also the matter of sources. John seems to have known Mark and Luke, but not Matthew, but mostly he relies on his own sources from which come the many stories we find in John but not in the synoptics. There is also a notable Hellenistic (Greek) and Platonic influence in John's Gospel and also, perhaps, an influence on John from the Gnostics and from the Essenes.

We have mentioned that John uses most of his stories as the basis for an extended discourse by Jesus. So extensive are these discourses that John's Gospel has generally been regarded as a didactic (teaching) Gospel. For this reason some biblical scholars say that the Fourth Gospel is more theological and the synoptics more historical. Yet the Fourth Gospel can also be surprisingly historical. For instance, John seems to be the only one who knows the name of the man whose ear Peter cut off — Malchus — and he includes this detail for no apparent reason except that it was a historical fact. He also gives us a minute description of the pool of Bethzatha, which appears to have been historically accurate. He was evidently intimately acquainted with the geography of Jerusalem, and Nicodemus and Joseph of Arimathea appear to have been his personal acquaintances. These historical details lend to the Gospel the ring of eyewitness truth.

While we miss the familiar parables of the synoptic Gospels, we do find in the Fourth Gospel, as we have noted, a great deal of symbolic language and many figures of speech. John's Jesus gives us long discourses based on images such as "the bread of life," "living water," "the true vine," and "the good shepherd." We also learn in John's Gospel about the special relationship of Christ to the Father: they are separate, yet one. Similarly, John's Gospel gives us a great deal of teaching about the Paraclete, the Spirit of Truth who will come to us after the resurrection of Jesus and lead us into all truth. Such theologically toned descriptions are only sparsely hinted at in the synoptics.

Perhaps most important of all is the systematic way the Fourth Gospel introduces various motifs in the Prologue and then weaves these motifs throughout the chapters that follow: light vs. darkness, above and below, seeing and not seeing, truth and falsehood, life and death, flesh and spirit. These dichotomies are absent in the synoptics.

The Fourth Gospel is tightly organized. It opens with a Prologue, which is followed by two introductory chapters. The next ten chapters (3–12) are about Jesus' public ministry; it is here that we find most of John's great stories. Then we have three chapters (14–16) devoted to Jesus' private ministry to the inner circle of disciples, followed by a single chapter (17), which is a soliloquy. Then comes the Passion story (18–20), which concludes the Gospel proper, although a later editor added chapter 21 as an appendix to deal with some unanswered questions. This structure gives us the impression that the Gospel was written by a single author who did his work quite carefully.

But who is this author? I've referred to "the Gospel of John" as a matter of convenience, but the fact is that we do not know for certain who the author is. Ancient texts seldom were identified by author, and if there was an author who was said to have written the document he was often not the actual author but a well-known person whose name was simply attached to the document. In the case of the Fourth Gospel, however, the text gives us some interesting information about a man who might well have been the author or, at least, a firsthand source of information: the "beloved disciple."

In chapter 21:20–23 we are told of "the disciple Jesus loved" who was following Jesus and Peter. Verse 21:24 seems to be a final ascription to the Gospel as it says, "This disciple is the one who vouches for these things and has written them down, and we know that his testimony is true." While this disciple is never named, other references to him (13:23; 18:15; 20:2f.) lead us to believe he was a close friend of Peter. Tradition has almost unanimously said that this man was the author of the Gospel and that he was, furthermore, the disciple John, son of Zebedee, the Galilean fisherman who was Peter's close companion.

However, there are serious objections to this viewpoint. Many scholars doubt that the simple and unlettered Galilean fisherman John could have written the polished Fourth Gospel, which shows all the signs of having been written by an educated man, trained in philosophical thought, with a sophisticated form of Greek at his disposal. Another objection is that whoever wrote the Gospel was intimately acquainted with Jerusalem. In fact, the author seems to have been well known in the inner priestly circles of Jerusalem; for this reason he has access to the chamber of the high priest.

Because of these facts, a number of scholars think the beloved disciple is not one of the twelve, but is an unknown disciple who lived in Jerusalem and was in a position of some influence. One possibility is that he was the friend of the man who owned the upper room in which the Last Supper was held. As a city-dweller he might have had a good education and been acquainted with the philosophical ideas current in his time. On the whole, this theory seems to account for more facts than the traditional theory, and we are left with the conclusion that the author of the Fourth Gospel is a man unknown to us, who partially reveals himself as the beloved disciple, who described Jesus' experiences in Jerusalem more than those in Galilee because he lived in Jerusalem, who had a wide circle of friends and contacts, possibly including such people as Nicodemus, and who wrote his Gospel in the latter decade of the first century C.E. However, for the sake of brevity and convenience we will continue to refer to the author of the Gospel as John and speak of John's Gospel, always keeping in mind, however, that we do not really know who the author is.

Whoever he was, the author of our Gospel was a religious genius who was uniquely in touch with the Christ. One possible outcome of his genius is that the Christ whose words we hear in the Fourth Gospel is not the historical Jesus from whom we hear in the synoptic Gospels, but the Risen or Cosmic Christ. This possibility will appear plausible to those who have experienced the technique of dialoguing with inner figures that C. G. Jung called "active imagination."

Jung showed that it is possible to bring into our living imagination figures or images from our dreams or other manifestations of our interior or spiritual life, and to engage these figures in a dialogue in which the image or figure interacts autonomously with the ego. In such a dialogue both the image or figure from an unconscious inner realm and the ego are autonomous and distinct. The resulting experience is active imagination. It must be made clear that nothing is made up in such an experience. The figures or images with which the ego dialogues are *real*. They simply have a different kind of reality than the materialistic reality we are used to.

There are some good examples of active imagination in the Bible. One is the dialogue between Elijah and Yahweh in the cave on Mt. Sinai after Elijah fled from Queen Jezebel. A second is Jesus' dialogue with Satan in the wilderness. Moses' dialogue with the voice of Yahweh coming from the burning bush is a third example.

This theory would account for the difference between the brief, pithy statements of Jesus in the synoptics and the lengthy discourses in the Fourth Gospel. It would also account for the abundant uses of images in the Fourth Gospel — for instance, the "true vine" and "living water" — and for the parable form of teaching that we find in Matthew, Mark, and Luke. Clearly the voice of Jesus in John's Gospel is more archetypal, and the voice of Jesus in the synoptics is more human. It is as though the synoptics recall the teaching of the man Jesus of Nazareth, and John brings to us the teaching he received from Christ in his personal postresurrection experiences with him. This being so, there is no contradiction between the messages of the Gospels. John's Gospel simply complements, and perhaps goes beyond, the other three.

This theory about the way in which the author of our Gospel derived his material may not be popular in our rationalistic age, but it is interesting that B. H. Streeter, a biblical scholar who wrote in the first half of this century, came up with much the same idea. Streeter expressed his dislike for the allegorical method of interpreting Johannine material that was commonly used in his day, because this method implied that John consciously invented or contrived many of his stories and discourses for the purposes of allegory. Instead he suggests that John's stories and discourses may have been seen and heard by him in a mystic trance. Streeter cites examples from the literature of mysticism in which the mystics show "a bewildering intermixture of history with dreams . . . which can hardly be understood save by those who realize the creative power of the mystical imagination." He concludes:

> A study of dream psychology and of visions recorded by mystics affords evidence that the solution of problems, on which the mind has pondered long and deeply, does sometimes come in the form of visions, the symbolism of which is quite as obvious and as elaborate in detail as that of allegories worked out by the conscious mind. And not infrequently these visions have a certain quality which, both at the moment of experiencing them and in subsequent reflection, compels conviction that they are veridical — that is, that they are not dreams or guesses, but revelations of actual fact.[5]

In short, the authority John relies on when he supplements the synoptic Gospels with unique material of his own may not be traceable to any historical sources, nor to consciously contrived allegories, but may come from his own intense inner experiences through some form similar to active imagination with the Risen Christ.

As far as I know, while B. H. Streeter was a highly regarded biblical scholar, his idea that John was in touch with an inner revelation and that his Gospel sprang from this has not been considered seriously in the world of biblical scholarship. From the psychological point of view, however, it is quite in keeping with what we know of the psychology of the unconscious.

In active imagination we find that ideas and insights emerge

---

5. B. H. Streeter, *The Four Gospels* (London: MacMillan and Co., 1936), 391–92.

in the dialogue that were not conscious to us before. We also find that we may not understand some of this emerging material. The spirit tends to anticipate consciousness, presenting us in our dreams and active imagination with psychic reality that we may not yet be in a position to comprehend. It is for this reason that the spirit chooses a symbolic language, for this leads us on to hitherto unknown truths and insights. Keeping this in mind, we must also hold to the possibility that the author of our Gospel may not have entirely understood everything that he was recording. A creative person such as our author would be a conduit for an influx of insights and understandings that were beyond the range of the conventional or collective understanding of his day. The history of the advance of scientific ideas is a case in point. We find repeatedly in the development of science that certain persons were "set aside," as it were, to receive from within a new understanding about the secrets of nature that was far in advance of the general thinking of the times. This being so, we should not be surprised to find in the Fourth Gospel spiritual insights that could be only partly understood at the time in which they were written. Of course this is one reason that a sacred document such as our Gospel has a living vitality throughout the ages. This vitality comes from its capacity to impart to readers of generations still to come new insights that only an advancing spiritual and psychological understanding can make possible.

The capacity of the unconscious to be in itself a source of knowledge also accounts for the fact that it is perfectly possible to conceive of ideas for which there are few if any historical antecedents. As we have noted, in most biblical scholarship there is a concerted effort to trace Jesus' teachings back to historical antecedents in Gnosticism, Platonism, the Essenes, or Jewish thinking. Such antecedents may exist, of course, but insofar as Jesus was in touch with the spirit he was capable of receiving new insights for which no historical antecedents can be found. The psychological depth of the parables of Jesus in the synoptics and the teaching stories in the Fourth Gospel point to the existence of Jesus of Nazareth as a person so in touch with the unconscious that he received his inspiration directly from God, not as a refurbished hand-me-down from previously known traditions. Similarly, the depth of the Johannine visions and discourses points to the existence in our author of such a connection with spiritual reality.

We are now almost ready to turn to the text, but first a few comments on how to read this book. A certain number of words will be used that are taken from the terminologies of C. G. Jung and Fritz Kunkel. "Individuation," "ego," "Center," and "Self" are examples. When these words are first introduced they will be defined. If the reader runs into them later and needs to refresh his or her memory s/he can look the word up in the index and find the original place where the word was discussed. The index will also be useful when a certain topic is being discussed that was previously discussed. Often when this happens the text will say, "As previously discussed...." If the reader does not recall the previous discussion, s/he can use the index in order to find it, for virtually all of the major topics and words are listed in the index.

Of course it is the preferred writing style today to avoid sexist language. In order to do so I will sometimes use expressions such as "s/he," as I have done above, or I may sometimes alternate between using "he" generically and "she" generically, since this often makes for smoother writing.

The Fourth Gospel, of course, was written in Greek. Experience has shown me that even people who do not know Greek can profit from an explanation of some of the Greek terms that underlie the English translations. The reader will therefore find that sometimes I may cite the original Greek word and discuss its meaning and appropriate translation into English. However, I give such discussions only the first time the word is presented. When we encounter the word later in the commentary I assume the reader has read about the word as described at its first usage. However, since this book is a commentary and is not meant to be read straight through, a reader might often read a section of the book out of its usual order. For this reason there is at the back of the book a list of the Greek words that are analyzed for their appropriate English meanings, which also lists the page where this analysis first takes place.

Regarding biblical translations: It will be found that sometimes one translation and sometimes another translation is used, according to which translation seems to best bring out the sense of the original Greek for that particular section of the Gospel. I will usually cite the translation that is used with the following abbreviations: JB: Jerusalem Bible; NJB: New Jerusalem Bible; KJV: King James Version; NEB: New English Bible; RSV: Revised Standard Version; JB: J. B. Phillips translation; LB: Luther Bible. When no translation is cited it means the translation is from the Jerusalem Bible, which is the "standard" English text I will be using. Occasionally I may suggest my own translation for a particular biblical passage.

The reader may be surprised at how often the early Church Fathers are referred to or quoted with reference to a particular part of John's Gospel. This is because these early Christian theologians were psychologists and philosophers as well and had a keen appreciation of the inward and mystical dimension of John's Gospel.

Keeping these things in mind we can now proceed to the Gospel itself, doing so in the spirit of that early Christian philosopher Origen who once said of John's Gospel: "We may therefore make bold to say that the Gospels are the first fruits of all Scriptures, but of the Gospels, that of John is the first fruit."[6]

---

6. Origen, *Commentary on John* 1.6.

∾ 1 ∾

THE CREATIVITY OF THE CENTER
The Prologue
John 1:1–18

SCHOLARS TELL US that the Prologue may be based on an old hymn. It is certainly true that there is a rhythm to the first fourteen verses. This rhythm is more apparent in the original Greek than in English translations, for in the Greek the concluding word of a sentence or phrase regularly becomes the opening word of the next sentence or phrase. While the best English translations try to duplicate this rhythm, it is not always possible to do so.

There is an exception to this poetic structure however. Verses 6–8, which concern John the Baptist, appear to be an intrusion into the original hymn-like text. They leave us with the impression that the information about the Baptist was a later insertion in the original text either by the author — John himself — or others. We will look at the reasons for including this material about John the Baptist in a later chapter.

A skillful novelist introduces her major characters in the opening pages of the story. In the same way, John skillfully introduces in his Prologue many of the major themes that he will discuss in detail later on: light and its contrast with darkness, the unbelieving people of this world with those who do believe, the possibility of becoming children of God, the importance of faith, and the relationship of the Son to the Father. In this chapter we will primarily discuss what John means in 1:14 when he says that *the Word became flesh,* and then proceed to discuss in some detail the origin and meaning of the idea of the Logos (Word) as we find it in the Fourth Gospel. The other issues John raises in the Prologue will be taken up in subsequent chapters.

John 1:14 is one of the most important verses in the New Testament, a cornerstone of the Christian religion: "And the Word was made flesh, and dwelt among us, full of grace and truth" (KJV). But how strange it sounds to the contemporary reader for whom a "word" is something a person speaks or writes, and "flesh" is what is covered by the skin on our bodies. In John's day, the Greek words we translate as "Word" and "flesh" had special meanings that defy the capacity for expression of our contemporary vocabularies, for they embody certain thought forms that are now alien to us.

The Greek word *sarx*, translated as "flesh," has five distinguishable meanings in the New Testament:

The first meaning is the substance of an animal body, beast or human. We still use the word "flesh" with this meaning.

The second meaning is the relationship of people by consanguinity or marriage. For example, we read in Matthew 19:5: "For this cause shall a man leave father and mother, and shall cleave to his wife: and they twain shall be one flesh" (KJV). This usage is antiquated today, so much so that the Jerusalem Bible translates "one flesh" as "one body." The use of "body" instead of "flesh," however, while it makes use of a word understandable today, loses the subtlety of the biblical expression because it concretizes an idea that in the original Greek expressed the thought of a spiritual as well as physical union.

The third meaning is one constituent of human nature to be contrasted with others. The principal distinction made in the New Testament is between "flesh" (*sarx*) and "spirit" (*pneuma*). The contrast was not between something morally bad and morally good, although the flesh was regarded as inferior to the spirit. An example of this usage of the word "flesh" is found in Matthew 26:41: " ... the spirit [*pneuma*] indeed is willing, but the flesh [*sarx*] is weak" (KJV; cf. Rom. 2:28, 29; 1 Cor. 5:5).

The fourth meaning, of special importance, is the idea of "flesh" as identical with the principle of sin in human nature. When used in this way, "flesh" denotes the existence of a propensity toward sin as the result of our fallen human nature. In psychological language this is a way of saying that it is part of the innate, archetypal structure of the human psyche that human beings tend to act in a way that is contrary to the will of God.

This is an idea of great psychological importance to which we shall return later.

It is important to note that *sarx* as the seat of sin within us does not refer specifically to our material nature or to our earthly bodies. In neither the Old Testament nor the New Testament is the body regarded as inherently sinful or as the seat of sin. Of course there are sins that have to do with our physical nature and bodily passions. St. Paul refers to some of them in Galatians 5:19–20. But the origin of sin is not the body as such; rather, it stems from a certain inclination of the will toward evil. Thus the long list of sins that Paul cites in Galatians not only refers to physical passions and lusts but also to hatred, envy, wrath, and many other purely psychological ills. It was an ancient understanding that when the word *sarx* was used in the New Testament as a synonym for the source of sin, it did not refer to bodily flesh. Methodius, early fourth-century bishop of Olympus in Asia Minor, wrote: "By flesh, he [Paul] did not mean [bodily] flesh itself, but the irrational impulse towards the lascivious pleasures of the soul."[1]

It is true that later the church acquired a prejudice against the body, and especially against sexual desires, but this is not biblical; it originates in Gnostic and certain Greek thinking, for it was a Greek idea that the body was a kind of prison for the soul, to be shed at death. The Stoic philosopher Epictetus once said of us: "Thou art a little soul bearing about a corpse [i.e., the body]."[2] The biblical point of view about the body is that God created both body and soul, so both are equally good. In fact, so essential an element is the body that rather than being rejected at death it also will be raised and transformed into a spiritual body in order that it may remain a fitting and eternal holy dwelling place for the soul (cf. Phil. 3:21; 1 Cor. 15:42ff).

Finally there is the fifth meaning of "flesh" as the equivalent of all created nature generally and human creaturely nature in particular. As such it is perishable and transitory. So Paul says that Jesus Christ was "made of the seed of David according to the flesh; and declared to be the Son of God with power, according to the Spirit of holiness" (Rom. 1:3, KJV; cf. Rom. 9:5, 7:5; 1 Tim. 3:16; Acts 2:17, 26, 31). This means that Christ's human generation came from the lineage of David, but his spiritual generation came

---

1. Methodius, *The Discourse on the Resurrection* 3.5.
2. Quoted from Bertrand Russell, *History of Western Philosophy* (New York: Simon and Schuster, 1945), 263.

from God. Here flesh is created, finite, perishable human nature. The Jerusalem Bible accordingly translates flesh when used with this significance as "human nature." It is the same meaning that Shakespeare had in mind when he wrote of the hardships of life that all of us must endure:

> ... and by a sleep to say we end
> The heartache and the thousand natural shocks
> That flesh is heir to ...
>
> *(Hamlet,* act 3, scene 1)

It is in this last sense that the word "flesh" is used in John 1:14. John is saying that the Word who is God himself became a human being and took upon himself our weak and mortal humanity and our physical nature. Theologically this verse is a cornerstone of the Christian teaching of redemption. If the Word had not become flesh, we would not have been able to see God, the saving acts of the crucifixion and resurrection would not have been possible, and our fallen human nature could not have been redeemed be- cause it would not have been infused, via the incarnation, with divinity. It is not too much to say that everything in Christian mystical theology hinges on John 1:14.[3]

John 1:14 is psychologically important. It is all well and good to say that when Christ became man one could see God, but how could this help persons born long after the incarnated Christ had ascended? It might seem that for those who did not see Christ-in-the-flesh his incarnation must be experienced only as a historical truth in which one must believe. However, early Christ- ian thinkers pointed out that this incarnated Christ lived on within each one of us. When God was incarnated as Christ, it was as though the divine Logos of which John speaks in his Pro- logue "was broken up and thinned out," as Origen once put it.[4] This is a way of saying that the creative Mind of God lives on within each one of us. It is for this reason that we are all parts of

---

3. John 1:14 also serves to distinguish Christian teaching from that rival teaching known as Gnosticism. The word "Gnosticism" is derived from the Greek word *gnōsis,* which means knowledge obtained through personal, even intimate experience. Many Gnostic teachers incorporated Christ into their teachings but denied that he had a real human body because the body and all material reality were evil. This was one of the many reasons why incarnational Christianity rejected the Gnostics, although Christianity, as we will see, has its own *gnōsis,* or secret, revealed knowledge.

4. See Origen, *Commentary on John* 1.42.

the "body of Christ," as Paul is fond of reminding us. Psychologically speaking this corresponds to the fact that the Center lives within each one of us. We could say that God incarnated in this world so Christ could be incarnated in each one of us. What this means for psychological development will become clearer as we delve more deeply into what early Christianity understood by "the Word" of God.

~ 2 ~

CHRIST AS THE WORD OF GOD
The Divine Logos
John 1:1–5

IN THE BEGINNING WAS THE WORD:
the Word was with God
and the Word was God.
He was with God in the beginning.
Through him all things came to be,
not one thing had its being but through him.
All that came to be had life in him
and that life was the light of men,
a light that shines in the dark,
light that darkness could not overpower.

Christians have heard these words so often that their minds may have become numb to their meaning; on the other hand those who hear them for the first time may be puzzled about their meaning. What is this "Word" of which John's Gospel speaks? We think we know what a "word" is; the dictionary is full of "words." But what can this "Word of God" be? The answer to the puzzle lies in the very special Greek word that is translated "Word" in our text, a word for which we have no satisfactory equivalent in English: *logos.*

Logos means much more than "word" in the ordinary sense. To signify words such as we find in a dictionary the Greek word *rēma* would be used, but the word *logos* includes the ideas of "thought," "deed," and "power." As used in the New Testament it signifies a personality more than it does an abstract idea. To translate *logos* into English at all is misleading to the English reader; it would be better, in fact, if *logos* was not translated but was accompanied by an explanatory footnote. Then readers would understand that they were confronted with an idea that was foreign to their modern outlook and would be impelled to dig deeper to discover its meaning.

In this case digging deeper means exploring how the word *logos* was used in Greek philosophy and comparing the word *logos* to its equivalent expression in the Old Testament, for when John selected the idea of the *logos* in order to explain something of what Christ meant he had in mind a vast psychological and spiritual heritage. It would take us beyond the scope of this work to go into detail on how *logos* was used in ancient times, but at least a brief explanation is essential if the modern reader is to gain a glimpse of the depth of meaning of John's statement "In the beginning was the *logos*." We will begin with the Greek philosophers.

Probably the earliest antecedent to the idea of the *logos* came from the philosopher Heraclitus, who saw the universe as constantly changing, stirred into constant motion by an all-pervading "reason," which he likened to a divine fire. This "reason" is the *logos*. Shortly after Heraclitus, the philosopher Anaxagoras spoke of the Divine Mind as it was immanent in the created order, which, like Heraclitus's divine reason, is also an antecedent for the idea of the *logos*.

Plato had the idea of a spiritual reality independent of the material reality of this world and believed that it was this spiritual reality that gave to the created world its form and being. The spiritual world was the world of Platonic "Ideas," an archetypal realm of changeless and universal patterns of which the material world is but an imperfect representation. The world of ideas was known by reason and enlightenment, the material world by the senses; the former gave true knowledge, the latter only ephemeral knowledge. Plato believed that the human soul knew this archetypal realm in a previous existence, prior to birth, and that attaining true knowledge in this world was found by a reawakening of this prior knowledge from which comes all knowledge of the good and the true. For Plato, a vision of this archetypal world from which we have our ultimate being constituted salvation. The *logos* partakes of the nature of this archetypal reality.

Aristotle regarded the visible world as more real than did Plato. For Aristotle, matter and form always existed together, the one never being present without the other. God alone, he said, is truly immaterial and exists as the "Prime Mover" of matter. God as the Unmoved Mover works with intelligent purpose; God is not only the source but also the goal of the world's developmental process. Aristotle was perhaps the first philosopher to postulate the teleological nature of the universe and of life's processes. Human beings, he said, consist not only of a material body, but also of a soul in which there resides a divine spark that the soul shares with God. This spark of divinity in human nature is an element of the divine *logos* — the shaping spiritual power and essence of God — and is eternal and impersonal. Thus in Aristotle we find a clearly formulated use of the word *logos*.

The idea of the *logos* of God expressing itself in the created material order and finding place in the soul of human beings came to its fullest expression in Greek philosophy among the Stoics. Stoicism believed the universe was composed of two kinds of matter: a gross or coarse matter, which is the stuff of material bodies, and an extremely fine matter, so fine that it pervades the coarse material realm and is virtually indistinguishable from the idea of spirit. The material, created order is thus pervaded with the spiritual substance, but it is also pervaded with a vital element — warm like the fire of Heraclitus — that shaped, harmonized, and interpenetrated all things. This was nothing less then an intelligent, self-conscious world-soul, an indwelling *logos*. This *logos* is God, and is the source of all life and all wisdom. Our human reason partakes of its nature, because this *logos* dwells within us. For this reason we can follow the God within and refer to ourselves as the offspring of God.

Finally we must mention the Jewish philosopher Philo (about 20 B.C.E. to 42 C.E.), who was himself greatly influenced by Greek philosophy. Philo sought to reconcile the Old Testament with Greek philosophy by means of an allegorical interpretation of Scripture that made great use of the idea of the *logos*. The *logos*, said Philo, flowed from God himself and was the instrument through which God created the world. Human beings, ideally speaking, are created in the image of and by the agency of the *logos*, though because of our fallen nature we are in fact but inferior copies of our divine origin.

When John adopted the term *logos* in order to explain his idea of Christ and his incarnation, he was influenced by Greek philosophy with its longstanding idea of an indwelling presence of God, and he also could count on his more educated readers to understand what this term meant. For John the *logos* referred to that expression of God's innermost nature which poured forth to create and be immanent in the world, giving the world order and expression, and which was most closely to be experienced within the human soul. It was a way of explaining how God, who was transcendent to creation, could also be immanent within the creation. It can be seen from this how inadequate modern translations of the word *logos* are and why it can be argued that it would be better to leave the word untranslated so the modern reader would know that she must dig deeper for its meaning. But if the word *logos*, as used in John's Prologue, *is* to be translated into English, perhaps the best of all translations is by J. B. Phillips: "In the beginning God expressed himself."

Turning now from the influence of Greek philosophy on John, we come to the equally important influence of the Wisdom literature in the Old Testament, for in the Old Testament we find an idea of God's creative spirit immanent within the creation and residing even in the human soul that is as old — or perhaps older — as that of the Greeks. Consider, for instance, what Moses says to the people of Israel just before his death when he admonishes them to keep the word of God that has been given them and that is in fact written in their very hearts:

> For this law that I enjoin on you today is not beyond your strength nor beyond your reach. It is not in heaven, so that you need to wonder, "Who will go up to heaven for us and bring it down to us, so that we may hear it and keep it?" Nor is it beyond the seas, so that you need to wonder, "Who will cross the seas for us and bring it back to us, so that we may hear it and keep it?" No, the Word [Heb.: *dabar*] is very near to you, it is in your mouth and in your heart for your observance. (Deut. 30:11)[1]

Later in the Old Testament we find the idea of the indwelling power of God beautifully represented in the Book of Proverbs and the Book of Wisdom. These books are part of the "Wisdom literature" of the Old Testament. Even though they are largely ignored

---

1. Paul quotes Moses' words in Romans 10:6-8.

by modern Christians they are in fact perhaps the most important parts of the Old Testament, for here we read of *Sophia:* the creative Wisdom of God by means of which God created the world and through which God dwells within the human heart. *Sophia* is a Greek word that means "wisdom." When ancient scholars wanted to translate the Hebrew Old Testament into Greek they translated the Hebrew word for wisdom (*chokmah*) by the Greek word *sophia*. This word in time became virtually a proper name for the eternal Wisdom of God of which the Old Testament literature speaks. It is also of more than passing interest that both the Hebrew and the Greek words for wisdom are feminine in gender, a point we will return to in a later chapter.

Space does not permit us to go into detail about the wonderful Wisdom literature of the Old Testament. For now we must content ourselves with noting that Wisdom/Sophia embodied or symbolized the feminine aspect of God that was part of that creative power which created the world, which dwelt immanent within the world, and which also dwelt within the human heart. This was the divine power that called people to know and live the truth, that was to be found wherever men and women were to be found, that took a delight in humankind but hated all pride and arrogance, and that offered people fruits and benefits far more to be desired than gold and jewels. She was above all the source of all human knowledge, whether knowledge of the workings of the world or spiritual and psychological knowledge, which she can likewise impart because she is mistress of the soul.

The significance of Wisdom/Sophia as the Word of God was not lost on the great minds of the early church, who saw in Christ the embodiment in a human being of what the Greek philosophers called the Logos of God and what the Old Testament spoke of as Wisdom/Sophia.[2] When we read "In the beginning was the Word" and later learn that this Word was in Christ, we are mystified, but for early Christians like Athenagoras, Irenaeus, Clement of Alexandria, Origen, Theophilus, Tertullian, Hippolytus, Cyprian, Methodius, Lactantius, Dionysius, and Gregory of Nyssa, to mention only a few, it was clear that to say Christ

---

2. Cf. Athenagoras, *A Plea for Christians* 10; Irenaeus, *Against Heresies* 4.20.1; Clement of Alexandria, *The Instructor* 1.10 and 3.6; Origen, *De Principiis* 1.2.3; and *Commentary on John* 1.21.39; Theophilus, *Theophilus to Autolycus* 2.10; Tertullian, *Against Praxeas* 6, *Against Hermogenes* 18; Hippolytus, *Fragments from Commentaries;* Cyprian, *Testimonies;* Gregory of Nyssa, *Against Eunomius* 3.2; Methodius, *Extracts from the Work on Things Created;* Lactantius, *The Divine Institutes* 4.6; Dionysius of Romane, *Against the Sabellians* 2.

was the Word was to assign to Christ a profoundly mystical and far-reaching reality. It meant that the utterly transcendent God, whom, as we will see, John later refers to as "the Father," created the world through that self-expression termed the Logos, and that this Logos, or Creative Word of God, is immanent within all of the creation. This Word of God was also believed to be the source of all truth. Whenever a person found the truth there was the Word of God to be found as the inspiration for that discovery and the guide to all true knowledge. For this reason many of the early Christian Fathers believed that the Logos was not only the source of inspiration for the prophets of the Old Testament but also was the source of inspiration for those Greek philosophers who had encompassed in their thinking some of the truth about God. They thus believed in the pre-existence of Christ, that is, that Christ as the Logos or Wisdom of God existed from the beginning before the incarnation, always stirring people to seek God and find the truth, even as the Wisdom books of the Old Testament in their descriptions of Wisdom/Sophia had declared. John, aware of all of this thinking about the Logos and about Wisdom/ Sophia makes the startling statement in his Prologue that this same Word of God was incarnated within an actual human life, enshrined with a human body, and had become an indissoluble part of a human personality. Thus "the Word became flesh" was for John the central Christian teaching and mystery.

The world-creating *logos* could be seen in the movements of the heavenly bodies, in the majesty of the skies, in the great ocean with its abundance of life, but also could be seen in the tiniest unit of life. John would have agreed with Nikos Kazantzakis when he wrote, "Everything is God's. When I bend over the ant, inside his black, shiny eye I see the face of God."[3] But the most important place where the Word of God was to be found for the early Christians was within the soul herself, where it lived as an *imago dei*, like a spring of water from which flowed the knowledge of God. All knowledge of God that comes from the words of others, or from an examination of the creation, or even from Scripture, comes from outside of us, but the knowledge of God that comes from within us is a direct knowledge inspired in us by the indwelling presence of the *logos* who resides within the human soul. This inner,

---

3. Nikos Kazantzakis, *The Last Temptation of Christ* (New York: Simon and Schuster, 1960), 157.

or inspired, knowledge of God is part of the Christian *mystērion,*
or "mystery." A "mystery" did not mean for the ancient mind a
puzzle to be solved, but a content of knowledge that one could
know only through being initiated into it by personal experience.
For this reason the Greek maxim "Know thyself" was also voiced
by almost all of the early Fathers of the Church, for in knowing
oneself one also came to know the divine Wisdom.

It was for this reason that the soul must be free from the domination of sin, for sin darkened the soul and thus obscured the
knowledge of God. No one can see if one's eyes are blinded or
vision distorted, but sin did exactly that: it blinded a person to
the truth and distorted a person's perception of himself and of
reality. Sin darkened consciousness and thus dimmed or even
obliterated that knowledge of God which Christian philosophers
like Tertullian called "the dowry of the soul," the soul's great trea-
sure. Indeed, it was for this reason that the church insisted that
Christ had to be sinless, not that he might represent for us an
impossible perfection we could never achieve, but that it might
be known that in Christ there was complete consciousness and
perfect awareness of God.

Because of this highly mystical understanding of the reality
of the Word of God, Christ was seen symbolically present in
many ways in the world. The wealth of symbols used in the early
church to denote Christ, many of them feminine in nature, are almost inexhaustible. To cite some examples: Christ was the "One"
who was everywhere in the creation. He was also the "beginning
and end of all things," like a divine "uroborus" (a symbol of a
snake biting its own tail and so completing a circle), and was
likewise referred to as a "good serpent" because the serpent in
the early church was a symbol for healing.[4] Gold symbolized the
divine Word because Christ endowed the soul with the quality
of incorruptibility and gold was the metal that would never cor-
rode.[5] Christ was also symbolized as a flower and was referred
to specifically as "the flower of Mary," a flower being a natural
and feminine mandala.[6] Another natural symbol for Christ was
the tree; in fact the cross was regularly referred to by the early
Christians as the tree.[7] Because of Christ's purity he was also

4. See Tertullian, *Against Marcion* 3.18.
5. See Hippolytus, *Fragments of Discourses or Homilies* no. 6.
6. See St. Ambrose, *On the Holy Spirit* 2.8.38–39.
7. See Methodius, *Banquet of the Ten Virgins* 9.3, and Tertullian, *Against Marcion* 3.19.

represented by milk, which was associated in the ancient mind with the feminine and with purity.[8] Another feminine symbol for Christ was the cave. Tradition said the stable in which Christ was born was a cave and also believed that many of Christ's important teachings to the disciples were transmitted to them in a cave. He was also represented as a beautiful youth[9] and as a divine fire.[10] As fire he was associated with the fourth person whom the prophet Daniel said was in the fiery furnace with Shadrach, Meschach, and Abednego.[11] Consequently Origen and others believed that Christ once made the statement, "He that is near me is near the fire."[12] Christ also had many theriomorphic representations and was seen as an eagle, as a calf, as a lamb, as a lion, and even as a worm, the last symbol harkening back to Psalm 22:6 and representing Christ as the lowest of the low who is yet the highest of the high.[13]

The most important animal representing Christ, however, was the fish, and, as we shall see, John makes much use of fish symbolism in his Gospel. But not only was Christ the fish; he was also the water and is likened by many to a "spring of water," a symbol drawn by the early church from the Gospel of John, as we will see later on. If Christ was the water, he was also the ship that crosses the sea safely, as Augustine pointed out.[14] The list of symbolic representations of Christ seems endless: he was symbolized by the sun, by a star, by the circle, by the number eight, and by a variety of mandalas (concentric designs that represent wholeness and integrity). He was also the uniter of the opposites who thus restored humankind to that wholeness which they lost in the Garden of Eden.[15] As the One who made all things whole Christ was also likened to a divine weaver.[16] Nor was Christ excluded from the realm of eros, for he was the bridegroom of the soul and was so represented in the Song of Songs, as well as in many other

---

8. See Clement of Alexandria, *The Instructor* 1.6.

9. See Socrates, *Church History* 3.19.

10. See Ambrose, *On the Holy Spirit* 3 and *Of the Christian Faith* 13.

11. See Ambrose, *Of the Christian Faith* 13.

12. See Origen, *On Jeremiah* hom. 3.3, and *The Gospel of Thomas*.

13. See Ambrose, *Of the Christian Faith* 2.8, and Cyprian, *Treatises* 2.13.

14. See Augustine, *On the Trinity* 4.15.

15. Irenaeus, *Against Heresies* 5.17.3, and Lactantius, *The Epitome of the Divine Institutes* 51.

16. Hippolytus, *Treatise on Christ and the Anti-Christ* 4. See the *Acts of Andrew* in *The Apocryphal New Testament*, trans. M. R. James (New York: Oxford University Press, 1960).

places of the Old Testament.[17] An especially important symbol of Christ was that of the city, a symbol harkening back to the Book of Revelation and the basis for Augustine's idea of the City of God.[18] And he was the stone, the solid foundation of all spiritual life that was firm and enduring.[19]

The above examples are only some of the most important of the multitudinous ways in which the early Christian imagination pictured this mystery of the divine Word made flesh whose presence was felt intimately in the soul. In this way the ancient mind struggled to represent in symbols the ineffable, mysterious, and wonderful reality of Christ and to reveal Christ as the mystical reality pervading all of life. This early Christian attitude is an antidote to stodgy and limiting overly rational formulations of the meaning of Christ and offers to free us from narrow preconceptions of what it means to speak of Christ. It also opens us up to seeing Christ in manifold areas of the creation and of human experience and so helps us relate to the reality of the miracle of the divine Word that is everywhere in creation but is most visible of all in the human soul.

---

17. Cyprian, for instance, cites Christ as the bridegroom in his comments on Psalms 24:3–6; Joel 2:15, 61; Jeremiah 16:9; Psalms 19:5, 6; Revelation 21:9–11; John 3:28–29. See Augustine, *Exposition of the Book of Psalms*, Psalms 23 and 131.

18. Augustine, *City of God* 10.7. See the apocryphal *Revelation of Paul*.

19. See Irenaeus, *Against Heresies* 3.11.8; Augustine, *On the Trinity* 3.1; Cyprian, *Treatises* 2.16; Origen, *Commentary on John* 1.41.

~ 3 ~

CHRISTIAN DISCIPLES
The First Disciples
John 1:35–51

As MENTIONED EARLIER, we are reserving a discussion of John the Baptist for a later time. Consequently we will pass over John 1:19–34 for the time being and proceed directly to the call of the disciples. First we will take up some preliminary considerations, then we will discuss the call of the disciples as the first stage of a triune initiation into the Christian mystery of salvation.

John the Baptist and two of his disciples are standing by when Jesus passes within sight. John the Baptist identifies Jesus to them with the words, "Behold the lamb of God!" So far the Baptist is the only one who has recognized Jesus for who he is: the redemptive son of God. Before we can proceed further with our analysis of this story, however, we must note that our author uses four different ways of expressing the English verb "to see," each with its own special nuance of meaning. We will have more insight into the story if we first take a look at these four Greek words.

We have already encountered the first word. John the Baptist uses it when he says "Behold [*ide*] the lamb of God." The Greek word involved is *orao*, which refers to the act of seeing when the emphasis is on the impression of what is seen on the mind of the observer. It is a word used when the intent is to heighten the *subjective* impression made upon the observer when that person sees either an inner or an outer reality. *Ide* (behold) is the imperative form of this verb, which occurs in John the Baptist's statement to his two disciples and again in verse 39. The nuance of meaning, therefore, is "let this man impress himself upon you!"

A second Greek word used for seeing is *blepō*. This word refers to the act of seeing without regard to its object. One could use this word without reference to anything that is seen. For instance, if someone lit a candle in a dark room he might say to a companion, "Can you see now?" This word occurs in verse 39 (in the future tense, *opsesthe*) and is a relatively neutral word.

The third word is found in verse 38. The Jerusalem Bible translates this verse, "Jesus turned around, *saw* them following, and said, 'What do you want?'" The Greek word involved here is *theaomai*, which means "to gaze upon, to discern with the eyes," and is akin to *theōreō*, which means "to gaze on, contemplate, view with interest and attention," even "to come to a knowledge of." Our word "theater" derives from these words. The use of this word in verse 38 implies that Jesus did not just see them in a casual way, but gazed on them intently and so beheld them for who they were, even to the point of coming to a knowledge of them.

The fourth word, *emblepō*, means "to look searchingly or significantly at a person." This word is used in verses 36 and 42. In verse 36 John the Baptist "sees" Jesus with the peculiar insight and intensity that the verb *emblepō* implies. In verse 42 Jesus "sees" Simon in this same intense way. The Jerusalem Bible translates *emblepō* as "stared hard at," which is a good English approximation of its meaning.

To continue with our story, first John the Baptist draws the attention of his two disciples to Jesus, and they then follow him because John did not use a casual word but a word that emphasized the importance of that which was seen. Jesus then sees them in such a way that it leads him to recognize their significance. This insightful seeing on the part of Jesus leads to his question to them, which is translated in the Jerusalem Bible, "What do you want?" The King James Version and Revised Standard Version, however, translate it, "What do you seek?" And the New English Bible, "What are you looking for?" The feeling tone between "What do you want" and "What do you seek" is different. A spiritually hungry person, for instance, might be described as a "seeker after truth" but not as a "wanter." The Greek word involved is *zēteo*, which has as its primary meaning "to seek, to look for." The distinction has psychological implications as well. If we "want" something it may be an egocentric wanting, but when we "seek" something it implies a genuine spiritual hunger.

The two men — soon to be disciples — answer simply, "Rabbi, where do you live?" The feeling is that they are a bit tongue-tied, that they may not even be able to answer the question "What do you seek," but that they are anxious to have a teacher and have recognized this teacher in Jesus whom they call "Rabbi," which means "teacher."

So the two disciples join Jesus and stay with him. The text tells us that it was "about the tenth hour" when all of this happened. The tenth hour would be approximately four in the afternoon. The detail about the time of day seems irrelevant except, as the Jerusalem Bible points out, that it identifies the story as a historical incident personally witnessed by the narrator or someone who personally gave him the information. It is one of many historical details in John's Gospel that leaves us with the feeling that in his narrative the personal-historical, and the archetypal-eternal, are interwoven.

John proceeds to identify one of the two who followed Jesus as Andrew, the brother of Simon Peter. Curiously enough the other one of the two is never named. One speculation is that the unnamed person is none other than the "beloved disciple" or "disciple whom Jesus loved," who may have been the author of the Gospel and the owner of the upper room in Jerusalem (see introduction). In this case, the author of our Gospel has included himself, albeit unnamed, in this portion of the story. This would account for the fact that it was known that all this took place about the tenth hour.

There then follow two insights that are not given in the synoptic Gospels until much later in the narrative. The first occurs in verse 41 when Andrew tells his brother, "We have found the Messiah." The second is the name given by Jesus to Peter: the rock. Here is the use of the word *emblepō*, which we have already discussed. The use of this word at this point means that Jesus looked into the heart of Peter. It is evidence that Jesus is one who sees beyond mere appearances into the inner person. In keeping with Simon's inner identity Jesus gives him another name: Cephas. In Matthew's Gospel it is not until the sixteenth chapter that Simon is given his "spiritual name" of Peter. The difference between the names "Cephas" and "Peter" does not appear to be important. The first word is Aramaic and the second word is Greek, but both

words mean "rock." In the epistles, Cephas and Peter are used
interchangeably. What is important is that Peter's inner being
was seen by Jesus to be firm and strong like a rock, although, as
we will see, Peter had to be sorely tested and his egocentricity
dissolved before this inner strength could emerge.

However, the use of a spiritual name by Jesus is interesting.
Among the American Indians, for instance, each person had his
or her individual name. That person's name came from some important aspect of his or her character or from a powerful spiritual
experience or dream that might have occurred during that person's vision quest or some other experience with the spiritual
world. The American Indian Crazy Horse, for instance (who defeated Custer at the Battle of the Little Big Horn) is the white man's
corruption of his Indian name Whirling Horses. Whirling Horses
received his spiritual name from a vision in which he saw many
horses whirling around a center. In like manner, Cephas/Peter is
Simon's spiritual name.

The story now moves quickly to the calling of Philip, and then
of Nathanael, whom Philip brings to Jesus. When Jesus meets
Nathanael he says, "There is an Israelite who deserves the name,
incapable of deceit" (v. 47). Jesus shows the same penetrating insight into Nathanael's character that he showed into Simon's; this
faculty in him can be ascribed to his psychological astuteness and
intuition. But in the next verse the matter goes farther than that.
Nathanael marvels that Jesus could know him so well, never having met him: "How do you know me?" he asks. The Greek word
here translated "know" is the special term *ginōskō*, which refers
to knowing something intimately through experience. Nathanael
uses this word because he is so amazed that Jesus could know
him so deeply in such a short time. Jesus replies, "Before Philip
came to call you, I saw you under the fig tree." This demonstrates
Jesus' faculty of supernatural insight, or, if you like, of extrasensory perception. Such a faculty is in keeping with the idea
that John's Christ shows forth more of the cosmic Christ than the
Jesus of the synoptics. Such extraordinary capacities are characteristic of John's Christ as is evidenced in many other places (see
2:24f; 4:17–19, 29; 6:61, 64, 71; 13:1, 11, 27, 28; 16:19, 30; 18:4; 21:17).

Such power on the part of Jesus overwhelms Nathanael, who
declares, "Rabbi, you are the Son of God, you are the King of Israel." The Jerusalem Bible's footnote assures us that we are, in
this context, to take the ascription "Son of God" as only a rough

equivalent of "King of Israel," not as an indication that Nathanael at this point knew Jesus' divine identity. Jesus replies, "You believe that just because I said: 'I saw you under the fig tree.' You will see greater things than that. . . . I tell you most solemnly you will see heaven laid open, and, above the Son of Man, the angels of God ascending and descending" (v. 51).

In this verse the important expression "Son of Man" is introduced into our Gospel. The expression occurs in John ten times. It is an expression shared in common with the synoptic Gospels, in which the phrase "Son of Man" also appears frequently. We will take up at a later point the psychological meaning. For now it is enough to note that by using the expressions "heaven opened" and "Son of Man" and by referring to the angels, John's Jesus has introduced us to the realm of the supernatural. To the modern ear such language seems strange, for it is not part of our collective conscious attitude to believe any longer in a supernatural realm. A knowledge of the unconscious, however, makes such an expression real to us again. Indeed, even the idea of angels takes on a new meaning when viewed in a psychological context. Such considerations, however, we will reserve for a later time. For now we must examine the meaning of discipleship as the first of several stages of introduction into the Christian mysteries.

Fritz Kunkel once observed that religion and psychology are concerned with the same thing: the evolution of consciousness. He regarded the Gospels as great textbooks of this evolution of consciousness, but pointed out that if we are to hear the message of the Gospels for ourselves we must have undergone its influence. This means that we cannot learn the depths of the message of the Gospels only by looking at them from a dispassionate, intellectual point of view. Instead, "we have to be in the test tube ourselves." Kunkel used the analogy of understanding the music of Beethoven: "Before we discuss Beethoven, we should have been stirred by his music."[1]

Kunkel believed that one of the best ways to put ourselves in the test tube of the Gospel experience is to see ourselves in the place of the disciples. In addition to asking ourselves, "What happens to Jesus?" we should also ask, "What is happening to

---

1. Fritz Kunkel, *Creation Continues,* original edition (New York: Charles Scribner's Sons, 1952).

the disciples?" For we cannot be Christ, but we can hope to be disciples. He believed that the best Gospel for helping us identify with the experience of the disciples was the Gospel of Matthew, and this is why he wrote his psychological commentary *Creation Continues* on this Gospel, rather than John's Gospel. He called John's Gospel a "great spiritual symphony" and believed that John's Gospel was written for those people who had already been initiated and were therefore ready for a deeper understanding. Nevertheless, John's Gospel does contain some significant experiences that occur to the disciples and so also speaks to those of us who are on the threshold of discipleship. In the spirit of Kunkel, we will examine the experiences that the disciples undergo that are described in the Fourth Gospel as paradigms of the experiences that we also may have to undergo in our own spiritual and psychological development. The story of the call of the disciples by Jesus is the first such story.

The call to the disciples is a call to initiation into the mystery of Christ. The idea of initiation is all but lost in our present culture, but it was an important one in the time of the inception of Christianity, for in the Roman Empire at that time there flourished a burgeoning number of "mystery religions." The Greek word translated in English as "mystery" did not mean to the ancient Greek-speaking person what it means to us. A mystery for us is a puzzle to be solved. A *mystērion* for the ancients was "a matter to the knowledge of which initiation is necessary." There are some things that can be known only by experiencing them; all in-depth spiritual or psychological understanding falls into this category. For this reason the word *mystērion* (mystery) is very important in the New Testament. In the synoptic Gospels, for example, Jesus says to his disciples, "To you is given the mystery [*mystērion*] of the kingdom of God" (Mark 4:11; Matt. 13:11; Luke 8:10). The versions in Matthew and Luke have the plural: *mystēria* (mysteries). In the Pauline literature the word *mystērion* occurs twenty-one times,[2] and Christ is spoken of as the "mystery (*mystērion*) of God" (Col. 2:2) whom we are called upon to understand with "full knowledge" (*epignōsin*).

In the Greek mystery religions the initiate was guided by a *mystagogue* (that is, one who leads the initiate into a deeper

---

2. Examples include Romans 11:25 and 16:25; Ephesians 3:3, 4; 5:32; 6:19; Colossians 1:26, 27; Romans 11:25; 16:25.

revelation of himself and God) into and through an experience in which a mythological figure's dramatic death and rebirth were portrayed. There were many mystery cults because there were many myths portraying death and resurrection. The earliest were the Greek cults of the Great Mother. They were held at Eleusis and centered on the myth of Demeter and Persephone. Others came from the East and centered on Aphrodite/Astarte and her dying and rising consort Adonis. Still others came from Egypt in which the central myth was that of the goddess Isis and her son/husband Osiris, who died and was restored again to life. By mystical participation in the life and being of the god who died and rose again, the initiate would also partake of renewed life. While a general knowledge of what happened in these rituals is known to us from reports by such ancient historians as Plutarch and Clement of Alexandria, exact details are obscure because those initiated into the cults were sworn to secrecy. In fact, the Greek noun *mystērion* is closely related to the verb *myō*, which means "to shut the mouth." As we will see later, Christianity is also a *mystērion*, in which we are called upon to be the initiates, and Christ is both *mystagogue* and the *mystērion* that can be known only to those who are properly initiated into this knowledge by their own experience.

In the Fourth Gospel, as in Matthew's Gospel, the disciples are the initiates, and we can see ourselves and our impending spiritual development mirrored in them. They are the ones whom Jesus instructs, and they are the ones who undergo experiences not unlike those through which we will have to pass if we are to come to know the *mystērion* expressed by Christ.

In his book *Soul Making: The Desert Way of Spirituality,* the Very Rev. Alan Jones tells us that in that ancient mystical path of Christian spiritual development that he calls "the Desert Way" there are three stages of Christian initiation or, as he calls it, conversion.[3] These stages of Christian initiation are concerned with what Jones calls "soul making," that is, they change and deepen the inner man or woman. Like many ancient Christians, Dean Jones believes that we partake of the life of Christ in a mystical way by being, as it were, grafted onto him. He also believes, as did

---

3. The Very Rev. Alan Jones, *Soul Making: The Desert Way of Spirituality* (New York: Harper & Row, 1985), 165.

Kunkel, that the paradigms for our own experiences were those of the first disciples.

Dean Jones identifies three stages of this Christian initiation or conversion and says that each stage is precipitated by and accompanied by a crisis. First comes the crisis of meaning, then the crisis of betrayal, and finally the crisis of absence or emptiness.[4] The call of the disciples is illustrative of the first stage: the crisis of meaning.

In order to arrive at a new psychological/spiritual insight we must be ready to receive it. This readiness requires that we be hungry for the new insight, and this hunger requires that we be dissatisfied with our present state of being and our present beliefs. As every psychotherapist knows, no new development can take place in people who are satisfied with themselves the way they are, or who do not doubt themselves, or whose belief system about themselves and life is heavily entrenched. Such people suffer from what the Bible calls "hardening of the heart," and it results in an impermeability to new consciousness and development. On the other hand, when we come to doubt ourselves, when our previous system of beliefs and previous way of coping with life are threatened or shattered, we find ourselves in a crisis. Then we no longer know who we are or where we are going or what our purpose is. It is the *crisis of meaning,* and people who are plunged into it often find themselves in the midst of great darkness and disorientation.

That the disciples were undergoing the crisis of meaning is evidenced by Jesus' first attitude to them. We have already seen that Jesus looked keenly into them, that is, that he perceived their inner state, and thus knew that they were dissatisfied with the existing collective belief systems of their times. This is why Jesus asks them the pointed question, "What do you seek?" No one seeks spiritually for something new if he has not lost what he had before. To be a seeker, therefore, is always to be somewhat spiritually or psychologically adrift, at sea on the great ocean of our inner life. Such a person is left with many doubts and few if any certainties; he feels vulnerable and often empty, with that inner emptiness that often precedes any experience of becoming inwardly filled.

The disciples were seekers after truth because they were aware

---

4. Ibid., 166.

that they did not possess the truth. They were evidently people who were not content with accepting in its entirety the traditional beliefs handed down to them, yet they did not yet have a new truth to follow. Thus they were in an uncomfortable interim state, suspended between the fading away of the power of old beliefs and the emergence of new convictions. South African novelist Nadine Gordimer once made a comment with reference to her native country that is also applicable to that person for whom the old psychological frame of reference has perished and a new one has not yet appeared: "The old is dying and the new cannot be born; in this interregnum there arises a great diversity of morbid symptoms."[5]

It is at this point in their spiritual lives that Jesus appears to the disciples. There is an old Chinese saying that when the student is ready the teacher appears. The disciples are painfully ready, and the teacher now appears. The disciples are overjoyed and tremendously impressed with their new teacher. So Andrew says to his brother in amazement and joy, "We have found the Messiah!" In the language of psychology, we call such an attachment on the part of one person to another the "transference." In psychotherapy the Self, or the image of the guide, becomes projected onto the therapist. From this transference comes the faith that is necessary if the work is to proceed. The wise psychotherapist knows that he or she is an unworthy recipient of this transference, but also knows that it must be carried for the time being until the client can find the guide within him/herself. However, sometimes the need for a savior or guide is so great that people project the Self onto people who are unworthy of it. In the Germany of the 1930s the widespread projection of the savior figure onto Adolf Hitler is a glaring extreme example. Much mischief and evil can come from such events because one person, or one group of people, idolizes another person who uses the power thus granted to him or her for unworthy evil purposes. But so badly do people need a repository for their faith that such tragedies can and do occur. If we consult our deepest instinct, however, our inner "dog" who can "sniff out" whether or not another person is to be trusted, we can avert much of this danger. Perhaps in the case of the disciples there had been previous occasions when someone unworthy of

---

5. Nadine Gordimer, *July's People* (New York: Viking Press, 1981). In the frontispiece Gordimer is quoting from *Prison Notebooks* by Antonio Gramsci.

their faith crossed their path, but they resisted the temptation to appoint that person their savior and guide because of the health of their spiritual instincts. This would seemingly have prolonged their painful crisis of meaning, but it also would have left them open to and ready to receive the Christ when he came into their lives.

The experiences that now came to the disciples in their association with Jesus were deeply meaningful and exciting. They had found the Master and they followed him happily, growing in consciousness and enthusiasm as they did so. But their full initiation was not yet complete. Before they could really truly *know*, deep within themselves, they would have to undergo two more crises even more painful than the first. But these crises still lay ahead of them.

~ 4 ~

THE EVOLUTION OF
CONSCIOUSNESS
The Witness of John the Baptist
John 1:6–8, 19–34; 3:22–36

WE HAVE ALREADY NOTED (chap. 1) that verses 6–8 in the first chapter of John's Gospel are believed to be later insertions into the original text designed to make it clear from the beginning that the central figure is Jesus and not John. Scholars believe that there was a powerful cult of followers of John the Baptist and that his followers may have resisted following Jesus because of their admiration for John. It is thought that John the Baptist's cult centered at Ephesus because the Book of Acts tells the story of Paul as going to Ephesus and finding that the disciples there had been baptized only with the baptism of John. There is also the account of Apollos, a learned and eloquent teacher of the way of the Lord, who had experienced only John's baptism (Acts 19:1–7 and 18:24–28). The Fourth Gospel also refers to a group of John's disciples in John 3:25.

The Greek helps us out a bit in ascertaining the importance of John the Baptist. In 1:7 we read, "A man came, sent *by* God." The preposition translated "by" could have been expressed in Greek in three ways. The preposition *ek* could have been used; this word denotes the idea of "out of" or "out from." Or the preposition *apo* might have been used; this word denotes the idea of "away from" or "separation from." The preposition chosen by our author, however, is the word *para,* which denotes "from as with regard to source or origin." Thus the text emphasizes that while John the Baptist is subordinate in importance to Jesus, nevertheless the source of his mission, power, and authority was God.

Much the same emphasis is found later in verse 7: "He came as a witness, as a witness to speak for the light, so that everyone might believe *through* him." The Greek preposition used here is *dia*, a word that is used with reference to the one who ministers as the agent of another person's will. Thus the ultimate agent is God, but the minister who carries out God's will in this particular instance is John the Baptist.

Verses 1:24–28, in addition to reinforcing the emphasis that John the Baptist is subordinate in importance to Jesus, refers to Elijah and "the prophet": "Why are you baptizing if you are not the Christ, and not Elijah, and not the prophet?" The question the men sent by the Pharisees are asking refers to two quotations in the Old Testament about the coming of the Messiah. Malachi 4:5–6 reads: "Know that I am going to send you Elijah the prophet before my day comes, that great and terrible day...." The Book of Deuteronomy 18:15 says: "Your God will raise up for you a prophet like myself [Moses], from among yourselves, from your own brothers; to him you must listen..." and in verse 18 again, "I will raise up a prophet like yourself for them from their own brothers; I will put my words into his mouth and he shall tell them all I command him."

The writers of the New Testament are steeped in, and very much aware of, the Old Testament. They wish to show that the prophecies and intimations of the Old Testament are fulfilled in Christ. If they can demonstrate this to be the case, the message of and about Christ will be more acceptable to the Jews, but more than that, if it can be shown that Old Testament prophecy is fulfilled in Christ, it also shows that God's overall plan of salvation is being completed. A distinguishing feature of the religion and faith of Judaism and Christianity is its linear dimension. There is a *telos*, that is, a goal, toward which all creation is moving. This goal is nothing other than the fulfillment of God's plan. This teleological (goal-seeking) aspect of Judaism/Christianity is one of the features that distinguishes it from virtually all of the other religious faiths with which it competed. We find nothing like it, for instance, in the Greek-originated paganism of the day, nor in ancient Egyptian or Babylonian religion. Only Zoroastrianism — with its cosmic struggle between the forces of darkness (Ahriman) and those of light (Ahura-Mazda) that one day would culminate in a conclusive cosmic battle, shared something of this teleological aspect. The author of the Fourth Gospel is anxious not only to show the supremacy of Jesus over John and not only to show that Old Testament prophecy is being fulfilled, but also to show that what transpired in Christ is the fulfillment of a divine intention, only dimly perceived by people of old, but now made clear in Christ.

The psychology of individuation also has a teleological aspect. It points out that the life in us is striving toward a goal that is usually unseen and unrecognized by consciousness but is known somewhere in the unconscious. The increasing recognition by consciousness that such a goal exists and the increasing cooperation of the ego with the fulfillment of this goal make up an important part of psychological development. The fact that the achievement of such a psychological goal seems to be intrinsically important fortifies the faith that there is an overall purpose to life. Philosophically this kind of thinking, rooted in the Old Testament and the New Testament, flowered in the ancient world in the thinking of a man such as Origen and in modern times in the thinking of Teilhard de Chardin. Psychologically it finds expression in the thinking of C. G. Jung and Fritz Kunkel.

The symbolism of immersion and washing in water has a widespread and ancient history. In the Old Testament there are a number of instances of a ritual bathing that is cleansing, healing, and renewing. For instance, in 2 Kings 5:14 we have the story of Naaman the Syrian whose leprosy was cleansed by bathing seven times in the Jordan River according to the instructions of Elisha. In the Septuagint (the Greek version of the Old Testament) several words for a ceremonial washing to cleanse oneself from moral or spiritual pollution were used. The simple verb *baptein,* which means "to dip," occurs frequently, as does the verb *louō,* which means to wash the whole body. But four times the intensive verb *baptizein* is used, one example being the story of Naaman just mentioned.

Virtually everywhere throughout the world baptismal ceremonies occur that involve initiation or ceremonial cleansing. So widespread are they that some form of baptism symbolism seems to be common to the entire human race. Some of these ancient forms of baptism continued to be used even among a people converted to Christianity. It is said, for instance, that in old Iceland and parts of Norway, when an infant was born, the father decided if the child should be destroyed or allowed to live. If the latter choice was made, water was poured over the child and the child was given a name. Henceforth, if anyone killed that person it was regarded by the community as murder. Even after Christianity was introduced into Norway about 1000 C.E. it is said that the ancient form of baptism continued along with Christian baptism.[1]

Scholars are quick to point out that there does not appear to be a direct historical connection between pagan baptism and Christian baptism. However, when a symbolic ceremony is as widespread as that of baptism we can be certain that it has an archetypal meaning. The archetypal meaning in this case is the universal need for spiritual cleansing and for the renewal of life that is represented by the immersion into and re-emergence from water. Psychologically the water symbolizes the waters of the unconscious out of which our psychic life originally emerged, and the immersion is a symbol for the death of an old ego state and emergence of a new one, which is a sine qua non if individuation is to take place.

This being the case, it is not surprising that our dreams are filled with symbols suggestive of ancient baptismal symbolism. Common baptismal dream motifs occur in dreams in which the dreamer is taking a bath or shower and sometimes in dreams in which the dreamer is swimming in a pool, stream, lake, or ocean. Such dreams suggest the importance of psychological and spiritual cleansing. What we need to be cleansed of may be our sins and errors, but it may also be our contamination from the psychological pollution of our times, that is, from what might be called "collective contamination." The ideas, attitudes, and egocentric emotions that we have and that other people around us have are highly contaminating. Consider, for instance, to take an extreme example, what it would have been like to have lived in Nazi Germany in the early and mid-1930s. The atmosphere would have been filled with highly emotionally toned and psychologically contaminating thoughts. Only the spiritually strongest and purest people could have survived in such an environment without becoming infected themselves. The need for a baptismal cleansing

---

1. James Hastings, ed., *Dictionary of the Bible* (New York: Charles Scribner and Sons, 1911), 1:239.

was urgent. The same situation exists in any social and political atmosphere in which there is a collective prevailing attitude. The need for cleansing from such psychic contamination is often stressed in dreams, as mentioned above.

The symbolism of alchemy is also rich in baptismal imagery. The ancient art and work of alchemy was an attempt to produce the marvelous and wonderful "philosopher's stone." This stone would bestow all manner of benefits on the human race including healing, renewal of life, and the attainment of incorruptibility. In order to fashion the philosopher's stone the alchemist placed in a sealed alchemical vas or retort an original substance called the "prima materia." This substance each alchemist had to discover for himself; it was symbolized in the literature in a wide variety of ways but always as something common, crass, and generally regarded as valueless (that is, the unconscious). The material in the retort was then heated, carefully watched, and prayed over and went through a wide variety of changes that the alchemists described in a bewildering number of fantastic images and symbols. If all went well, after many efforts and failures, and after great energy had been poured into the work by the alchemist and his female companion, known as the "soror mystica," the philosopher's stone would emerge. Before the age of enlightenment, alchemy was widespread and many famous Christians were alchemists, including Albertus Magnus and Thomas Aquinas. The church apparently saw no conflict, and while not actively espousing alchemy, managed to look the other way. For the Christian alchemists it was clear that the philosopher's stone was nothing other than Christ himself. It's fair to say that for many medieval Christians, alchemy carried the esoteric, mystical side of the faith. That is, it was a way of appropriating to Christianity the psychology of the unconscious.

One of the great works of C. G. Jung was to rescue the rich symbolism of alchemy from the rubbish heap of the world where it had been thrown along with myths, fairy tales, and the like. Jung has shown in his works *Psychology and Alchemy* and *The Mysterium Coniunctionis* that the symbols of alchemy are symbols of the individuation process and that the philosopher's stone is a symbol for the emergence of that wholeness of personality he called the Self. He also showed that at least seven typical stages of transformation of the elements in the retort took place, and that these seven stages of transformation are symbolic of typical

processes of change and development that underlie the process
of individuation. One of these stages was known in alchemy as
the *solutio*.

In the *solutio* the fixed, rigid form of the elements in the retort are dissolved; this allows for their reformation in a new way.
Edward F. Edinger has done a masterful job of presenting the
psychological meaning of alchemical symbolism, quoting as an
example of the *solutio* an ancient text: "Bodies cannot be changed
except by reduction into their first matter."[2] Psychologically this
corresponds to the need for the periodic dissolving of a personality formation and ego state that is too rigid and fixed so that
nothing new can emerge. This process of psychological dissolution is, in practice, often a frightening time, for when we feel
our old personality dissolving we are not always confident that
something else is coming to take its place. At this point a certain
amount of faith is required as well as, quite often, the moral and
psychological assistance of another person.

Edinger says that one effect of analysis is to dissolve the old
personality structures that are no longer adequate for life and
growth: "This [dissolving] is done by the analytic process, which
examines the products of the unconscious and puts the established ego attitudes into question."[3] It is accomplished by life
itself, which constantly calls on us to question ourselves and by
producing suffering tends to dissolve the old personality and
force the development of a new one. As mentioned, when this particular stage of psychic development is indicated, various forms
of water symbolism may appear in our dreams, for water symbolizes the dissolving element, just as in our waking life every
time anyone sheds genuine tears he or she has undergone a bit
of the ancient alchemical *solutio*.

The church has formalized all of this into its sacrament of baptism. Originally, in the early church, baptism was a numinous
ceremony. It was, in fact, a *mystērion*, in the sense in which it was
discussed in chapter 3. As Hugo Rahner has pointed out and as
we mentioned before, there were two Christian "mysteries": that
of baptism and that of the cross. What was understood in the
early church as the *mystērion* of baptism will be discussed at a
later time. Suffice it for now to say that for most people today

---

2. Edward F. Edinger, *The Anatomy of the Psyche* (La Salle, Ill.: Open Court Publishing
Co., 1985), 47.
3. Ibid., 48.

the church's present ceremony may be a meaningful and socially significant event but it lacks the numinosity that baptism once had for people.

When the numinosity has left an ancient ceremonial it vanishes back into the unconscious, so for some people their baptism now consists of an immersion into the unconscious. As a priest once said to me after he had experienced his own inner depths, "My journal and my dreams are now my baptism and confirmation." Most people no longer feel the power of ancient ceremonies, nor even believe in them any more, but our psychological need for them remains. Now some people have to dip into the waters of the unconscious in order to find the power once again.

After chapter 3, John the Baptist is mentioned in the Fourth Gospel only in passing (John 4:1; 5:33ff; 10:41). His death is not recorded for us in this Gospel, but we are told in Matthew 14:3ff and Mark 6:24 that he was beheaded by Herod the King at the behest of his wife Herodias and her daughter, Herodias being furious with John the Baptist because he criticized Herod for marrying her. (John the Baptist said it was against the law for Herod to marry Herodias because she had been the wife of his brother Philip.) It is interesting to note that John the Baptist died because of a woman. It may be that his ascetic life and somewhat aloof bearing angered women. Whatever the reason, it is worth noting that there is no record in the Gospels, as far as I know, of any woman ever being angry at or having anything against Jesus, with the possible exception of the Samaritan woman by the well, which incident we will consider later. To the contrary, we meet many women in the Gospels who knew Jesus and they all had either a fruitful encounter with him or a warm relationship with him. It is to the subject of Jesus and his relationship with women and the feminine principle that we now turn.

~ 5 ~

THE FEMININE GOSPEL
The Wedding Feast at Cana
John 2:1–11

THE STORY OF THE WEDDING FEAST AT CANA is one of the most perplexing and yet most beautiful stories in John's Gospel. On the third day after the day on which the disciples were called, Jesus and his disciples are invited to a wedding that his mother is attending. After an interesting interchange with his mother, Jesus performs the kind of physical miracle that we find almost incredible. It is similar to the miracle of the loaves and fishes, except there is the added feature that, as the Abingdon Bible Commentary notes, "the occasion does not seem adequate for such a display of supernatural power." One explanation is that the story is an allegory: just as Jesus changed the water into wine, so Christ changes the old religion of Judaism into the new wine of a religion based on his forthcoming resurrection. The difficulty here is that John uses symbolic discourses to convey his message and not allegories.

Scholars are helpful with regard to certain of the details of the story. For instance, we are informed that the six jars of water would hold about one hundred gallons — quite a bit of wine. The Jerusalem Bible also tells us that the Greek idiom *ti emoi kai sol* (verse 4), which it translates "why turn to me?" and the King James Version translates, "what have I to do with thee?" is a Semitic-based idiom common to both the Old Testament and the New Testament that is used in expressions in which the desire is to turn away interference from another person. The Jerusalem Bible also assures us that in verse 12 the reference to "brothers" does not refer to blood brothers of Jesus, but to the "inner circle of the first disciples." To reinforce their point they translate this verse: "After this he went down to Capernaum with his mother and the brothers...." However, the King James Version and other translations say: "After this he went down to Capernaum, he, and his mother, and his brethren, and his disciples." Since the Greek refers to both "brothers" (*adelphoi*) *and* "disciples" (*mathētai*), the Jerusalem Bible would seem to be out of line here. One suspects that the translators of the Jerusalem Bible may be trying to protect the Roman Catholic idea that Mary was a virgin all her life, in which case Jesus could not have had brothers.

All the commentators seem to agree that verses 11–12 are an "aside" from the author to substantiate the fact that Jesus performed miracles. This seems curious, since in many places in the Fourth Gospel Jesus disparages the efficacy of miracles in producing and maintaining faith (3:1, 6:29–30; 7:3, 31; 9:16, 33). It may be, however, that John felt the need to tell this story because the Old Testament said that every true prophet must be associated with "signs" (see Isa. 7:11ff).

Two aspects of this story have important psychological significance. First is the joyful nature of the event in which Jesus participated and the way he added to the festivities by providing an abundance of excellent wine. Unlike John the Baptist, Jesus was not an ascetic, leading a quasi-hermitlike existence. To the contrary, he evidently participated in and encouraged human warmth of fellowship and joy of spirit. He is also shown here as quite different from the Essenes, with whom he has often been compared. Indeed some scholars argue that Jesus himself was an Essene and took his teaching from them, a point we will comment on later.

The emphasis in this passage on joy is also a reminder that the process of individuation has its joyful side. Jungian descriptions of the individuation process often emphasize its dark and painful aspects, of which there are a great many, but it is not all darkness and pain. For one thing, the process of individuation puts us in touch with "what we are all about," and thus with our creative energies. As Marie-Louise von Franz once pointed out, "When someone does what he or she is created to do that per-

son experiences joy or satisfaction."[1] Life is hard enough without
psychological pessimists overlooking the fact that the life of individuation does offer times of spontaneous and creative joy in
diverse ways. It also must be said that a life in which someone is
individuating, hard though it is, is more rewarding than a life in
which one does not individuate. John's story of the changing of
the water into wine reminds us of this.

The second aspect of this story, which speaks to the nature of
individuation, concerns Jesus' relationship to the feminine, and
it is to this that we now turn.

In verses 3–4 there is an interchange between Jesus and his
mother that sounds severe to the modern reader. Mary says to
Jesus: "They have no wine." Clearly the implication is that Jesus
should do something about it. Jesus replies, "Woman, why turn to
me? My hour has not yet come." The Abingdon Bible Commentary tells us that the use of the term "woman" in this way was
not at that time derogatory or discourteous. The Jerusalem Bible,
however, says it was an unusual form of address, repeated, however, in a highly positive light in John 19:26. The fact that Mary
implied Jesus should do something about the lack of wine suggests that she believed her son had unusual powers. The main
thrust of Jesus' reply to Mary is that he cannot follow the will
or prodding of any human being, but takes direction from God
alone. In spite of Jesus' seeming bluntness Mary is not the least offended or discouraged, and in the manner of a woman who knows
she is going to get her way, confidently tells the servants to do
what he tells them to do. The story depicts an intimate and warm
connection between Jesus and his mother and a friendly participation by Jesus in the festivities of the wedding. Now, weddings are
celebrations in honor of the bride and of the feminine, so the story
raises the question of Jesus' relationship to the feminine principle and to women, a subject of importance since in the process of
individuation a man's or woman's relationship to the feminine
is of paramount importance. In order to understand where the
Fourth Gospel stands on this matter we must first understand
the situation with regard to the feminine in the Bible as a whole.

The psychology of individuation in our times is calling for a re-

---

1. Paraphrased from memory. Marie Louise Von Franz was a close colleague to C. G.
Jung and is the author of many books on Jungian thought.

emphasis on feminine values, the emancipation of women from masculine domination, and the rediscovery of feminine archetypal images in the psyche. It also calls for the end to patriarchy and patriarchal values, that is, to the end of a psychological situation in which men dominate women, social structures are weighed in favor of men, feminine values are denigrated, and feminine images eclipsed in value by masculine ones.

Because patriarchal systems and values have dominated Western culture — including the church — for so long, as women struggle for social and economic equality with men and as they become conscious of the way patriarchal values have dominated our society and injured their sense of and respect for themselves, they often become resentful of anything that smacks of male domination. This often includes the Bible, Christianity, and the church, since many women — and a good many men too — see the Bible as a patriarchal document. After all, is not God a "he"? Is not Yahweh a fiercely masculine God, of whom the God of the New Testament is an outgrowth? Is not Jesus, in whom God was incarnated, a male? Does not St. Paul denigrate women and assign them to inferior social and spiritual roles? In commenting on this, Sandra Schneiders writes: "The tenacity of the patriarchal God-image is such that many feminists have decided that the only course open to women whose self-image has been healed of gender inferiority and whose world-image has been healed of hierarchy in general and patriarchy in particular is to abandon the Christian God altogether."[2]

Schneiders, who is what might be called a "biblically informed feminist," has written a remarkably insightful and lucid treatment of the sex and gender of God in the Bible, the reason why God was incarnated in a male, and why women who seek a grounding for their spirituality do not have to reject the Christian Scriptures. It is not possible to include all of the tightly packed argument she includes in her book, but certain salient features that are especially relevant to our concerns can be touched upon.

Schneiders begins by pointing out that theology never assigned sex to God, for the Bible says that God is pure spirit and spirit does not have sex. She quotes John 4:24 in this connection, in which Jesus says to the Samaritan woman: "God is spirit, and

2. Sandra M. Schneiders, *Women and the Word: The Gender of God in the New Testament and the Spirituality of Women* (New York: Paulist Press, 1986), 19.

those who worship must worship in spirit and truth." As for the language that denotes God as the *Father* and the *Son*, she says that Gregory of Nyssa "well represented the tradition when he affirmed that the terms 'Father' and 'Son' as applied to persons of the Trinity were not names of natures or essences but of relations and ... [furthermore] ... the terms are used metaphorically."

But when we leave the realm of theology and venture into the world of religious imagination the situation becomes more complicated. Our God-image, as Schneiders points out, is determined largely by our imagination, and our imagination is shaped by the metaphors that are used to depict the nature of the God that Judaism and Christianity espouse. Because the church and, purportedly, the Bible use so many masculine metaphors with reference to God, it produces a situation in which a woman who reads the Bible "must see herself as an inferior version of humanity subject first to human men and ultimately to the infinite divine male who established the patriarchal world organization."[3] What is needed, she says, is "a therapy of the religious imagination."

Schneiders proceeds to explore the metaphorical language for God in the Old Testament. First she notes that the only name for God that we have — the Hebrew YHWH, a "word" never meant to be pronounced — seems to translate out into "I am" and has no gender attached to it at all. Second, she notes that the most important personification of God in the Old Testament is feminine, and this is that of Wisdom/Sophia, which we have already discussed at length in chapter 2. There is also the name given by the Rabbis to the mysteriously visible manifestations of God among his people as found in the Bible: the Shekinah. Shekinah and Sophia are feminine both in grammatical structure and in imagination. Third, when it comes to metaphors, the majority that are used are masculine, but many of them are sexually neutral, and a significant number are feminine. For example, God is metaphorically described as a spring (Jer. 2:13), a she-bear (Hos. 13:7–8), and a mother eagle (Deut. 32:11–12). God as a parent to Israel is indeed frequently described as a father (Deut. 1:31), but often the father-image is combined with maternal metaphors. For instance, Moses says that God, not he, "conceived" the people of Israel, and that God carries them like a "foster-father carrying an unweaned child" (Num. 11:12), or, in some translations, that

3. Ibid., 18.

God carries the people of Israel in the "hidden place," that is, a divine womb or bosom (Hebrew *chob*, "hidden place"). Again, in Isaiah, God says to Israel, "As a mother comforts a child, so I shall comfort you" (Isa. 66:13). Indeed, as Schneiders points out, the typical word in the Old Testament for the mercy or compassion of God is *rehem*, the Hebrew word for womb (see Isa. 63:15). Another interesting feminine metaphor for God is found in Isaiah 42:14 in which God's anguish for Israel is compared to the anguish of a woman in childbirth: "I have kept quiet, held myself in check, groaning like a woman in labour." Furthermore, and here she makes an important point, the number of feminine metaphors for God is all the more remarkable because they fly in the teeth of a predominantly patriarchal culture.[4]

Another important aspect of the feminine nature of God is found in the idea of the "grace of God." The English word "grace" is a translation of the Greek word *charis*, which is feminine in gender.[5] *Charis* means "favor, gracious care or help which is rendered from one person to another on a voluntary basis, an action which is given freely and to which the person who renders the help is not bound." It is an important word in the New Testament, found twenty-one times in the Epistle to the Romans alone. God's grace is one of the Deity's primary attributes, but more than that, the divine *charis* is often personified and hypostasized in much the same way that Wisdom/Sophia was personified and hypostasized. This comes out in the Greek more clearly than in the English. For instance, in Romans 3:24 we find a construction in Greek known as "the dative of means." In such a construction a noun is placed in the dative case in order to demonstrate its instrumentality as an agent of action. So the King James Version translates this verse. "Being justified freely by his grace..." (*dikaioumenoi dōrean tē autou chariti...*). In Acts 15:11 the quasi-independent status of *charis* is put even more strongly in a Greek construction that uses the preposition *dia*. This preposition is used to denote the quasi-independent agency through which something is accomplished. The English translation is "But we believe that through the grace [*dia tēs charitos*] of the Lord Jesus Christ we shall be saved...."

When it comes to Jesus' use of metaphors we find that a sur-

---

4. All biblical quotations in this section are from the NJB.
5. Among the Greeks there were three goddesses who bestowed gracious favors among humankind. They were the three *Charitae* (Graces).

prising number of them were feminine. For instance, take the
story in John 3 in which Jesus talks with Nicodemus. In this passage, as elsewhere in the Fourth Gospel, God is referred to as
spirit, which, as we have noted, has neither sex nor gender. But
he does say that Nicodemus must be born again through water
and, in an image we will explore in more depth later, likens this
rebirth to entering again into a great divine maternal womb.

In a particularly interesting passage of Schneiders's book, she
compares the parable of the shepherd who looks for his lost sheep
with the parable that follows it, of the women who searched for
her lost coin. (Both appear in Luke 15.) It is remarkable, she points
out, that in the first parable commentators and tradition have not
hesitated to identify the shepherd in the first parable with God
(hence male), but they have not identified the woman in the second parable with God, even though that would appear to be the
logical thing to do. It is clearly Jesus' intent that both "shepherd"
and "searching woman" are to be understood as metaphors for
God but so blinded are we by our assumptions that the biblical
God must be masculine that we overlook the obvious: i.e., that
both masculine and feminine images portray the Deity. The same
thing is true of the parable of the bakerwoman in Matthew 13:33
and Luke 13:20–21. In this parable *we* are the flour through which
the yeast is leavened all through, and the woman who does the
mixing is a metaphor for God. As for himself, in Matthew 23:37,
Jesus describes himself as a "mother hen longing to coddle her
chicks under her wing." These and many other feminine metaphors are striking and make it clear that in spite of the numerical
preponderance of masculine metaphors for God still, as far as
the biblical image is concerned, the full description of the divine
nature requires them both.

However, we still have to contend with the use of the father-
son relationship, used by Jesus himself, to describe his relationship with God. If God is to be thought of as feminine as well as
masculine, why does he not use a mother-son relationship image
as well as one based on the relationship of father and son? Schneiders's answer is that the exclusive use of the father-son image is
because of the dominance of the patriarchal culture. She argues
that in the Jewish culture of the day no other parental relationship could have been used because Jesus was described as having
been *sent* into the world by God, and in that day women and
mothers lacked the social standing to have enabled them to have

trained and sent their sons into the world to fulfill a purpose. She writes, "In the patriarchal culture of Jesus a mother-son relationship could not have carried this meaning [of being sent] because mothers had no independent trades and they did not train their male children for adult work."[6] If Jesus had used any other parent metaphor than the one he used to explain his relationship to God, it would not have been understood. Moreover, even though he spoke of this relationship as that of a son to a father, he did not use *patriarchal* language or imagery, for a father is not necessarily a patriarch.

In a patriarchal system, the ruling person is a male who has domination and control over all property, goods, and members of his household and dominion, even to the point of life and death. Jesus never speaks in this way of God when he refers to him as "father," for a father is not necessarily a patriarch, and, like a mother, can be protective, self-sacrificing, and nurturing. In fact, Jesus often uses the Aramaic term "Abba" when referring to God, an informal term of endearment that means something like "Dad." Schneiders notes that modern translators are so uncomfortable with the idea that Jesus spoke of God as "Dad" that they refuse to translate the Aramaic term into its English equivalent even though the meaning is clear. In fact, she notes, in the parable of the prodigal son, which is the only parable in which Jesus presents his idea of the fatherhood of God, the image of God with which we are presented is the "very antithesis of patriarchy."[7] She points out that rather than endorsing patriarchy and patriarchal values, Jesus radically challenges them. She concludes:

> In Jesus' culture the father-son metaphor was the only one capable of carrying the meaning of his integral involvement in the work of salvation originated by God. Second, by his use of "Abba" for God and his presentation of God as the father of the prodigal, Jesus was able to transform totally the patriarchal God-image. He hailed the father metaphor which had been patriarchalized in the image of human power structures and restored to it the original meaning of divine origination in and through love. Third, he delegitimized human patriarchy by invalidating its appeal to divine institution.[8]

---

6. Schneiders, *Women and the Word*, 43.
7. Ibid., 46.
8. Ibid., 48.

But was not Jesus himself a male, and since he was in the incarnation of God does this not tip the scales in favor of male versus female images of the divine? Schneiders makes a shrewd response. One of the purposes of the incarnation was to undermine the patriarchal domination that had gripped the whole culture. This could not have been done had God been incarnated as a woman because as a woman he would have been rejected in his role by one and all. In his culture, only men were listened to, and for this reason alone the incarnation had to take place in a man.[9] She concludes:

> Only as a man could he have subverted the accepted definition of masculinity, validated the so-called feminine virtues despised by men but dear to God, redefined the relationship between women and men as one of equality and mutuality, and destroyed patriarchy's claim to divine sanction.[10]

The positive relationship of Jesus to feminine values to which Sandra Schneiders calls our attention is nowhere more exemplified than in the Fourth Gospel, in which Jesus is portrayed as having a remarkably close relationship to several women, and in which the women play a more spiritually developed role than the men. There are four good examples of this, plus a good example of a careful attempt by John to avoid sexist language, which we will examine in the next chapter.

First is the encounter between the woman of Samaria and Jesus, recorded for us in chapter 4. We will examine this story in detail later on; suffice it for now to note that at the end of the story the Samaritan woman had become convinced that Jesus was a remarkable person, so much so that when she told her experience to the townspeople they "believed in him on the strength of the woman's testimony" (4:39). So impressed were they at what she said that they went to Jesus and implored him to spend some time with them, and Jesus did stay with them for two days, teaching them so that many more came to believe. This led the townspeople to say to the woman, "Now we no longer believe because of what

---

9. While the incarnation was in a man there is an ancient Christian tradition very much alive in Eastern Christianity today that the first human being to reach perfection ("deification") was a woman: Mary, the mother of Jesus.

·10. Schneiders, *Women and the Word*, 63.

you told us; we have heard him ourselves and we know that he really is the saviour of the world" (4:42).

Schneiders's argument is reinforced by Raymond E. Brown, who, in his book *The Community of the Beloved Disciple*, argues that the Samaritan woman was the first apostle, since the Samaritans of the town believed in Jesus because of what she told them and the convincing way in which she spoke.[11] Like an apostle, her belief and her words led others to faith. It is true, of course, that the villagers were not fully persuaded until they met Jesus themselves, but this is not the fault of the woman as an apostle; no one fully believes until they meet Jesus themselves. Brown feels that this apostleship of the woman was consciously intended by John. He points out that in the high priestly prayer of chapter 17 Jesus refers to those people who are to believe in him "through their word," that is, through the word of the disciples (17:20). In John 4:42 the people believe because of the words of the Samaritan woman. In Greek the grammatical construction that refers on the one hand to the words of the woman and on the other hand to the words of the apostles is almost identical.

The second example is that of Jesus' mother, whom we have already met in the story of the wedding feast at Cana. This is not the last we hear of Mary in the Gospel; she reappears at the crucifixion scene in which she is one of the three women who stayed at the foot of the cross while her son died. In 19:26, Jesus, looking down from the cross, united his mother and the disciple whom Jesus loved (who, as we have noted, is probably either the author of our Gospel or its major source) with the words: "Woman, this is your son." Then to the disciple he said, " 'This is your mother.' And from that moment the disciple made a place for her in his home." According to Brown, Jesus did much more than provide a home for his mother after his death. He believes that after the resurrection a unique Christian community developed whose main spiritual center was the Gospel of John and that the leaders of this community were both the beloved disciple *and Mary the mother of the Lord.* In short, Brown believes that on the cross Jesus elevated Mary to a position of authority in the Johannine community equal to that of the male apostles. Brown's thesis is corroborated by the fact that in the Eastern Orthodox Church Mary is regarded as

11. Raymond E. Brown, *The Community of the Beloved Disciple* (New York: Paulist Press, 1979), 187.

the first human being to have achieved deification — the ultimate goal of the Christian life — a point we will have occasion to return to later.

A third example is found in the fact that the first person to see the Risen Christ was a woman — Mary of Magdala. In John's account, there were four women who stayed by the cross during Jesus' agony, and one of these, Mary of Magdala, after Jesus died and had been buried, returned to the tomb on the first day of the week while it was still dark. She found it empty and ran to tell Peter and the others that someone must have taken the body from the tomb. The disciples go back with her to the tomb and see for themselves that it is empty. Later Mary returns to the tomb again alone, and there in the tomb she encounters the risen Christ. She runs to tell the disciples, to whom Jesus later appears himself.

This incident is of great importance, for in the early church to have seen the risen Lord was the mark of apostleship. John's version differs from the version found in the synoptic Gospels in which it is Peter who is the first to see the risen Christ. What we have then, in John's account, is the elevation by the evangelist of a woman to a place of primary importance both spiritually and in terms of her authority in the church.

The fourth and fifth examples come from the story of Mary and Martha, who, along with their brother Lazarus, were close friends of Jesus, so close that Jesus visited with them and stayed in their home. We will examine this story in detail later; what is important for our present consideration is that the first confession of faith in Jesus' messianic identity comes in the Fourth Gospel from the lips of a woman, for Martha says to Jesus: "I believe that you are the Christ, the Son of God, the one who was to come into this world" (11:27).

As is well known, the confession of faith by Peter is an event greatly celebrated in the Christian church. In fact, the Roman Catholic Church bases its claim to primacy on the fact that Peter was the first to recognize the messianic nature of Jesus and that Jesus was the Christ. Peter was therefore the "rock" on which the church was founded, and since Peter started the church in Rome, the Roman Church is preeminent. But why was there no similar claim for Martha's confession of faith? We can only lay the responsibility for this omission at the door of the patriarchal attitudes that were part of the culture out of which the church developed but were not part of the biblical account.

A final event that emphasizes the importance of women in the Fourth Gospel and in the eyes of Jesus is also found in the story of Mary, Martha, and Lazarus. In 11:5 we are told that "Jesus loved Martha and her sister and Lazarus." Curiously enough, we never hear in any of the Gospels that Jesus declared that he loved the disciples. No doubt he did, but the lack of a specific statement to this effect makes his declaration of love for the two women stand out all the more clearly. Not only were they given by Jesus a place of spiritual authority and eminence equal to men, but they were given a special place in his affections.

On several occasions we have referred to the patriarchal culture of the times. Now we need to look at this culture more closely. Only then can we appreciate the radical social consciousness of Jesus in the Fourth Gospel and how remarkable is the defense of women and feminine values that we find in the New Testament. We will examine the role of women in the Old Testament and Jewish culture at the time of Jesus, in Arabic cultures of the time, in Roman culture, and in Greek culture, and then compare these attitudes to those of John's Gospel.

The Old Testament has many examples of remarkable women, ranging from the gentle Ruth to the aggressive leader Deborah, who became one of the judges of Israel.[12] There are also examples of relationships in the Old Testament in which a man deeply loved and honored his wife, for example, Jacob's love for Rachel. Among the Rabbis, though most of them regarded women as inferior to men and taught accordingly, some of them were surprisingly enlightened. Nevertheless, the fundamental legal and social status of women in the Old Testament and also in the Judaism of the time of Jesus was distinctly inferior to that of men. For instance, it was required by law that boys be educated, but education for girls was not legally required and seldom undertaken, except for the training given to them in matters of running the household. Legally a woman belonged to a man, little better off than his property or chattel. In all important respects her husband was her lord and master. She had nothing to say about the man whom she would marry. Her father had the right to give her to any man he chose; or she might become a concubine or be taken

---

12. For further background information see Morton and Barbara Kelsey, *The Sacrament of Sexuality* (Warwick, N.Y.: Amity House, 1986), 75ff, and John T. Bristow, *What Paul Really Said about Women* (San Francisco: HarperCollins, 1988), 18.

in war. The man ruled in the home too. Women were not to eat with men. The good wife would prepare and serve her husband's food but would eat separately from him.

A man had the legal right to divorce his wife for any cause. In fact, Jewish law required a man whose wife had been barren for ten years either to divorce her and marry again or take a second wife. Elaine Pagels, in her book *Adam, Eve and the Serpent*, suggests that this law stemmed from ancient times when it was imperative to maintain a high birth rate.[13] It did not, of course, occur to anyone in that era that the reason for childlessness might have something to do with the man.

When it came to adultery, it went unpunished in the man, but if a woman was taken in adultery she might be killed. This law was still in effect at the time of Jesus, which is why, in John 8:1–11, we read that the woman taken in adultery was to be stoned to death. This makes Jesus' attitude toward divorce and adultery all the more remarkable. It must have been a surprise even to his disciples when he refused to condemn the woman who was to be stoned for her adultery and shocking to all who heard him say: "The man who divorces his wife and marries another is guilty of adultery" (Mark 10:12; Matt. 5:32; Luke 16:18).

The role of women in the Arabic culture of Jesus' time has been well summarized by Will Durant. After noting that the Arab man greatly valued the "consuming beauty" of women, Durant continues with these words:

> Before Mohammed — and after him only slightly less so — the career of the Arab woman passed from a moment's idolatry to a lifetime of drudgery. She might be buried at birth if the father so willed; at best he mourned her coming and hid his face from his fellows; somehow his best efforts had failed. Her winsome childhood earned a few years of love; but at seven or eight she was married off to any youth of the clan whose father would offer the purchase price for the bride. Her lover and husband would fight the world to defend her person or honor; some of the seeds and fustian of chivalry went with these passionate lovers to Spain. But the goddess was also the chattel; she formed part of the estate of her father, her husband, or her son, and was bequeathed with it; she was always the servant, rarely the comrade, of

---

13. Elaine Pagels, *Adam, Eve and the Serpent* (New York: Random House, 1988).

the man. He demanded many children of her, or rather many sons; her duty was to produce warriors. She was, in many cases, but one of his many wives. He could dismiss her at any time at will.[14]

Most of this fiercely masculine patriarchal attitude toward women passed into the Koran, and much of it is still in force in Arabic cultures today.

In Rome things were not much better for women than in the Semitic cultures. In the days of the Republic the rule of *paterfamilias* prevailed, and the ruling patriarch (father of the family) was absolute. He was the only one in the family with any legal rights, the only one who could buy, hold, or sell property. If his wife was accused of a crime he stood in judgment over her. If she was caught in adultery he could sentence her to death. He chose his daughter's husband, but even if married she remained under her father's legally sanctioned domination. So strong was his power that it endured even if he became insane. As for the woman, she was never free; at each stage of her life a man ruled her: father, brother, husband, son, guardian. Nevertheless, this harshly patriarchal code was mitigated by the effect of public opinion, the natural love often prevailing between a man and woman, and the dignity accorded her status as the woman of the home.

As wealth increased in Rome greater liberties were given to women, but things went too far for Augustus who, in the year 18 B.C.E., reaffirmed the father's right to kill an adulterous daughter and bring his adulterous wife to court. Convicted of adultery, a woman under Augustus's law was banished for life and forfeited the bulk of her wealth, such as it might have been. On the other hand, a man could not be charged with adultery and was also legally permitted to have relations with prostitutes.

In certain parts of Greece from the Homeric era until the inception of Christianity, the position of women was relatively good. It would appear that the influence of the early matriarchal mythology that predated the mythology of the Olympian gods left a legacy for women that was one of the most favorable in the ancient world. For instance, in Sparta men and women were equal under the law, and women could inherit property, own it in their

---

14. Will Durant, *The Age of Faith* (New York: Simon and Schuster, 1950), 158.

own name, and bequeath it upon their death. Divorce was rare, and there was no one-sided punishment for adultery.

In Athens, however, the situation was markedly different. Some people ascribe this difference to the influence of Greek philosophy. For example, John T. Bristow points out that such Greek philosophers as Socrates, Aristotle, Demosthenes, Zeno, and Epictetus all regarded women as inferior to men; they said women were important only for their usefulness to men, and that for the philosopher (who was the noblest of men of course) they were distractions and temptations. In fact, for a woman in Athens there were three alternatives: she could be a prostitute, one of the *hetairai*, or a wife. The *hetairai* consisted of a small class of women especially set aside to be trained to be the companions of men: they were the only women who received any education, except in matters of household duties, and most of them were not Greeks but foreigners. Legally the Athenian woman had no standing in court and could not inherit her husband's property. She was expected to live a quiet life in the home, produce children, and see to the needs of her husband. Men participated in sports, circulated freely in the *agora* (marketplace), were educated, and debated philosophy. Women were virtually secluded, never leaving home except to visit members of the family, and even at home they were not to be seen through the windows of the house. If a man came to visit her husband, she removed herself to the women's quarters. It is not surprising that while Greece during the age of Pericles had many notable women who contributed to literature and poetry, there were none in the age of the philosophers.

Consider, for instance, the speech by Medea in Euripides' play by that name. Medea, betrayed by her husband Jason, makes this angry lament about the loss of her husband and the bitter lot of women in ancient Athens:

> But me — the blow ye wot of suddenly fell
> Soul-shattering. 'Tis my ruin: I have lost
> All grace of life: I long to die, O Friends.
> He, to know whom well was mine all in all,
> My lord, of all men basest hath become!
> Surely, of creatures that have life and wit,
> We women are of all unhappiest,
> Who, first, must buy, as buys the highest bidder,
> A husband — nay, we do but win for our lives

> A master! Deeper depth of wrong is this.
> Here too is dire risk — will the lord we gain
> Be evil or good? Divorce? — 'tis infamy
> To us: we may not even reject a suitor![15]

Unfortunately, it was the patriarchal culture of Athens, not the culture of Sparta, that influenced the eastern part of the Mediterranean world. When Alexander the Great conquered Asia Minor, Persia, Judea, Syria, and Egypt, he took Attic culture with him. Greek culture, language, and attitudes became the norm throughout the whole area of what became the eastern portion of the Roman Empire. This process is known as "Hellenization," and it affected Jews and Gentiles alike.

Another influence that had an antifeminine bias that influenced the attitudes of people in the early years of Christianity comes from certain forms of Gnosticism. About the year 150 C.E. the influential Gnostic philosopher Valentinus promulgated a teaching about the Fall in which a feminine aspect played the crucial role. According to Valentinus, there were many emanations from the primordial source of all being. The last of these was Sophia, but Sophia acted foolishly. Instead of being content with her place in the cosmogonic scheme of things, she longed to be close to the Source (the Father). Because she was not content with her place, sufferings, fear, confusion, grief, and ignorance came into existence.

The same Gnostic devaluation of the feminine is found in certain Gnostic writings in which it is made clear that women cannot be saved. For instance, the *Gospel of Thomas,* one of the documents found at Nag Hammadi in 1945, concludes with a discussion between Simon Peter and Jesus. Peter says to Jesus, "Let Mary go out from among us, because women are not worthy of the Life." But Jesus generously replies, "See, I shall lead her, so that I will make her male, that she too may become a living spirit, resembling you males. For every woman who makes herself male will enter the Kingdom of Heaven" (Logion 114). The difference between the attitude toward women ascribed to Peter and Jesus by the Gnostics and the attitude that we find in the Fourth Gospel is striking.

Now it is true that the patriarchal laws and attitudes we have summarized may not always have been observed in practice.

---

15. Since the parents of a Greek girl chose her husband for her. The quote is from *Medea,* lines 225ff, translation by A. S. Way, in the Loeb Classical Library edition.

Women found ways to have adulterous relationships in spite of the death penalty that could be applied to them. Men no doubt genuinely loved their wives and treated them well even though the law did deny them their legal rights. They were certainly often honored in the home, and they certainly must have found ways to exert their psychological and emotional influence on men and get their own way when they so desired. Nevertheless, the social, legal, and marital status of women in the culture in which Christianity emerged was distinctly inferior to that of men. It was into this atmosphere that Christ came bearing his message about the importance of women and feminine values, a message made evident in words, in his relationships with women, in his appeal to women, and in the fact that women were the first to recognize the divine reality within him. This positive valuation of women and the feminine is all the more remarkable because its values are so different from those of the dominant patriarchal culture.

But how about St. Paul? Is he not an embodiment of patriarchal values, and does not his attitude stand in sharp contrast to that of Christ? So it would seem upon a superficial examination of certain of his writings, for did he not seem to say that women were beneath men? that they must be submissive to men? and (if you concede that Paul wrote 1 Timothy) even that they could only be saved by childbirth while men were saved spiritually through Christ? The fact is, however, that Paul's words have been distorted. John Bristow, in his book *What Paul Really Said about Women*, makes a cogent argument that the situation is quite the contrary, that Paul, far from being against women, was almost as much of a feminist as Christ himself. It is to this issue that we now turn.

First it should be pointed out that Paul disregarded the prevalent social conventions that called for the segregation of women socially and in religious functions, that he appointed many women to positions of influence in the early church, and that he was in favor of the equal education of women. Bristow summarizes Paul's record in this regard by pointing out the following facts:

- The first convert Paul made in Europe was a woman, Lydia (Acts 16:11–15).

- His message was always aimed at both men and women, and both sexes responded to it (Acts 17:4, 11–12).

- Many women believers are mentioned by name and were known by Paul personally (Acts 17:34).

- Paul frequently and openly recognized the importance of women as leaders in the churches (Phil. 4:2–3).

- Paul often describes women as his co-workers, and in at least one reference to a Christian couple he names the woman first, indicating her primary importance (Rom. 16:3–4).

- In the closing portion of Romans, of the twenty-six people whom he mentions by name, seven are women, and the first one on the list is a woman.

- In Romans 16, Paul names as an apostle a woman, Junias, of whom John Chrysostom later declared: "Oh how great is the devotion of this woman, that she should even be counted worthy of the appellation of apostle![16]

These references are impressive, but how about those places in the epistles in which Paul, as noted, seemed clearly to regard women as inferior to men? The three most important such references are Ephesians 5:21–23, 1 Corinthians 11, and 1 Timothy 2:9–15. Bristow gives these passages special scrutiny in his book, looking at them with a view to their original meaning in Greek and their setting in the cultural context of their day. His findings are illuminating and well worth reading in their entirety in his book. The gist of his linguistic argument is as follows:

In the passage from Ephesians, the key verse is 5:21–24:

> Give way to one another in obedience to Christ. Wives should regard their husbands as they regard the Lord, since as Christ is *head* of the Church and saves the whole body, so is a husband the *head* of his wife; and as the Church *submits* to Christ, so should wives to their husbands in everything.

I have emphasized the key words in this passage, which seems to relegate to women a submissive role inferior to that of men. The first word is "head." Of course the New Testament was not

---

16. *Nicene and Post-Nicene Fathers*, 11:554 and 13:515.

written in English but in Greek, so to be accurate we must refer
to the original Greek translated in English as "head." Here we
discover that while there is only one English word for "head,"
there are two Greek words, and they have distinctly different
meanings. One of these words is *archē*, which means "first in point
of importance, power, and origin." The second Greek word is
kephalē, which means "head, as in the head of the body." *Kephalē*
is never used in the sense of "to rule over" but sometimes is used
in military parlance to mean "one who goes into battle at the head
of his troops." Bristow points out that an English reader who is
not aware of the separate meanings of these two Greek words will
conclude that Paul is saying in Ephesians that the man is to rule
over the woman. But if Bristow is correct, Paul is not saying that
the man should rule over and dominate his wife, but that he is to
be the leader in going out to meet dangerous situations as a person
who is protective and courageous. Moreover, Bristow adds, Paul
was perfectly aware of the two Greek words *archē* and *kephalē* and
deliberately chose the latter in order to avoid the connotations of
the former.

This leads us to the apparent reference in Ephesians 5:24 to
"submission" or, as we find it in some translations, "be subject
to" (RSV, NEB): " . . . and as the Church submits to Christ, so should
wives to their husbands, in everything" (JB). Once again we have
two Greek words with different meanings, both of which could be
translated with the same English expression. One of these Greek
words is *hypakouō*. It means "to obey" or "to be subject to" and is
the word that would be used if one referred to the necessity for
a slave to obey his or her master. This is not the word that Paul
used with regard to a woman's relationship to her husband, even
though he does use this word in Ephesians 6:5 in another context.
Instead Paul uses the word *hypotassō*, a word that, in the active
form, could be translated "be subordinate to." But in this case the
word is neither active nor passive (two "voices" that we have in
English) but "middle" (a voice we do not have in English). Now,
if a verb is active, it means that the subject of the verb is acting. If
the verb is passive it means the subject of the verb is being acted
upon. But in Greek if a verb is in the middle voice it means that
the subject is acting upon itself. In this case, it means the woman
is requiring a certain attitude of herself; it is not being imposed
upon her. It is therefore a voluntary action that Paul is asking for
in which the woman willingly and actively subjects herself to her

husband.[17] But "subject to" is an awkward and misleading translation of the Greek word in question. If subjugation was what was called for, Paul would have used the previously mentioned verb *hypakouō*. A better translation of the word in this context would be "to place oneself at the disposition of" or "be supportive of or responsive to." It will be noted that in Ephesians 5:21 Paul asks the members of the church in Ephesus to "give way to one another in obedience to Christ." In this verse we have the same verb *hypotassomai*. It is clear that among a group of people it would not make sense to say that they should all submit to the domination or authority of everyone else in the group. But it would make sense to say that they should be responsive to the needs of one another and that each of them should place himself or herself at the disposition of others. The way Paul used *hypotassomai* in verse 21 is the same way he used it in verse 24.

In 1 Corinthians 11:1–16 we have various statements by Paul that seemingly give to women an inferior status to men. As with the passage in Ephesians, so with this passage Bristow argues from the Greek terms that the English translations are misleading and give the wrong impression. We will take just one example. In 1 Corinthians 11:9 the Jerusalem Bible reads: "Man was not created for the sake of woman, but woman was created for the sake of man." Bristow follows the lead of certain modern translations that think this verse should be translated: "Neither was the man created for the sake of the woman, but the woman for the sake of the man." The bottom line of meaning here is that *men need women*. Therefore women do not exist simply for childbearing, as a means for men to reproduce themselves, but from the beginning men have a deep, soulful need for woman, even as God observed, "It is not good that man should be alone" (Gen. 2:18). This being so, such a statement on Paul's part does not denigrate women; rather it elevates them, especially in a culture that was based on the idea of man's emotional and psychological self-sufficiency.

The final passage to be considered occurs in 1 Timothy 2:9–15. This passage has to do with the role and place of women when Christians of both sexes were assembled for the purpose of instruction. First it is to be noted that women were included in the instruction. While this might not seem extraordinary to us, it was extraordinary for that era, since, as mentioned before, in the tra-

---

17. Bristow, *What Paul Really Said about Women*, 40.

ditions of both the Jews and the Greeks of the times, women were
not educated except in homemaking skills. What the Christians
were doing therefore, in including women in the classroom, was
scandalous, and Paul knew this. It was for this reason, Bristow
asserts, that the men were admonished to keep silent because the
whole idea was scandalous and might easily lead to false accusa-
tions and malicious rumors about the intentions of the Christians
in including women in such a gathering.

Bristow vigorously defends this argument with further elucidations on the meaning of the Greek words involved. The one
verse we will concentrate on here is the final verse in this discussion of women in the assembly, 1 Timothy 2:15, which says
"Nevertheless *she* will be saved by child-bearing, provided *she*
lives a modest life and is constant in faith and love and holiness" (JB). I have emphasized "she" in order to call attention to
this word, for we have here an important nuance of meaning that
does not appear in most English translations. In Greek the subject
of a verb may be expressed by the use of a personal pronoun or
simply by the way the verb is declined, that is, the verb ending
will tell us whether the subject of the verb is singular or plural. In
the case of 1 Timothy 2:15 the subject of the verb in the first clause,
that is, the subject of "will be saved," is singular and clearly refers
back to "the woman who was led astray" in the previous verse.
However, the subject of the verb in the second clause is plural.
The literal and obvious translation of the original Greek would
be: "But *she* will be saved through childbearing, if *they* remain in
faith and love and holiness with soundness of mind" (emphasis
and translation mine).[18]

The curious thing is that only a few English translations of the
Bible have 1 Timothy 2:15 translated accurately in strict accord
with the Greek. Among these are the King James Version and
Phillips. Most other English translations show it in the manner
of the Jerusalem Bible, changing the plural of the verb in the second clause to the singular, as the Revised Standard Version for
instance: "Yet woman will be saved through bearing children, if
she continues in faith and love and holiness, with modesty."

One wonders what the justification can be for taking such
license with what appears to be a perfectly clear and straight-

---

18. The Greek is *sōthēsetai de dia tēs teknogonias, ean meinōsin en pistei kai agapē kai hagiasmō metia sōphposynēs.*

forward Greek text. Bristow says that modern translators do such things in order to make sense to the modern reader out of a confusing sentence. It certainly is true that the Jerusalem Bible translation of the sentence seems to make more sense than that of the King James Version. For after all, who are these mysterious people referred to in the Greek and the King James Version as "they"? It would appear that to avoid confusing the reader, or taxing his or her intellectual powers too much, the Jerusalem Bible and other translations take liberties with the biblical text.

If we reject the tendency of modern translators to overcome the difficulties in the biblical text by arbitrary means, we are left with the problem of explaining the shift from "she" to "they." Who are these other people who will, by remaining constant in faith and love and holiness, enable a woman to be saved in childbearing? Bristow says that the "they" refers to those women who are faithful carriers of the Christian life. What's more, he believes that Paul, or whoever wrote 1 Timothy, had in mind by childbearing, not the giving birth in an ordinary way to babies, but to woman as the bearer psychologically of the Christ-child. He supports this position by pointing out that the Greek text of 1 Timothy 2:15, literally translated, should be "Or saved through the birth of *the* child," a rendering the New English Bible has in a footnote. Putting this in modern language we would say that the meaning of 1 Timothy 2:15ff is that if a woman is faithful to that deepest process within herself, she will be saved by giving birth to Christ via her own individuation.

If Bristow's suggested interpretation of this text is correct, Paul is pointing out that women are themselves instruments of salvation through Christ. This point of view elevates women and is markedly different from the prevailing point of view in the biblical era that we have examined, which regarded women as inferior to men in spiritual matters.

Bristow argues that Paul's statements about women were misunderstood by gentile converts who had been heavily influenced by the antifeminine Hellenistic thinking that we have summarized previously. It is also his belief that later Christian thinkers were also heavily influenced by the Hellenist attitudes that depreciated women, and that these theologians not only erroneously perpetuated within the church the idea of the moral and psychological inferiority of women, but also misinterpreted what

Paul said. The later Christian theologians whom he cites as conspicuous examples include Tertullian, St. Augustine, Clement of Alexandria, and (much later) the highly influential Thomas Aquinas.

Much of the patristic contention of the moral inferiority of women was based on their interpretation of the story of Adam and Eve. The influence of this story and its antifeminine interpretations were powerful and longlasting in the church. The usual position taken was to point out that Eve was the first to sin, and that this was evidence of her moral weakness and psychological inferiority. There are many examples of this, but perhaps the most scandalous comes from the early third-century theologian Tertullian, who wrote:

> Woman, . . . do you not know that you are (each) an Eve? The sentence of God on this sex of yours lives in this age: the guilt must of necessity live too. *You* are the devil's gateway: you are the unsealer of that (forbidden) tree: *you* are the first deserter of the divine law: *you* are she who persuaded him whom the devil was not valiant enough to attack. *You* destroyed so easily God's image in man. On account of *your* desert — that is, death — even the Son of God had to die.[19]

This has had a long and tenacious life in the postbiblical thinking of the church. As late as the sixteenth century no less a person than Erasmus says, in his analysis of the story of Adam and Eve, that whereas Adam's will was weakened by his immoderate love for his wife, Eve's weakness of will extended also to her reason and intellect:

> . . . in Eve obviously not only the will was weakened, but also reason and intellect, the fountain of all good or all evil. It seems that the snake succeeded in persuading her that the Lord's prohibition to eat from the tree of life was vain. In Adam it seems rather that the will was weakened more because of his immoderate love for his wife to whose desires he gave preference over obedience to God's commandments.

However, he then adds:

> . . . yet also his reason had, I think, been weakened, which is the source of the will.[20]

---

19. *On the Apparel of Women* 1.1.
20. Erasmus, *Discourse on Free Will* (New York: Continuum, 1988), 22.

Whether the story of Adam and Eve shaped the way the later Church Fathers thought or the patriarchal attitude of these Fathers shaped their interpretation of the story is hard to say. In either case the result was a devaluation of women's importance relative to that of men. Consider, for instance, this statement from Augustine:

> Thou [God] subjectest women to their husbands in chaste and faithful obedience, not to gratify passion, but for the propagation of offspring, and for demotic society. Thou givest to men authority over their wives, not to mock the weaker sex, but in the laws of unfeigned love.[21]

The notion that woman was responsible for sexual enticement was widespread. It never seemed to occur to the Fathers that men might have seduced women, or that it was their own sexual wantonness that led men to sexual excesses. The responsibility for seeing to it that sex didn't get out of hand was given over to women, as is exemplified in this passage from Clement of Alexandria in which he admonishes women to be completely clothed:

> Let the woman observe this, further, let her be entirely covered, unless she happen to be at home. For that style of dress is grave, and protects from being gazed at. And she will never fall, who puts before her eyes modesty, and her shawl; nor will she invite another to fall into sin by uncovering her face.[22]

As noted, there was a determined effort in the postapostolic church to blame Eve for original sin, for, after all, did not the serpent tempt Eve first? However, Bristow astutely points out an alternative way of understanding this story that the Fathers of the Church — with their preconceived notion of feminine inferiority inherited from the inclination toward Greek philosophy — never considered. According to this way of looking at the story, it is entirely possible that the serpent tempted Eve first because she was morally stronger, not weaker, knowing that if he could win Eve over, Adam was a pushover. This point is supported by the fact that while the serpent had to use all his wiles to seduce Eve,

---

21. Augustine, *On the Morals of the Catholic Church* 30.
22. Clement of Alexandria, *The Instructor* 3.11.

all Eve had to do to bring Adam along with her was to offer him
the fruit she had plucked from the tree.

There is a great psychological distance between the statements
by Tertullian and St. Augustine and that of St. Paul, who wrote
in Galatians 3:27–28:

> All baptized in Christ, you have all clothed yourselves in
> Christ, and there are no more distinctions between Jew and
> Greek, slave and free, male and female, but all of you are one
> in Christ Jesus. (JB)

Influenced as we are today by the later development in the
church of an antifeminine, patriarchal psychology that traces its
origin back to Hellenistic philosophy and Gnosticism, it is easy
to suppose that Jesus and Paul were responsible for this state of
affairs. However, the situation, as we have now seen, was quite
to the contrary.

Moreover, even granting the patriarchal attitude in the later
church that we have just mentioned, we should also note that the
picture was not entirely one-sided. The same Clement of Alexandria, for instance, whom we have just quoted with reference to
the proper attire for women, also was of the belief that in their
essentials men and women were equal. He was of the belief that
in the matter of the perfection of the soul man and woman shared
equally, and that women were to philosophize equally with men.
He also said that since men and women possess the same nature
they possess the same virtue. To quote his own words:

> Accordingly woman is to practice self-restraint and right-
> eousness, and every other virtue, as well as man, both bond
> and free; since it is a fit consequence that the same nature pos-
> sesses one and the same virtue. We do not say that woman's
> nature is the same as man's, as she is woman. For undoubt-
> edly it stands to reason that some difference should exist
> between each of them, in virtue of which one is male and
> the other female. Pregnancy and parturition, accordingly,
> we say belong to woman, as she is woman, and not as she is
> a human being. But if there were no difference between man
> and woman, both would do and suffer the same things. As
> then there is sameness, as far as respects the soul, she will
> attain to the same virtue but [he then adds in patriarchal
> fashion, according to today's standards at least] as there is

difference as respects the peculiar construction of the body she is destined for child-bearing and house-keeping.[23]

Finally we should note that the church espoused many of the causes of women. The church fought for and eventually won equal marital and property rights for women, vigorously attacked one-sided laws against adultery, defended the right of women to an equal standing with men in courts of law, and extinguished the practice of disposing of infants (almost all of whom were girls) at the whim of the father. It is not too much to say that all of this is the legacy of the New Testament, beginning with the attitudes of Jesus.

From the point of view of the psychology of individuation the issue of the feminine is of great importance. The wholeness of both men and women calls for the recognition, honoring, and re-specting of their feminine sides as well as their masculine sides, and also for the opportunity in life for a full expression of their femininity. Men, insofar as they identify themselves with a one-sidedly masculine psychology, lose contact with that feminine core of their being that C. G. Jung called the *anima* and that leads men to their *soul*. The anima in a man, when she has been related to properly, leads a man into his inner depths, makes possible a contact with the unconscious and places him in touch with subtle but powerful psychic forces that can correct, balance, and com-plete his masculinity.[24] Women who have been cut off from their femininity or led to depreciate its value and importance need to have their feminine self-assuredness reinforced from valid psy-chological perspectives and religious traditions. For those women who find the Bible spiritually nourishing it will be helpful to know that the New Testament point of view is in accord with their striv-ing for the cultural and psychological expression of themselves as women, and nowhere in the Bible is this reinforcement and validation more clearly present than in the Gospel of John.

Nevertheless, having said all this, it should be noted that certain other religious traditions may have archetypal represen-tations of the feminine that are lacking in the New Testament.

---

23. Clement of Alexandria, *The Stromata* 4.8.
24. John A. Sanford and George Lough, *What Men Are Like: The Psychology of Men for Men and the Women Who Live with Them* (New York: Paulist Press, 1988). Also John A. Sanford, *The Invisible Partners: How the Male and Female in Each of Us Affects Our Relationships* (New York: Paulist Press, 1980).

Some men and women, therefore, who are searching for a broader understanding of the feminine may wish to turn to archetypal material found in mythology. A rich source is Greek mythology, for while Greek philosophy had a distinctly masculine bias, Greek mythology is rich in images of the archetypal feminine. Among the Olympians, for instance, we have the goddesses Aphrodite, Athena, Artemis, Hera, and others. Psychology regards these goddesses as personifications of the archetypes of the collective unconscious, and therefore as primordial images of the feminine within our own psyche. And while it is true that the Olympian deities of Greek mythology had a certain masculine bias, insofar as Zeus was the Father God over all, one can also go to the pre-Olympian era of Greek mythology and find in such ancient deities as Gaia (Mother Earth), Demeter, Kore, the Erinyes, and many others archetypal representations of the feminine as they appeared in a matriarchy.

~ 6 ~

THE PSYCHOLOGY OF ANGER
The Cleansing of the Temple
John 2:13–25

SCHOLARS TELL US that it was not unusual for people to be in the precincts of the temple selling various items and changing money; what was unusual was Jesus' angry reaction. Jesus' abrupt action — driving the money-changers and merchants out of the temple with a whip and overturning their tables — was a challenge to the temple authorities who condoned such practices. His antagonists therefore challenged Jesus' authority with their question: "What sign can you show us to justify what you have done?" Jesus replies with an enigmatic answer: "Destroy this sanctuary, and in three days I will raise it up." In typical Johannine style, the evangelist has Jesus' questioners take him literally: they ask him how he could raise up the temple in three days when it took forty-six years to build it.

Scholars believe that the forty-six years referred to is the time that elapsed between the year in which Herod began to rebuild the temple in approximately 20–18 B.C.E. and the time in which the incident John is describing took place. If so, then the date of this narrative would be about 26–28 C.E. If Jesus was born in 4 B.C.E., as is commonly supposed, he would be about thirty or thirty-two years old at the time of his ministry. The answer that Jesus gave to his opponents that was so baffling to them may have been intended for the future support of the faith of the disciples during the crucifixion, for clearly Jesus was referring to the temple of his

71

body, which would be destroyed on the cross and raised again at the resurrection.

Verses 23–25 are interesting because they again show Jesus as a psychologist. John tells us that many people were impressed by the signs that Jesus gave, but he also tells us that Jesus was suspicious of them, and he did not need anyone to give him evidence about people because he could size them up either by his own powers of intuition or by a power of supernatural cognition. Jesus had the capacity to perceive not only the surface appearance of people (the "persona") but also the hidden unconscious aspect of a person's personality (the "shadow"), which so often contradicts a person's conscious aspirations and pretensions. He does not trust these people because people who present a certain face to themselves and the world, but are unaware of their unconscious motives and intentions, cannot be trusted, appearances to the contrary.

But perhaps the most striking aspect this story shows us about Jesus' personality is that he was angry. We often hear it said that anger is bad and should be avoided. How can this be if Jesus himself became angry? This question of anger is worth a closer look.

It will help us understand the psychology of anger if we examine the four different Greek words for anger that are used in the New Testament.

The first of these words to be considered is *parorgismos*. This word means "excited anger," "provoked anger." It is generally disapproved of in the New Testament and regarded as dangerous. We can identify *parorgismos* in many New Testament usages with egocentric anger.

Egocentric anger erupts in a person when that person's egocentric attitudes or defenses have been challenged or exposed. To the extent that we are egocentric there is always a weak spot in our psychology; if someone confronts us in that weak area we will experience either fear or a blind rage. We will be vexed, like Rumpelstiltskin in the fairy tale by that name when the princess succeeded in guessing his name and foiling his demonic intentions to take her child. The intent of the anger is to destroy the person who has enraged us by exposing our hidden guilt, weakness, or demonic intentions. Murders are committed under the impetus of this kind of rage, and it is small wonder that it is condemned in the Bible.

There is also a verbal form of this word that is used in the New Testament: *parorgizō,* which means "to provoke to wrath." It is found in the charming statement by Paul in Ephesians 6:4: "Parents, never drive your children to resentment [*parorgizō*] but in bringing them up correct them and guide them as the Lord does." In this instance, the egocentricity lies in the parents who, because they have not dealt with their own complexes, transmit to the child their own rage. Once again Paul shows himself as a good depth psychologist; if he had lived in the modern era he would have made a good family counselor.

Egocentric anger is further exemplified in the Bible with a second Greek word, *diapriō,* which means literally "to divide with a saw" or "to grate the teeth in a rage," or passively "to be cut to the heart" or "to be enraged." In the Book of Acts, when Peter speaks to the members of the council who are accusing the apostles, he tells them things they do not want to hear. We are then told: "When they heard that, they were cut to the heart [*dieprionto*]" (Acts 5:33, KJV). We find the word used in the same way in Acts 7:54 (KJV): Stephen replies to the high priest and his accusers who, hearing what he had to say, were so enraged, they "were cut to the heart, and they gnashed on him with their teeth."

The third Greek word for anger we will consider is *thymos,* which means "a strong passion or emotion of the mind, anger or wrath," or even "the swellings of anger." Examples occur in Luke 4:28, Acts 19:28, 2 Corinthians 12:20, and Galatians 5:20. The word generally denotes impulse and passion. It is interesting that in classical Greek the word *thymos* also means "soul." As soul, it represents the seat of anger but also the seat of spirit and courage.

This kind of anger is dangerous, but it is also warm, passionate, and understandable. For instance, let us say that you are an elderly man living in a small house and caring for your sick wife, whose condition sometimes requires that you take her to the hospital for emergency treatment.[1] However, the young men who live across the street callously park their cars in front of your driveway. You have asked them not to do so, and they ignore you. You have called the police, but they were busy with more important crimes. You try to approach the young men in the right way

---

1. This example is taken from an actual case.

but only meet with arrogance. You also have reason to suspect that they are dealing with drugs. One day when again their car is parked across your driveway you go across the street to ask them to move it — but this time you take your loaded revolver with you. Once again they scorn your request. Words are exchanged. Shots are fired. The two young men are gunned down.

It is a tragedy. The old man will have to be prosecuted and serve some kind of sentence for murder. But who would not be sympathetic with him? Who would not understand why he killed the young men? Society cannot condone his action, but who among us will not weep for him rather than condemn him?

In such a case the anger does not come from our egocentricity, but from a passionate response deep within us. It can be likened to a basically healthy anger that has gone too far or been too rashly applied. For there is such a thing as healthy anger. It has been described as a healthy response to an intolerable situation. This kind of anger endows a person with courage in the face of danger and with the capacity for moral outrage and indignation. It can impart to us courage and moral resolve, but also it can so overwhelm us that it can lead to tragedy.

For *thymos* to attain its proper goal it must be combined with the right kind of consciousness. The Greeks recognized this and had two different deities who had to do with warfare. One was the god Ares, a brawling god, who relished blood and gore and fighting and was despised by human beings and gods alike. Ares, interestingly enough, almost always lost. The other deity was the goddess Athena. Athena was the cool-headed goddess of culture, of heroes, and also of defensive warfare. She did not fight because she liked to fight, however, but because it was necessary. When she fought she used a cool head and shrewd strategy, and she always won her battles. Small wonder the city of Athens took its name from her. *Thymos*, combined with the spirit personified by Athena, serves a useful purpose. This is why occasionally, as in Romans 2:8, it is used interchangeably with the next word for anger we will consider — *orgē*.

It takes a strong ego to experience *thymos* and retain the coolness of Athena. This is in contrast to egocentric anger, which is always characterized by a person whose ego is weak (all egocentricity is a form of ego weakness). A strong ego is capable of directing anger consciously and purposefully in order to attain the desired result. When anger is directed in this way the New

Testament used the Greek word *orgē*, which means "the settled purpose of wrath."

It is interesting that when the New Testament refers to Jesus' anger, or to the anger of God, *orgē* is usually the word that is used. For instance, Mark tells us a story in which Jesus meets a man with a withered hand, but it is the Sabbath and Jesus knows that the people standing around will accuse him if he heals the man. Then we are told:

> And when he [Jesus] had looked round about on them with anger [*orgē*], being grieved for the hardness of their hearts, he saith unto the man, stretch forth thine hand. And he stretched it out: and his hand was restored whole as the other. (3:5 KJV)

This kind of anger is used by God and Jesus in the New Testament as the instrument by means of which evil is destroyed. It is the essence of anger as a "healthy reaction to an intolerable situation." It serves God's purposes, and in a human being it proceeds from the innermost Self (not from egocentric anger). With the help of this anger the innocent can be protected and evil can be destroyed.

We are now in a position to understand the meaning of the best known biblical reference to anger — Paul's statement in Ephesians 4:26 when he said:

> Be ye angry, and sin not: let not the sun go down upon your wrath: neither give peace to the devil. (KJV)

or

> Be angry but do not sin; do not let the sun go down on your anger, and give no opportunity to the devil. (RSV)

The King James Version and the Revised Standard Version are preferred translations in this case because they faithfully translate the Greek word *parorgismos*. That, as we have seen, is the dangerous egocentric anger that emerges from our unconsciousness. When this anger comes up we are bidden by Paul not to let the day end before we get to the bottom of it. This is the anger that we need to understand so we can deal with our complexes and egocentricity. Good advice from a master psychologist.

~ 7 ~

BEING BORN AGAIN
Dialogue with Nicodemus
John 3:1–8

THE STORY OF NICODEMUS bears the mark of a historical event, an actual reminiscence. The little detail that Nicodemus appeared "by night" is an indication that the event took place much as John described it. However, John does not tell the story only for its historicity; in typical Johannine fashion he uses the story as the "launching platform" for a symbolic discourse on light and darkness and on eternal life, the dividing line being verse 9. In this section we will first discuss the actual encounter between Jesus and Nicodemus and reserve the longer discussion regarding light, darkness, and life for the next chapter.

There are two theories among scholars about Nicodemus: first, that he was a sincere inquirer; second, that he came as a representative of the pharisaic class, of which he was a member, either trying to find a way to come to terms with Jesus or a way to disparage what he stood for. If the former is the case, we have to assume that Nicodemus was a man looking for a deeper truth but was limited by his literalism and concretistic way of thinking. If the latter is the case, we have to assume that his questions to Jesus and demeanor toward him were not sincere.

The case for the second point of view is strengthened by the fact that Jesus' replies to his questions sound curt and that Nicodemus's replies appear to be argumentative and even to ridicule what Jesus is saying. Thus when Nicodemus says "How can a grown man be born? Can he go back into his mother's womb and be born again?" this can be interpreted as sarcasm. Similarly, Jesus' final statement to Nicodemus in verse 10 — "You, a teacher in Israel and you do not know these things?" — can be thought of as a curt dismissal of a man whom Jesus perceived to be insincere.

If this is the case, it is a study in the futility of a spiritually minded person trying to carry on a discussion about spiritual matters with someone whose underlying motive is to refute and ridicule spiritual beliefs. People who find themselves in such a situation would do well to follow Jesus' example and cut the conversation short.

However, there is also a good argument for the other point of view: that Nicodemus was sincere. First is the little detail that he came by night. It is reasonable to suppose that he came by night to avoid being seen, but if he was sent by the Pharisees he would not have cared if he was seen or not. The night visit to Jesus suggests a man who is nervously inquiring about something that he senses might have some truth to it, but does not want to risk offending or angering his associates who see Jesus as the enemy, and so goes to some length to keep his visit secret.

Second is the fact that Nicodemus also appears later in the Gospel. John 19:39 says that after Jesus had died and was being buried by Joseph of Arimathea, "Nicodemus came as well — the same one who had first come to Jesus at night-time — and he brought a mixture of myrrh and aloes, weighing about a hundred pounds" (with which to embalm the body). If it is true that Nicodemus was a hostile inquirer in the story John tells in chapter 3, we have to assume that he went through a radical change of heart later on. In view of John 19:39 it is more credible to believe that Nicodemus was an awkward but sincere and somewhat nervous inquirer, that his statements to Jesus do not reflect hostility but the difficulty his literal mind has in understanding what Jesus is saying, and that Jesus is not rebuffing him but going to some lengths to try to enlighten him. For our purposes, we are going to assume that the latter situation is the way it really was.

Nicodemus does not begin the dialogue with a question but with a statement of admiration for Jesus. Jesus, sensing his hunger for spiritual truths, says to him:

> I tell you most solemnly, unless a man is born from above, he cannot see the kingdom of God.

This seemingly simple statement has many nuances of meaning in the original Greek. The first concerns the nonsexist language that John uses in reporting this incident. Consider the statement "unless a *man* is born from above...." This expression certainly implies a sexist attitude. A "man"? How about the women? Even if the word "man" is used here in its generic sense to refer to either a man or woman it still has sexist implications. To understand why this expression is not sexist we must examine the Greek.

In Greek, there are three words that could have been used in this sense. The first is the word *anēr* ("andros" is a conventionalized English translation of this Greek word, as in "androcentric"). *Anēr* means "a mature male person"; it is also the word for "husband." It is the opposite of *gynē,* "woman," from which our word "gynecology" is derived. But this is not the word used in John 3:3.

Second is the word *anthrōpos,* which is also usually translated "man" and is the source for our English word "anthropology." This word means "a human being," but because it takes the masculine article (*ho anthrōpos*) it is usually translated "man" or "a man." If *anthrōpos* were the word used in John 3:3, this word would have been less sexist than *anēr,* though it would still have had some sexist overtones. But in fact still a third Greek expression is used in John 3:3.

This third expression makes use of the Greek impersonal pronoun *tis,* which means "a certain one," "anyone." No sex whatsoever is attached to the word *tis.* When *tis* is used neither sex, nor age, nor any other humanly divisive category is implied, and this is the word used in both John 3:3 and 3:5. The use of this word in a context such as the one we are considering is unusual: as mentioned, *anthrōpos* would be much the more convenient expression. In fact, when Nicodemus replies, "How can a grown man be born? Can he go back into his mother's womb and be born again?" he uses the word *anthrōpos.* The implication is clear: our author has gone out of his way to find the one and only word available that has no sexist or any other divisive implications to it. *Anyone* can be born again providing the right spiritual conditions are met.

And yet we find the word "man" used in the King James Version, Phillips, the New English Bible, the Jerusalem Bible, and in other translations. However, the Revised Standard Version and the New Jerusalem Bible use the impersonal English pronoun "one" or "no one," and Martin Luther translated the Greek with the impersonal German word *jemand*. It can only be said that some translators are more sensitive to the original Greek and its important contemporary nuances of meaning than others, at least in this case.

But there is still another nuance of meaning to the Greek in this verse that is important for us to consider. The Greek word in the expression "unless a man is born *from above*" is the word *anōthen*, a word which can mean either "from above" or "again." Which meaning is correct in this instance? Some translations (for example, the Jerusalem Bible) use "from above," but others (for example, the King James Version and the Revised Standard Version) use "again." A good guess is that *both* meanings are intended by John. The interpretation "born from above" leads us to consider the matter of "celestial geography"; the interpretation "again" leads us to consider the Christian mystery. Let's begin with the matter of celestial geography as we find it in the Fourth Gospel.

Above/below constitute one of the motifs of the Fourth Gospel of which we spoke in the introduction and briefly in a previous chapter. "Above" implies "up, heaven, sky," and, perhaps, "higher" in terms of value. "Below" implies "down, earth, and what lies under the earth," and perhaps, "lower" in terms of value. The fact that one is born in this case "from above" (not "from below") sounds prejudicial to the earth and the "things that lie below." And, in fact, in the Fourth Gospel, God is from above, but we are from below, and at the end Christ "ascends," he doesn't "descend." We suspect that we have here a Christian bias against the earth, perhaps even an association of what lies below with evil.

To a certain extent this is true. The Christians shared with the Greeks, the Jews of the Old Testament, and others the idea that Hades, or the place of the departed soul, was below, in, or under the earth. So in Deuteronomy 32:22 we read that Yahweh's wrath "will burn right down to the depths of Sheol" (NJB). And in Luke 10:15 Jesus says to unrepentant Capernaum: "And as for you, Capernaum, did you want to be raised as high as heaven? You shall be flung down to hell." (The expression Jesus used is adapted from Isaiah 14:13.)

This bias in favor of heaven above as against earth below is reflected in Christian architecture, for on top of our churches are steeples, and the steeples point "up" into the sky, for that is where heaven is and where God is to be found. You could say that steeples are like spiritual lightning rods meant to direct divine energy from the sky. Some Christian worshipers exemplify this attitude and, when praying, they hold their palms up and gaze upward to receive the divine grace that will come to them from "on high" (instead of from within themselves). This is all so commonplace that Christians by and large take it for granted, but among some other peoples the matter is reversed. Among the Hopis, for example, and other Pueblo Indian people, the "church," or kiva, is a round chamber that is under the ground. To enter it you have to climb down a ladder. On the floor of the kiva is a small hole, which is known as the *sipapu,* and this is the entrance to a narrow tunnel that leads down into the earth, because the divine comes from below, not from above.

All of this is psychologically instructive. Our contemporary Western conscious attitude has been shaped by many centuries that regarded that which is above as superior to that which is below, favored heaven over earth, and pointed human consciousness up toward a heavenly spirit and away from an earthly spirit. On the psychological level this has had its implications for it denigrated the chthonic (earthly) man or woman, devalued instinct, tended to see the spirit in us that comes from the earth as demonic, favored the masculine over the feminine, and, on the environmental level, subordinated Mother Earth and her considerations to the power aspirations of the ego.

In the process of individuation this exaggerated conscious posture must be compensated for and adjusted, and a person must learn to value "Mother Earth" with all that this means.

However, we can push this matter too far. Neither John's Gospel nor Christianity denigrates the earth as such. In the New Testament as in the Old Testament the earth is God's creation and it is good. In Christian history and tradition many important events took place on and in the earth, not the least of which is the incarnation itself. For example, Christ, as we have noted, was believed to have been born in a cave (the stable in which the Lord was born was almost certainly a cave), and Christian tradition says that many of the most important teachings of Jesus were imparted to his disciples in caves. The supposed underground tomb of Mary is likewise a sacred Christian spot in Israel, and with regard to church architecture a spiritually valued area of the church is the crypt, an underground chamber that gets its name from the

Greek *kryptos* — "hidden, secret." The crypt is the place where the hidden and secret teachings of the church are symbolically stored, the psychological undergirding of the Christian superstructure of faith and doctrine. In fact, in Cairo one can visit the Church of the Holy Family, a Coptic Christian church built over the cave where the holy family is supposed to have taken refuge when Joseph fled with Mary and the babe from Herod. Actually, it is likely that the contemporary spiritual prejudice against the earth and what lies below is not from original Christianity at all, but from Gnosticism, which *did* denigrate the earth as inferior and the realm of evil and the wicked Demiurge who kept the children of light imprisoned in his material realm through the darkness of ignorance. The Gnostic negative attitude toward the earth and the material world and what lies below was a major reason that Christianity rejected Gnostic teaching.

Therefore it is best to understand that "above" and "below" in the New Testament do not refer to literal geography but to inner or spiritual geography. "Higher things" refers to insights and truths that transcend our presently limited awareness, and if God comes from "on high" it is because God brings superior insight and power. Certainly in the Fourth Gospel, all such "geographical" language is to be taken symbolically in this way.

We find that the idea of aboveness is used in much the same way in shamanistic spirituality. Among people all over the world who shared a common shamanistic culture, such as the American Indians, there was a world above and a world below. The shaman or shamaness was the person who through a unique spiritual experience had journeyed from the earth plane to the worlds above or below and there obtained unusual spiritual insight. Usually the journey was to the upper world. An example is Black Elk, who in a vision that came to him when he was in a coma and that initiated him into his future role as a shaman or healer was transported to a great high mountain where he talked with the "Grandfathers" who instructed him in the things he was to know.

We have examined the significance of the word *anōthen* in its meaning of "from above"; now we will look at what this word means with reference to being born "again." To be born again implies a complete psychological and spiritual change and renewal of the individual. It is such a fundamental change that in the epistles it is likened to the death of the old person and the emergence of a new person (Rom. 6:1–7). Another New Testament compari-

son is that the outer human nature falls away and there emerges
a strengthened inner human nature (2 Cor. 4:16). In this new person, the center of the personality is no longer the old ego, but
Christ as the inner Center of our being (Gal. 2:20). This radical
transformation of personality through Christ is the essence of the
Christian *mystērion* (mystery).

In a previous chapter we noted the importance in the New
Testament of a *mystērion*, that is, an initiatory rite leading to a
change of personality and an infusion of a revealed knowledge.
The Christian *mystērion* takes the individual soul through a process of dying to the old ego and into a renewal through a new
Center (Christ). In John's Gospel the word *mystērion* as such does
not occur, but the idea is there in the concept of being born again.
Being born again is an identifiable and describable psychological
experience. It is at the heart of every process of individuation.
While it can be described in a general way it cannot be achieved
in a collective way. Each individual passes through the process
of dying and being born again in his or her own way. Yet though
the different ways this is accomplished are as many as the people
who undergo them, there is always at the heart of each rebirth
the same central archetype: the replacing of the ego as the sham
center of the personality by a new and genuine Center.

Kunkel and Jung call this new Center to the personality the
"Self," or "Real Self"; the New Testament calls it the Christ
within. The psychology of individuation describes empirically
the process that the New Testament describes in a mythological
or supernatural language. Psychology uses the more neutral language of science because it addresses itself to people from a wide
variety of cultural and religious backgrounds, so it must find a
language that is both scientific and universally acceptable. Religion chooses a language that speaks to the soul and connects
psychological processes to a metaphysical background. If it is
true, as the New Testament says, that there is a process of transformation so fundamental that it is described as being born again,
then it should not be surprising that empirical psychologists such
as Jung and Kunkel stumble across this process in their examination of the human soul and its metamorphoses. In fact, if this
were not the case we would have to seriously question if religious
statements to this effect were not after all mere wishful thinking
or metaphysical statements with no basis in lived reality. Some
people are averse to this idea of the Self because they believe it

"psychologizes" religion, but others see it as a vindication of what Christianity has been saying all along. As one cleric put it, "There is in man enough of God to prove that God is."[1]

Jesus goes on to make rebirth a condition for "seeing" the kingdom of God: "Unless a man is born from above [again] he cannot see the kingdom of God." The expression "kingdom of God (or heaven)" is found many times in the synoptic Gospels but only once in John's Gospel. Elsewhere John uses "eternal life" as an equivalent expression. The kingdom of God would appear to be an ineffable reality affecting people psychologically and spiritually that can be "seen" only by those whose "spiritual eyes" are opened. The verb "to see" in the New Testament is closely associated with the idea of knowing. We have already commented on the fact that the Greek language has many words that refer to knowing, each one expressive of a certain aspect of knowledge. One of these words is *oida*. *Oida* is the perfect tense of the word *eidō*, which means "I see," but, as sometimes happens in Greek, in this case the perfect tense is used with the meaning of the present. So *oida* means "I know" in the sense of having seen something that has objective reality, but that becomes an item of knowledge because it now registers inwardly. The impact of John 3:3 is that the kingdom of God is a spiritual reality that can be known only when certain inward conditions are met.

The literal-minded Nicodemus finds all of this hard to understand. Like many of us today, his spiritual understanding is limited by his inability to think symbolically. Symbolic thinking enables us to comprehend truths that otherwise would escape us. As we have seen, enigmas such as we find in our dreams, and in this case in Jesus' teaching, compel us to "reach farther" so we can grasp hold of psychological and spiritual meanings of which we were previously unaware. Still, incredulous though he is, Nicodemus is trying to understand, so he asks Jesus: "How can a grown man be born? Can he go back into his mother's womb and be born again?"

Consider what a powerful image we have here! — the image of going back into the maternal womb to be born again as a new person. Nicodemus took this idea concretely; Jesus will take it

---

1. Origen, *Commentary on John* 2.2. Cf. the comment by Greek scholar Samuel G. Green, "It is utterly impossible that the Article should be omitted where it is decidedly necessary, or employed where it is quite superfluous or preposterous" (Samuel G. Green, *Handbook to the Grammar of the Greek New Testament* [New York: Fleming H. Revell, 1912], 181).

symbolically. Jesus is referring to what can be called "the womb of God," and here we have one of the biblical feminine metaphors for God that Sandra Schneiders has pointed out to us. If God is like a great psychic womb in which we are reborn, then God must be "feminine" as well as "masculine," "maternal" as well as "fatherly."

We cannot be sure whether Nicodemus actually asked this question of Jesus or if our author put it into his mouth as an artistic device. In either case, the question gives Jesus an opportunity to expand on the meaning of being born again:

> I tell you most solemnly,
> unless a man is born through water and the Spirit,
> he cannot enter the kingdom of God:
> what is born of the flesh is flesh;
> what is born of the Spirit is spirit.
> Do not be surprised when I say:
> You must be born from above [or "again"].
> The wind blows wherever it pleases;
> you hear its sound,
> but you cannot tell where it comes from or where it is going.
> That is how it is with all who are born of the Spirit.
>
> (John 3:5–8)

Jesus says that a person must be born again through "water" and the "spirit." We will now examine what is meant psychologically by these words "water" and "spirit."

In the expression "born again through water and [the] spirit" we have another instance in which the subtleties of Greek grammar add important nuances of meaning that are easily lost in translation. In Greek the presence or omission of the definite article "the" is always significant. This is especially true in John's Gospel, as Origen once noted with reference to the use of the article in the Prologue:

> We next notice John's use of the article in these sentences.
> He does not write without care in this respect, nor is he
> unfamiliar with the niceties of the Greek tongue.[2]

---

2. Origen, *Commentary on John* 2.2. Origen was perhaps the most brilliant of all the early Christian thinkers and was largely responsible for the development of the famous Christian catechetical school in Alexandria. In the later centuries of the church, however, he was repudiated because of his doctrine of the pre-existence of the soul. Erroneously, he

When the definite article "the" appears before a noun it sets that noun off as distinct from its general class and calls attention to it as a distinct entity. When the definite article is missing, the noun in question is less distinctly distinguished from other nouns or from other members of its class. In the Jerusalem Bible translation we have just quoted we read "water and *the* Spirit." Other translations, such as the King James Version, the Revised Standard Version, and the New Jerusalem Bible, also include the definite article before the word "Spirit." However, in the Greek the definite article is not found before either the word "water" or the word "spirit." And in the New English Bible and Phillips the translation is simply "water and spirit."

The impact of this seemingly subtle difference is significant. If the definite article is present with one or both of the words "water" and "spirit," it suggests that the experience of rebirth has a dual significance: it is accomplished first as an experience with water, then as an experience with the spirit. The fact that the article is not there suggests that though the experience of rebirth has a twofold aspect, it is one experience in which we pass through water-spirit, as it were.

A second implication of the lack of the article is to lend emphasis to the translation of the Greek word *pneuma* in this case as "wind" rather than as "spirit." The word *pneuma* means "wind," "air in motion," or "spirit." By thinking of *pneuma* in this case as like a divine wind we are led to a living image, just as water is a living image.

More of the implications of this distinction will be considered shortly, but first we will turn to the idea of being born of "water."

Most scholars say that when Jesus said one must be born through water he was referring to Christian baptism. This would imply, of course, that Jesus had in mind the forthcoming church with its sacraments, creeds, clergy, and rules of order. While it is natural that the church would later read back into Jesus' saying this meaning (eisegesis), it is likely that, in keeping with the

---

was also later associated with the doctrine of reincarnation. (See my book *Soul Journey: A Jungian Analyst Looks at Reincarnation* [New York: Crossroad, 1991], chapter 5.) The Eastern Church holds him in high esteem but does not regard him as one of the Fathers of the Church. He had a highly mystical bent and inquiring mind that was bound to lead him to differences of opinion with some of his Christian associates. Origen regarded himself as a Christian, however, and died from the effect of tortures he endured because he refused to recant his faith in Christ. That is good enough for me, and I count him as a genuine speculative early Christian theologian.

whole tenor of this passage, Jesus used water as a symbol for a spiritual reality that was the agent of transformation. Not that baptism in the early church did not have a powerful effect on a believer; it was certainly one of the main expressions of the Christian *mystērion*, as we will see in another chapter. But today the numinosity has vanished, for most people at least, from the ceremony of baptism, and baptisms are ceremonies that often have more social and conventional meaning than religious meaning for those who participate in them. In order to understand what "water" may refer to symbolically, let us reflect on the nature of water and examine the way water appears as a symbol in our dreams.

Water is the dark, the moist, that which enlivens desert wastes and makes life fruitful; it is the womblike, the cool, the feminine. Water overcomes all obstacles: when confronted by an obstruction it goes under, over (through evaporation), or around the obstacle on its downward course toward the sea. It is feminine. In terms of ancient Chinese psychology it is *yin*.

As we have already observed, in our dreams water is the most prevalent of all symbols for the unconscious. It appears frequently in our dreams as a stream, to symbolize the life-giving energy of the unconscious (just as it appears in the Psalms in this way, for example, Psalm 46:4: "There is a river whose streams bring joy to God's city," NJB). It appears as a spring to symbolize the emergence from our inner depths of that which heals and brings life. It comes as the rain to symbolize God's blessing and the release from painful inner tension. It appears as large bodies of water in which we must swim, symbolizing the importance of learning enough psychology so that we can safely swim in the sea of our own psyche. And it appears as the ocean itself, symbolizing the unconscious as the great Mother of all life, the matrix from which all forms of life originally emerged, both the life of living organisms and the life of the soul. Here it is the "Old Sea Mother," the original source of all psychic life.

Now we will compare the image of water with that of wind. Wind is penetrating. It finds its way through the tiniest cracks of our houses and penetrates the thickest parts of the forest. It affects all creatures and objects with which it comes in contact: forcing the traveler to pull his cloak around him, rustling the leaves, shaping the eroding rocks, driving the sailing ship through the sea. The strong wind carries aloft the hawk and the eagle, and, as the hurricane, rips up and destroys. But it also brings with it the rain, with which, as in our biblical image, it is closely associated. As the rain-bringer the wind moves across the face of the earth bringing the substance for all life. In a similar way God, "like a divine wind," brooded over the face of the waters in the account of creation in the first chapter of Genesis, bringing the world into being. If water is the moist and receptive *yin*, wind is the moving, spermatic *yang*.

In our dreams the wind enters our dream-houses, creates disturbances, produces numinous effects. Sometimes it appears in dream life as a dangerous whirlwind — an image of the Center speaking to us, just as God spoke to Job from the wind: "Then the Lord answered Job out of the whirlwind" (Job 38:1, RSV). It symbolizes all that about the psyche which is "spirit," that is, which is unpredictable, creative, dangerous, inspiring, that which "blows where it pleases, you hear its sound, but you cannot tell where it comes from or where it is going." It symbolizes the creative irrational masculine power of the psyche, which comes from a source within us so deep and so connected to the power of life itself that we are justified in calling it the Spirit of God. Small wonder then that this wind changes us from "flesh" to "spirit." Flesh, as we have already noted in an earlier chapter, signifies, among other things, our ordinary human nature, which is transformed by the "wind of God," the spirit. Then we become, in the language of the New Testament, changed from an unconsciously living and acting human being to an *anthrōpos pneumatikos* — a spiritual human being.

These two forces together — the *yin* and the *yang* of the psyche, the two energetic polarities of all creation — work within us to effect that transformation of being that John's Gospel likens to being "born again" and "from above" via the agency of a higher consciousness. It is a process not only well known to the author of the Fourth Gospel but capable of empirical description by those who study the mysterious processes of individuation.

There is one more nuance of meaning to Jesus' idea of rebirth that appears in the Greek but can be lost to the English reader. John 3:5 — " ... unless a man is born through water and spirit" (NEB) — involves the Greek preposition *ek*, which means "out from the center of." The one who is born again is therefore one who has come "out from" water and wind as though he or she has made a passage through a psychic or spiritual element.

The idea of rebirth in John's Gospel contains within it the idea of such a passage. Originally all of us at birth went through the "tunnel" of the vagina. Everyone who is reborn likewise goes through a dark and narrow passage (analogous to the "narrow way" of which Jesus speaks in Matthew 7:14) and emerges on the other side. Whether we are assisted in making this passage by divine help or the help of a spiritual and psychological doctor or both, we are, as it were, pushed and pulled through the tunnel of rebirth to emerge on the other side a new person. The "newness" that we now experience is expressed in the Greek word *kainos*, which means not new in point of time, but new in quality. The physician, divine or otherwise, who helps us in this process "pulls us through." Jung notes all this in the following words:

> Our language is full of the most extraordinary things of which we are not aware, we use them without stopping to consider. For example, when you say, "I am under the treatment of Dr. So-and-so" you are using the Latin word *trahere*, to pull. The doctor is pulling you through the hole of rebirth, and when he makes you whole and sound, you say, "The doctor pulled me through."[3]

The inner wisdom of this passage from John has an ancient history. "Water" and "wind" together, experienced as one living reality with two aspects to it, are both the passage of rebirth and the agency of rebirth. In the imagery of the Wisdom literature in the Old Testament and Apocrypha, which we have already considered, this reality is none other than Sophia herself, and Sophia, as we have seen, is the Logos, or Mind of God, in action. It is fitting, therefore, to quote a passage from the Book of Wisdom in which we see the divine Sophia as a power "penetrating" (like the wind) all living things and an influence that, like water, is "irresistible":

> I learned both what is secret and what is manifest,
> for wisdom, the fashioner of all things, taught me.
>
> For in her there is a spirit that is intelligent, holy,
> unique, manifold, subtle,
> mobile, clear, unpolluted,
> distinct, invulnerable, loving the good, keen,
> irresistible, beneficent, humane,

---

3. C. G. Jung, *Dream Analysis: Notes of the Seminar Given in 1928–30 by C. G. Jung*, edited by William McGuire (Princeton: Princeton University Press, 1984), 65.

steadfast, sure, free from anxiety,
all-powerful, overseeing all,
and penetrating through all spirits
that are intelligent and pure and most subtle.
For wisdom is more mobile than any motion;
because of her pureness she pervades and penetrates all
    things.
For she is a breath of the power of God,
and a pure emanation of the glory of the Almighty;
therefore nothing defiled gains entrance into her.
For she is a reflection of eternal light,
a spotless mirror of the working of God,
and an image of his goodness.
Though she is but one, she can do all things,
and while remaining in herself, she renews all things;
in every generation she passes into holy souls
and makes them friends of God, and prophets;
for God loves nothing so much as the man who lives with
    wisdom.
For she is more beautiful than the sun,
and excels every constellation of the stars.
Compared with the light she is found to be superior,
for it is succeeded by the night,
but against wisdom evil does not prevail.
She reaches mightily from one end
of the earth to the other,
and she orders all things well.

(Wisd. 7:21–8:1, RSV)

~ 8 ~

LIGHT AND DARKNESS
The Discourse with Nicodemus
John 3:9–21

NICODEMUS REPLIES TO JESUS' WORDS about being born again with a question, "How can that be possible?" Phillips gives us a freer translation: "How on earth can things like this happen?" Jesus replies with a question of his own: "You, a teacher in Israel, and you do not know these things?" The word used for "know" is *ginōskō*, with which we are already familiar and which implies knowledge that comes through experience. So Jesus is saying, "You have not yet experienced these things and made them part of your knowledge?" Jesus' question is more than irony or sarcasm; it implies that Jesus believes Nicodemus *should* know these things because they are implicit in the religious faith that he represents.

The teaching about being born again is esoteric. It refers to the inner psychological process that underlies the faith of the believer. This mystical or psychological process is found in the Old Testament as well as in John's Gospel, and that is why Jesus thinks Nicodemus should know about it. But Nicodemus represents the institutionalized religion of Judaism, and when a religion becomes institutionalized it tends to lose its inner, psychological dimension. The usual pattern is that certain persons have dynamic, transforming psychological experiences with God, which then become generally accepted but transcribed into an institution with authority, doctrines, and fixed rituals. This has the advantage of offering a wide range of people the benefits of the religious experiences that originated with the few, but

90

has the disadvantage of substituting an outer order for an inner experience.

Nicodemus's question gives the author of the Fourth Gospel another opportunity to move from historical reminiscence to spiritual discourse. The discourse that now takes place in John 3:11–21 is clearly intended for all future readers of the Gospel. We will examine some of the issues raised in this discourse, with special attention to the question of the Son of Man and to the important motif of light vis-à-vis darkness.

Verse 11 introduces a contrast between "we" and "you":

> Truly, truly I say to you,
> *we* speak what *we* know,
> and bear witness to what *we* have seen;
> but *you* do not receive our testimony.
> (RSV; emphasis mine)

In English the pronoun "you" is ambiguous as far as number is concerned; it can either mean one person or a number of people. In Greek, as we have seen, each verb form has "number," leaving no doubt about whether the singular or plural is intended. In this case the expression "you do not receive" refers to a number of people. This means that Jesus is not only referring to Nicodemus but to all those people who think the way he does. We are tempted to identify the "you" of this verse with the Pharisees, for Nicodemus is a member of that group, but for our present-day purposes we can understand Christ's words to refer to all those people whose religious understanding is literal and whose perspective is conventional and who as a consequence do not experience the deeper meaning of religious truths.

But who are the people to whom Jesus is referring when he says "*we* speak what *we* know"? One possibility is that Jesus is referring to himself and his disciples; however, since the disciples have not yet begun to teach on their own this doesn't seem to be a likely explanation. Another possibility is that the "we" refers to the members of the Christian community whose spiritual life was centered on the Fourth Gospel and whom Raymond Brown calls the Johannine community. In support of this position is Brown's assertion that the Johannine community often had to contend with Jewish disbelief. But from the psychological point of view, the "we" refers to all those people who have experienced and know of the inner realm.

Understood in this way, the reference in the Fourth Gospel to "the Jews" is to be understood symbolically and refers to all persons who have an entrenched consciousness that excludes direct experience with the inner world. Such persons might consciously adhere to the Christian faith or Jewish faith or any other faith. The expression refers to a psychological attitude, not a religious or ethnic class of people.

Verse 3:12 introduces a special idea in the Fourth Gospel, the idea of "this world":

> If you do not believe me
> when I speak about things in *this world*,
> how are you going to believe me
> when I speak to you about heavenly things?
> (emphasis mine)

To the casual reader of an English translation of the Fourth Gospel the reference to "this world" seems innocuous enough. We all know what it means to speak of the world, or we think we do. But the Greek expression used in the Fourth Gospel is very special; in fact, we find "this world" or "the world" referred to three times in John 3:17 and once again in 3:19. We also found it three times in the Prologue ("He was in the world, and the world was made by him, and the world knew him not"). In fact, John uses this expression sixty-seven times in his Gospel, usually contrasting "this world" with the heavenly world, as he does in verse 12, which we are now considering.

As might be expected, such an important idea employs a special Greek word: *kosmos*. The *kosmos* does not refer simply to the earth on which we human beings live, but also to the spiritual order that prevails among humankind and that is often in opposition to God's will. The people of Jesus' time believed there was a prevailing spiritual attitude among people that was inimical to God's purposes. This is what is referred to in the Fourth Gospel by the expression "this world."

In fact, there is among us human beings a prevailing "collective consciousness" or "collective state of mind" (not to be confused with the collective unconscious). This collective consciousness consists of the generalized way of thinking of a large group of people, the sum total of the prevailing attitudes, beliefs, and prejudices that a people possess in common. Sometimes this collective consciousness appears to be more or less benign, but sometimes it is actively and malignantly evil. For instance, in Germany of the 1930s a malevolent collective consciousness prevailed throughout a whole people. "The world" is thus a compendium of opinions, limitations on human thought, egocentric pretensions enshrined in the culture, and general unconsciousness. To the extent that a group of people are contained unreflectingly in a generalized and unexamined collective consciousness they constitute a "world" more or less presided over by unconscious forces. As we progress through our Gospel we will find more occasions to note the importance of the idea of "this world" as contrasted with the world of a higher consciousness that God seeks to bring about.

In the next two verses we find a striking image:

> No one has gone up to heaven
> except the one who came down from heaven,
> the Son of Man who is in heaven;
> and the Son of Man must be lifted up
> as Moses lifted up the serpent in the desert,
> so that everyone who believes may have eternal life in him.
>
> (vv. 13–14)

The story of the serpent that Moses lifted up in the desert is told in the Book of Numbers 21:4–9. The people of Israel have escaped from Egypt and have wandered for a long time in the wilderness with little food or water. They have lost their courage and have become impatient with their weary journey and speak out against God and Moses, saying they would rather they had never been freed from Egypt and forced to undergo such a terrible journey. God is angered by their attitude and sends poisonous serpents among them; many people are bitten by these snakes and die. Repentant, the people come to Moses and ask him to intercede with Yahweh that they might be saved from the serpents. Yahweh relents and tells Moses to make a serpent out of bronze and raise it on a rod; anyone who is bitten and looks at the bronze serpent will be healed.

In John 3:14, John compares Christ with Moses' serpent. Just as the serpent was lifted up on Moses' rod, so Christ will be lifted up on the cross, and even as the sight of the serpent healed, so all those who see and comprehend Christ on the cross will be healed. The healing of the serpent, however, only cured the people from the poisonous bites, while the healing of Christ leads to eternal life.

Because of the dubious role of the serpent in the story of Adam and Eve, the snake has usually been associated in Christian minds with evil. For this reason it may come as a surprise that Christ was called the "good serpent" by many of the Fathers of the early church. In the mythology of other cultures, however, there is no prejudice against the serpent, which often is shown in a positive light. For instance, in the Babylonian story of Gilgamesh, the hero Gilgamesh is told by the God Utnapishtim that at the bottom of the sea there is a wonderful plant whose name is "the-old-man-becomes-young," and whoever eats of this plant will regain his youth. Gilgamesh swims to the bottom of the sea, finds the plant, and brings it to the surface. But overcome with weariness from his exertion he falls asleep, and when he awakens he sees a snake devouring the last portion of the plant. Ever since then it has been said that the serpent has the gift of immortality, as exemplified in its ability to shed its old skin and emerge in a new one.

In Greek mythology, the god of healing, Asklepius, was often represented in the form of a serpent or with a serpent companion. This serpent was the symbol of the god's power of healing.

In our dreams the serpent is a common but always impressive symbol with many shades of meaning. In its broadest sense the serpent symbolizes the uncanny, objective, natural ways in which the unconscious works to either bring about our undoing or our healing. Which way we experience the serpent power within us will depend on our attitude toward our inner world. In our dreams when a serpent approaches us as though to make contact, it usually symbolizes the "intention" of the unconscious to bring about our individuation. This always has fateful consequences, but when we accede to the inner demand for consciousness and growth it brings about our healing. In fact, sometimes the appearance of a serpent in a dream anticipates healing in a very definite way.[1] The healing aspect of the serpent appears in Christian lore in the Chalice of St. John, a prevalent symbol for healing in the early church. According to the legend, St. John was condemned to die by drinking from a poisoned chalice, but the poison departed the chalice in the form of a serpent and the Apostle drank safely.[2]

The next verses are among the most beautiful and important

---

1. See chapter 3 of my book *Healing and Wholeness* (Ramsey, N.J.: Paulist Press, 1977), esp. 52.
2. This story is told in the apocryphal *Acts of John* 20. See *The Apocryphal New Testament*, trans. M. R. James (New York: Oxford University Press, 1960), 263.

in the Gospel. We will refer to them now, but take them up in more detail later on when we are more prepared to examine them for their inner meaning:

> Yes, God loved the world so much
> that he gave his only Son,
> so that everyone who believes in him may not be lost
> but may have eternal life.
> For God sent his Son into the world
> not to condemn the world,
> but so that through him the world might be saved.
> No one who believes in him will be condemned;
> but whoever refuses to believe is condemned already,
> because he has refused to believe
> in the name of God's only Son.
>
> (vv. 16–18)

We can note especially the importance of the idea of condemnation, with its implication of judgment. At this time we will examine the idea of the Son of Man, spoken of in verse 13, and then the idea of light vis-à-vis darkness.

Verses 13 and 14 reintroduce the idea of Jesus as the "Son of Man," which we briefly discussed in a previous chapter and which now merits our closer attention. The question of the expression "Son of Man" (*ho huios tou anthrōpou*) in the New Testament is a complicated matter, and New Testament scholars have reached no uniform agreement about its meaning; in fact, sometimes it seems as though there are as many ideas about it as there are scholars. First we will consider some of the historical background to this expression and then suggest what the expression means from the point of view of the psychology of individuation.

It is important to note that the expression "Son of Man" occurs frequently in the Old Testament. In the Hebrew expression translated Son of Man — *bar nasha* — the expression is understood as a poetical synonym for "man," in the sense of Psalm 8:4: "What is man that thou art mindful of him?" (KJV). An example of this usage is Psalm 144:3:

> Yahweh, what is a human being for you to notice.
> child of Adam for you to think about? (NJB).

The expression is used in a more specific sense in the Book of Ezekiel, in which the prophet Ezekiel is addressed as "Son of

Man" (Ezek. 2:1, 2; 3:1). A third usage of this expression occurs in
the Book of Daniel. The prophet has a heavenly vision in which
he saw:

> ... coming on the clouds of heaven,
> as it were a son of man. (Dan. 7:13, NJB)

There is a progression here: from a poetical, generic name for
human beings as a species, to a term for a chosen and inspired
prophet, to a title for a mysterious heavenly being.

In the New Testament the term "Son of Man" is found sixty-
nine times in the synoptic Gospels, twelve times in the Fourth
Gospel, once in Acts (7:56), twice in Revelation (1:13, 14:14), and
not at all in the epistles. That the expression is not used in the
epistles may be explained by the fact that, with the exception of
the references in Revelation and Acts, the term is used exclusively
by Jesus with reference to himself. There appear to be various
ways in which he uses the term. For instance, sometimes he uses
the term "Son of Man" to refer to his earthly work. An example
is in Matthew 9:6–7 when Jesus says to the people who criticized
him for healing the paralytic by forgiving his sins:

> Why do you have such wicked thoughts in your hearts? Now
> which of these is easier to say, "Your sins are forgiven," or to
> say, "Get up and walk?" But to prove to you that the Son of
> Man has authority on earth to forgive sins — he said to the
> paralytic — "get up, and pick up your bed and go off home."

At least once Jesus used the term as a way of referring to his
lowly state. For instance, in Matthew 8:20 he says:

> Foxes have holes and the birds of the air have nests, but the
> Son of Man has nowhere to lay his head.

On other occasions this lowly state referred to and included a
reference to his forthcoming crucifixion, as in Matthew 20:28:

> ... just as the Son of Man came not to be served but to serve,
> and to give his life as a ransom for many.

These uses of the term "Son of Man" all refer to his work on
earth, but there are also those places in which Jesus refers to himself as the Son of Man in an eschatological, metaphysical sense,
much in the spirit of Daniel 7. With reference to the end of the age
Jesus says in Matthew 13:41–42:

The Son of Man will send his angels and they will gather out of his kingdom all things that provoke offences and all who do evil, and throw them into the blazing furnace, where there will be weeping and grinding of teeth. Then the virtuous will shine like the sun in the kingdom of their Father. Listen, anyone who has ears!

As noted, scholars have struggled through the centuries to come up with a consistent theory of what is meant by this phrase. The various theories that have been devised take us beyond the scope of this work. However, there is one point on which almost all scholars agree: that the Greek expression *ho huois tou anthrōpou* and the English translation, "Son of Man," are linguistic barbarisms. This fact is explained by the hypothesis that the Greek expression is an attempt to render an original Aramaic expression into Greek. Scholars generally agree that Jesus spoke Aramaic (a particular dialect of Hebrew spoken in Judaea). This matter is of some importance, for as we have already noted the Hebrew expression *bar nasha* has the significance of "man" in its generic sense. Unfortunately, the Greek translation of the Hebrew/Aramaic and the English translation of the Greek shift the emphasis from "Man" to "Son." Actually, "Man" is the primal focus of this expression, and "Son of Man" is a particular way of speaking of what could be called the "archetype of man." Some scholars believe the better translation would be simply *ho anthrōpos*, "the Man."

One scholar in particular has argued that the expression "Son of Man" denotes the idea of a primal or archetypal human being. Frederick H. Borsch has traced the idea of a Son of Man to sources that far antedate the Christian era. He has noted a core of ideas and images about an Original Man of a legendary character in parts of the world as disparate as China and Scandinavia, though they are particularly abundant in the Near East. This First Man was depicted in myths throughout many ages and in many places as a Man who had to fight a great battle, in which he was temporarily overwhelmed by the powers of darkness and evil, but from which powers he was eventually rescued to emerge a victorious and heroic champion. According to the legends, this primal hero, who was once on earth, is also a Cosmic Man who lives in the heavens. This Man shared in human fate and existence, but emerged triumphant from evil and death, and his adherents can

benefit from his victories. Borsch believes that Christ combined
all of the aspects of this primordial legendary Man in his own
being. In Christ we see the ancient Primal Man reborn in a new
way and in a new context.

Borsch calls his book *The Son of Man in Myth and History.*[3] It is
worth noting that he does not add *and Psychology* to the title. This
is understandable since scholars are not concerned with psychology as such. However, we *are* concerned with psychology, and so
we are interested in the psychological meaning of legends about
a Cosmic Man who lived as a hero on earth, whose story was told
in ancient legends, who was referred to in the Old Testament, and
with whom Christ identified in the New Testament. The psychological explanation is that this "Son of Man" is an archetype. It
is interesting that in a number of places Borsch himself uses the
word "archetype" in order to do justice to his idea of the Primordial Man. At one point he concludes, "One might hold that there
is a quality that is almost archetypal in the Man's story." Now,
by an archetype we mean a typical and universal pattern. Borsch
no doubt had in mind a typical and universal pattern found in
mythology, but from the psychological point of view such patterns occur in mythology when there is an archetype in the psyche
from which the archetypal myths and legends emerge.

From the point of view of psychology, the Son of Man is a way
of referring to the archetype of our complete humanity, which
exists within the soul and is the guide for and the goal of our
individuation. Christ as Son of Man relates us to our humanity;
Christ as Son of God relates us to God. This point was made by
Gregory of Nyssa, who wrote:

> For as He is called the Son of Man by reason of the kin-
> dred of His flesh to her of whom He was born, so also He
> is conceived, surely, as the Son of God, by reason of the
> connection of His essence with that from which He has His
> existence.... The word "Son" claims for Him both alike —
> the human in the man, but in the God the divine.[4]

This helps us understand the relationship between the historical Jesus and God. The historical Jesus can be understood as a
person who was uniquely aware of what we would call today the

---

3. Frederick H. Borsch, *The Son of Man in Myth and History* (Philadelphia: Westminster
Press, 1967), 407. Cf. 68, 87, and 98.
4. Gregory of Nyssa, *Against Eunomius* 3.4.

Self, or, in religious language, the reality of the *imago dei* within the soul. From this there emerges a radically unique consciousness, a consciousness that transcended that of others of his time, as is clear from the parables and sayings in the synoptic Gospels.[5] In the language of the late Hebrew scholar and Jungian analyst James Kirsch, he was a man who could "read the unconscious directly."[6] The historical Jesus was uniquely in touch with the archetype that he lived and expressed so completely. In him the human and the divine natures were distinct, yet intimately related into one being. This mystery is reflected in the Fourth Gospel in the relationship between the Father and the Son, passages we will consider as they come up.

Theologians may choose to derive other meanings for the expression "Son of Man" as well, but the psychological meaning is our primary concern. In order to realize this psychological meaning in our lives and psychological development, however, we must not only contemplate the metaphysical or theological meaning of Christ as the Son of Man but also realize that this reality exists in us as the Word of God and therefore as an intimate part of our psychological structure. Operating from the unconscious and drawing the ego into a relationship with it, the Son of Man archetype affects us like an inner magnet, unites our human nature, and relates it to a transcendental reality.

Clement of Alexandria puts the matter succinctly in these words:

> The power of the Word, which is given to us, being strong and powerful, draws to itself secretly and invisibly every one who receives it, and keeps it within himself, and brings his whole system into unity.[7]

The discourse with Nicodemus concludes with the important Johannine motif of the light and the darkness, a motif that was introduced in the Prologue in the words: "a light that shines in the dark, a light that darkness could not overpower." This discussion begins:

> On these grounds sentence is pronounced:
> that though the light has come into the world

---

5. See my book *The Kingdom Within: The Inner Meaning of Jesus' Sayings*, rev. ed. (San Francisco: HarperCollins, 1987).

6. From a private conversation.

7. Clement of Alexandria, *The Stromata* 5.13.

men have shown they prefer
darkness to the light
because their deeds were evil. (v. 19)

In John's Gospel the words "light" (*to phōs*) and "darkness" (*hē skotia*) do not refer to natural phenomena, such as in "it is light in the day and dark at night," but to spiritual phenomena. The words are used metaphorically to signify the light of truth and spiritual illumination on the one hand, and the principle of moral and spiritual darkness on the other. The Jerusalem Bible points out that in the New Testament there are three related but distinguishable uses of the light/darkness dichotomy. First, "Just as the sun lights man on his way, so anything that shows him his way to God is 'light.' "[8] Second is light "as symbolic of contentment and joy, as darkness is of death, unhappiness and misery." Third is the use of light and darkness "for the mutually hostile worlds of Good and Evil." Examples of the first usage in John's Gospel occur in John 1–9, 9:1–39, and 12:35. There are no clear examples of the second usage in John's Gospel, but the third usage is represented in John 12:36, 9:39, and 12:46, and in the passage under present consideration. In this passage "sentence is pronounced" according to whether we choose the light or the darkness, that is, it is of vital importance to the soul of each individual where one stands in this matter. The passage continues by making it clear that both the principle of light and the principle of darkness exist in the world (*kosmos*).

The distinction between light and darkness as natural phenomena on the one hand and light and darkness as spiritual principles on the other hand needs to be kept clearly in mind. There is nothing wrong with the darkness of night. In fact, our souls crave this darkness, and if it were light twenty-four hours a day we would be crying out for the psychic shelter of the night. In the natural order, light and darkness balance each other like *Yang* and *Yin:* they alternate with each other, giving balance and order to life. But as spiritual principles the light and the darkness struggle against each other, and constitute a pair of moral opposites that requires us to choose between them. As spiritual principles we cannot follow both the light and the darkness, for the darkness seeks to overcome the light. As we will see in more

---

8. See the Jerusalem Bible, footnote "b" of chapter 8.

detail later, the judgment of which the Fourth Gospel speaks has to do with this choice.

In verse 19 there is another subtle but important distinction between the Greek and the English. English translations read "men loved darkness rather than light" (RSV) or "men have shown they prefer darkness to the light" (JB). The thing to note here is that the Revised Standard Version and other English translations do not include the definite article before "darkness" and "light," and the Jerusalem Bible includes the definite article before "light" but not before "darkness." In the Greek the definite article is included before both light and darkness. As we have seen, the use of the definite article in Greek is always there for a specific purpose.[9] In the context of this verse the presence of the definite article before both of these words means that the Fourth Gospel is singling them out for special emphasis, distinguishing "the" light and "the" darkness from the general notion of light and darkness, and thus hypostatizing them as independent spiritual principles. The same usage of the article with light and darkness was employed in the Prologue (John 1:5, 9) and is almost always used throughout the Gospel whenever these two words occur.

The psychological sense of the light as a spiritual principle is that it brings consciousness, illumination, knowledgeableness, and enlightenment. The psychological sense of the darkness as a spiritual principle is that it darkens the mind and brings ignorance and moral and psychological obtuseness and unawareness. The psychology of this can hardly be overestimated and is of crucial importance for the psychology of individuation, for individuation can proceed only when one walks in the light. Indeed, the whole process of the examination of one's life and the analysis of dreams, which psychological analysis employs to assist in the process of individuation, is an exercise in living in and by the light.

It must not be supposed, however, that the light of which the Fourth Gospel speaks is a quality of the ego as such. In this case we have to think of the ego as analogous to a candle that gives forth light when it is lit by a flame. The light comes from a deeper reality than the ego; it is that which enlightens us and greatly expands our consciousness. To belong to the light is to become conscious; to refuse the light is to become dark. It is this light to which C. G. Jung referred when parting from his friend Mary Mellon in those

9. See footnote 1 in chapter 7 above.

dark years when Europe was being engulfed by Nazi Germany: "I think the night has descended on Europe. Heaven knows if and when and under which conditions we shall meet again. There is only one certainty — *nothing can put out the light within.*"[10]

The psychology of individuation stresses the importance of becoming conscious and enlightened. For this to take place the ego needs to be in touch with the light that comes from within and exercise its capacities for consciousness. Thus the light is important in psychology and in the New Testament and for the same reasons. As Clement of Alexandria put it some eighteen hundred years ago:

> Let not us, then, who are sons of the true light, close the door against this light; but turning in on ourselves, illuming the eyes [the unconscious], and gazing on the truth itself, and receiving its streams, let us clearly and intelligibly reveal such dreams as are true.[11]

However, it must not be imagined that a person becomes enlightened by concentrating exclusively on the light. John's Gospel is filled with admonitions to understand the works of darkness as well as to contemplate the light. Jung put this very well when he wrote, "One does not become enlightened by imagining figures of light, but by *making darkness conscious.*"[12] The darkness we are to make conscious, first and foremost, is our own darkness, beginning with a thorough knowledge of our egocentricity.

Three other issues that revolve around the Greek words in this passage merit attention. The first has to do with "men" and "prefer": "men have shown they prefer darkness to the light...." Regarding "men," once again the Greek has the definite article. It also uses the word *anthrōpos,* which, it will be remembered from our discussion in an earlier chapter, refers to the human race in general, not to the males of the species. Thus the strict translation of this would be "the members of the human race." So the Fourth Gospel is referring to a general and ingrained tendency in human nature.

The Greek is much stronger than the English, and this stronger

---

10. C. G. Jung in an article in *The Princeton Alumni Weekly* on the Bollingen Foundation, 17 (emphasis mine).

11. Clement of Alexandria, *The Instructor* 2.9.

12. C. G. Jung, *Psychological Reflections* (Princeton: Princeton University Press, 1970), 220 (emphasis mine).

meaning is brought out even more in the Greek word translated "preferred" in the Jerusalem Bible (also the New English Bible and Phillips, but not the King James Version and the Revised Standard Version). This word is none other than the well-known word *agapaō*, the verb from which is derived the noun *agapē*, which, as every Bible student knows, means "love" in the deepest and most complete sense. Now, to "prefer" something is one thing; to "love" it is another. Our passage is saying that human beings are inclined to love (or one could say "be firmly or passionately attached to") the darkness rather than to the light. This proclivity of human beings for unconsciousness rather than consciousness, for darkness rather than light, is well known to the student of the unconscious and is evidenced from even a casual reading of the daily newspaper.

It was also well known to St. Augustine, who once wrote a comment on the use of the terms "light" and "darkness" in the Prologue, a comment we are now in a position to understand. He wrote of the light that shines in the dark, a light the darkness could not overcome:

> Now the Darkness is the foolish minds of men, made blind by vicious desires and unbelief. And that the Word by whom all things were made, might care for them and heal them, "The Word was made flesh and dwelt among us." For our enlightening is the partaking the Word, namely, of that life which is the light of men.[13]

There is also in the concluding portion of this sentence the use of a Greek word for evil that is important for us to understand in order to grasp further subtleties of the Gospel. We find this word in the text that reads: " . . . because their deeds were evil."

There are several words that might have been used to express the idea of evil. One is the word *kakos*, but this word simply denotes that which is bad in any way, morally or otherwise. There is also the word *phaulos*, which means "sorry, vile, evil, wicked," and which, in fact, is the word that is used in the next verse when it refers to "everybody who does wrong. . . . " But neither of these words is strong enough to convey the meaning that is intended, so we find instead the word *ponēros*, a word that is used in the New Testament to refer to evil as an active agency of principle. It

---

13. St. Augustine, *On the Trinity* 4.2.

is this word that is used in the Lord's Prayer, where it can be translated "deliver us from evil" or "deliver us from the Evil One." In
either case it describes evil as a malignant principle at work in
the world. In using this special word for evil the text says in the
strongest possible way that insofar as humans love the darkness
more than the light, their actions — and their souls — come to
partake of the nature of evil itself.

Our text now continues with an explanation for this profound
tendency in us to avoid consciousness:

> And indeed, everybody who does wrong
> hates the light and avoids it,
> for fear his actions should be exposed;
> but the man who lives by the truth
> comes out into the light,
> so that it may plainly be seen that what he does is done in
>   God.
>
> (vv. 20–21)

The matter is clear: we prefer the darkness of unconsciousness because we do not want to have to face up to our own evil.
Specifically, we do not want our actions in life to be exposed —
not even to ourselves, or, we should say, especially to ourselves.
The only way to protect ourselves from this self-revelation is to
endorse the principle of darkness by refusing the light and the
consciousness that it inevitably brings.

As we have noted, Jung once said knowing the light comes
from making darkness conscious. What he meant was that when
we make ourselves see the darkness that is in us, then we can espouse the principle of the light. In the language of individuation
this is accomplished by facing the shadow — our own dark side,
which we ordinarily do not want to see because such an insight
would be counter to our egocentric pretensions and ambitions.
Confrontation with the shadow is essential for individuation, as
Jesus made clear in many passages in the synoptic Gospels.[14] The
shadow prefers to operate in secrecy, but God is the "knower of
all secrets," and God's light strives to bring into our awareness
all those deeds we have done that were done under cover of the
darkness, deeds of which we are ashamed and afraid to face because they would force us to change. But the person who "lives by

---

14. See my book *The Kingdom Within*.

the truth" comes under the power and influence of the light. Such a person can then live in the open, with himself, and with others. He is not afraid to be seen by God and having faced his shadow is no longer afraid to see who he is. He has become conscious. Evil seeks the darkness in which to hide; self-honesty, that most essential of all qualities for individuation and the truly religious life, seeks the light.

"The truth": once again we have a special Greek word used in conjunction with the definite article. It is *the* truth, *hē alētheia,* a word that means that which is free from error, that which is genuine and has integrity. The truth we are to discover is the truth about ourselves. To live by the truth is to live with inner self-honesty, exposing oneself and one's actions to the light. It cannot be attained by rationalization, by blaming other people, or by projecting our shadow onto others.

Becoming conscious — "living in the light" — is hard work. It sometimes seems easier to follow the way of the darkness. All of this was well known to our author, who uses two different Greek words for "to do" something. One word, as we have noted before, is *prassō,* and the other word is *poieō.* The word *prassō* is usually used in connection with doing that which comes easily, and in the New Testament is almost always the word that is used in connection with doing something evil. On the other hand, the word *poieō,* which can also mean "to create," is almost always used in connection with doing anything that takes an effort. In the New Testament when someone does something that is good or creative, the word *poieō* is the word of choice. For instance, Jesus, to the best of my knowledge, is never said to perform an act with *prassō* but always with *poieō.*

A good example is in our present passage. In John 3:20 we have a reference to "everybody who does wrong." The Greek word used here is *prassō.* A little later we read of the "man who lives by the truth." The word here is *poieō.* The distinction is clear: the life of consciousness and truth requires an effort; the life of unconsciousness and evil is following the path of least resistance.

Those who undertake the process of individuation know this to be a fact. It takes an effort to live consciously. To subject one's inner and outer life to scrutiny and examination does not come easily. If a person uses as an aid the following of dreams and keeping of a journal, that also requires an expenditure of time and energy. However, there is a compensation for the effort that is put out by the person who follows this life, for that person receives energy and support from within. In religious language, "God goes with us" when we try to live consciously. Furthermore, we also experience the creativity of the unconscious. By using energy we gain energy. By facing our difficulties we also find the inner path becomes easier. In contrast, the person who does evil is opposed from within; that person lives as though an invisible force was standing in the way.

~ 9 ~

LIVING WATER
Conversation with the Samaritan Woman
John 4:1–42

AS WE HAVE SEEN in our discussion of John 3, our author introduces us to the contrast between the literal mind and the symbolic mind and shows that the capacity for symbolic thinking enables us to be born again through the waters of transformation. He enlarges on this theme in the conversation between Christ and the woman of Samaria. The story begins with the account of a journey Jesus took that required him to return from Judaea to Galilee through Samaria (vv. 1–3). Samaria was a fertile land north of Jerusalem. At one time it was occupied by the ten tribes of Israel, while the two tribes of Judah occupied the southern region. However, when the Assyrians conquered the northern kingdom of Israel, the people were mostly deported and people from other countries were brought in to settle the area. This was part of the Assyrians' policy intended to discourage future insurrections. The Samaritans, as these people came to be called, eventually began to worship Yahweh, the God of the Jews whose land they now occupied, but they did not honor the temple in Jerusalem, worshiping God on various altars set up on high hills in Samaria instead. The fact that the Samaritans were of foreign extraction and did not worship as the Jews did created hostility between the two groups of people even though they worshiped the same God. The story tells us:

On the way he came to the Samaritan town called Sychar,
near the land that Jacob gave to his son Joseph. Joseph's well
is there and Jesus, tired by the journey, sat straight down by
the well. It was about the sixth hour.

The sixth hour would be noon, the hottest time of the day, so
Jesus was tired and thirsty from his journey. Moreover, since the
disciples had gone into the town to buy food (v. 7), Jesus had
no way to draw up water from the well as they evidently had
taken the rope and bucket with them. The whole setting is hoary
with sacred history, for in the Old Testament many important
meetings and encounters took place at wells or springs (see Gen.
24:10f, 29:1f; Exod. 2:15f). This was natural since in the dry land
of Israel wells and springs were important places and were often
regarded as sacred. Symbolically we could say that a well represents a "place where things come together." The result is that
when a Samaritan woman came to the well to draw water Jesus
said to her, "Give me a drink" (v. 7).

The woman was startled and replied, "What? You are a Jew
and you ask me, a Samaritan, for a drink?" To this our narrator
added, evidently for the benefit of readers who might not be familiar with the hostility between Jews and Samaritans, "Jews, in
fact, do not associate with Samaritans" (v. 9). Jesus replied:

> If you only knew what God is offering
> and who it is that is saying to you:
> "Give we a drink,"
> you would have been the one to ask,
> and he would have given you living water.

"Living water" — the Greek is *hydōr zōn*. The word here for
"living" is related to the word we met in the Prologue: "All that
came to be had life [*zōē*] in him and that life was the light of
men" (John 1:4). We have considered the meaning of water in
the symbolism of the unconscious; now we find an analogous
symbolic meaning for water in the Bible. In the Old Testament
the prophet Isaiah speaks of the water of salvation:

> And you will draw water joyfully
> from the springs of salvation.
> (Isa. 12:3; cf. Isa. 55:1;
> Jer. 2:13, and others)

Water is also a biblical symbol for the gift of Wisdom, which we discussed earlier. So Baruch speaks of the "fountain of wisdom" (Bar. 3:2), and Sirach speaks of "the water of wisdom" (Ecclus. 15:3). Something wells up from within the human soul which is the refreshment of the soul and from which pours forth life and wisdom. This is symbolized by water, and it is this of which Jesus speaks in his image of "living water."

The Samaritan woman, however, can only take Jesus' words literally, so she is perplexed:

> You have no bucket, sir, and the well is deep: how could you get this living water? Are you a greater man than our father Jacob who gave us this well and drank from it himself with his sons and his cattle?

Our story now introduces a subtle nuance of meaning that is bound to escape the reader who has only the English text. When the Samaritan woman speaks of the well that is deep, the Greek word *phrear* is used. This word refers to a man-made well or cistern, but Jesus always uses the word *pēgē*, which, as we noted earlier, means a natural source of water that gushes up from the ground, like a spring. This is the image of water that Jesus uses when he answers her:

> Whoever drinks this water
> will get thirsty again;
> but anyone who drinks the water that I shall give
> will never be thirsty again:
> the water that I shall give
> will turn into a spring [*pēgē*] inside him, welling up to eternal
>   life.

So we have a contrast in the Greek. The woman says:

> You have no bucket, sir,
> and the well [*phrear*] is deep ...

Jesus says:

> ... the water that I shall give
> will turn into a spring [*pēgē*] inside him. ...

The first source of water is man-made, and like any well is subject to becoming dry or losing its contents when the cistern

is cracked; the second source of water gushes up from an inexhaustible source and never runs dry. It is a contrast noted by the
prophet Jeremiah, to whom Yahweh said of his people:

> They have abandoned me,
> the fountain of living water,
> and dug water-tanks for themselves,
> cracked water-tanks
> that hold no water. (Jer. 2:13, NJB).

There is a reality within us that we can directly experience and
that is analogous to the spring of water of which Jesus is speaking.
We noted earlier that Etty Hillesum knew of this and spoke of "a
really deep well inside me, and in it dwells God." It is this source
of life within us, for instance, from which our dreams well up, an
unending source of life from and for our souls.

The early church psychologist-theologians did not hesitate to
identify this water with Christ, whom they termed "the fountain of life."[1] Speaking in his inimitable mystical, psychological
way, Clement of Alexandria writes of water that not only is it the
natural source of all life, so that "without the element of water,
none of the present order of things can subsist," it is also a spiritual element without which the life of the soul cannot exist. In
fact, this water is none other than "Christ, the maker of all," who
came down as the rain[2] and was known as a spring (John 4:14),
diffused himself as a river (John 7:38), and was baptized in the
Jordan. Christ is the "boundless River that makes glad the city of
God . . . " (Ps. 46:4), the illimitable Spring that bears life to all men
and has no end, who is present everywhere and absent nowhere,
who is incomprehensible to angels and invisible to human beings. He concludes with words that could well have been spoken
to the Samaritan woman: "When you hear these things, beloved,
take them not as if spoken literally, but accept them as presented
in a figure."

This is the healing water that comes up from within, heals the
weary ego, and replenishes the soul. This water was also known
to the Greeks, who built their healing shrines, homes of the god
of healing, Asklepius, over or near sources of water, particularly

---

1. This and the succeeding quotations regarding water are from Clement of Alexandria, *The Discourse on the Holy Theophany*, Part 2.
2. Hosea 6:3: "He will come to us like a shower, like the rain of springtime to the earth"
(NJB).

springs and running streams, shrines that were taken over by the church and rededicated to various healing saints when Christianity replaced paganism in the Graeco-Roman world. It is a water that was also known to the Greek playwright Sophocles. In his play *Oedipus at Colonus,* the stricken Oedipus asks the Greek chorus how to make atonement to the deities he has offended. They answer him:

> Make a libation first of water fetched
> With undefiled hands from living spring.[3]

The water, then, of which Jesus speaks has the following characteristics: First, it is a special water, not earthly water, but spiritual water. As such it is, as noted, often represented in our dreams, sometimes appearing as a water that is of unusual clarity. One man, for instance, dreamt of a service of Holy Communion in which he participated with a companion: "We have regular communion wafers that we dip into some incredibly clear water from a tiny mountain stream. This water is so clear that it is most marvelous." Another man dreams of arriving in a certain city and coming upon a remarkable body of water: "It might be part of the sea, or maybe it is a river that goes through the city. What makes the water so amazing is its remarkable clarity, which gives it a most unusual quality. It might also be salt water, which, combined with the clarity, adds to its unusual and inviting quality."

Second, we are told that Christ is the source of the water. This is the water that *he* will give us, and is to be contrasted with the ordinary water that one receives from a well or municipal water supply. As we noted, Clement of Alexandria is of the opinion that Christ not only gives the water but is, in a mystical way, the water itself.

Third, we are told that this water will be like a spring of water welling up from within ourselves; as such, no one can ever take this water away from us.

We can see what an esoteric and mystical document the Fourth Gospel is. It is this esoteric quality of the Gospel that has led some people to term it the "Gnostic Gospel." However, we have already noted that there are reasons why the Fourth Gospel cannot be said

---

3. Line 470, from the translation by F. Storr. Sophocles uses another Greek word for a spring: *krēnē,* akin to *pēgē* and used in the opposite sense of a *phrear* (Liddell and Scott's *Greek-English Lexicon*).

to belong to Gnostic literature that flourished in the early Christian era and became known as Gnosticism. As we have noted, Gnosticism taught that materiality is the cause of sin and error; the Fourth Gospel says that the source of sin and error comes when the will inclines toward the darkness and refuses the truth and the light. For the Gnostics, the body and the material creation were evil in themselves; for the Fourth Gospel God's Word created everything, including the material world. For the Gnostics, the saving efficacy of Christ was minimized; for the Fourth Gospel Christ as the enduring Word alive within the soul is essential for salvation. For the Gnostics the source of the fall into sin was laid at the door of Sophia, a feminine aeon whose cosmic blunder brought about the tragedy of human life. For the Fourth Gospel, as we will see, the problem lay in the active agency of evil in the world.

What Gnosticism and early Christianity did share was a belief that *gnōsis*, that is, knowledge through experience of inner truth, had a saving efficacy. In an attempt to acquire this *gnōsis*, early Christians sought insights from dreams and visions, interpreted the Scripture symbolically, believed that knowledge of the Word came through the soul, and taught the precept "Know thyself" as the way to the knowledge of God. The Fourth Gospel is thus not a "Gnostic Gospel"; rather, Christianity in its inception was a Gnostic religion, that is, a religion that said that at the heart of the meaning of Christ was a *mystērion* that could be known through inner experience.

Our text now continues with the following interchange between Jesus and the Samaritan woman:

> "Sir, give me some of that water, so that I may never get thirsty and never have to come here again to draw water." "Go and call your husband," said Jesus to her, "and come back here." The woman answered, "I have no husband." He said to her, "You are right to say, 'I have no husband'; for although you have had five, the one you have now is not your husband. You spoke the truth there." (vv. 15–19)

The answer the woman makes to Jesus shows two things: First, that she is not yet free of her literal thinking; she still thinks of water of which Christ speaks as similar to the water from a well. Second, it shows that she is still caught in her egocentric attitude, since for her the important thing is that if she had this water of which Christ speaks, it would relieve her of the burden of going to the well and pulling drinking water up with a bucket. As long as we approach the inner world from a purely egocentric point of view, we cannot imbibe its essence, nor understand its mysteries.

One sees this a good deal in the process of analysis. Most of us begin analytical work because the ego is hurting somewhere. We *want* something — relief from a painful state, emergence from a depression, the resolution of a relationship problem. This is understandable, and for a while in the analytical work it seems to be allowed by the unconscious. But in time, the emphasis of the work must shift from ego to soul. We are called upon no longer to do the psychological work just for our own sake, but for the sake of something else within us. The need for this shift of emphasis is sometimes indicated in dreams in which the dreamer comes to the analyst for an appointment only to find that the analyst is engrossed in conversations with other people. Much to the anger of the dreamer, she is treated casually and forced to wait while the analyst she is paying for her appointment gives his attention to these strangers. The message of the dream is something like this: "Look, you, the ego, aren't the only one who is important." This work is being done for the sake of the soul, which appears in the form of these other persons in the dream. You need to place your soul first and your ego second, remembering what the Lord said, "What is a man profited if he gain the whole world, and lose his own soul?" (Matt. 16:26, KJV).

In order for the ego to change its attitude, a person must see the darkness that is in him because of his egocentricity. This means facing up to that shadow side of his personality, of which we spoke earlier. When the shadow problem has not been dealt with, people often dream of polluted water. The dreams we just noted in which the water was incredibly clear could only come to someone who had faced his darkness and not pushed it aside into the unconscious where it pollutes the inner life.

One place in which we can see our shadow is in our unresolved relationships, and this is why Christ continues the dialogue with the woman by confronting her with the fact that she has had five husbands. Drawing on his capacity for an uncanny knowledge of what lay in a person's heart, he brings up this uncomfortable matter of her broken relationships (much as an analyst might do). He does so by laying a bit of a trap (the unconscious will also lay traps for us to make us confront unpleasant realities about ourselves) with his request that she go and get her husband and bring him back with her. When she reports "I have no husband," it gives Jesus an opportunity to penetrate her defenses with his thrust: "You are right to say, 'I have no husband'; for although you have had five, the one you have now is not your husband." Then he adds (a bit sarcastically we may assume), "You spoke the truth there."

Just as many of us would do under similar circumstances, the Samaritan woman tries to avoid discussing an uncomfortable subject by diverting the conversation to something else, so she brings up the old issue between Jews and Samaritans about where God is to be worshiped. It is a favorite trick many people use even today: if topic "A" makes you uncomfortable, shift the conversation to topic "B."[4] So she says:

> I see you are a prophet, sir. Our fathers worshiped on this mountain, while you say that Jerusalem is the place where one ought to worship. (vv. 20–21)

But Jesus is not to be thrown off the track so easily. True, sensing that her resistance is so strong that further discussion of her shadow is not possible, he drops the matter of her five husbands and present lover who is not her husband, but uses her question as a way to try to teach her — and us — things about God that neither she nor her forefathers had ever considered:

> Believe me, woman, the hour is coming
> when you will worship the Father
> neither on this mountain nor in Jerusalem.
> You worship what you do not know;
> we worship what we do know;
> for salvation comes from the Jews.
> But the hour will come — in fact it is here already —
> when true worshipers will worship the Father in spirit and
>   truth:
> that is the kind of worshiper
> the Father wants.
> God is spirit,
> and those who worship
> must worship in spirit and truth. (vv. 21–24)

4. See my book *Between People* (Mahwah, N.J.: Paulist Press, 1982), chap. 6.

This striking statement by Jesus is the culmination of the story, the high point toward which our author was aiming from the beginning. Starting with a historical reminiscence of an actual conversation between Jesus and a Samaritan woman, the story concludes with a statement by Jesus that radically changes the prevailing ideas — held by both Jews and Samaritans — of the nature of God and how God is to be worshiped. The text is worthy of close examination.

In verse 22 Jesus connects worship with knowledge. It is hard to worship in a valid way what one does not know from personal experience. Who are the "we" to whom Jesus refers, those who are neither Samaritans nor Jews when it comes to this matter of worship? The implication is that "we" refers to all of those who know something of God and for whom, as a consequence, the way of worshiping has been transformed.

Then in verse 22 comes the interesting statement: "salvation is from the Jews." Here there is an important nuance of meaning from the Greek. The Greek in this case is *hē sōtēria ek tōn Ioudaiōn estin* — "*the* salvation [is] from the Jews." The important thing here is the inclusion of the definite article "the" before "salvation," a point that does not come out in most English translations (Phillips excepted). This inclusion of the article means that the salvation referred to is not a general kind of salvation, but a specific salvation, *the* particular way of salvation that has been embodied in the religious history of the Jews. That is why Jesus can go on to say that this salvation comes from the Jews.

From the point of view of the psychology of individuation something tremendously important happened in the religious history of the Jews: there came about a direct connection between the human ego and God. Psychologically, this laid the groundwork for a relationship between ego and Self, and this marks such an advance in ego development and consciousness that individuation in a modern way now became possible. In fact, as we have noted, the New Testament has the first extant and surprisingly complete cases of individuation to be found anywhere in the world in the stories of Jacob, Joseph, and Moses.[5] This living relationship between human consciousness and the numinosum of God is continued in the relationship that existed between the

5. See my book *The Man Who Wrestled with God*, revised paperback (Mahwah, N.J.: Paulist Press, 1987).

prophets and Yahweh. Persons such as Isaiah, Jeremiah, Elijah, and Ezekiel are spiritual giants who have a talking relationship with the Center. From their experiences of relationship with God emerges the idea of the corporate relationship of Israel as a people with God, a relationship that is enshrined and maintained through the Covenant. But here the individual relationship with God became submerged in the corporate relationship with God, and the individual ego was lost in the national consciousness and identity. The same thing happened in Judaism as in Christianity: a religion born from the immediate experience of certain individuals (the patriarchs and prophets in the Old Testament; the disciples, faithful women, and St. Paul in the New Testament) becomes collectivized (Israel/the church), and eventually turned into a doctrine (law/church) and concretized (necessity of temple worship/idolization of ecclesiastical authorities). With this development, the impetus toward individuation leaves the collective area and disappears underground once again, waiting to emerge whenever possible in those individuals who are willing and able to carry the process, be they Jews, Christians, or otherwise.

Jesus goes on to the matter of worship, and he does not refer to either the Samaritans or the Jews but to the true "worshipers." These true worshipers will not be concerned with where they worship God, but with the inner state from which they worship. They will worship "*en pneumati kai alētheia*, in spirit and truth." The use of the one preposition *en* to refer to both spirit and truth suggests that "spirit and truth" comprise one experience, that spirit and truth in this instance cannot be separated. The word "truth" — *alētheia* — refers to that which is morally true, genuine, and real. The implication is that one can worship God only in an inner spirit of moral integrity, genuineness of character, and reality of self-perception. Issues about where this worship is to be performed — on mountains or in temples or cathedrals — is secondary to the issue of the spirit of the worshipers and their psychological integrity. In verse 24 we are told again that we must worship in spirit and truth because that is the nature of God: God *is* spirit. While this latter statement might seem conventional enough to us today, it was radical in Jesus' time, for in the Old Testament God had never been addressed as spirit.[6]

---

6. See article by A. B. Davidson, in *Dictionary of the Bible*, ed. James Hastings (New York: Charles Scribner and Sons, 1911), 1:95.

It should also be noted that as spirit, God has no sex, a point made by Sandra M. Schneiders.[7] As spirit God permeates all creation, and especially the human soul. As spirit God is everywhere, and one is never separated from the divine reality. As spirit God's nature and reality cannot be contaminated by the psychic pollution of a culture. And since God is spirit, worship can be made anywhere, provided one's inner condition is correct. Out of our psychological state emanates the true (genuine) worship, and other considerations are secondary: this is the radical message Jesus brings us in this passage.

The woman's reply to this powerful and searching statement by Jesus is one more attempt at diversion: "I know that Messiah — that is, Christ — is coming, and when he comes he will tell us everything." The implication is: "I don't have to listen to you telling me these uncomfortable things about God and myself, for one day Christ will come and he will tell me what I want to hear." This is the entry for Christ to make another powerful statement: "I who am speaking to you is he" (John 4:26).

The significance of this statement is almost certain to be lost on the casual reader, for the Greek text does not say "I am he," but "I am." The phrase "I am" in Greek would usually take a predicate such as "I am he," or, "I am the Christ," or "I am the good shepherd" (as in John 10:11: *ego eimi ho poimēn ho kalos*). The Greek expression "I am" is *ego eimi*, and it occurs several times in the Fourth Gospel without any predicate. Biblical scholars call this the "absolute I am," and regard this Greek construction as both grammatically peculiar and extremely important. The reason for its importance is that in the Old Testament, when Moses asks God whom he shall tell the people has told him these things, God says to him, "Say to the Israelites, 'I am has sent me to you'" (Exod. 3:14). The phrase *ego eimi* is the Greek equivalent expression for the Hebrew phrase translated "I am." Thus Christ is using the sacred name of God with reference to himself. The importance of this for both psychology and for an understanding of the Fourth Gospel will be discussed in more detail later on.

At this point the discussion between Jesus and the woman ends because the disciples reappear. Significantly, they are surprised to find him speaking with a woman, though they don't ask

---

7. Sandra M. Schneiders, *Women and the Word: The Gender of God in the New Testament and the Spirituality of Women* (New York: Paulist Press, 1986), 186.

him about it (perhaps by now they are used to having surprises from this unusual mentor of theirs). The woman, meanwhile, hurries back to town and tells the people:

> Come and see a man who has told me everything I ever did: I wonder if he is the Christ? This brought people out of the town and they started walking towards him.

It would seem that in spite of herself Jesus has made an impression on this woman, especially perhaps in his last statement, *egō eimi*, "I am," for she now has an intimation that maybe he is the Christ. It is remarkable in John's Gospel that the first intimation of the nature of Christ appears on the lips of a woman; it is she who has an insight that not even the disciples have at this point. Furthermore, as we find out in verses 39–41, she turns out to be a persuasive evangelist in her own right:

> Many Samaritans of that town had believed in him on the strength of the woman's testimony when she said, "He told me all I have ever done," so, when the Samaritans came up to him, they begged him to stay with them. He stayed for two days, and when he spoke to them many more came to believe; and they said to the woman, "Now we no longer believe because of what you told us; we have heard him ourselves and we know that he really is the saviour of the world." (vv. 39–42)

Here we see again the radical nature of the Jesus of the Fourth Gospel: he disregards social conventions with regard to talking with a woman; a woman is the first one to have an intimation about the Christ and is the first evangelist for him; hoary traditions on worship are broken; God is referred to as spirit; Christ uses the sacred *egō eimi* to refer to himself; true worship is defined in inner categories; and God is spirit and therefore is "located" everywhere, as a wind moves everywhere through all creation.

It is a new message, bringing with it a new psychology, but the times are ready for it as is made clear in verses 34 to 38:

> My food
> is to do the will of the one who sent me,
> and to complete his work.
> Have you not got a saying:
> Four months and then the harvest?

Well, I tell you:
Look around you, look at the fields;
already they are white, ready for harvest!
Already the reaper is being paid his wages,
already he is bringing in the grain for eternal life,
and thus sower and reaper rejoice together.
For here the proverb holds good:
one sows, another reaps,
I sent you to reap
a harvest you had not worked for.
Others worked for it;
and you have come into the rewards of their trouble.

These verses speak of a psychological development that has reached its time: "Look at the fields! Already they are white, ready for harvest." Important new ideas have a history. Each new idea — in science for instance — builds upon previous ideas. That is why Einstein once said that if he could see further than others it was because he stood on the shoulders of giants. New psychological developments likewise emerge because they develop out of a previous psychological condition. Consciousness evolves just as the various species of life have evolved from more primitive to more sophisticated forms. The psychology of individuation is an evolving process too. Like a lamp it appeared briefly in the lives of certain persons in the Old Testament, but it first finds complete expression in the life and consciousness of Christ. But Christ's words tell us that human consciousness has evolved, at least in part, to the point where many people are ready to receive the new thought. In fact, many people did receive a share of it, and this provided the energy for the emergence of Christianity as a remarkable phenomenon in the ancient world. True, not everyone caught the new spirit or emerged with a new awareness, but this is the way it always is, for consciousness of the sort we are describing cannot be transmitted collectively. We cannot learn it in school, or be spoon-fed it in church. Each individual must acquire it for him/herself through hard work, the development of painful insights, and the grace of God. Furthermore, like all new developments, this new psychological development is certain to run into resistance. New scientific ideas often meet with such resistance from a scientific community because the old patterns are deeply entrenched and do not want to give up their power. A new psychological development in an individual may also meet with resistance on the part of those persons who are her companions — for it will force them to change too. And new religious and spiritual ideas likewise meet with new resistance, especially when the old ideas have become enshrined in an institution, collectivized teaching, and personal power structures. As we progress further into our Gospel story we will see how this resistance is constellated — and leads eventually to the crucifixion.

～ 10 ～

CURE OF THE NOBLEMAN'S SON
Faith and the Healing Process
John 4:43–54

WE COME NOW to the first healing story in John's Gospel: the cure of the nobleman's son. Some scholars believe this story is a variant of the story of the healing of the centurion's servant found in Matthew 8:5–13 and Luke 7:1–10. This may be so, but there are notable differences. In John's Gospel it is a high official of the court (or nobleman) who comes to Jesus, not a centurion; it is his son who is ill, not his servant; and the healing takes place in Cana of Galilee, not Capernaum. In both stories, however, attention is called to the close connection between faith and healing. In the synoptic versions Jesus is so astonished at the faith of the centurion that he says, "I tell you, not even in Israel have I found faith like this." In John's version, the faith of the court official is so great that he is convinced that if Jesus would only come down to see his son he would be cured, and after Jesus told him that his son would live we are informed by the evangelist that "the man believed [had faith in] what Jesus said."

John prefaces his healing story with an explanation for why Jesus, after he left Samaria, went to Galilee instead of to Nazareth: "He himself had declared that there is no respect for a prophet in his own country." The Greek syntax changes the reference from a general statement to a specific truth (*en tē idia patridi*). The force of the New Testament sentence is that while it is generally true that a prophet has no honor in his own country, it was specifically true for Jesus. We will examine more of the implication of this statement shortly, but first we must understand the nature of this faith that is so important for healing.

In psychology there is a great emphasis on knowledge. Both Freud and Jung agreed that if a person only knew what forces had shaped her personality and could only know what lay in the unconscious, healing would result. "Making the unconscious conscious" is the hallmark of all depth psychology, and "the truth will make you free" is the maxim under which the psychotherapist proceeds. The very word "analysis" suggests the importance of knowing for healing. The word comes from two Greek words *ana* and *lysis*. The word *lysis* means to dissolve or loosen, so analysis is that process which dissolves the whole into its parts. Thus in analysis we see what are the individual component forces that underlie our behavior or distress, and this has the effect of "loosening things up" so that our underlying personality structures can be re-formed.

In contrast, for the most part faith is simply disregarded as a factor in psychotherapy, for, after all, psychotherapy purports to be something of a science and faith is a religious term, is it not? And when faith is mentioned it is usually disparaged and is even seen as the enemy to our attempts to come to self-knowledge. For instance, Stephen A. Hoeller, in his work on Gnosticism in its relationship to Jungian psychology, stresses the merits of arriving at inner knowledge and identifies it with the meaning and purpose of life in contrast with faith, which he sees as opposed to knowledge. He writes:

> for the meaning and purpose of life thus appears to be neither faith, with its emphasis on blind belief and equally blind repression, nor works with their extraverted do-goodism, but rather an interior insight and transformation, in short, a depth-psychological process.[1]

It is interesting to note that Hoeller's depreciation of faith has its roots in the Gnostic attitude of the second and third centuries B.C.E. Some eighteen hundred years ago Irenaeus objected to the Gnostics because, in his view, they claimed haughtily to be "spiritual men who have attained to the perfect knowledge of God."

---

1. Stephen A. Hoeller, *The Gnostic Jung and the Seven Sermons to the Dead* (Wheaton, Ill.: Guest Books, 1982), 11.

Irenaeus said that these Gnostics contrasted themselves to the Christians whom they termed "animal men" because of their lack of knowledge, and who were characterized by "mere faith" in contrast to the "perfect knowledge" of the Gnostics.[2]

Clement of Alexandria said the same thing: "The followers of Valentinus," he once wrote, "assign faith to us, the simple, but will have it that knowledge springs up in their own selves through the advantage of a germ of superior excellence, saying that [their knowledge] is as far removed from faith as the spiritual is from the animal."[3]

Jung himself often spoke disparagingly of faith and saw it in opposition to knowledge. He once wrote, "Faith and knowledge can no more agree than Christians can with one another." Faith is "blinding"; it is "childlike" and encourages people to "*remain* children instead of becoming *as* children." As such it always involves us in the "conflict between faith and knowledge."[4]

Jung's disparagement of faith came from his personal experiences as a child with the faith of his father. He tells us in his autobiography, *Memories, Dreams, Reflections,* that when he was a boy he eagerly anticipated his confirmation instruction from his pastor father, for then he would be told the meaning of the enigmatic doctrine of the Trinity, which had long puzzled and fascinated him. But alas! when the confirmation classes came his father quickly passed over the matter of the Trinity, and when the young Carl asked him about it he was told not to try to understand it, but to believe it "on faith." That finished Jung with regard to faith, for Jung was not a man to go around believing in something one could not understand, nor was it in his spirit to cease inquiries and believe through blind faith. Small wonder Jung, and others such as Stephen Hoeller, concluded that faith encouraged a childlike attitude and precluded conscious understanding and inquiry. It can be said that for Jung, from that time on, the path to healing and wholeness lay not through faith but through knowledge.

It is true that certain theological attitudes have distorted faith to the point where it became inimical to the spirit of knowledge and inquiry. The example of Jung's father is a case in point. How-

---

2. Irenaeus, *Against Heresies* 1.6.2.
3. Clement of Alexandria, *Stromata* 2.3.
4. C. G. Jung, *Aion,* in *The Collected Works of C. G. Jung,* trans. R. F. C. Hull, 20 vols. (Princeton: Princeton University Press, 1953–79), vol. 11, para. 269; *Psychology and Religion,* in *Collected Works* 11, paras. 765 and 864.

ever, as we noted earlier, in early Christianity faith and knowledge were not seen as opposed to each other but were regarded as close partners. In the Fourth Gospel especially, faith is not hostile to knowledge but is an adjunct to it. Faith, as the early Christians understood it, had nothing to do with making oneself believe in things that could not be understood or blindly assenting to doctrinal formulations one could not understand. In this regard it is noteworthy that Jesus showed little interest in anyone's theological beliefs, although he was greatly concerned with the quality of someone's faith, as we have seen in our story of the healing of the court official's son. In the biblical view faith is not a category of the intellect but of the soul. The mind needs to know so it does not live in darkness, the soul needs faith or it loses its strength and will to live, and mind and soul need each other and the gifts of knowledge and faith that they bring to one another.

The Greek word *pisteuō*, translated "to believe," is instructive when it comes to understanding what the Fourth Gospel means by faith. The word can mean simply "to be convinced" of something. So if we said, "I believe the earth goes around the sun, not the sun around the earth," we would be making a statement regarding our scientific convictions. But when the word is used in a religious sense it is used in a more complicated way. *Pisteuō* in a religious sense means to trust in something. In this case the object of that trust may be in the dative case, which denotes that in which one's trust is placed. Or, the verb *pisteuō* may be accompanied by the preposition *eis* which means "into." *Pisteuō eis* means "to put one's trust *into* something." This Greek construction occurs some twenty-six times in John's Gospel.[5] It shows that faith is not an intellectual act of making oneself believe in something that cannot be proven, but is an action from the soul that enables a person to place her trust into a living reality.

When it comes to the noun *pistis*, translated "faith," the Greek constructions are also instructive. In English we think of "having faith" as though it were a certain possession. We also imagine that this "faith" is something we can conjure up for ourselves if we only try hard enough. In the New Testament, however, the word *pistis* when referred to Christ or God is usually part of a particular grammatical construction known as the "object genitive." As noted before, in Greek, nouns are declined, which means

---

5. Examples: John 2:23, 3:36, 6:35, 7:31, 11:25, 14:12, 17:20, and so forth.

they have certain case endings. One of these cases is the genitive. The genitive is the only special case we have in English and it usually denotes possession. So if we say, "The house's roof needs to be repaired" we are using "house" in the genitive case to denote possession or "belonging to." In Greek the genitive case is also used to denote simple possession, but it also has more subtle meanings, and one of these subtle meanings is found in the use of the object genitive in connection with the word "faith."

The way it works is as follows: Sometimes two nouns are combined in such a way that the second noun appears to be the object of the energy of the first noun, but is also the source of the energy of the first noun. As an example, consider Mark 11:22, where Jesus says to the disciples, "Have faith in God." That sounds straightforward enough. How often have preachers exhorted us to do the same? In Greek, however, the wording is: *exete pistin theou.* In this construction the word for God is *theou* and is in the genitive case. This signifies that the faith we are to have in God is itself originated from or excited by God. As Greek scholar Samuel G. Green put it: "The fundamental meaning of the Genitive is very apparent, the object of a sentiment being, in another view of it, the source or occasion of its existence. Thus *exete pistin theou* (have faith in/toward God) really means, 'have such faith as his character excites.' "[6] This kind of faith occurs many times in the New Testament in connection with having faith in God, Christ, the name of Christ, and so on.[7] The Greek grammatical construction helps us see that this faith is a vital living quality, that it has nothing to do with blindly believing in something, but is a quality of the soul that springs from the soul and is nourished in the soul by the object of the faith.

One can think of the energy of this kind of faith the same way we think of the energy contained in a battery. A battery contains energy that we can use for our purposes, but this energy must be put into the battery from some greater source of energy. And if the energy in the battery is not to be depleted it must be renewed from time to time by its energy source. So it is with faith in God.

That it is this idea that Jesus has in mind when he speaks of faith is shown in the healing stories that occur in all four Gospels.

---

6. Samuel G. Green, *Handbook to the Grammar of the Greek New Testament* (New York: Fleming H. Revell, 1912), 218.

7. Examples include Romans 3:22, 26; Galatians 2:16; Ephesians 3:12; Philippians 3:9; James 2:1; and so forth.

In the biblical healing stories, various Greek words are used to refer to the healing that Jesus gave to the sick person. Two of the most common of these words are *therapeuō* and *iaomai*. *Therapeuō* is the source for our word "therapy." In classical Greek, for example, *therapeia* was the word for the divine worship of, or service to, the gods. It also could mean to heal or cure, and to cultivate the land or tend a garden. *Iaomai* is related to the noun *iatros*, which is the Greek word for a physician. Today we have a new expression based on this Greek word: "iatrogenic." It refers to a disease caused by the doctor. In the New Testament *therapeuō* and *iaomai* often appear to be interchangeable. For instance, in Acts 28:8 (*iaomai*) and 28:9 (*therapeuō*) we see both words used with much the same sense. In Luke 14:3 and 14:4 we again find both words used, in this instance by Jesus, in a way that suggests their interchangeability. In fact, these words would be the usual ones employed with reference to the healing of a person who had been ill, and Jesus often used them or some equivalent expression.

However, there was another word that Jesus used to refer to healing: *sōzō*. This word did not mean healing as such, but rather it meant "to save." To be saved is different from merely being healed. For instance, if we had an infected toe that was cured we might say it was "healed," but we would not say that we were "saved." *Sōzō* is a much more complete word than *therapeuō* and *iaomai* and signifies not only the alleviation of a distressing symptom, but also the total renovation of someone's personality, hence the usual English translation of this word "to be made well or whole."

An examination of the healing stories in the Gospels shows that Jesus used the word *sōzō* only in instances in which the suffering person made a personal, individual effort to seek him out for healing.[8] On other occasions, when Jesus healed someone at the behest of someone else, Jesus used one of the lesser words for healing. In the story of the cure of the court official's son, for instance, Jesus does not use *sōzō*. In contrast consider the story in Luke 8:40–48 (Matt. 9:18–26 and Mark 5:21–43). In this story a woman who had been suffering from an issue of blood for twelve years and had sought healing from many doctors without success struggles through a crowd to reach Jesus so she can touch

---

8. For more on this see my book *Healing Body and Soul* (Louisville: Westminster/John Knox Press, 1992).

the hem of his garment. Immediately Jesus knows that someone touched him with the intention of being healed, for he said that at that moment "power went out of me." Discovered, the woman is fearful of a rebuke, but Jesus says to her, "My daughter, your faith [*pistis*] has restored you to health [*sōzō*]; go in peace."

Here we see exemplified the quality of biblical faith: the woman was led to persevere until she found healing because of her faith. It was faith that brought her to Jesus, the ultimate source of her healing. Jesus was the receptacle into which her faith was placed. She had faith "into" him. She could not "know" what would happen when and if she found her way to him, but her soul had faith and this led her to the right source.

This kind of faith is also the quality that makes it possible for psychotherapy to succeed. It is well known to psychotherapists that if the healing work is to succeed there must be a relationship between the client and the therapist. We call the quality the client brings into this relationship the transference. The transference has been analyzed backward and forward by psychologists and has been found to include many elements. People can bring all kinds of factors into the relationship with the therapist or project onto the therapist various psychological images, such as that of the anima or animus or Self, but the bottom line to the transference, as we noted in a previous chapter, is faith. The client must bring at least a modicum of faith into the therapeutic relationship or he would not be there in the first place, and certainly if the work is to succeed the quality of faith must be present. Therefore it is important in therapy that a person select his own therapist if possible, for this means that the element of faith is most likely to be present. If the client does not "have faith in" the therapist, the therapy will be fruitless and will soon be given up.

Interestingly enough, it is not only the client who must have faith, but also the therapist. The therapist needs to have faith that her work with the client can succeed. This requires a certain faith in the ultimate integrity and honesty of the client and also a faith in the process of healing. It is often the faith of the therapist that sustains the faith of the client when the latter begins to weaken. The faith of the therapist is strengthened if she herself has been ill and has been healed. When one has been ill and then become well one *knows* that healing can take place and has a sense for the process that leads to it. In the psychotherapeutic relationship we have a good illustration of the Greek object genitive. The therapist is both the recipient of the faith of the client and also, at least in part, the source of that faith.

It is worth noting that dreams also play a significant role in sustaining faith. In the process of analysis, dreams are remembered, written down, and studied for their meaning. Some of our dreams prove to be positively uncanny in the way they show us our inner situation and sometimes point the way out of a difficult situation. Our dreams give us the feeling that we are "being spoken to"' from a voice within. However, we must have a bit of faith to begin with or we would not bother to record them. This initial faith may be supplied by the therapist who says, "You know, your dreams may help you; I suggest you begin to remember them and write them down." Because we have faith in the therapist we are willing to risk it with the dreams. But in time the situation is reversed. As we see the meaningfulness of the dreams, they themselves increase and sustain our faith that a meaningful process is going on within us and that all is not hopeless after all. Thus the dreams are both the object and the source of our faith, a good example of the "object genitive" at work.

It also follows that if at any point in the therapy the client were to lose faith in the therapist, the efficacy of the therapy would come to an end. This might happen, for instance, if the therapist demonstrated his lack of knowledge, skill, or integrity, in other words, if he proved to be an unsuitable receptacle for the faith of his client.

As the carrier of the projection of the Self, guide, or healer for the client, the therapist must always know that she is only an ordinary human being doing the best she can with her skill, concern, and knowledge. Otherwise she can fall into an inflation that is destructive to the client. She must also realize that eventually the client must discover the Self within herself and withdraw the projection from the therapist. It is as though the therapist agrees to hold the projection of the healer for the time being until such a time as the client discovers that the true healer is within her own soul.

We could say that faith is that quality of the soul that opens us up to healing. It is like rain that falls on hard ground, and by moistening it makes it amenable to receiving the seeds that will grow into a new life. It is this faith that enables the soul to persevere, and it is also the perseverance of the soul that nourishes faith. Indeed, the soul can hardly live without faith, which is why, as we noted earlier, we can be so desperate for faith that if we cannot find a suitable receptacle for our faith we may place it in someone or something that is unworthy of it.

As we noted earlier, faith and knowledge, which are so often artificially separated in the thinking of people today, were, along with love, part of one process in the thinking of the New Testament. So St. Paul wrote:

> so that Christ may live in your hearts through faith, and then, planted in love and built on love, you will with all the saints have strength to grasp the breadth and the length, the height and the depth; until, knowing the love of Christ, which is beyond all knowledge, you are filled with the utter fulness of God. (Eph. 3:17–19)

This quotation about the process of salvation is filled with the symbolism of individuation. It begins as a process, described as the implanting of Christ in one's heart (innermost being). This process is initiated through faith (*pistis*), for before one can know, one must follow the energy and longing of the soul with perseverance. The process having started, it is increased through love (*agapē*), and this leads to the formulation of a mandala, the four-fold directions of breadth, height, and depth, being grasped by consciousness. Finally comes knowledge, which is *gnōsis*, knowledge gained through intimate experience, and this in turn leads to the full experience of God (*plerōma*, which means fullness or wholeness), which began with the seed implanted by Christ within the heart.

So it is that the religious process of development involves a complex relationship among faith, knowledge, and love. Clement of Alexandria had a great deal to say about this. "Now neither is knowledge without faith, nor faith without knowledge." And, "Faith is discovered by us to be the first movement toward salvation... which leads us to love and knowledge." For "knowledge cannot be attained without faith." On the other hand, "Knowledge... is characterized by faith; and faith, by a kind of divine and mutual reciprocal correspondence, becomes characterized by knowledge."[9]

This connection between faith and knowledge comes out clearly in the Fourth Gospel, in which there are some 90 refer-

---

9. Clement of Alexandria, *The Stromata* 5.1, 2.5, 2.4.

ences to the importance of faith and 118 expressions that relate to the importance of knowledge; in fact, in some cases the relationship between faith and knowledge is so close that the distinction between the two is not very clear. This is because faith, far from being an attitude that precludes the desire to know, is that which energizes and strengthens the desire to know. Faith yearns for knowledge, and knowledge strengthens faith. The faith of the New Testament and of the early Church Fathers is not the "blind faith" that Jung so rightly disparaged, but is that which impels us to diligently search for the truth. Once again Clement of Alexandria puts it adroitly when he says, "Faith . . . must not be inert and alone, but accompanied by investigation." He goes on to reject any attitude that leads to lack of inquiry: "For I do not say that we are not to inquire." And he supports his argument by quoting from Jesus, "For 'Search and you will find' " (Matt. 7:7). He then proceeds to quote the Greek playwright Sophocles as well, who once wrote: "For what is sought may be captured, but what is neglected escapes." And also the Greek poet Menander, "All things sought, the wisest say, need anxious thought."[10]

It is this same spirit that pervades all seekers for truth, including those seeking scientific truth. The scientist does not begin with knowledge but with faith that knowledge can be found. Jung himself began his work with certain intimations of the reality of the unconscious. His own experiences, his dreams, the intimations from his soul, led him to defy collective opinion, and, with no outward support for his research, he arrived at a knowledge of the existence of the collective unconscious. Jung can be said to have been proceeding in that kind of faith of which St. Augustine spoke when he said, "Faith is only faith when it waits in hope for what is not yet seen in substance."[11]

That faith and knowledge are partners in one process is not to be wondered at since they have one and the same source in Christ, who as Wisdom and Logos both inspires the faith of the soul and teaches us the way of understanding.

10. Clement of Alexandria, *The Stromata* 5.1.
11. St. Augustine, *The City of God* 13.4.

~ 11 ~

ILLNESS AND SIN
The Cure of the Sick Man at the Pool of Bethzatha
John 5:1–18

THE SECOND HEALING STORY in John's Gospel is the story of the man by the pool of Bethzatha and follows on the heels of the first. The first nine verses (5:1–9) are concerned with the healing miracle; the succeeding verses (5:10–18) are concerned with the dispute with the Jews that stemmed from the fact that Jesus performed the healing work on the sabbath. Many scholars believe that this passage marks a transition in John's Gospel from the theme of testimony (chaps. 1–4) to the theme of controversy (chaps. 5–11).

John gives us a detailed description of the pool of Bethzatha (the name is spelled in various ways in different ancient manuscripts), which suggests, once again, that our author was intimately familiar with Jerusalem and is reporting a historical reminiscence. It is thought by many scholars that verses 3b and 4, which describe how and why the water moved from time to time, are not original with the most preferred ancient manuscripts and were a later addition. Nevertheless it appears that the water in the pool was periodically disturbed either by an underground disturbance or by the influx of new water at certain intervals. The fact that this disturbance was attributed to an angel gives us a glimpse into how people in the biblical era thought about angels and also into the tendency of the human psyche to mythologize

131

its world. This mythological tendency gave rise to the idea that the first person to enter the pool after the angel had disturbed the water would be healed (perhaps by the angel himself). It is entirely possible that people had such faith in this that certain persons entering the water at this time were healed, so strong can be the influence of *psychē* on *sōma*. It is also an example, as noted before, of the close association between water on the one hand, and healing and renewal on the other.

Many sick people were gathered around the pool — blind, lame, paralyzed — but Jesus' attention was drawn to one man in particular, a man who had suffered from an unspecified illness for thirty-eight years and who we may surmise had spent most of this time waiting by the pool, without, however, ever being the first one to enter the water after it was disturbed. There was something about this man that caught Jesus' attention, for he was the one among the many people there to whom he spoke. The question he addressed to him is pregnant with meaning: "Do you *want* to be well again?" I have emphasized the word "want" because the Greek word translated as "want" is *thelō*, which means to will, to exercise conscious volition. The question Jesus asked the man does not involve simply desire or preference, but will and choice. It is what can be called a consciousness-raising question, that is, if the man had reflected honestly on the question he could have arrived at some important insights about himself.

However, the fact is that he did not do so. Instead his answer deflects the question with what sounds like an excuse for his inability to get into the pool first; evidently he had a guilty conscience: "Sir, I have no one to put me into the pool when the water is disturbed: and while I am still on the way, someone else gets there before me."

For thirty-eight years this man has been by this pool and has not yet made it into the water! The implication is clear: the man does not want to be cured: he prefers the suffering of his disease to the rigors that a healthy life entails. For of course, the price of being healthy is to live a healthy life, which for most of us means taking on work, responsibility, and life's tensions and burdens. Remarkably enough, some people would rather be ill than pay the price of being healthy. Evidently Jesus, with the amazing capacity to see into the heart of people that we have already noted, perceived that this man's physical illness was intertwined with his deficient conscious attitude. In short, we have here an example of a psychosomatic illness.

Kunkel helps us at this point with his description of the four major egocentric types. One of them — the Turtle — is a person who is so afraid of life that he withdraws into a protective shell and environment in order to shield himself from life's demands. In some cases a Turtle may encase himself in a psychological defense system that protects him from unwanted intrusions into his emotional life; in other cases he may seek out a life-situation in which as few demands as possible are made upon him. Such a situation might be an illness. A person whose egocentric defense system includes an illness will resist getting well, for he perceives health and life to be more dangerous and demanding than illness. At the same time that such a person may complain about his illness and use it to win sympathy, he may also secretly (keeping it secret even from himself) carefully nurse his illness along so as to prevent a cure. It is clear from the context of the story that the man by the pool of Bethzatha was such a man.

This being the case, what Jesus said to him must have been alarming: "Get up, pick up your sleeping-mat and walk!" The verbs in the Greek are in the imperative voice, indicating that what Jesus said was not a suggestion but a command. On hearing these words the man was instantly cured — quite against his will! — and had no alternative but to pick up his mat and walk away, without, it should be noted, thanking his unwanted benefactor.

The story now broadens to include not only the fate and response of the sick man, but also the controversy that this healing engendered with the Pharisees. Noticing that the man who had been ill is carrying his sleeping-mat, the Pharisees confront him: "It is the sabbath; you are not allowed to carry your sleeping-mat." The man's reply reveals once again his passivity and his refusal to take responsibility for himself, his actions, and their consequences: "But the man who cured me told me, 'Pick up your mat and walk.'" Greeted with the information that someone had performed a work on the sabbath, the authorities demand to know who he was, but the man who had been sick cannot tell them since Jesus had disappeared quickly into the crowd after performing the miracle.

However, later Jesus met the man again and made a stern statement to him that reveals to us the light in which Jesus saw him: "Now you are well again, be sure not to sin any more, or something worse may happen to you." The Greek translation would, more literally, be: "See, you have become well...." The Greek word translated "well" is *hygiēs,* which means hale, sound, healthy. It is not *sōzō,* discussed in chapter 10, because the man did not make a personal effort to find health, thus exercising the faith of the soul.

Jesus also says in this sentence "...be sure not to *sin* any more, or something worse may happen to you." In a footnote, the Jerusalem Bible reassures us that Jesus is not implying that the man's illness was the result of sin. However, when the above statement is taken in the context of the whole story it is hard to escape the conclusion that in Jesus' mind the man's sin and his illness were connected. Evidently the Jerusalem Bible disclaims the idea that Jesus meant to connect sin and illness because in John 9:2 he does reject the connection between the two. But in John 9:2 it is with regard to another man and another situation, as we will see later when we get to John's ninth chapter. In the present circumstance it seems clear: the man's sin and his illness were intertwined.

But what is the sin of which the man was guilty? In the New Testament there are at least eight different words for sin, each with its own special nuance of meaning. In this case the Greek word used for sin is *hamartanō.* While usually simply translated into English "to sin," the literal meaning of the word is "to miss the mark or aim." It is the most commonly used of all words in the New Testament for the idea of sin.[1] *Hamartanō* is the same word that was used in archery. If an archer shot an arrow at the target and missed the mark, it would be *hamartanō.* The word is to be contrasted with another Greek word, *tynchanō,* which means the opposite: to hit an object. It is used in 2 Timothy 2:10 with reference to attaining salvation.

The idea of "hitting the center with an arrow" implies consciousness, good aim, and steadfastness of character, for if the arrow does not find the mark it is the fault of the archer, not of the arrow. The impact of this idea of sin is that wrong actions and attitudes spring from a wrong inner condition that causes us to "miss the mark" in life.

We find this same idea in other religious points of view. In classical Greek thought the same word — *hamartanō* — is also

---

1. Found in 1 Corinthians 15:34; Titus 3:11; John 5:14; and Matthew 18:75, and in noun form in Romans 7:7, 17:20; John 9:41; Hebrews 9:26; 2 Corinthians 5:21, and so forth.

used with reference to sin. Greek scholar Walter F. Otto says: "We know that the Greeks habitually pictured recognition of what is right and wrong under the image of an accurate bowshot."[2] In Sophocles' play *Oedipus at Colonus,* the stricken Oedipus says with reference to the unfortunate fate he brought upon himself when he unwittingly killed his father and took his mother as his wife:

> For which in retribution I was doomed
> To trespass [*hamartanō*] thus against myself and mine.[3]

Thus *hamartanō* has to do with failing to act from one's Center, thus sinning against oneself. It is the result of our unconsciousness, of the sort that springs from unresolved egocentric attitudes that consistently cause us to "miss the mark." It is sin as it emerges from a faulty and egocentric psychology. Interestingly enough, the Chinese sage Confucius employed the same image of missing the mark, as in archery, to represent a faulty psychological state. Writing about 500 B.C.E., he said:

> In archery we have something like the way of the Higher Man. When the archer misses the center of the target he turns around and seeks for the cause of the failure in himself.[4]

Not many of us like to be confronted with our egocentricity, and the man by the pool of Bethzatha is no exception. Instead of being grateful that he was cured, he was resentful of the exposure of his egocentricity and promptly told Jesus' enemies who it was who cured him on the sabbath. The result is as expected: Jesus' enemies began to persecute him. The man's vindictive action toward his benefactor confirms our diagnosis that he was encased in his egocentricity and resented being cured. His attitude will be seen all the more clearly when we compare his reaction to Jesus to the reaction of the man born blind whom we will meet in John 9. The result of the man's turning informer is the heightened antagonism between Jesus, representative of a new point of view, and those who represent an old point of view. It is to this controversy that we now turn.

---

2. Walter F. Otto, *The Homeric Gods* (London: Thames and Hudson, 1955), 77.
3. Sophocles, *Oedipus at Colonus,* lines 967–68.
4. Confucius, *Doctrine of the Mean,* XIV 5.

~ 12 ~

EGO AND SELF
Jesus Replies to His Accusers
John 5:19–47

IN TYPICAL JOHANNINE FASHION we now move from a story to a discourse. The lengthy monologue of Christ in this section is both spiritually rich and difficult for the modern mind to grasp. We can understand it better if we do as we have done before and regard it as an active imagination between the author and the Risen Christ and understand that though the discourse is couched in the form of a diatribe to the Jews, it is in fact intended for us, the readers. As we have done before, so we will do now and understand that by "the Jews" we mean not those who espouse the faith of Judaism, but all those people who remain so entrenched in old attitudes that they are not open to the new life of the spirit. Since we all are partly, or perhaps even largely, caught in our old psychological structures, we are the ones to whom Christ is speaking.

In this section we will also examine the Greek words *poieō* and *prassō*. Both of these words mean "to do" something, but as a rule *poieō* means to do something that requires an effort while *prassō* means to do something that comes easily. For this reason, when the Greek refers to an act of evil the word *prassō* is usually used, whereas a creative act is expressed by the word *poieō*.

In verses 19 and 20 there is a discussion of how the Son does what he sees the Father doing, and in verse 21 there is a discussion of how even as the Father raises the dead and gives them life, so does the Son. In these verses and also in verse 29a, the word John uses for "to do" is the word *poieō*. In verse 21 he uses

136

a word derived from *poieō: zōopoieō*, which means "to engender living creatures" or "to make alive, to vivify." The inclusion of *poieō* in this word fortifies the idea that the making of life is a creative action, and God is a creative God. In contrast, in the latter part of verse 29, where the reference is to those who did evil, the Greek word used is *prassō*, connoting the carelessness and unconsciousness with which evil deeds are committed.

Psychologically we can say that the creativity of God is expressed in the human psyche in the creativity of the Self or Center. Kunkel believed creativity to be the essential quality of the Center and that from the Center came the impetus toward and the energy for a creative life. He did not use the term "good" to describe the Center since everyone has his own idea of what constitutes goodness and what appears to be good to one person may appear evil to another. It is interesting in this connection that in the New Testament God is understood to be first and foremost the Creator, but neither God nor Jesus is referred to as good except on one occasion: the story of the rich young man who said to Jesus, "Good [*agathos*] master, what must I do to inherit eternal life?" To which Jesus replied, "Why do you call me good? No one is good but God alone" (Mark 10:17–18, with parallels in Matt. 19:17 and Luke 18:18). The word "goodness" [*agathōsynē*] is, to the best of my knowledge, never used in the New Testament with reference to God, although it is used with reference to Christian character. The word "kindness, generosity" (*chrēstotēs*) occurs more frequently (Rom. 2:4; 11:22; Eph. 21:7) and the word *kalos* is indirectly used by Christ to refer to himself in the Parable of the Good Shepherd (John 10:11, 14, 32).

This passage is also rich in its allusions to judgment and life, which it contrasts with death. As we have noted, the theme of life vis-à-vis death is one of the major motifs in John's Gospel, a theme introduced at the very beginning, in the Prologue ("All that came to be has life in him and that life was the light of men"). Our major discussion of this motif will come later, but we can anticipate this discussion by noting that it is not the death of the body to which our text is referring but the death of the soul. The "dead who will leave their graves at the sound of his voice" (v. 28) are all those whose souls once were dead to the things of the spirit.

The primary focus of the discourse, however, is on the relationship of the Father to the Son. Like the theme of life vis-à-vis death, the theme of the relationship of the Father to the Son was

presented to us in the very beginning of the Gospel ("In the beginning was the Word: and the Word was with God and the Word
was God"). We will now comment on this important theme with
special reference to its psychological symbolism.

There are some nineteen sections or verses in which the Fourth
Gospel speaks of the relationship of the Father and the Son. In
eleven of these the relationship between the two is extremely
close, as in 17:21 — "Father, may they be one in us, as you are
in me and I am in you ... " — to the point of virtual identity as in
10:30 — "The Father and I are One."[1] In eight verses or sections
the relationship is still close, but a qualitative distinction can be
drawn as in 14:28 — "If you loved me you would have been glad
to know that I am going to the Father, for the Father is greater
than I."[2]

Theologians have pondered the meaning of these uses of the
term *egō eimi* deeply, but from the psychological point of view
they can be seen as representative of the structural relationship
between the ego and the Center. At the risk of repetition, it may
be helpful to summarize this relationship at this point.

The psychology of individuation shows that there are two centers to the personality: the ego, and Self or Center. The ego is,
roughly speaking, the center of consciousness, but the Self is the
center of the whole personality embracing the conscious and the
unconscious. The Self is thus the larger reality including the ego
within it. As long as the ego is unconscious and encased in its egocentricity, it deviates from the Self. For individuation to take place
the ego needs to be aligned with the Self, reflecting the Self in its
life and embodying the creativity of the Self. This Self presents
itself in dreams and religious experiences as an *imago dei*, and so
I have compared it with the early Christian idea of Christ as the
indwelling Logos or Wisdom of God, which the Fathers of the
Church said resided in the soul. To do the will of the Logos or
Self is tantamount to doing the will of God, to depart from this
will leads to a life of error or sin. Thus the ego can be viewed
as something other than the Self; yet it also has an identity with
the Self and partakes of the same nature. This mysterious relationship of Father to Son and Self to ego is part of the Christian
mystērion, which we discussed in a previous chapter and which

---

1. See John 1:1; 5:19ff; 8:28; 17:5, 21; 10:30, 38; 14:6, 9, 10.
2. John 3:16, 35; 5:17, 43; 6:40, 44; 12:50; 14:28.

was summarized by St. Paul when he said: "I have been crucified with Christ, it is no longer I who live, but Christ who lives in me" (Gal. 2:20, RSV).

As we have noted, the Self is also referred to as the Center. When we speak of the Self we tend to think of the *imago dei* within us as that which includes all of our totality, as though it were in a circle. When we speak of the Center we tend to think of it as the center of the circle, where everything included within the circle finds its unity. This psychology of the Center was anticipated in the early church by some of its most brilliant thinkers. A striking example is found in the writings of Gregory of Nyssa. Gregory was contemplating the soul. "For who is there," he asks, "who has arrived at a comprehension of his own soul?" He goes on to describe the great variety of operations of the soul and its great diversity that results in its "anger and fear, pain and pleasure, pity and cruelty, hope and memory, cowardice and audacity, friendship and hatred, and all the contraries that are produced in the faculty of the soul." He continues:

> Observing which things, who has not fancied that he has a sort of populace of souls crowded together in himself. . . . Is it [the soul] a unity composed of them all, and, if so, what is it that blends and harmonizes things mutually opposed, so that many things become one, while each element, taken by itself, is shut up in the soul as in some ample vessel? . . . For if these have an independent existence, then, as I have said, there is comprehended in ourselves not one soul, but a collection of souls, each of them occupying its position as a particular and individual soul.[3]

Gregory correctly perceives what our dreams indicate, that our nature is made up of a great plurality. The Center is that mysterious factor that Gregory intuits that "blends and harmonizes things mutually opposed." It is because of the Center that we are a unity in spite of our diversity, provided that we realize the multiplicity of our nature consciously so that the Center can operate. In Christian parlance, this unifying Center is Christ, who is our Peace.

That the relationship of the Son to the Father is also to be understood as a paradigm of the relationship of the ego to the

---

3. Gregory of Nyssa, *Answer to Eunomius's Second Book*.

Self is corroborated by the fact that there are certain places in the Fourth Gospel that say that even as the Son is in the Father and the Father in the Son, so also is Christ in us, and we in Christ. For instance, see John 14:20:

> On that day
> you will understand that I am in my Father
> and you in me and I in you.

And in chapter 17 Christ says to the Father with reference to the disciples:

> Father, may they be one in us,
> as you are in me and I am in you,
> so that the world may believe it was you who sent me.
> (John 17:21)

and

> With me in them and you in me,
> may they be so completely one
> that the world will realize that it was you who sent me
> and that I have loved them as much as you loved me.
> (John 17:23)

Such reasoning raises the issue of the legitimacy of seeing psychology in the Bible as well as theology. It is feared by some that if one sees psychological meaning in Scripture it is a denial of theological validity, a way of saying "it is all 'nothing but' psychology." The psychology of individuation, however, in no way denies that there is a metaphysical reality beyond the psychological reality. It merely says that as a matter of empirical fact there is such a thing as individuation and there is such a thing as a real Center to personality.

In his better moments, Jung was careful to draw the line between what was empirically verifiable in psychology and what belonged to the world of theology and metaphysics. He frequently said that he was describing the reality of the psyche and not denying metaphysical reality beyond it. Nor did he limit God to the empirical Self observable in the psyche. God is a reality that lies beyond what can be empirically observed. As the Fourth Gospel says, "No man has known the Father." Jung liked to describe the Self not as God but as a "vessel filled with divine grace."

Neither did he confuse the unconscious with God, though he did say that the unconscious was the medium through which God can be known:

> This is not to say that what we call the unconscious is identical with God or is set up in his place. It is the medium from which the religious experience seems to flow. As to what the further cause of such an experience may be, the answer to this lies beyond the range of human knowledge. Knowledge of God is a transcendental problem.[4]

and

> In order to clear up any misunderstandings, especially from the theological side, I would like to emphasize yet again that it is not the business of science to draw conclusions that go beyond the bounds of our empirical knowledge. I do not feel the slightest need to put the self in place of God.[5]

One would think that Christians might be glad to know that what theologians have said for centuries about the reality of the Divine Logos and the immanence of God in the created order through Christ is observable as a reality in the *imago dei* in the human soul. To the Fathers of the Church, as we have seen, this came as no surprise but was a natural consequence of the idea of the Logos as the immanence of God in the creation, but, of course, they were not as frightened of being introspective as many people are today. In fact, the empirical discovery of the Center, indeed, the whole psychology of individuation, confirms what Christian theology and psychology said long ago. Psychologically, to be in Christ (*einai en Xristō*) is to be related to our psychic Center, even as Christ as the Son was related to the Father, and from this emerges that striving toward wholeness which we call "individuation" and the Bible called *teleiōsis* — completion, fulfillment.

No examination of this passage from John's Gospel would be complete, however, without a few comments on the important sayings of Jesus in verses 5:25–29. Here we learn that at the voice of the Son of God the dead who hear it will live. This can be taken as a reference to the Christian belief in life after death and a coming judgment. For it is said in verse 28 that the dead will

---

4. From an article in the *Atlantic Monthly* entitled "God, the Devil and the Human Soul."

5. C. G. Jung, *Mysterium Coniunctionis, Collected Works* 14, para. 273.

leave their graves and rise again, those who did good to life, and those who did evil to condemnation. It would appear, however, that John intended these verses to be understood as a spiritual rising to life as well as a more literal one. The "dead" are those among us whose souls are dead through lack of consciousness and connection to God, who alone truly makes the soul alive. The grave thus understood is the grave we fall into when our souls have effectually died through lack of light and love, killed, as it were, by our egocentricity and lack of understanding, but when the soul hears the inner voice of God it rises from its self-imposed grave and lives again.

~ 13 ~

TWO MIRACLES
Jesus Feeds the Multitude
John 6:1–15
Jesus Walks on the Water
John 6:16–21

THE STORY OF THE FEEDING OF THE MULTITUDE is the only story (other than the account of the crucifixion) to occur in all four Gospels. In fact, since Matthew and Mark both have two separate but similar stories of the miracle of the loaves and fishes, it can be said that the story is found six times. This suggests that this story was regarded as unusually important in the early church. Certainly John gives it added prominence by attaching to it the lengthy discourse that we will consider in the next section.

The story of the miracle of the loaves and fishes can be regarded as John's eucharistic story. Unlike the synoptic Gospels, the Fourth Gospel has no story of the Last Supper; the footwashing story is found instead. However, in adding to the story of the miraculous multiplication of the loaves and fishes the account of the heavenly food, John has laid the foundation for the theology and psychology of the Eucharist.

In the story of the loaves and fishes, and the succeeding story of Jesus walking on the water, we are confronted with the difficulty imposed on our rationality by a physical miracle. We have already encountered a miracle of healing in the story of the man by the pool of Bethzatha. This story may challenge our credulity, and yet we are familiar with the irrationality of healing, and spontaneous cures are known in the annals of medical science. Somehow it is not so hard to believe, given the close connection between body, mind, and spirit, that illnesses can be cured in a seemingly miraculous way. But how can a few loaves of bread feed five thousand people? And how can anyone actually walk on water?

Some interpreters, in an attempt to explain the miracle and salvage the story from the incredible, come up with the theory that the loaves of bread and the few fish, generously given to Jesus to distribute to the multitude by the boy, moved others who had been concealing their own food supplies to give of what they had, and in this way everyone was able to eat. Of course this interpretation has no basis in the story itself, which says nothing about others among the multitude offering up their hidden food supplies. It is better and more honest to let the story confront us with all of its difficulties.

Miracles such as this one tend to divide people into the scholars on the one hand, and the literalists on the other. Generally speaking, New Testament scholars appear to be bothered by the irrational. For instance, when it comes to the teachings of Jesus, a concerted effort is made by scholars to "trace" his teachings back to historical sources. The idea seems to be that what Jesus taught about the kingdom of God, his parables, his radical ethic, must have come from antecedent sources, such as the Essenes or the Old Testament. The idea that Jesus could have arrived at his message through his own process and via his own relationship to God seems to make rationally minded people uncomfortable. Psychologically, however, we know that gifted people arrive at new insights and knowledge via the unconscious. Jesus, as we have already noted, was a person who could read the unconscious directly. This is like having a pipeline to God. In my book *The Kingdom Within*,[1] I have shown that Jesus' psychological insights were startlingly new. They came from within himself, not from historical antecedents, and made him, among other things, the first great depth psychologist. Many scholars, in their effort to turn the scrutiny of careful thought and the scientific method onto Scripture, have become so uncomfortable with the irrational that wherever it appears it is denigrated and, if possible, explained

---

1. *The Kingdom Within: The Inner Meaning of Jesus' Sayings*, rev. ed. (San Francisco: HarperCollins, 1987).

away. What is left, of course, is the corpse of what was once a living reality. As a result, churches whose teachings rest entirely on a rational, "scientific" approach to Scripture have lost spiritual power.

In the opposite camp are the literalists. These people sacrifice intellectual scrutiny in order to preserve what they see as the Bible's integrity and meaning. Unabashedly they accept everything in the Bible in its most literal form. One must admire such dogged determination to hang onto biblical essentials, but the price to be paid is a large one. Not only must one give up the ability to scrutinize, examine, and evaluate Scripture in the light of scientific information; it also leads to intolerance for everyone whose point of view differs from that of the literalists (including other literalists who quote conflicting biblical passages in support of a divergent position). Everyone with a different opinion is seen to be not just in error but to be diabolical and opposed to divine truth. The greatest difficulty with the hermeneutic of the literalists, however, is that it aborts the possibility of seeing more deeply into the meaning of Scripture.

The method of the early church, as we have seen, was different. Because of its multilevel interpretation of Scripture, biblical passages could be examined for their historical, ethical, and psychological/mystical teachings. It is often helpful to have input from scholars in which they compare parts of the Bible to other historical movements and to historical antecedents, and much is to be learned. And certainly the ethical teaching of the Bible, with its food for our social conscience and concerns, is of great importance. But in addition there is the psychological or mystical content, and for this one needs the symbolic approach.

Applying the symbolic approach to our present discussion, we will be able to find great wealth in this story quite apart from the issue of its historicity as a miracle, and we will be within the parameters of the hermeneutic of the early church in so doing. It is to this that we now turn.

All variations of this story stress the great number of people who were fed. John refers to a "large crowd." Matthew, Mark, and Luke say the crowd numbered five thousand people, and Matthew, in a burst of sexist-tinged enthusiasm for the vast number who were fed, adds "to say nothing of women and children." The emphasis on the large number of people who were fed is sym-

bolic of the vast hunger of humankind for spiritual food. There is
a huge spiritual emptiness in the human race. We suppose in our
Western culture that if only people had all the material blessings
of life they would be satisfied, but they are not. The emptiness
of our souls and our spiritual craving for nourishment surfaces
in our alcohol and drug addictions and in the restless way we
move from one material craving to another, not realizing that this
restlessness is a symptom of the deep-down longing within the
human soul for the real food of life. Even more specifically, the
variety of eating disorders (overindulgence, anorexia, bulimia)
with which our culture is afflicted may have their fundamental
source in this inner emptiness.

However, the emptiness of the soul today leads not only to
psychological illnesses but also to evil. If the soul of a person is
not filled with the spirit of God it will tend to be filled with a spirit
of evil. Jung once wrote that as long as the soul is empty a person
is a prey to evil either as a victim of evil, or as its perpetrator. In a
letter to Bill W. (one of the cofounders of Alcoholics Anonymous,
who consulted with Jung in the early 1930s when he was thinking
of founding A.A.), Jung wrote:

> I am strongly convinced that the evil principle prevailing in
> this world leads the unrecognized spiritual need into perdi-
> tion, if it is not counteracted either by a real religious insight
> or by the protective wall of human community. An ordinary
> man, not protected by an action from above and isolated in
> society, cannot resist the power of evil.[2]

Verses 5 and 6 add an interesting nuance to the story. When
Jesus saw the crowd approaching (the great human need) he said
to Philip, "Where can we buy some bread for these people to
eat?" Why Philip? Why not some other disciple? Philip is mentioned only once in passing in each of the synoptic Gospels, but
in John's Gospel he is prominently featured in several places. In
1:43ff we learn that he was the third disciple whom Jesus called.
In this present passage (v. 6) we learn that he is singled out to
be tested. In 12:20ff those who want to see Jesus approach Philip
first (suggesting Philip was a leader of the group). In 14:8ff we
learn of Philip's thirst to know God ("Lord, let us see the Father

2. C. G. Jung, *Letters*, vol. 2, *1951–1961*, selected and edited by Gerhard Adler in collaboration with Aniela Jaffe, translated from the German by R. F. C. Hull (Princeton, N.J.:
Princeton University Press, 1975), 624.

and then we shall be satisfied"). Perhaps it was precisely because Philip had a thirst to know that he is, along with Peter, the most prominent of the disciples in the Fourth Gospel. We can take him as a stand-in for ourselves. As Fritz Kunkel taught in his psychological commentary on the Gospel of Matthew, it is valuable to view the Gospel narratives not only from the vantage point of Jesus, but also from the vantage point of the disciples.[3] We — like the disciples themselves — are the ones to be transformed by the events of the Gospels and the analogous events in our own lives.

When it comes to the deeper symbolism of this story, Jungian analyst and biblical student Edward F. Edinger is of great help. In the biblical story the loaves and fishes are multiplied many times over in such a way that what was originally a small amount of food becomes more than enough food to feed all the hungry people in the crowd. Edinger points out that one feature of the Self as it has been symbolized in various traditions is its capacity to transform and multiply its effects.[4] For an example he cites the story in 1 Kings 17, in which Elijah, in the midst of a drought, asks a poor widow for water and bread. She is willing enough but explains that she has only a tiny portion of water and the meal and oil for making the bread for herself and her son. Nevertheless, she did as the prophet told her, and lo! even though all three of them drank of the water and ate of the bread, "The jar of meal was not spent nor the jug of oil emptied."

In comparing the story of the widow whose jar of meal was never spent nor whose jug of oil emptied to Christ's feeding of the multitude, Edinger is keeping company with Tertullian. Tertullian said not only was Christ the agency who could multiply the few into the many, the small into the abundant in these stories, but it was the same Christ who nourished the six hundred thousand Israelites with manna as they wandered through the desert, and the same Christ who so multiplied twenty scant barley loaves and some fresh grain that they fed one hundred hungry men, saying "They will eat and have some left over" (2 Kings 4:42–44, NJB).[5] He is also keeping company with Origen, who, as we already noted,

---

3. Fritz Kunkel, *Creation Continues* (Mahwah, N.J.: Paulist Press, 1987).

4. Edward F. Edinger, *Anatomy of the Psyche* (La Salle, Ill.: Open Court Publishing Co., 1985), 227.

5. Tertullian, *Against Marcion* 4.21.

said of the Logos, that he was "broken up and thinned out" in order to become incarnated and available to each of us.[6]

Edinger also draws from the symbolism of alchemy to make his point. Alchemy, which during the Middle Ages carried the mystical undercurrent of official Christianity and which numbered many well-known Christians among its adherents, has been shown by C. G. Jung to be a gold mine of symbols that relate to the process of individuation. In alchemy, the goal of the alchemical process was to produce the philosopher's stone, as the result of a great *opus,* or mystical labor, which in the eyes of Christian alchemists of that time was nothing other than Christ himself, who was often symbolized by the stone. One of the many miraculous and beneficial qualities of the philosopher's stone was its capacity for *multiplicatio.* This is evidenced in the way the emergence of the Center into consciousness has the effect of multiplying (increasing) the extent of consciousness. The Center, when consciously experienced, reproduces insight, knowledge, and intuition endlessly. Moreover, the personality of an individual in whom the Center is activated, and who therefore is undergoing the individuation process, has an effect on others. Others are influenced by our increasing consciousness and wholeness without our even being aware that it is happening. This is why the influence of a great personality continues to live on throughout history. This is also the psychological truth expressed by Jesus in the Parable of the Talents:

> For unto every one that hath shall be given, and he shall have abundance: but from him that hath not shall be taken away even that which he hath. (Matt. 25:29, KJV)

In our story, the loaves and fishes not only multiplied themselves, they also were broken into pieces (in order to be distributed). Edinger points out that this motif of being broken is another symbol of the Self. Just as the loaves and fishes were broken into bits in order to be distributed and then multiplied themselves endlessly, so the Self is broken into portions and distributed among humanity. If we think of the Self as the archetype of human nature ("the Son of Man"), then we understand that each one of us *embodies* a portion of that within our own nature. What portion of the Self is included in our particular psychologi-

---

6. Origen, *Commentary on John* 1.42.

cal nature varies. Beethoven was a great composer of music, while Einstein was a great mathematician and scientist. One person may be skilled at art, while his neighbor across the street may have a gift for repairing automobiles. All of these creative abilities come from the Self, but they are apportioned out differently. From this comes the idea of the early church that the church is the Body of Christ, for each one of us *embodies* a portion of Christ. Of course this symbolism is a prominent feature of the Eucharist. Part of the process of individuation involves the discovery of what portion of Christ, that is, what aspects of the Self, we are to live out in our lives.

In the story of the feeding of the multitude we were confronted with a mystical miracle. In this story we have another miracle — walking on water — which likewise strains our credulity.

In the previous story we noted that there was a rationalistic way to explain the miraculous feeding of the multitude with the few loaves and fishes; similarly in this story a rationalistic interpretation has been offered. Some scholars have pointed out that the words "they saw Jesus walking on the lake" could have meant "saw Jesus walking *by* the lake." The matter hinges on the Greek preposition *epi*, which usually is translated "on" but sometimes could be translated "by." The notion is that the disciples were closer to shore than they thought (as might be suggested by verse 6:21), and that when they first saw Jesus he was *by* the lake, not on it. This not-very-convincing argument may satisfy the rational intellect, but not the soul, neither our own souls, nor the soul (inner truth) of the story. It is quite clear from the total context that in this story the disciples were confronted with a numinous and therefore frightening event.

The word "numinous" is worth exploring. It was originated by religious philosopher Rudolf Otto who, in his book *The Idea of the Holy,* was trying to get at the essence of holiness. Otto concluded that the essence of holiness was to invoke in the observer a feeling of awe, wonder, and even dread. He called such an emotion "numinous," coining the word from the Latin word *numen,* which means a "divine majesty" or "presiding spirit." If, for instance, someone were to return home late at night, enter the house, hear a chain clanking upstairs and a ghostlike groaning sound, and see a white globe of light moving mysteriously through the air, the resulting emotion would be "numinous." It is clear from this example that there is positive numinosity (when confronted by the awesome majesty of God or an angel) and negative numinosity (when confronted by the spirit of archetypal evil). In either case, one essential characteristic of a numinous experience is that it produces not only awe and wonder, but also, at least to some extent, a sense of dread.

Dreams are also sometimes numinous. An example would be a nightmare. After a vivid nightmare we are all believers, at least for a few seconds after awakening from the frightening dream, no matter how much of a scoffer and skeptic we may be when we are fully awake.

This sense of dread is found in our biblical story in verse 6:20. The English translation, "This frightened them," hardly seems adequate. The Greek word is *phobeō* — "to terrify, to fear reverentially." It would be more accurate to say "they are terrified almost out of their wits."

Jesus reassures them: "Do not be afraid." He is not simply trying to make them feel better. He knows they cannot approach more closely to the experience they are having unless they lose some of the intensity of their fear. We find the same thing when approaching the unconscious. There is something uncanny about it, and sometimes we are so afraid of its numinosity that our fear keeps us from exploring our experiences further. This would be unfortunate, for, as Jung once pointed out, if we will stick with our inner experiences and not panic in the face of them, we will ultimately make it through. On the other hand, to approach that which is holy without an appropriate sense of awe and deep respect is to incur the sin of *hybris:* wanton disregard of the power of the divine. This sin, so prominent in classical Greek usage, is also found in the New Testament.[7] The disciples' experience of seeing Jesus walk on the water was an effective antidote to any tendency toward *hybris* that they might have had.

Another nuance of meaning in the story that suggests the intensity of this experience for the disciples is found in verse 6:19: "They *saw* Jesus walking on the lake...." Here we have the Greek word *theōreō*, which, like the word *theaomai*, which we have met before, means not simply to "see" but to "gaze intently upon."

Finally, in verse 6:20, "It is I," we have another use of the mysterious *egō eimi*. To us the expression "It is I" sounds casual enough,

---

7. See Matthew 22:6; Luke 11:45; 2 Corinthians 12:10; Acts 17:10.

but, as we have seen, to the hearer of the Fourth Gospel in the first century C.E., the expression *egō eimi* would have suggested that something highly mysterious was at work.

If Rudolf Otto is correct, the experience of the numinous is at the heart of all true religions. This we might expect, but Jung went further than that and said that an experience with the numinous was also at the heart of all valid psychotherapy. It was Jung's belief that only an experience with the numinous could truly heal us. Since he believed God communicated through the unconscious, he believed this experience could be found through working with the unconscious, and the facts seem to prove that he was right. The process of psychotherapy consists of many elements, but if that therapy includes the unconscious, then at the heart of it is the experience with the numinous. It is this that properly orients the ego toward God, for when we meet the numinous we know we have met with a greater reality than our ego and it must be respected, listened to, and carefully observed for its meaning. Psychologically, this is the "fear of the Lord" that is "the beginning of wisdom."

Dreams can be one way in which the numinous is communicated to us. The obvious example of the nightmare we have already mentioned, but even an ordinary dream, if we have seen and been affected by its meaning, can have this effect on us. From what source did the dream get this meaning? What is the intelligence within us that devised the dream's clever plot and timely message? Such questions inspire in us that respect for the dream, and its unseen Creator, which is due to the power of the numinous.

However, conventional religion and conventional psychotherapy both try, consciously or unconsciously, to deny their roots in the numinous. The sense of the numinous is all but lost upon modern Christians, and in psychology the mysteries of the soul are dismissed in favor of rationalistic explanations for human behavior and problems. This sentiment was once expressed by Jung in one of his letters, in which he said: "The clinical practice of psychotherapy is a mere makeshift that does its utmost to prevent numinous experiences."[8] In contrast he stated, "The fact is that the approach to the numinous is the real therapy and inasmuch as you attain to the numinous experiences you are released from

---

8. C. G. Jung, *Letters* 2, 118.

the curse of pathology."[9] This is why he made his now-famous statement that in his experience no one over thirty-five was ever healed of her problems without acquiring a true religious attitude. The fact that our word "therapy" is, as we noted earlier, derived from the Greek word *therapeuō* should be a reminder to those who practice the healing arts that they are servants of a Higher Power that must be respected by both doctor and patient if the patient is to become whole.

---

9. C. G. Jung, *Letters*, vol. 1, *1906–1950*, selected and edited by Gerhard Adler in collaboration with Aniela Jaffe, translated from the German by R. F. C. Hull (Princeton, N.J.: Princeton University Press, 1973), 377.

~ 14 ~

INNER FOOD
The Discourse on the Heavenly Bread
John 6:22–71

THE LONG DISCOURSE that follows the stories of the feeding of the multitude and the walking on the water touches on most of the major theses in John's Gospel, but the thread that holds it together is the image of the heavenly bread. After we have undertaken a textual analysis we will observe what Christ said about himself as the heavenly bread, what the early church thought about this, and its psychological import for today.

Verse 6:27: This verse introduces us to the image of food. In a dream, the appearance of food often means, as Edward F. Edinger once pointed out, that something is ready to be assimilated by consciousness. The miraculous feeding of the multitude by Christ and the later identification of Christ as the heavenly food signified that a new development had now become possible for humankind. Christ is that new development and new consciousness that is now ready for emergence in the human psyche. This heavenly food of a new consciousness is contrasted with the old food. The old attitudes are a food that cannot last, while the food that will be of lasting life and value is the food offered by the Son of Man. It is clear that this food is symbolic of that which nourishes the soul, the innermost person. To eat this food involves doing the will of God, which on the psychological plane means being faithful to one's innermost truth. In his comment on this verse Clement of Alexandria compares it to John 4:34, in which Jesus says to the

Samaritan woman: "My food is to do the will of the one who sent me, and to complete his work." Clement says of this:

> Thus to Christ the fulfilling of His Father's will was good; and to us infants, who drink the milk of the word of the heavens, Christ Himself is food.[1]

Note that we are to "*work* for food that endures to eternal life." The food is a gift to us, but we also have to work for it. As mentioned earlier, individuation is a work, an *opus;* the inner treasures do not yield themselves to those who will not work for them. The key to this work, as always, is psychological honesty with oneself and others and diligent attention to inner processes.

Verse 27 concludes with the words: " . . . for on him the Father, God himself, has set his seal." The Greek word involved is *sphragizō* — "to stamp with a seal; to set a mark upon, to distinguish by a mark." A seal enables an observer to recognize to whom something belongs. In this case, the Christ has on him the seal of the Father. If we understand that our individuation is generated by Christ, then we can also understand that this is none other than the work of God. A seal is something definite. It is a definite mark. Individuation is a process of becoming a definite (defined) person. To become whole is to become someone, to achieve a consistency and unity of character. The word "character" comes from the Greek word *charaktēr,* "an impress; exact expression." To have character, therefore, is to become the exact expression of one's innermost reality.[2]

Verse 6:28: The people are intrigued by Jesus' words and they ask that most natural of all questions: "What must we *do*. . . . " The answer Jesus gives must not have seemed very helpful: " . . . you must believe in the one he has sent." Yet we can understand that he is saying, "You must follow your innermost faith, the faith that comes from your soul and that seeks God."

But even this may not seem helpful to us. How do we "follow our faith"? We want specific instructions, not broad directives. We want to be told "how to achieve salvation, not to be left with open-ended directives. We want a sign pointing in the direction we are to go, not a road map. For this reason religious systems that offer people definite answers and precise instructions on "how to" achieve salvation are always popular.

---

1. Clement of Alexandria, *The Instructor* 1.6.
2. This word is used in this way in Hebrews 1:3.

The same thing is true in psychology. We want a psychology that tells us exactly what is wrong and exactly what needs to be done. In psychological work people also ask, "What can I *do?*" There are always those people who presume to know what others should do, and often we are happy to follow them. It never occurs to us that if they should be wrong we would be going the wrong way. The fact is, only something inside of us knows what it is *we* are to do and what is the way to follow.

For these reasons many people find their dreams frustrating and elusive. They look at a dream and again the question is asked, "What shall I *do?*" As Jung once pointed out, dreams don't tell us what to do, but they do tell us the direction in which we are heading.[3] They are not a book of instructions on how to make individuation work, but they are a faithful compass telling us where we are headed and when we have lost the way. But dreams leave the final choices up to us, and they make us search for the deepest meanings from what appears to be an enigmatic language.

The great minds of the early church were aware of the enigmatic way in which the Spirit speaks, but they perceived that by speaking in apparent enigmas the Spirit forced them to deepen their understanding in the search for their meaning.

The only spiritual truth worth having is the truth we have to dig for. So Clement of Alexandria wrote:

> Dreams and signs are all more or less obscure to men...in order that research, introducing us to the understanding of enigmas, may hasten to the discovery of truth.[4]

And Augustine wrote:

> The presentation of truth by emblems [symbols] has a great power; for, thus presented, things move and kindle our affection much more than if they were set forth in bald statements, not clothed in sacramental symbols. Why this should be, it is hard to say; but it is the fact that anything which we are taught by allegory or emblem affects and pleases us more, and is more highly esteemed by us, than it would be if most clearly stated in plain terms.

He adds that if the soul is

---

3. C. G. Jung, *Seminar on Dream Analysis*, 208.
4. Clement of Alexandria, *The Instructor* 2.9. Cf. Origen, *Against Celsus* 1.48.

brought to those corporeal things which are emblems of spiritual things, and then taken from these to the spiritual realities which they represent, it gathers strength by the mere act of passing from one to the other, and, like the flame of a lighted torch, is made by the motion to burn more brightly, and is carried away to rest by a more intensely glowing love.[5]

Verse 6:32: A subtle meaning to this verse centers on the presence of the definite article (the) before the words "bread from heaven" and "true bread." In English the use or disuse of the article is a matter of indifference, but in Greek, as we have seen, the use of the article is always significant ("It is utterly impossible that the Article should be omitted where it is decidedly necessary, or employed where it is quite superfluous or preposterous.")[6] In this case, the use of the definite article before the word "bread" and "true" lends emphasis and distinction. It is not any kind of bread that is referred to, but *the* bread, the one and only bread of its kind. The extraordinary quality of this bread is emphasized by the fact that it is *the* true bread (not just "true bread"). What makes this bread so unique is that it "comes down from heaven." As previously noted, the celestial geography in John's Gospel refers to levels of consciousness. The bread from heaven is a reality that comes from, and bestows, a higher consciousness.

In the verses that follow there is some repetition. It is in the nature of archetypal language that such repetition occurs. This repetition is necessary if the full comprehension of meaning is to be achieved.

Verse 6:33: The text says that this bread that comes down from heaven "gives life to the world." The present tense is employed and the Greek makes this emphasis on the present tense even stronger by employing a present participle. This Greek usage denotes *continuous action*. To translate the Greek more accurately one would have to say something like: "This bread from heaven is in a continuous process of giving life to the world."

Verse 6:35: "*I am* the bread of life." Here we have *egō eimi* once again, which we have previously discussed briefly. This is not, however, the "absolute" *egō eimi*, which was the Greek equivalent of the Hebrew "I am," because in this sentence there is a predicate (that is, "the bread of life"). Nonetheless, the use of this

5. Augustine, *Letters* 50.11.21.
6. See footnote 1 in chapter 7 above.

construction is probably intentional on the part of our author, a reminder of things to come in connection with the absolute use of the phrase.

The verse continues with the assurance that the one who eats this food will "never be hungry." The Greek uses here a "double negative" (*ou . . . mē*) which is the strongest possible way to put the idea. Underline the word "never" for emphasis and the full meaning in Greek is more distinctly rendered.

Verse 6:37: Here we have a peculiar thought: "All that the Father gives me will come to me." The suggestion is that some people might not be given to Christ by the Father. There seems to be an irrational factor at work, even an elitist concept, and we will have more to say about this later. The verse concludes: "I shall not turn him away." We have here the same double negative construction that we had in verse 6:35. Mentally, we should underline the word "not."

Verse 6:40: First we are to "see" the Son. The word used for seeing is, once again, *theōreō*. This kind of seeing is virtually equivalent to knowing. It is an act of consciousness. But in addition we are to "believe in him." We have here a good example of the New Testament idea of faith as something invested in someone. The literal Greek translation of this verse would be: "in order that everyone who sees the Son clearly in such a way that it registers distinctly on his consciousness, and who puts his faith into him [*eis auton*] will have eternal life."

Verse 6:40 ends with a reference to the "last day." We will not go into the metaphysical aspect of this teaching here, but can make the comment that the "last day" is part of the teleological aspect of the Fourth Gospel. The word "teleological" comes from the word *telos*, which means "an end attained; a consummation; a closing act." All of the words in the New Testament that embody the word *telos* in some way have to do with a process that goes in the present time, but is moving or working toward some consummate goal. We already mentioned one of these words (*teleiōsis*) in a previous chapter. The New Testament has a great many others. These are "individuation" words, for individuation is a process that moves toward a goal.

Certain of the Church Fathers extended this idea of the movement of life toward a goal to the metaphysical realm. Not only human life, but all life, indeed, of creation, was said by Origen, Gregory of Nyssa, and others to be moving toward a consummate goal. As all beings move toward completion, the plan or goal of God is gradually realized. Indeed, at the end, even the devil himself will be hanged, for his role in the divine drama as the spur to salvation will no longer be needed. In this view of things, Origen and Gregory anticipated Teilhard de Chardin.

Verse 6:44: In this verse we are told that no one can come to God unless he is "drawn" by God. The Greek word is *helkuo*. The word means "to be drawn toward; to draw mentally or morally." This same word occurs also in John 12:32: "I shall draw all men to myself."

The word as used in this context is important because it rests on an archetypal image. Jung has shown that the Center operates within the psyche like a magnet that draws all the disparate parts of the personality toward itself; in this way it forges a unity out of our multiplicity.

This "compelling power" also works on the ego. This is essential, for, as we have seen, the will of the ego must be drawn toward the will of the Center. The ego may, of course, resist this inner drawing power of the Center. The usual way this resistance is expressed is to deny the reality of the magnetic influence of the Center by repressing an awareness of the "inner voice." When this happens, the magnetic influence of the Center sets up a psychic disturbance, for the inner balance has now been disturbed. If the will of the ego has become corrupted by evil, then the inner voice of the Center cannot be heard. Thus for healing to take place the will must be free from its slavery to the power of evil.

In an early Christian document known as the *Recognitions of Clement*, the apostle Peter comments on the difficulty involved in curing the evildoer Simon Magus of an illness. Peter says of Simon that he

> is seized with such disease and cannot now be healed, because he is sick in his will and purpose. Nor does the demon (of evil) dwell in him against his will; and therefore, if anyone would drive it out of him, since it is inseparable from himself, and, so to speak, has now become his very soul, he should seem rather to kill him.[7]

Notice the subtlety of all this. God acts upon us like a magnet drawing us to him. Yet our will is also involved and our free will

---

7. *The Recognitions of Clement* 1.72.

is not abrogated. In the final analysis, we must consent to the power of God. From the point of view of the psychology of early Christianity, this was essential, for otherwise one's love toward God would not be freely given and would therefore be of no value.

Verse 6:46: This important verse will be discussed when we consider chapter 14 of John's Gospel.

Verse 6:53: In this verse the image of eating Christ's body is amplified by the image of drinking his blood. It is the primary Christian symbol for integration and has been enshrined in the Christian eucharistic ritual. The outward and visible sign in the sacrament is the wafer of bread and the chalice of wine; the inward spiritual event is the relationship of Center to ego and the incorporation of Christ into oneself. The language of the church in this regard is virtually cannibalistic: we *eat* the body and *drink* the blood.

Among certain primitive people it was the custom to eat the body of a slain enemy who had displayed unusual valor, strength, or skill. In the cannibalistic act the motive is not physical hunger, but the psychological yearning to incorporate into oneself the virtues of the slain enemy. In the Christian sacramental action we are incorporating into ourselves the virtues of Christ. Psychologically this corresponds to incorporating the strength of the Center into our conscious being.

Verse 6:54: The result of this process is something called "eternal life." What this means we will consider shortly. So also verse 6:58.

Verse 6:56–57: These verses speak once again of the mystery of the relationship of the ego and the Center, which we have discussed before.

Verses 6:59–62: In these verses John tells us that Jesus had many followers in addition to the twelve disciples, and that some of them found his language intolerable, refused to accept it, and, as we learn in verse 66, left him. Their complaint was, "This is intolerable language. How could anyone accept it?" The English of the Jerusalem Bible, in trying to make this verse more readily understandable to the modern reader, reduces the impact of the Greek. The more literal translation would be: "Hard is this saying. Who is able to hear it?" The word for "hard" is *sklēros*. Our medical word "arteriosclerosis" uses this word for "hardening of the arteries." So the saying of Jesus is hard; it does not go down easily.

In the expression "Who is able to hear it?" we have emphasis on *hearing*. This is significant because in the Bible God is known much more through hearing than through seeing. One *hears* God's voice. In fact, one word for sin in the Bible is *parakouō*, which means "to fail to listen, to hear amiss." Psychologically, one also hears one's inner voice. Even our dreams, visual though they are, are said to "speak to us." For this reason, in the Bible, to have one's hearing hardened means that this person is shut off from God. All of these overtones of meaning were certainly known to the author of the Fourth Gospel when he wrote the words, "Who is able to hear it?"

Verse 6:63: "It is the spirit that gives life, the flesh has nothing to offer." Or, in Phillips, "the flesh will not help you." This verse brings up the matter of that peculiar New Testament word *sarx*, literally translated "flesh." In chapter 1 we noted that this word has five distinct meanings in the New Testament. The five meanings, briefly reviewed, are:

1. The substance of an animal body; literally flesh.

2. The relationship of consanguinity or by marriage (two people being "of one flesh," as in Matthew 19:5 or 1 Corinthians 10:18).

3. Creaturely nature generally or human nature in particular. So, for instance, when Christ became incarnate he took upon himself "flesh" (human nature). John uses the word with this meaning in 1:14: "And the Word became flesh."

4. With reference to one constituent of human nature in contrast to another. The usual contrasts would be between flesh and soul, or flesh and heart, or flesh and spirit. This contrast is not made with the idea of depreciating the flesh or casting moral aspersions on it.

5. Finally there is the ethical sense of "flesh" as a synonym for fallen human nature. In this sense flesh is seen as the seat of sin, and is contrasted with spirit, which refers to the divine life in human nature.

In our present context, the fourth meaning of *sarx* is the one that is indicated. The "flesh" would refer therefore to our physical nature with its limitations. When Clement of Alexandria said that the multitude who were fed by the five fishes were limited in vision and consciousness to their "sensible nature," that is, to those impressions brought to them by their physical senses, he is talking of those who are only "in the flesh" and without benefit of the spirit. It would be our "common human nature," which we discussed earlier.

Spirit is different. As we saw in a previous chapter, the spirit of God permeates everything, just as the wind blows through the trees. The spirit is generic. It is not *our* spirit, but God's spirit, but it can come to reside in us. For our lives to be renewed we cannot remain only in the flesh, that is, have a consciousness that is limited to and by our ordinary human consciousness. This consciousness of ours must be fructified and influenced by the "wind of God" that comes into consciousness from a source beyond the ego. Psychologically speaking, this "wind of God" is an archetypal energy mediated to us through the unconscious.

Verses 6:67–69: These verses are the equivalent in John's Gospel of Peter's confession of faith in Matthew 16:6. In Matthew, Peter said, "Thou are the Christ, the Son of the living God." In John's Gospel Peter says, "We have believed, and have come to know, that you are the Holy One of God" (RSV).

The reference to Christ as the "Holy One" has at least two nuances of meaning. First it shows us that Christ is a numinous reality, an awesome experience. Second, the word "holy" in Greek is *hagios;* this word was not very important in classical Greek. It never occurs, for instance, in either Homer or in the Greek playwrights, who favor the word *hagnos* instead, but it looms large in the New Testament. This may be because the word *hagios* comes from a Greek word meaning "to separate." Thus one who is holy is one who is separated, or "set apart."

It is a psychological fact that in the individuation process, as a person develops consciousness, she becomes separated from the collective psychology of the culture and people around her. When a person becomes herself, she becomes a distinct personality and so no longer lives in a "participation mystique," that is, an unconscious identification with other people, groups, or collective movements. Thus individuation makes us as persons "set apart." Christ, as the Holy One of God, emphasizes the importance of this quality; such a person is able to relate to others as individuals (not collectively) and also has an individual sense of morality founded on the Center and is not identical any longer with the collective morality of the group or culture in which she lives.

Another depth of meaning in these verses is found in the

use of the Greek grammatical construction we examined earlier
known as the "object genitive." It will be remembered that in this
construction one noun is regarded as deriving its source from a
second noun, which is also the object of its action. Thus in the
expression "the holy one of God," the source of the holiness is
found in God. So also, if we become someone set apart by our
developing consciousness, this separation is engendered by the
influence upon us from the Center. It is not an act of separation
that the ego alone can accomplish.

Verses 6:70–71: These verses introduce Judas for the first time.
Judas, one of the twelve disciples chosen by the Lord himself, is
now termed a devil. Why was he a devil, and why did the Lord
have him as one of the twelve if he knew this about him? Verse 70
is the first clue in John's Gospel that something is amiss in the
inner circle of the twelve disciples. We will hear more about it as
the Gospel continues.

Although the themes in this discourse are varied, the overall
theme is that of Christ who has made available for us the living
bread that has come down from heaven. The Fourth Gospel in
this way presents us with the image of *eating*.

The motif of eating appears frequently in our dreams. Usually
eating is a dream symbol that appears only after a person has
worked on her own self-understanding for some time. The reason for this is that eating in a dream means that psychic elements
within us are now ready to be assimilated, and this requires extensive psychic preparation. Generally speaking, we are called
upon to eat what is set before us in a dream — though there are
exceptions. Edward Edinger has pointed out that eating is part of
the symbolism of the alchemical *coagulatio*. *Coagulatio* symbolism
makes something real and solid. In the process of individuation we are to become real and "solid" people. Fundamentally,
he notes, eating symbolism denoted the need to "assimilate a
relationship to the self."[8]

Just as the body must have food in order to survive, so must
the soul have spiritual food in order to survive. There is healthy
food that is nourishing and bad food that poisons the body. It has
been said that sick body cells crave sick food, and healthy body

---

8. Edward F. Edinger, *The Anatomy of the Psyche* (La Salle, Ill.: Open Court Publishing
Co., 1985), 11.

cells crave healthy food. The physical craving of addiction can be thought of as the craving of body cells that have been made sick. When people cleanse and purge their bodies of drugs and debilitating foods, they find their tastes in food change, that they now desire those foods that are healthy for them. It is the same way with the souls. Sick souls also crave sick foods in the form of egocentric strokes of reassurance, power, an addiction to more and more wealth, and so forth. Healthy souls, on the other hand, yearn for the inner food that nourishes spiritual health. But the process is also reversed; the healthy spiritual food has the power to cure the soul of its ills. The fact that there is sick food and healthy food in matters of the spirit as well as of the flesh is, as we have noted, the reason why Jesus spoke in verse 6:32 of *"the true* bread," in order to distinguish it from ordinary or corrupt spiritual food.

It is also interesting to note that bread is generally regarded as feminine, or *yin* in quality, because it derives from the earth, which is typically regarded as "Mother Earth." What about the fish? Christ also fed the multitude with the fish, but no further mention is made of them. However, in chapter 21 the motif of the fish is reintroduced, and we will examine it in more detail later on.

Clement of Alexandria referred to John's chapter 6 as the study of "the mystery [*mystērion*] of the bread." Clement cites a wide variety of biblical passages that relate to eating symbolism and concludes that "the Word is figuratively described as meat, and flesh, and food, and bread, and blood and milk. The Lord is all these, to give enjoyment to us who have believed on Him."[9] Clement believed that by assimilating Christ in this way we are brought into union with him, and that this unification with Christ is what saves us. The unconscious also mediates to us this same imagery of eating and offers us a process in which we can assimilate the Center to ourselves, and, in turn, be assimilated to the Center.

Origen elaborated on the themes introduced by Clement's discussion of John 6. Origen believed that God, acting through the soul (that is, the unconscious), by means of images, brings many impressions before the mind (that is, into consciousness). Through the soul, Origen notes, there comes "a kind of general divine perception which the blessed man alone knows how to

---

9. Clement of Alexandria, *The Instructor* 1.6.

discover." Origen believed that this divine perception is what is meant in Proverbs 2:5, which refers to the saying of Solomon "Thou shalt find the knowledge of God."

In the language of mysticism the senses of smell and taste are interior ways of perception. Through exercise of spiritual smell and taste one takes something into oneself and there perceives its nature and reality. According to Origen and others of the Church Fathers, the soul has her own means of perception; just as the body has its senses, so the soul also sees, hears, feels, smells, and tastes. Origen once called this "dove's eyes."[10] The faculties of taste and smell in particular help us "sniff out" the spiritually false from the spiritually true and valid. So also, something that is evil will leave a "bad taste" within us. For this reason Origen once noted, with reference to the discussion in our Gospel of the nature of living bread, that it is the "sense of taste which can make use of the living bread that has come down from heaven." In much the same vein, St. Paul said of those who know the Lord, "We Christians have the unmistakable scent of Christ . . . " (2 Cor. 2:15).

Origen proceeds to give many examples of perceptions of spiritual reality that can be found in the Bible. His point of view is that the reality of God can be known through faith, and that faith is sustained by the perceptions of the soul. And in fact, one of the chief benefits of working with the unconscious is that it sustains our faith that there is something meaningful at work in us that we can contact no matter how bad or impoverished are the material and circumstantial realities of our outer life.

We can now comment on why Jesus calls this bread "living" bread, or the "bread of life." We have already noted that an important motif in the Fourth Gospel is the motif of life vis-à-vis death. Indeed, so important is this theme that "eternal Life" is the equivalent in John's Gospel of the kingdom of God (or Heaven) in the synoptic Gospels. The important thing to remember is that for John eternal life begins now. At this present moment it can be said that the soul in each of us is moving either toward life or toward death.

This is brought out more clearly in the Greek than is possible in the English. As we noted earlier, the Greek language has two words for life: *zōē* and *bios*. The word *bios* (from which we derive our word "biology") denotes life in its various earthly manifes-

---

10. Origen, *Against Celsus* 1.18.

tations. Insofar as we are a living organism, we have a *bios* or life, as do animals and plants. *Zōē* on the other hand denotes the principle of life. When John uses the word "life," it is *zōē* of which he is speaking. The "living bread" is the inner food that is filled with the principle of life itself. This is the word that was used in John 1:4, "All that came to be had life [*zōē*] in him, and that life was the light of men." It is this living principle that can fill the soul and that leads to eternal life. While a *bios*, a purely natural life, perishes, *zōē* is an eternal element that never perishes. Insofar as we fill the soul with *zōē*, we come to belong to that which is imperishable.

Jung and Kunkel believed that in the individuation process a person comes to partake of this inner aliveness. In contrast are those people who are already dead but don't know it. Jung spoke of the "living dead." He believed that if a person lived an unconscious life, that person was as good as dead already:

> It is death to the soul to become unconscious. People die before there is death of the body, because there is death of the soul. They are mask-like leeches, walking about like spectres, dead but sucking. It is a sort of death. I have seen a man who has converted his mind into a pulp. You can succeed in going away from your problems, you need only to look away from them long enough. You may escape, but it is the death of the soul. Go into the lobby of a hotel — there you will see faces with masks. These dead people are often traveling on the wing, to escape problems; they look hunted and wear a complete mask of fear.[11]

Origen and Jung agree on this idea of death. Origen, in commenting on John's Gospel and its theme of life and death, writes:

> All are dead who are not living to God ... their life is to sin, and therefore [it is] a life of death.[12]

And Gregory of Nyssa sums it up even more completely:

> God is ... the life of the soul. But seeing that ignorance of the true good is like a mist that obscures the visual keenness

---

11. Jung, *Dream Analysis*, 90.
12. Origen, *Commentary on John* 2.10.

of the soul, and that when that mist grows denser a cloud is formed so thick that Truth's rays cannot pierce through these depths of ignorance, it follows further that with the total deprivation of the light the soul's life ceases altogether; for we have said that the real life of the soul is acted out in partaking of the Good; but when ignorance hinders this apprehension of God, the soul which thus ceases to partake of God, ceases also to live.[13]

The question arises about the metaphysical implications of this process of moving in this lifetime into life and away from death. Do we carry the life we gain through individuation into the next life? We will pursue this question in another chapter.

In order to understand what the Fourth Gospel means by images such as that of the living bread, we must be open to wider spiritual vistas. If our minds can think only literally, if we have refused any insight into ourselves, if our only means of perception are through the physical senses, if we become theologically and psychologically rigid, then we cannot appreciate the tremendous subtlety and variety of the images of Christ that we find in John's Gospel. Origen was quite aware of this. He was unhappy because "the general run of Christians" content themselves with the simple affirmation that Christ is the Word of God. He claimed that we can begin to contemplate what the Word of God means only if we admit into consciousness the manifold images that the Gospel uses to describe this Word. As in our dreams, so in the Fourth Gospel, many images are used to describe Christ, each one seeking to bring us closer to one more facet of the meaning of this incredible reality. So Origen writes in words with which we will conclude our discussion of the living bread:

The Son of God says in one passage, "I am the light of the world," and in another, "I am the resurrection," and again, "I am the way and the truth and the life." It is also written, "I am the door"; and we have the saying, "I am the good shepherd," and when the woman of Samaria says, "We know the Messiah is coming, who is called Christ, when He comes He will tell us all things," Jesus answers, "I that speak unto

---

13. Gregory of Nyssa, *On Infant's Early Death.*

thee am He." ... We also have read the words, "I am the true vine and my Father is the husbandman," and again, "I am the vine, ye are the branches." Add to these testimonies also the saying, "I am the bread of life, that came down from heaven and giveth life to the world."[14]

---

14. Origen, *Commentary on John* 23.

~ 15 ~

THE CREATIVE EGO RESPONSE
The Adulterous Woman
John 8:1–11

SCHOLARS TELL US that the story of the woman who committed adultery, found in the first part of later manuscripts of John's Gospel, was not part of the original text. There are good reasons for this belief. First is the fact that not all the ancient manuscripts contain this story. Second is the fact that the story breaks the continuity of narrative and discussion that begins with John 7:52 and then resumes again with John 8:12 (eliminate John 8:1–11 and there is a more or less continuous flow). Third is the fact that the language sounds more like that of the synoptic Gospels than like the language of John's Gospel. Nevertheless, the story is part of valid Christian tradition and was included in John's Gospel by people who had their reasons for feeling it belonged. Whether or not it was originally in the Fourth Gospel, it is a profound story and is within the spirit of John's message, so we will regard it for practical purposes as part of the text.

First we can note that the story is an excellent example of the role of women in society at the time in which Jesus lived, which we discussed in an earlier chapter, and that it shows Jesus' unique and independent stand with regard to the importance and equality of the feminine. In John 8:5 we are told that the Mosaic Law condemned women to death by stoning if they committed adultery. John T. Bristow tells us that some rabbinic tradition equated

adultery with idolatry and murder.[1] However, all of this condemnation only fell on the woman who committed adultery; no
mention is made of the man, although, of course, it takes two
people to commit adultery. The double standard is glaring.

Jesus' attitude toward her is in marked contrast to this prevailing point of view. It is clear that while he does not condone her
adultery (neither would he condone it in a man; cf. Matt. 5:28),
his sympathies are with the woman, and his attitude toward her
sin is in startling contrast to the prevailing legalistic code.[2]

Jesus' enemies use the woman's plight as a way of attacking
him. Evidently Jesus' attitudes toward such things must have
been known or the scribes and Pharisees would not have used
the woman's adultery as a way to try to trap him. Their question
to him — "Moses has ordered us to condemn women like this to
death by stoning. What have you to say?" — is clearly an attempt
to expose him before the people as one who denied the Law, and
they could later use this as evidence against him. To everyone's
surprise, Jesus made no answer right away but bent down and
began to write on the ground with his finger. What he wrote we
are not told. Commentators suggest that he might have done this
to show disdain for his questioners, or possibly he was trying to
hide his embarrassment or perplexity over this difficult situation.
Still a third possibility is that he was trying to gain a little time as
he searched within for the "creative ego response."

In a previous chapter we talked about the source of creativity
and noted that God, working through that inner spiritual realm
known as the collective unconscious, produces creative responses
to life's difficult situations. Putting it in a slightly different way,
if the ego is in touch with the inner Center, it can act creatively
no matter how difficult is the life situation, but isolated from the
Center the ego lacks creativity. An analogy can be made between
the ego and a candle. A candle by itself produces no flame, but
lit by a fire from another source it burns brightly. So it is with the

---

1. John T. Bristow, *What Paul Really Said about Women* (San Francisco: HarperCollins, 1988), 96.

2. The same legalistic code evidently prevails in Islam. Jacques Jomier says of the story of the woman taken in adultery: "In the Muslim tradition there is a similar incident when Muhammad is in the oasis of Khaybar. Some Jews bring before him a woman caught in the act of adultery: she is one of their people. They ask him what they should do. Muhammad calls for a copy of the Torah. Since it is formally stated there that the adulteress should be stoned, he orders her to be stoned. Obedience to the Law comes before everything" (*How to Understand Islam* [New York: Crossroad, 1989], 137). The incident Jomier is describing is found in the Qur'an 5, 42.

ego. The more egocentric the ego is the more it is cut off from the creativity of the Center, and the more stilted, unproductive, and conventional are its responses. Confronted by a bewildering or difficult situation, the egocentric ego will respond in only a completely conventional way, or may collapse altogether and not be capable of any response. In touch with its Center the ego is capable of enduring the most extraordinary hardships and coming through with the most creative and courageous responses.

We owe these insights to Fritz Kunkel. Kunkel believed there were two kinds of ego responses. The first, the response the ego makes out of its egocentricity, is "characterized by inflexibility, panic, defensiveness, rage, and sterility." In contrast, the creative ego response is a response "that is exactly appropriate to the kind of situation with which the person is faced. It cannot be stylized or characterized because the creative Ego response is always unique and one-of-a-kind."[3]

When his enemies persist in demanding an answer to their question, Jesus comes up with a creative ego response that is exactly suited to the situation: "He that is without sin among you, let him first cast a stone at her" (KJV). This answer has four important functions. First, it throws the ball back to his detractors without the need for any defensiveness on Jesus' part. Second, it shows compassion for the woman taken in adultery without condoning her actions. Third, it gives his detractors something to think about that, if they do so, may lead to their own greater consciousness and growth. Fourth, it leaves no room for his enemies to use his answer against him. Most of us might have attempted all of this with some lengthy and more or less unsuccessful speech. Jesus accomplished it in one sentence.

C. G. Jung once noted the importance of this story and commented on it in one of his private seminars. He was talking of the need to accept things into our system, that is, to become conscious of things and be able to face them without being destroyed by them. He noted, "That is what Christ did for the adulterous woman, and, as he was the son of God, it worked; he changed her so that she could accept it [her sin] into her system, so that she could stand herself, and no longer be morally destroyed by it."[4] We could say that Jesus related to her as a wise and concerned

---

3. John A. Sanford, ed., *Fritz Kunkel: Selected Writings* (New York: Paulist Press, 1984), 315.

4. C. G. Jung, *The Visions Seminars*, book 1 (New York: Spring Publications, 1976), 134.

psychotherapist whose deep and overriding concern was for the spiritual and psychological health of her soul, not for the condemnation of sin as such, with all of the feeling of alienation from God that such condemnation brings.

Jesus' actions on behalf of the adulterous woman helped her find that elusive and holy state of freedom. When she left him she was a free woman because she was creatively related to herself. Jung once said, "The real Christ is the God of freedom."[5] Part of the genius of John's Gospel is that John was aware of this, and the Christ of his Gospel on virtually every page, by his creative actions, shows his freedom. This is also the genius of Paul, for whom Christ brought the living Spirit, which was a Spirit of life and freedom: "Before God, we are confident of this through Christ: not that we are qualified in ourselves to claim anything as our own work: all our qualifications come from God. He is the one who has given us the qualifications to be the administrators of this new covenant, which is not a covenant of written letters but of the Spirit: the written letters bring death, but the Spirit gives life" (2 Cor. 3:4–6).

But it should be stressed that this freedom is not license to do as one pleases. The egocentric ego likes to fancy that it can do anything it wants and equates this with freedom. A person who is hedonistic in his outlook looks only to his pleasure, and justifies this on the basis of freedom. The mystery is that there is only one freedom for the ego and that is to serve the Center within. Practically speaking this is tantamount to serving the will of God. That is the paradox: to serve one's deepest inner truth is to become free. All else is an egocentric illusion and leads not to freedom but to neurosis or, if someone is completely wanton and consumed by the sin of hubris, to enslavement to evil. The author of the Fourth Gospel is aware of this, and we will discuss in a later chapter the mystery of the free relationship of ego to Center in those sections in the Gospel that deal with the relationship of Christ to the Father.

---

5. Jung, *Dream Analysis*, 519.

～ 16 ～

THE SOURCE OF CREATIVITY
Jesus Goes to Jerusalem and Teaches
John 7:1–52

THE FIRST HALF OF JOHN 7 gives us some important historical information about Jesus' third journey to Jerusalem. The first visit (John 2:13–25) centered around the cleansing of the temple. The second visit (John 5:1–47) told the story of the cure of the man by the pool of Bethzatha. This story involves the matter of Jesus' authority, and, as we shall soon see, this leads us to the question of the source of creativity. But first let us examine the text.

In 7:2–4, so the Jerusalem Bible tells us, Jesus' brothers are probably to be understood as his relations in a general sense. The disciples of 7:3 refers to Jesus' followers in a broad sense, not to the twelve. What the brothers say to Jesus is probably to be understood as a taunt. The implication of what they say is something like: "If you are such a great man, then don't stay hidden here in Galilee, go on up to Judaea where everybody can see how great you are!" It is not surprising that members of Jesus' family are unable to see his greatness. Family members, even though they are in many ways so close to each other, often are unable to see each other for who they are. There are too many projections, rivalries, illusions, and hopes that family members place on each other to enable them to be objective.

In verse 7:7 we read "The world cannot hate you, but it does hate me...." Here we have another example of the Greek word *kosmos*, which, as we have already seen, meant the material and visible world of human beings, often in opposition to the kingdom of heaven. The "world" in this sense is equivalent to the general state of consciousness that prevails among people, a state of consciousness that is rooted in what is immediate and at hand, in the framework only of the ego, and that has no contact with higher sources of knowledge and illumination.

In verse 7:6 we have a special Greek word for "time": *kairos*. The New Testament uses two Greek words for time. *Chronos* (from which we get our word "chronometer") refers to the duration or flow of time. The second word, *kairos*, means "opportune time," a "time that is ready," or a "time that is fulfilled according to divine plan." So when Jesus says that the right time has not yet come, he is referring to that timing that would be in accord with a divine plan. The meaning of what Jesus says next is not so clear. The Jerusalem Bible translation reads " ... but any time is the right time for you." This seems questionable. The Revised Standard Version reads "but your time is always here" (*ho de kairos ho hymeteros pantote estin hetoimos*). This could mean that while Jesus' fulfilled time to go to Jerusalem is not yet here, the opportune time for brothers to understand higher things is here right now and ready for them at any moment.

In verse 7:7 we have the Greek word *ponēros*, which, as we have seen, is the word the New Testament uses when it wishes to refer to evil as a malignant spiritual principle. When Jesus says the ways of the world are evil (*ponēros*), he means that if we linger in unconsciousness, motivated only by our egocentricity, we are open to the malignant spirit of evil that pervades our world and directs our actions.

In verse 7:8 we read in the Jerusalem Bible: "I am not going to this festival, because for me the time is not ripe yet." The Greek word translated "ripe yet" is *plēroō*, a word used in the New Testament with reference to the accomplishment or fulfillment of a divine plan or purpose. The Revised Standard Version would again seem to be preferable: "My time has not yet come." The word "ripe" implies a purely natural or vegetative process; the Revised Standard Version translation conveys the idea of the fulfillment of God's intentions better and is more consistent with the overall attitude of John's Gospel.

In 7:10 we learn that Jesus went up to the feast after all. No explanation is given. Some commentators believe that after his brothers left, the awaited divine indication did come to Jesus that his time was now ready to go to Jerusalem. That seems as good an explanation as any.

In 7:20, after Jesus has told the crowd that someone is trying to kill him, the crowds say in the Jerusalem Bible translation: "You are mad! Who wants to kill you?" While this is a technically correct translation, it misses the expressiveness of the Greek. The Greek expression translated in the Jerusalem Bible as being "mad" is *daimonion echeis*, literally, "you have a demon." Now, in our time if a man stated his belief that someone was out to kill him when nothing of the sort was the case and he had no real reason for believing this, we would suppose he was a paranoid and would say he was insane or mad. In Jesus' day if someone acted that way they would say he was possessed by a demon. The Revised Standard Version translation "you have a demon" seems more faithful to the text and to the spirit of the times.

Verses 7:23–24 sound obscure to the modern reader. Scholars tell us that the argument is rabbinic. The Jerusalem Bible notes: "Circumcision was reckoned the 'healing' of one member [i.e., of the body]; if this 'healing' of one member was allowed on the sabbath, how much more the healing of the whole man?"

The main import of this complicated text has to do with the authority of Jesus and of his teachings. The core of the argument is found in verses 7:13–19. The people are puzzled by two things. First was the question of how this apparently unlettered man from Galilee had learned to read. Galilee was sort of the back-country area of Judaea in those days. It was not expected that someone from the "backwoods," who had not received special instruction, could read, but Jesus was a notable exception. The answer to their question does not require the idea of divine intervention. We may suppose that if a person was bright enough and desirous enough, that person could learn to read regardless of the lack of official schooling.

The second problem the people have with Jesus is about the source of his teachings. It is clear that Jesus did not derive his knowledge from rabbinic teachings and sources. The rabbis were the "Fathers" of the time, the guardians and interpreters of divine truth, but Jesus does not say what he learned from them; he comes up with a strange teaching that he apparently originated himself. Jesus' words in verses 7:16–19 are his reply to their doubts and questions. The essence of his answer is that the source of his teaching is not from himself, nor is the source of his teaching from some human authority. Rather, he obtained his teaching from God, who sent him into the world to speak God's words and truth.

One interesting thing about this passage is that even today many scholars approach the teachings of Jesus with the question: From what human source did his teachings originate? A great deal of energy has been expended by biblical scholars to trace the sources of Jesus' teachings to historical antecedents. Since the Old Testament cannot really account for a great deal of what Jesus had to say, many scholars search rabbinic literature for these sources. For instance, they note that parables, in something like the form of Jesus' parables, were occasionally taught by the rabbis of old. Still, there was nothing in rabbinic lore to account for the radically new nature and message of Jesus' parables. When, therefore, the Dead Sea Scrolls were found and the teaching of the Qumran community was available, a great deal of energy was devoted to showing that Jesus' teachings might have emerged from that of the Essenes. There was even speculation that Jesus himself might have been an Essene, although there is little evidence for this hypothesis.

These historical efforts are important and worth pursuing because new ideas and insights do not just come out of the air but have their precedents. Nevertheless, there is little evidence that the teachings of Jesus as we find them in the synoptic Gospels can be accounted for by the teachings we find in the Old Testament, or rabbinic literature, or the Essenes, or any other historical source that is known to us. When it comes to the far more esoteric teachings of Jesus in the Fourth Gospel, the gulf between what Jesus teaches and historical antecedents is even greater. Jesus himself recognizes this when he says, in the passage under consideration, that his teachings do not have a human source at all but come directly from God.

Many people today have difficulty accepting the Gospel at face value and ascribing the source of Jesus' teachings to God, perhaps because they do not believe in a God who actually communicates with people or because they do not believe in spiritual reality. If someone believes in spiritual reality, that person believes there is a nonmaterial reality, which exists independently of the body and of the ego and which is capable of manifesting God's truth. In psychology we call this realm the "collective unconscious" because it is common to all people and is largely unconscious to them. Jung once said of this realm that while it was certainly not God yet it was the vessel through which the divine grace might be mediated.[1] Psychology has shown that there is indeed a spiritual realm. The angels, demons, principalities and powers, dreams, visions, extrasensory experiences, healings, and a multitude of other phenomena well known in the era of early Christianity is the ancient way of describing what we would call today the collective unconscious.

The interesting thing is that new truths emerge from this spiritual realm. A study of the way in which scientific ideas develop is a case in point. One can take virtually any important scientific idea today and trace its history. It is known, for example, that long before Darwin wrote his *The Origin of Species* there were a few people here and there who had the seeds, as it were, of the ideas that were brought to fruition in him. Similarly, Einstein could not have come up with his general or special theory of relativity had he not — to use his own words — "stood on the shoulders of giants." It seems that there is something like Truth in the spiritual realm, and that it seeks to be discovered and realized in human consciousness. Through the collective unconscious a power works to bring into consciousness important new ideas and insights. This power works until a human being is found in whose consciousness the new ideas can take root. Someone like Einstein takes the new idea and makes, as it were, a new leap with it. Knowledge proceeds, so to speak, by *quantum* leaps that have their genesis in a source beyond the ego. Thus advances in consciousness and knowledge can be said to be made from two sources: (1) the reflections of the human ego (2) the impetus to knowledge and inspiration for knowledge from the collective unconscious, or spiritual realm if one prefers that term, which seems to take a keen interest in the matter. We could use the example of a football game: Sometimes ground is gained by running with the ball, and sometimes a player catches a long pass thrown from a distant source.

Jesus could not have taught as he did if there had not been a certain spiritual development that preceded him. The New Testament could not have emerged if there had not first been an Old Testament. Nevertheless, in Jesus there is a pronounced quantum leap in spiritual knowledge, and it does not come from the Essenes or some other human group but from God himself. In

---

1. Note the quotation cited earlier from Jung (p. 141 above): "This is not to say that what we call the unconscious is identical with God or is set up in his place. It is the medium through which the religious experience seems to flow."

psychological language we would say that a largely unknown divine power, working through the collective unconscious, finds its way into the consciousness of certain people and inspires in them a new consciousness. In the passage under consideration Jesus is saying, to use psychological language again, that his un-aided human ego is not the source of what he says, but that his knowledge and his insights, that is, his doctrine, come from a divine source — God himself.

In John 7:28–29 Jesus elaborates on the source of his knowl-edge. The people, he says, do not know the one who sent him. This was literally so. But Jesus does know because for him spiritual reality — and hence God — is an immediate experience.

It was also real to the author of the Fourth Gospel. We have seen that John knew a lot of historical facts. He knows the name of the man who cut off Peter's ear (Malchus), and he knows about Nicodemus and the details of the pool of Bethzatha. We think he may have been the man who owned the upper room in Jerusa-lem where Jesus met with his disciples for the last time. He is a thoroughly historical character. But in a process of inner dialogue with the spiritual realm, which we have hypothesized was akin to what we might call active imagination today, our unknown au-thor made a quantum leap and there came into his consciousness a knowledge of the Christ that had no purely human origin but came from the Lord himself.

Here we have another example of the importance in John's Gospel of symbolic thinking. For John, as we have seen, the deeper dimension of Jesus' teachings can be, and often must be, approached symbolically. Literal thinking leaves a person spiri-tually in ignorance; psychological and spiritual truth is opened up only through symbolic thinking. This is why John does not let his reader forget for a minute the narrowness of literal think-ing. So in verses 7:35–36 John shows us how the inability of the people to think symbolically prevents them from understanding Jesus' words. When Jesus says, "You will look for me and will not find me; where I am you cannot come," the people can only say, "Where is he going that we shan't be able to find him? Is he going abroad to the people who are dispersed among the Greeks [that is, those Jews who live outside Judea in the Greek-speaking world] and will he teach the Greeks? What does he mean when he says 'You will look for me and will not find me; where I am, you cannot come'?"

Immediately after this Jesus makes another statement that permits only a symbolic interpretation: "If any man is thirsty, let him come to me! Let the man come and drink who believes in me" (7:38). Scholars tell us that the background for these words from Jesus comes from the Old Testament liturgy of the Tabernacles, which included rites and prayers for rain. These rites drew from various Old Testament sources. For instance, in Exodus 17:1–7 we read the story of how when the people of Israel were wandering through the desert and in danger of dying from thirst, Moses, following divine instruction, struck a rock at Mt. Horeb with his rod and water gushed forth. As we have already noted, the Church Fathers did not hesitate to say that in a mystical sense this rock was Christ, as did St. Paul in 1 Corinthians 10:4. Other passages from the Old Testament that are relevant to what Jesus says in 7:38 include Zechariah 14:8 and Ezekiel 47:1. According to John, Jesus' teachings, taken symbolically, can bring us to the spiritual water that we must drink in order to have a spiritual life. Hence the importance of overcoming our literalness and cultivating our capacity for seeing, as it were, through the "eyes of the soul."

There is much at stake. Entrenched authorities jealously guard those doctrines from which they derive their power. The ego in its egocentricity resists those new truths and insights that will bring inner development because it means the end of the old egocentric order. John understands all of this, and that is why at the end of this chapter he returns us to the resistance of the Pharisees to Jesus and his message. For the Pharisees embody and personify that ego resistance that is in all of us to new truths, as we have already noted.

At this point Nicodemus emerges again. It will be remembered that we first met him in John 10. His reappearance here is part of the evidence that Nicodemus is a historical person, someone known to John. In this passage Nicodemus is still one of the Pharisees, but he is no longer identical with their collective opinion. So he challenges them when they condemn Jesus without an investigation, saying to them in verse 7:51, "But surely the Law does not allow us to pass judgment on a man without giving him a hearing and discovering what he is about?"

The Pharisees are confronted with the troubling fact that, contrary to their own law, they are arriving at a judgment about Jesus without having given him a hearing. The egocentric ego when "caught in the act" tends to respond by trying to disparage those who bring up disquieting information, so they turn on Nicodemus, saying to him scornfully, "Are you a Galilean too? Go into the matter and see for yourself: prophets do not come out of Galilee." They are relying on the old handed-down teaching that no prophets could come from Galilee. What they do not know is that Christ came not from Galilee but from Bethlehem, and, what is more important, from God. But John knows, and we, his readers, also know.

~ 17 ~

THE OLD CONSCIOUSNESS
AND THE NEW
Controversy with the Pharisees
John 8:12–30

As we noted in a previous chapter, John 8:12 continues the discussions between Jesus and the Pharisees on various issues. John uses these discussions as a way to instruct his reader more deeply on the mysteries that Christ brings into the world. We will begin with a textual analysis and then probe the main theme: the new consciousness that is brought by Christ.

Verse 8:12 is an important statement of Christ as the light:

> I am the light of the world
> anyone who follows me will not be walking in the dark;
> he will have the light of life.

We are now in a position to understand this saying of Jesus in depth. In a previous chapter we discussed the three meanings of light in John's Gospel. In John 8:12 we have a good example of the first of these three meanings: the idea of light as that which shows a person the way to God by enabling that person to have an enlightened consciousness and no longer to walk in the darkness of ignorance and sin. The soul in its journey through this world hungers for this light, which brings us to enlightenment, new awareness, and consciousness on many levels of our being. We also see exemplified here the way this light is contrasted with its spiritual opposite: darkness, which in this context is the spirit of not knowing, of dwelling in ignorance and hence in sin. We also are told in this verse that this light is special in another regard: it is the light of "life." The life to which John is referring is not mere existence (*bios*) but is the living, flowing principle of life itself (*zōē*), spiritual as well as physical. Hence the connection between light and life: each one brings the other with it.

On the psychological level, the growth of consciousness is vital to the individuation process. All insight into one's own inner processes, as well as into the meaning of life in its larger sense, brings the light, and all insight is the product of the light. This in turn brings an increase in life.

John 8:13 reintroduces the controversy between the Pharisees and Jesus. We have already noted in previous chapters that in the context of John's Gospel, Jesus' adversaries are to be understood not only historically but also symbolically. They personify the old consciousness in its opposition to the new consciousness. We will look more deeply into the meaning of this struggle shortly.

John 8:15, "You judge by human standards," is a translation of the word *sarx* (*kata tēn sarkan* = "according to the flesh"). It will be remembered from our discussion of John 1:14 ("and the word became flesh") that the word *sarx* in the New Testament has five different meanings. In our present context, *sarx* refers to that limited state of consciousness that prevails when our consciousness is conditioned only by information brought us by our senses and by the collective opinions of our culture. In contrast, Jesus' consciousness is influenced by his relationship with the Father and so he does not evaluate circumstances only from the limited human point of view.

Verses 15–19 take up the important Johannine theme of judgment. The word translated "judgment" is the Greek word *krisis*, from which our English word "crisis" is derived. Judgment is a crisis, and the issue of whether we belong to the light (consciousness) or the darkness (unconsciousness) involves us in this crisis. How we live our lives, whether consciously or unconsciously, in the light or in the darkness, is a critical matter of such great importance that it is justifiably referred to as a crisis involving judgment. In a later chapter we will take up this important theme in John's Gospel more fully.

John 8:21: The Pharisees cannot go where Jesus is going because their consciousness is part of the collective consciousness of "this world." For this reason their souls will die, for the soul lives by the light of new consciousness and the freedom from the darkness and sin that the light brings.

John 8:22–24 brings together themes we have already considered. Since the consciousness of the Pharisees is "of this world," they belong to that which is psychologically and spiritually "below." It is for this reason that they will die, as indicated in the previous verse, since living in the darkness means the death of the soul. In verse 24 we have another reiteration of the *egō eimi*, the "I am," the full import of which remains to be discussed. However, it is important to note that when the Jerusalem Bible says "I am He" the word "He" is not found in the Greek text. Translators have a difficult time translating the text literally as simply "I am." The Revised Standard Version also says "I am he." Phillips says "I am who I am." The New English Bible says "I am what I am." The King James Version, which as usual follows the Greek more closely, says "I am *he*," but puts the "*he*" in a different script to indicate that this is inferred from the context and not literally there in the Greek. The same syntax is found in John 8:28.

The remaining verses in this discussion, 8:22–30, continue the important Johannine theme of the Father and of the relationship of Christ to the Father, which we examined in some detail in a previous chapter. The Pharisees ask him the question, "Who are you?" We may imagine that John includes this question from the Pharisees because Jesus' answer gives John an opportunity to inform the reader who Jesus is. The first part of Jesus' answer, scholars seem to agree, is somewhat obscure. He says, "What I have told you from the outset." Or, as in the Revised Standard Version, "Even what I have told you from the beginning." What is this "beginning" of which Jesus speaks? One answer may be that as the Logos, Jesus pre-existed the incarnation and, as we saw in chapter 2, spoke through the prophets and in many manifestations of the divine presence in the Old Testament. Jesus then says that he has many things to say to the Pharisees and much about them to condemn. These are hard words, but they may need to be hard because the Pharisees purport to be the spiritual leaders of the people, but what they teach comes from their darkness and not from the light. In contrast to them, we discover in verse 8:26, Jesus is sent into the world by one who is truthful, and he speaks to the world only what he has learned from this one who is truthful. (The word "truthful" here is the same truth as *alētheia*, a

Greek word we have considered before, which means "genuine" and "without error.")

When the Pharisees do not understand him, Jesus explains what he means in a different way. In 8–27 John, in a kind of aside to the reader, tells us that when Jesus spoke of one who has sent him he is speaking of the Father. Jesus goes on to explain to the Pharisees that the one who sent him is indeed none other than the Father whom they have worshiped and acknowledged all along. In an earlier chapter we noted that there are nineteen passages in the Fourth Gospel that discuss the matter of the relationship of the Father and the Son, and that in eleven of them there is a virtual identity between the two, while in eight of them there is a close relationship but also a distinction. This passage would belong to the latter category: Jesus and the Father are so closely related that Jesus does and says what the Father wants, and yet we are led to think of Father and Son as separate realities.

It will be helpful to summarize what we have already said about the Father/Son relationship, and then to add a new dimension. First, we noted that Father and Son are not the names of essences but of relationships; they are meant metaphorically and do not connote sexual gender identity. Second, we observed that the relationship of the Son to the Father is a heavenly or metaphysical paradigm of the psychological relationship of the ego to the Self. Third, we can now note that the term "Father" expresses the nature of God as the Transcendent and the Absolute, which is essentially unknowable to human consciousness, while the Son as the Logos represents that same divine reality expressing itself in the created order. As such, the Son can be known. In fact, the son is so close to us that the Son or Logos dwells within the soul herself. In this way did Johannine Christianity work out the problem of God's immanence and transcendence: that is, how can the utterly transcendent God also be known as God immanent within creation? It also offers what could be called a spiritual epistemology. In answer to the question, "How can God, who is the Absolute, ever be known to a human being?" John answers that God can be known because the Divinity is in the creation as the Son, a manifestation of the Divine Logos, or Wisdom. About this important matter we will have more to say when we come to the fourteenth chapter of John's Gospel.

This section ends in John 8:30 with an interesting statement:

"As he was saying this, many came to believe in him." The word
"believe" is the Greek word *pisteuō*, which we examined in an
earlier chapter. There we saw that the act of believing was a "believing *into*" something, faith being put into the object of that faith.
John 8:30 is a good example since the verbal construction here is
polloi episteusan eis auton. The translation would be: Many (*polloi*)
believed (*episteusan*) into (*eis*) him (*auton*). The force of this is that
faith was put *into* Jesus, who was both the object of that faith and
its inspiration.

The faith of these people, however, was not aroused by any
rational argument; rather it was aroused by the numinosity of
Jesus and what he was saying. As we saw earlier, that which
is numinous partakes of the quality of the holy, which arouses
in a person awe, wonder, and even dread. In the presence of the
numinous we are all believers, for the numinous bypasses rational
or logical thought and awakens deeper centers of understanding.
Faith when inspired by the numinous is the response of the soul to
the object of its deepest yearnings. Then we are truly "persuaded";
then we believe through faith.

The primary focus of this chapter, however, is another encounter between the old consciousness, personified by the Pharisees, and the new consciousness that is brought by the Christ.
As we have already noted, it is best to approach such dialogues
as "active imaginations" that became alive in the mind of John
because two primordial archetypes were constellated in his imagination: the archetype of the old and that of the new. Approaching
the dialogue portions of John's Gospel in this way we free ourselves from being caught in ethnic controversies and move to the
more vital area of the spiritual collision that takes place when a
new awareness comes to supplant the old. This is not to say that
there were not historical encounters between Jesus and his detractors; it is to say that the important element is the archetypal
or spiritual dimension of which such historical encounters are
passing illustrations.

There are innumerable examples from mythology, the Bible,
and history of the collision between the old and the new consciousness. From Greek mythology we have the stories of Uranus,
Cronus, and Zeus. Uranus, the original father god of the sky, fa-
thered many children, but as each one was born the infant was
shut away by Uranus in the depths of the earth, except for his son
Cronus, who succeeded in eluding Uranus and eventually un-

manning him, casting his bleeding genitals into the sea.[1] Cronus now became the ruler of the gods, but he also tried to destroy his progeny by swallowing them as soon as they were born. Cronus's wife, grief-stricken Rhea, however, succeeded in giving birth to her son Zeus secretly in a cave. She then gave Cronus a stone wrapped in swaddling clothes, which he swallowed, thinking it was the newborn infant. Later Zeus, grown to manhood, forced Cronus to drink a draught that caused him to vomit up the children he had swallowed. These children became the gods of Olympus. Zeus then banished Cronus from the sky and sent him away to the farthest regions of the universe. This myth of the "devouring father" is a variant of the archetype we are considering that causes the old entrenched power to try to destroy the new.

In the Bible the story in Matthew's Gospel of the slaughter of the innocents is a good example of this same archetype. Herod has learned from the Wise Men of the birth of the baby Jesus in Bethlehem and that this baby is to be the "new king." Herod does not understand that the kingdom of Christ is a spiritual kingdom and fears for the loss of his throne and power. To guarantee his grip on his personal kingship he decrees that all the children in Bethlehem under the age of two shall be destroyed. The baby Jesus escapes Herod's tyranny, however, because his father, Joseph, was warned of the danger by an angel in a dream and the holy family escaped to Egypt. In similar ways, modern dictators such as Stalin and Hitler have been driven to destroy the innocent in order to maintain their power.

The church, which is supposed to be the carrier of the power of Christ and new consciousness, has also at times lapsed into the role of the devouring father who destroys the new awareness. A good example is the story of the collision between Galileo and church authorities in the seventeenth century during the Inquisition. The church during this era of its history had founded its teachings on the principles and authority of Aristotle. One of Aristotle's beliefs was that the sun revolved around the earth. The brilliant Italian thinker Galileo, however, through his studies

---

1. From the black drops of blood that fell from Uranus's wound upon the earth sprang the redoubtable Erinyes, or Furies, female divinities who took merciless revenge on those who broke the old code of law; and from the place where Uranus's severed penis fell into the sea sprang Aphrodite, goddess of love. In such a way did the ancient Greeks explain the origin of those archetypal powers that govern human life.

of the movements of the heavenly bodies, opposed many of the teachings of Aristotle. In particular Galileo argued publicly for the radical theory of his predecessor Copernicus: that the earth revolved around the sun, not the other way around. However, the church, fearing that to admit that if this was so it would diminish its authority, preferred repression rather than truth. Galileo was forced to recant his ideas for fear of his life and was sentenced to an indefinite term in prison.[2] The tendency of the church to defend its dogma to the extent that the truth is denied was observed by Jung, who once wrote: "Science seeks the truth because it feels it does not possess it. The Church 'possesses' the truth and therefore does not seek it."[3]

Science isn't always as loyal to the truth, however, as Jung supposed, and the history of science, like that of the church, is full of examples in which people with entrenched ideas and power structures knowingly or unknowingly destroyed people with new ideas that challenged them. A striking example is that of the Hungarian gynecologist and obstetrician Ignac Semmelweis. In the year 1847 puerperal fever was rampant in certain places. It was generally believed to be a separate disease, like smallpox, except it attacked only women who had recently given birth to their children. Semmelweis observed that the disease struck only those women whose deliveries had been performed by obstetricians and medical students; women attended by midwives rarely got the disease, and even mothers delivered at home, or in alleyways and streets, rarely contracted puerperal fever. These facts, plus a number of other more technical observations, led Semmelweis to conclude (correctly as it turned out) that there was no separate disease "puerperal fever" but that the women were being infected by the unwashed hands of the physicians who had been in direct contact with the bacteria from cadavers or other patients. Later he himself directed an obstetric clinic in which careful attention was paid to cleanliness. Puerperal fever in Semmelweis's clinic was virtually unknown. The facts seemed to speak for themselves, but it was many years before the medical establishment recognized the truth of Semmelweis's conclusions

---

2. His sentence of imprisonment was remitted to house arrest, but he was under constant surveillance by the church's version of the Gestapo. He became blind and lived only five more years. Fifty years later a grateful city erected a monument to him and placed it in a church; evidently the church had at least partially repented of its former error.

3. Jung, *Letters 1*, 347.

and changed its ways. Some biographers of Semmelweis say this was because of a bitter power struggle and the intransigence of those in power; others say that Semmelweis brought it on himself because he failed to disseminate his information properly. At any rate, he died an early death in an insane asylum. No doubt his madness was hastened by having to watch many women die when the disease could have been so easily prevented.

In the individuation process, the old egocentric ego is constantly being challenged to change by admitting into its awareness new insights, perspectives, and information that come from life experience or from the unconscious. Time and again the daemonic side of the egocentric ego, energized by the destructive archetype we have been describing, rejects and destroys the new truth. Quite often such changes in consciousness are finally accepted only under the aegis of painful necessity.

Individual carriers of new truths, like Semmelweis and Galileo, can be destroyed, and the ego can destroy new insights for a while, but the truth itself can never be destroyed. Ultimately it will always emerge triumphant, which is why John 1:5 tells us that the power of the light can never be overcome by the power of the darkness. On the psychological level, our dreams persist in presenting us with the truth about ourselves, and our dreams, fortunately for us, cannot be controlled by the ego. When the ego persists in denying the new insights that it should appropriate and in refusing to alter accordingly its attitude and course in life, dreams may take place in which the dreamer is accused of a crime (the crime of unconsciousness) and even in which the execution of the dreamer is called for (because the old ego is standing in the way and must be eliminated).

The resistance of the old ego to the new truths is the reason, as we have seen, why Kunkel made the statement, "The secret is, that the ego is the devil." He was thinking, of course, not of the ego when it is functioning in alignment with the Self, but of the egocentric ego. But behind and beyond the ego lies a great and more sinister psychic power, an archetypal or spiritual power.

In the Bible, archetypal powers are represented and portrayed in what sounds to us like mythic language. The modern mind may disparage such "mythological thinking" as unscientific and fanciful, but the fact is that there is psychological truth in it. The Bible ingeniously weaves together personal and historical elements with mythic or archetypal elements in a way that is psychologically correct, for the human psyche consists not only of the transitory individual ego, but it also has an archetypal basis to it which is universally present in all human beings and which the ancients described in mythic language.

This archetypal structure to the psyche has both a beneficial and a daemonic aspect to it. In the Bible, its daemonic side is represented in the "principalities," "authorities," and "rulers" of this world. Gerd Theissen, professor of New Testament at the University of Heidelberg, is one of the few biblical scholars to see the importance of the intersection of the human and archetypal worlds in New Testament psychology and has written about this in his challenging book *Psychological Aspects of Pauline Theology.*[4] While it constitutes a brief digression from John's Gospel, a summary of his insights will help us understand John's teachings in more depth and integrate them into a modern psychological perspective. But in order to understand what John is saying and what Theissen is saying about the New Testament, we will have to look at a few more Greek words.

The Greek word *archōn* is another of those biblical words that is virtually impossible to translate into English. The most frequent English word used to translate *archōn* is "prince," but "ruler" or some other word denoting a royal power might also be used. But frequently the *archōn* is no earthly prince; rather the term denotes an autonomous spiritual power, less in authority than God, but greater than any human being or agency. Examples of its usage can be found in Matthew 9:34, 12:24, 20:25; Mark 3:22; 1 Corinthians 2:6, 2:8; Ephesians 2:2; Revelations 1:5; and, in John's Gospel, 12:31, 14:30, and 16:11.

While the word *archōn* is the most important word used to refer to spiritual powers, many other Greek words are also used in the New Testament with much the same meaning, for instance, *exousiai* (plural), which denotes "authorities, potentates, or powers." *Exousia* (singular) denotes someone who has the freedom to choose. Consequently an earthly ruler might be represented by this word, for such a person has authority to make decisions. But the word might also refer to a spiritual power that has a certain amount of autonomy. When so used, the word is generally in the plural and the reference is to *the exousiai* as the authorities and

---

4. Gerd Theissen, *Psychological Aspects of Pauline Theology* (Philadelphia: Fortress Press, 1983).

rulers and powers of the spiritual world. Examples of this usage can be found in Ephesians 2:1, 3:10, 6:12; 1 Corinthians 15:24; Colossians 1:16, 2:10, 15; and 1 Peter 3:22.

Another word is *dynameis* (plural), which can be translated "spiritual powers" or "heavenly luminaries." The stars would be examples of heavenly luminaries, or *dynameis*, but they were also identified with spiritual entities or influences virtually identical with the stars. Examples of the word *dynameis* with reference to "spiritual powers" can be found in Matthew 14:2 and Mark 6:14. Their identity with heavenly luminaries that also were spiritual powers can be found in Matthew 24:29, Mark 13:29, Luke 21:26, and Galatians 4:3, 9. However, a *dynamis* (singular) could also be a "power as a personal supernatural spirit or angel." Examples can be found in Romans 3:38; 1 Corinthians 15:24; Ephesians 1:21, 13:1; and 1 Peter 3:22.

There is also the word *stoicheion* (singular), which means "a straight rod or rule," but is often used in the Bible to refer to an autonomous, spiritual element of the natural universe. An example of this usage can be found in 2 Peter 3:10, 12. Sometimes the *stoicheia* (plural) are also associated with the heavenly bodies, as in Colossians 2:8, 20, where they are the heavenly bodies, but also "the natural ruling elements of this world" (*stoicheia tou kosmou*).

There is also the Greek word *angelos*, or angel, which usually refers to a spiritual power operating in the affairs of humankind as the agents or messengers of God or God's will. Often the *angeloi* (plural) sent dreams, as in the case of the dreams that came to Joseph, the earthly father of Jesus. But sometimes the angels were also thought of as dark angels, who might act contrary to God's will. Examples of this usage can be found in Romans 8:38; 1 Corinthians 11:10; 2 Corinthians 11:14; 1 Peter 3:22; 2 Peter 2:4; and perhaps also 2 Peter 2:11.

As can be seen, there are many words in the New Testament that refer to spiritual powers or authorities, but we will concentrate on the most important word, *archōn*, so that we can benefit from the excellent discussion of this word by Gerd Theissen. In biblical scholarship, there has for a long time been a debate about whether the *archontes* (plural) in the New Testament are to be understood as specific human beings who wielded political power and spiritual influence, or as spiritual or heavenly powers. Theissen rejects this "either-or" approach to the subject that has primarily prevailed among biblical interpreters. He argues that the *archontes* must be regarded as both personal, human, historical figures, *and* autonomous spiritual realities with a collective significance, which we would call in psychological language "archetypes." (Theissen himself uses this word occasionally in order to describe them.)

Theissen believes that the *archontes tou kosmou*, the "rulers of this world," so often referred to in the New Testament, represent the "dominant consciousness of society, which is experienced as a compulsive power." They "symbolize the psychic resistance" to new consciousness and God's word, which acts as a "deforming censorship" and which is personified as "hostile guards in front of the human heart." They are a psychic resistance deeply entrenched in the human psyche that obstructs God's light and consciousness, so that the message of God has to "force its way into the unconscious human depths against an inner resistance."[5] Because this psychic resistance is well-nigh universal among human beings, the *archontes* transcend any individual person, as is exemplified in passages such as 1 Corinthians 2:6ff, which reads as follows:

> Yet among the mature we do impart wisdom [*sophia*], although it is not a wisdom of this age or of the rulers [*archontes*] of this age, who are doomed to pass away. But we impart a secret and hidden wisdom of God, which God decreed before the ages for our glorification. None of the rulers of this age [*archontes*] understood this, for if they had, they would not have crucified the Lord of glory. (RSV)[6]

Clearly in this passage the *archontes* are not human individuals, but are to be understood as archetypal powers that shape collective human thinking under regressive and destructive lines, who are doomed, by God's *sophia*, or wisdom, to ultimately pass away, but not before they try to crucify God's Son or light using the agency of particular human beings as instruments of their purpose.

The *archontes*, however, may appear to be identical with specific people who are in positions of rule or authority because "the consciousness of the rulers is usually bound up with the dominant consciousness (of the times) — the collective convictions and

5. Ibid., 380–81.
6. Cf. Philippians 2:5–11; Colossians 2:15; 1 Thessalonians 2:14–15; 1 Corinthians 8:5–6.

evaluations that inescapably mark every member of a society."
Thus an *archōn* "often appears as a compulsive power marking the
individual . . . as something demonic." It is for this reason that "the
archontes are heightened to cosmic powers present everywhere"
functioning in such a way that God's message is contradicted because it comes into conflict with collective dominants of human
consciousness.[7]

As *archetypal* powers, the *archontes* have an entrenched and
autonomous existence within the human psyche from which vantage point they profoundly influence consciousness. It is for this
reason that they are, quite correctly, described in mythic language
in the Bible and personified as autonomous spiritual entities,
projected by the ancients sometimes into the stars. They also appear, as Theissen has pointed out, as human rulers and potentates
because human rulers identify with the archetypal powers and become exponents of their negative energy that devours and limits
new consciousness. This is the reason Theissen refused the usual
"either-this-or-that" argument found in most biblical scholarship
regarding the matter of the identity of the archons and argued that
the archons must be regarded as both personal and collective or
archetypal.

Readers of the New Testament need to keep in mind the New
Testament worldview. Modern readers, quite naturally, identify
Christianity with monotheism: the belief in one God. There is
indeed only one God in the New Testament and only one power
to be worshiped. But it is a mistake to suppose that this means
there is God on the one hand and human beings on the other
hand and that this embraces all spiritual reality. To the contrary,
as we have seen, there is a vast and multitudinous spiritual realm
in which humankind is immersed and which is so real that it
profoundly influences the course of human consciousness. While
the spiritual reality is often helpful to humankind and in the form
of angels acts on behalf of God's will, it can also be harmful and an
obstruction to God's will. There is thus an autonomous spiritual
power at work in the world that tries to offset God's will and that
is supremely manifested in the idea of the devil, with which we
will be concerned in the next chapter.

The modern reader may be tempted to dismiss all such biblical
talk as outmoded mythology and superstition. Even some bibli-

---

7. Theissen, *Psychological Aspects of Pauline Theology*, 383.

cal scholars today tell us that to get at the contemporary meaning of the Bible we must disregard all biblical references to autonomous spiritual reality as part of a mythological worldview that no longer makes sense. But from the point of view of depth psychology the biblical viewpoint is entirely correct. There are archetypal powers in the human psyche, some working for good and some for evil, and the mythic descriptions of them in the New Testament are entirely in keeping with modern psychological findings.

What we have in the eighth chapter of John's Gospel is a good description of exactly the kind of process that Theissen refers to. The Pharisees are identified with the old consciousness that fights against the Light, the new consciousness being brought by Christ. But it is not only their individual psychology that is at work here. Behind the individual resistance of the Pharisees to the new consciousness is the archetypal resistance, represented in many myths both in the Bible and elsewhere, which we have briefly summarized. It is for this reason that all new awareness fights against a great resistance. This resistance can be manifested on the level of the individual who resists insight into himself or herself and on a collective level, when it can devour a whole people, as happened in the era of World War II. The reader of John's Gospel must keep in mind that behind every word the author writes is his keen awareness of this psychological background and of the spiritual resistance to growth that the new consciousness in Christ often must struggle against. It is not too much to say that it is a cosmic struggle, when viewed in its collective dimensions, in which the powers of darkness try to destroy the new Light entirely, as we will see as we progress further along.

~ 18 ~

THE PROBLEM OF EVIL
The Devil as the Father of Lies
John 8:31–59

CHAPTER 8 OF JOHN'S GOSPEL continues in verse 31 with another statement that Jesus makes to those who now believe in him, but then shifts quickly in verse 33 to the continuing dialogue between Jesus and his opponents, a dialogue that concluded with a description by Jesus of the nature and machinations of the devil. We will explore Jesus' comments on the devil in some depth, but first we will make a brief analysis of the text.

John 8:31–32 makes a powerful statement. To make Jesus' words their "home" would mean the disciples should bring the meaning of his words into themselves and act upon them. Then they will learn the truth. We have here again the word *alētheia*, which means that which is genuine and true. In the Jerusalem Bible, the word translated "learn" in verse 32 is the verbal form of the word *gnōsis*, which, as we now know, refers to knowledge that is learned by intimate experience. "You will *know* the truth" thus means not a mere intellectual knowledge, but a deep inner knowing. This kind of knowing of the truth leads to freedom, and it was evidently Jesus' statement about freedom that led his adversaries to challenge him further, which they do in verses 33ff.

John 8:33–36: In typical Johannine fashion, our author uses the question Jesus' adversaries put to him as an opportunity to explain to his readers that the freedom is found in serving God. As we have already suggested, psychologically this is the equivalent of the ego serving the creative inner Center rather than its own egocentricity. If we do this, we experience the Son who makes us free. The only real freedom we have is to choose God's will: everything else is a form of slavery; this is part of the Christian *mystērion*.

The word for sin in verse 34 is the word *hamartia*, which we discussed earlier and which means literally "to miss the mark." Psychologically it denotes a failure of consciousness. It is characteristic of John's Gospel that freedom, faith, knowledge, and consciousness all go together and lead to life, while servitude, ignorance, unawareness, and lack of understanding also go together but lead to spiritual death. Verse 36 reminds us again of Jung's comment that Christ is the God of freedom.

John 8:37: Jesus recognizes that nothing he has said has penetrated (more literally "found a dwelling place") into the hearts of his detractors. We now are in a position to understand why this is so. As Gerd Theissen put it, as long as a person's heart is dominated by the *archontes*, the collective dominants of the thinking of this world, the word of God cannot penetrate except by force. This sets the stage for evil. What lies within a person's soul is of crucial importance to that person's spiritual welfare. Jung once commented that the power of evil was so strong that only two things could keep a person from being overcome by it: if a person is contained in a warm and related human community it keeps evil from taking complete possession, and/or if a person's soul is filled with a spirit stronger than that of evil.[1] But if the soul is left empty or is filled with that destructive energy the Bible calls the princes and rulers and powers of this world, then the soul is in grave spiritual danger.

John 8:38–41: These verses show us that behind and beyond the personal opponents — Jesus on the one hand and his adversaries on the other hand — lie the archetypal opponents, the "fathers." Jesus' Father is God, but Jesus knows that the father of his adversaries is a power quite different from that of God. His detractors can only assume that Jesus must be preferring to Abraham, but Jesus makes it clear that it is not Abraham to whom he is referring. We have here a collusion between the creative power of God the Father, and the devouring, negative destructive father who de-

---

1. See the letter Jung wrote to Bill W., one of the founders of Alcoholics Anonymous. It is cited above on p. 146.

stroys new consciousness. As we will soon see, the essence of this father is that he is the father of lies, while God is the Father of truth.

The remaining portion of chapter 8 is a discussion of the devil. The word translated "devil" in this passage is the Greek word *diabolos*, which means literally "to throw something across one's path" (from the verb *diaballō*, "to throw over"). A little later we will see why the devil has the quality of one who throws something across our path.

First we must note that in the Johannine discussions of the devil as the author of evil it is psychological or moral evil that is in question, and not natural evil. In any discussion of the problem of evil it is important to keep this distinction in mind. Natural evil would include calamities such as earthquakes, disease, floods, and the like, which humankind deems to be evil. These evils do not proceed out of a sinister intentionality but are natural occurrences, however undesirable they may be. They are examples of *kakos*, which we noted in an earlier chapter referred to anything that was deemed to be bad. Psychological or moral evil, however, proceeds from a human being or spiritual power who has evil intentions. This kind of evil, as we have noted, is referred to by the Greek word *ponēros*; it is this evil with which John's discussion of the devil is concerned.

The devil also appears in the synoptic Gospels where his presence in the world is assumed without question. The Gospels give no reasons for the presence of the malignant evil power, rather as though no reason needs to be supplied. It is a "just-so" story: this is just the way it is. It was left to later Christian thinkers to try to fit the devil into God's plan of salvation. It is also clear in the synoptic Gospels that for a human being to fall under the power of the devil is a matter of great concern, and in this John's Gospel heartily agrees.

We have seen that the ego in its egocentricity is a kind of devil, but it is not *the* devil. Behind the deviltry of the egocentric ego is the archetype of evil. The essence of this evil, John states, is that evil lies, and so destroys the truth. The egocentric ego has a tendency to lie because it wants to avoid facing the truth about itself, but behind this personal evil lies the archetype, that collective power within all of us that leads the ego into the tendency to twist, distort, and deny the truth. It is this evil power that causes the ego to block out the word of God, to be incapable of "hearing" the voice of truth, as John makes clear in 8:47. It is also a device of this evil power to lead us to project our own evil onto others, that is, to see in others what in fact lies in ourselves, as John makes clear in verse 48 when Jesus' detractors project their own state of possession into Jesus. ("Are we not right in saying ... that you are possessed by a devil?")

And what if we are not aware of all this? What if we are truly blind to the machinations of our ego as it seeks to avoid the truth, and so increasingly we fall into the power of the archetype of evil within us all? As far as the practical spiritual consequences are concerned it makes no difference. As we have discussed previously, the moral and spiritual consequences of our actions are as inexorable as are the physical ones; spiritual law has its consequences just as does natural law. Unawareness of what we are doing not only is no excuse, but it adds to our sin, as is made clear in Hebrews 9:7. In this verse we are told that once a year the high priest entered the Holy of Holies to offer a sacrifice on behalf of "the people's sins of ignorance" (NEB). The word translated "sins of ignorance" is the Greek word *agnoēma*. This word is a compendium of the letter *a* (alpha) and the word *gnōsis* (knowledge). The letter alpha in Greek negates what follows it. So an *agnoēma* is a sin of not knowing, hence a sin of ignorance.[2]

The ego may be blind to its sins and blunderings, but the unconscious registers everything we do, as we know from our dreams, which characteristically reveal to us all about ourselves that hitherto has been hidden. In the Bible, this knowledge of all that goes on within us is part of the nature of God, who is the knower-of-the-heart and who knows all the secrets of the soul, even those that have been kept carefully hidden by the egocentric ego.[3] In Egyptian mythology this faculty of universal knowledge of the individual soul was ascribed to the ibis-headed god Thoth, who kept a record of every person's deeds and thoughts. When a person died it was believed that his or her soul journeyed via the Nile River to the underworld, for the Nile River was thought to flow in a great circle, disappearing for a while from human sight in order to journey through the land of the dead and thence to return again to flow once more through the world of conscious-

---

2. Unfortunately most modern translations render this interesting and important word simply as "fault" or "error." In this case the New English Bible has the more literal and spiritually meaningful translation: "for the people's sins of ignorance."

3. Biblical references to the indwelling God who knows the secrets of the heart include: Luke 17:21; Romans 2:15–16, 8:9–11; 1 Corinthians 3:16, 4:5; 2 Corinthians 6:16, 13:5, 14:25; Colossians 1:27; Ephesians 3:16–17; Galatians 2:20, 4:19; Hebrews 4:12–16; 2 Tim. 1:14.

ness. As the soul journeyed through the land of the dead it passed twelve gates guarded by twelve deities, all of whom had to be satisfied about the righteousness of the departed soul. But the final test came when the soul arrived at the court of Osiris, judge of the dead. Here Thoth read the record of the soul's sojourn through life while Osiris pondered from this information whether or not the soul deserved eternal life or punishment. Finally Osiris held up a scale, and Thoth placed the soul on one side and a feather on the other. If the soul was lighter than the feather that soul went to everlasting life, but if the soul was weighted down by sins it would be heavier than the feather, in which case it went to eternal punishment. In this way nothing escaped the notice of God, and divine justice was meted out according to one's deserts.

Now we are in a position to understand why one meaning of the name of the devil (*diabolos*) is to throw something across our path. What the devil throws across our path is *choice*. Jung often admonished us to "stand between the opposites" in life. What he meant was that we should not strive to be so one-sidedly and egocentrically "good" that we lose touch with our shadow. But it also must be said that we have to *choose* between the opposites. It is the standpoint of John's Gospel that life constantly confronts us with such choices. We may surmise that God permits the devil to operate in order that souls are confronted with choices, for without choices it would not be possible to develop morally or psychologically. Many of the choices that we make are quite small; in themselves they do not seem to be important, although if added together they amount to a life that is lived either well or badly. At times, however, we may be confronted with a highly significant choice in which our very souls appear to be at stake.

A moving example of such a choice was told to me by a Jewish client of mine who was explaining to me why he had no extended family. "They were all killed in the holocaust," he explained. Then he qualified his statement, "Except for one aunt." When I asked for more information about this aunt he told me the following story: His aunt was among a group of Jews led out to be shot by a German firing squad during World War II. The execution was to take place near the German-Polish border at the dusk of the day. As this woman was marched by the German soldier assigned to shoot her he whispered to her: "When I shoot, run." He shot in the air and she ran and lived to tell the story. Here is a dramatic example of someone confronted with choice. The soldier could shoot to kill, or not shoot to kill. The other soldiers in the firing squad shot and killed their victims. If asked why they did so they might well have said, "We had no choice." Or they might have said, "If we had not killed that person someone else would have." Or, "We had to follow orders." The fact is that one soldier in the group chose not to shoot, and the others did. Who can criticize those soldiers who shot to kill? If we had been in their shoes would we have done any differently? Small wonder we pray in the Lord's Prayer, "Do not put us to the test."[4] Surely this is also what Jesus had in mind in Matthew's Gospel when he said, "And do not fear those who kill the body but cannot kill the soul; rather fear him who can destroy body and soul in hell" (Matt. 10:28, RSV).

From the point of view of John's Gospel, Christ is there at every moment of choice, regardless of a person's religious belief system. Those who protest a belief in Christ and those who do not are likewise confronted with his reality in their choice, for every choice has its judgment, that is, its inevitable spiritual consequences. In each life situation Christ as the Light can bring consciousness, and those who follow the Light follow Christ whether they realize it or not. This consciousness is essential if we are to confront choices correctly. What we would call today insight and psychological development cannot be separated from ethical awareness, nor the other way around. It is all part of one path.

To choose the path of unconsciousness and evil is slowly but surely to corrupt the soul. In his novel *The Picture of Dorian Gray*, Oscar Wilde dramatically represented the same path of death that John's Gospel discusses. In Wilde's story, the handsome young man, Dorian Gray, has been blessed with the gift of eternal youth; no matter what he does, it will not change his appearance. Everyone marvels at how pure and fresh the young man appears even as the years go by. Unfortunately, the young man uses his gift as a screen for his selfish life and evil deeds, but while his face does not change, a marvelous painting of him does. With each dark deed, the once beautiful face in the painting becomes more distorted. Not wanting anyone to see it, Dorian Gray hides the painting in an attic room and visits it only from time to time. At length, no longer able to abide the dreadful face he now sees in the painting, he takes a knife and slashes it to pieces. But with the destruction of the painting, Dorian Gray himself dies.

---

4. An alternative translation to "Lead us not into temptation."

Now we are able to see more clearly the meaning of the final two verses with which chapter 8 concludes and in which we hear again the great "I am." In John 8:58 Jesus says to his adversaries, "Truly, truly I say to you, before Abraham was, *I am.*" Here we have again the *egō eimi* of which we have spoken before, but now we can see that this expression in John's Gospel marks the break between the old consciousness and the new consciousness, for when Jesus uses this expression he not only identifies himself with the Father; he confronts our consciousness with a divine reality that none of us can avoid.

～ 19 ～

THE MEANING OF ILLNESS
The Cure of the Man Born Blind
John 9

IN CHAPTERS 10 AND 11 ABOVE we examined two healing stories: the story of the healing of the nobleman's son and the story of the healing of the man by the pool of Bethzatha. In the first story we saw the importance of faith, and in the second we saw the connection that sometimes exists between illness and sin. In John's chapter 9 he will show us still another meaning that illness can have. Then, in typical Johannine fashion, he will move from the historical incident involving the cure of the man born blind to a general spiritual truth.[1]

The powerful opening verses of the chapter draw the reader immediately into a gripping story involving important issues:

> As he went along, he saw a man who had been blind from birth. His disciples asked him, "Rabbi, who sinned, this man or his parents, for him to have been born blind?" "Neither he nor his parents sinned," Jesus answered, "he was born blind so that the works of God might be displayed in him."

The question the disciples put to Jesus has a history behind it. In the Old Testament the prevailing belief about illness was that it came from God, because everything in life came from Yahweh, good or ill. It was a consequence of the strict monotheism of the Old Testament. For example, we read in Isaiah:

---

1. For a further exploration of the themes of this chapter see my book *Healing Body and Soul* (Louisville: Westminster/John Knox Press, 1992).

> I am Yahweh, and there is no other,
> I form the light and I create the darkness,
> I make well-being, and I create disaster,
> I, Yahweh, do all these things. (Isa. 45:7, NJB)

So Yahweh sent illness as well as health, but being a just God Yahweh would not visit a person with illness unless that person had sinned. A just person would not suffer illness or misfortune because of God's justice. It followed from this that illness must be the consequence of a sin: some act of faithlessness or the breaking of a divine ordinance. In short, the Old Testament idea was that illness had a theological origin, not a natural one.

It was no doubt for this reason that the Hebrews had virtually no physicians and no natural science of illness. Doctors are rarely referred to in the Old Testament, and when they are it is usually in a disparaging way (see 2 Chron. 16:12.) As for natural medicine, that was left to the Greeks to originate. In the fifth century B.C.E. Greek physicians such as the famous Hippocrates repudiated the idea that the gods caused disease and looked for rational, natural explanations. They became careful observers of the working of the human body and began the study of anatomy. One of them, Empedocles, was the first person to recognize that the heart was the center of the vascular system and that the blood carried a vital element (oxygen) throughout the body. Greek doctors prescribed remedies for illness that included diet, fresh air, massage, ointments, fastings, and, in some cases, surgery. Nothing like this took place in the Old Testament because the whole phenomenon of illness was the direct consequence of sin. As the psalmist put it,

> Your indignation has left no part of me unscathed,
> my sin has left no health in my bones.
> My sins stand higher than my head,
> they weigh on me as an unbearable weight.
> I have stinking, festering wounds,
> thanks to my folly. (Ps. 38:3–5, NJB).[2]

Remarkably, this connection between illness and sin is alive and well today; it simply wears slightly different theological

---

2. Conrad L'Heureux, in his book *Life Journey and the Old Testament* (Mahwah, N.J.: Paulist Press, 1986), has described the Old Testament view very well and collected many Old Testament references to illness and its connection with sin.

clothing. Until the recent revision of the Episcopal *Book of Common Prayer*, the Office of the Visitation of the Sick made it clear in the prayers the priest was to offer on behalf of the patient that the patient was ill because of sin and should implore God for forgiveness. In Christian Science illness is a direct result of "wrong thinking," for which one should make amends. In spiritual healing the inability to recover from illness is due to one's lack of faith. In Jungian psychology one sometimes hears the opinion expressed that if you are properly individuated you would not get sick. In "New Age" thinking one often hears the view that if you are sick it is because you "chose" it. This belief no doubt comes from the Eastern idea of reincarnation: whatever you are suffering from in this life is the karmic result of your sins in a past life.

The result of such beliefs is that if we are ill we also feel a sense of guilt or shame about it. We readily find ourselves in the position of Job, whose friends, however sympathetic they appeared to be, fundamentally believed his sufferings and misfortune were all his fault. The brilliance and importance of the Book of Job is that Job refused to accept this theological theory of illness and demanded justice from God. But Job's point of view was the exception in the Old Testament.

Of course there is some truth in these ideas, as everyone knows who has studied psychosomatic medicine. There certainly are many instances in which a physical illness is the result of our psychological unconsciousness or spiritual sins. Nevertheless, as one doctor friend of mine once put it, "You must never forget that everything that is alive is under constant attack."[3] This includes animals and plants, which also become diseased, for reasons that can hardly be ascribed to sin. The fact is that illness, like health, is archetypal, and belongs to all of life. As Aeschylus once put it, "Of a truth, lusty health rests not content within its due bounds; for disease ever presses close against it, its neighbor with a common wall."[4]

In this case of the man born blind the disciples were applying the collective theological theory of illness of their day, but they came up against a difficulty: if illness came from sin, what of a man who was born blind? How could a tiny baby have sinned?

---

3. My thanks to Robert P. Sedgwick, M.D.
4. Aeschylus, *Agamemnon*, lines 1000f.

Examples of infants born into the world with maladies posed a problem for the traditionalists who believed that all illness was due to sin. One explanation often given was that in such a case the parents of the infant had sinned, but this hardly seems to be justice, and, in fact, while the older parts of the Old Testament believed sins could be handed down through the generations, the more advanced prophets rejected that view and held that the individual was held guilty only for his or her own sins, not for those of parents or grandparents.[5]

In contrast to those who held to the theological view of illness, Jesus was not bound by any particular theory or collective viewpoint, but looked at each case of illness individually. Sometimes the person was ill because of sin, and at other times the person was ill for entirely different reasons. In the case of the woman with the issue of blood (Luke 8:40–48) the illness evidently served the purpose of bringing her to Jesus so that she could not only be cured of her malady but made whole. In her case it could be said that the illness served the purposes of her individuation. In the case of the man born blind Jesus says that he was born blind so the glory of God might be made manifest in him: "Neither he nor his parents sinned; he was born blind so that the works of God might be displayed in him" (9:3). This tells us that the man's illness provided the means that enabled God's greater power to become apparent. It is certainly true that in many cases of illness or natural deformity an opportunity is provided for what we could call psychologically the emergence of the Self. A conspicuous example would be Helen Keller, whose deafness and blindness were the context in which the remarkable depths of character inherent in a human being could be conspicuously seen. In the case of the man born blind, God's glory was revealed in him, not only because Jesus cured him but because the man himself was spiritually transformed in the process, as we will soon see.

The method of the cure strikes us as curious: "Having said this, he spat on the ground, made a paste with the spittle, put this over the eyes of the blind man, and said to him, 'Go and wash

---

5. Interestingly enough, no one in this story suggested that the man's blindness was the result of a previous life. It is sometimes suggested by believers in reincarnation that the New Testament, and Jesus in particular, believed in reincarnation. Going into this issue would take us beyond the scope of this work, but it is worth noting that if Jesus had believed in reincarnation this certainly would have been the time to say so. For a thorough treatment of Christianity and reincarnation see my book, *Soul Journey: A Jungian Analyst Looks at Reincarnation* (New York: Crossroad, 1991); also my *Healing Body and Soul.*

in the Pool of Siloam (a name that means 'sent'). So the blind man went off and washed himself and came away with his sight restored" (9:6).

Why the use of spittle? Perhaps the use of spittle for a cure goes back to the ancient tradition among the Greeks and Hebrews that the life-essence or soul of a person was contained in certain fluids of the body, specifically the blood and the spittle. Jung also noted that saliva among ancient people symbolized the living Spirit of a person and pointed out that this is why Christ used spittle to heal the blind man.[6] The spittle then would symbolize the life essence of Jesus himself, which had a healing efficacy. At any rate, the use of mud and spittle for a cure leaves no room for inflation on the part of the man who was cured. Like Naaman the Syrian who was cured of his leprosy by Elisha who sent him to wash in the muddy waters of the Jordan River (1 Kings 5), so the blind man was cured through the humble element of mud and saliva and sent to wash in the common pool of Siloam.

There is a nuance of meaning at this point in the story that would escape the reader of an English translation. In Greek there are several words that mean "to wash." One word, *plynō*, means to wash a garment. A second word, *louō*, means to wash the whole body. A third word, *niptō*, means to wash only a part of the body. In this story the word *niptō* is used in verse 9:7. All the man is required to wash is his eyes, not his whole body. If the word *louō* had been used it would have suggested the man's need for ritual cleansing, that is, cleansing from sin. The choice by John of the word *niptō* over the word *louō* reinforces the point that this man's illness is not the result of sin.

The pool of Siloam was evidently a place known to John, a pool no doubt well known to his readers. Scholars hypothesize that its name, which means "sent," referred symbolically to Jesus who was sent by the Father. The reader of John's Gospel in ancient times would have recognized the pool of Siloam as a familiar place and would also have caught the symbolic meaning of the word "sent."

The fact that this man was born blind so the glory of God might be revealed in him does not, however, answer all of our questions. Why was this man chosen and not another? After all, this man had to suffer many years from blindness before he was finally

---

6. Jung, *Dream Analysis*, 221.

cured by Jesus. Why was *he* chosen for this experience rather than some other person? The story gives us no explanation, but a Greek would have said that it was fate. In the thinking of the ancient Greeks, *moira*, or fate, played a great role. There were three goddesses, known as the Moirai, or Fates, whose task it was at the conception of each human life to determine the fate of the person. Clotho spun the thread of life for that person, Lachesis measured it, and Atropos cut it at the predetermined moment of death. Their names in Greek, the Moirai, came from the word *moira*, which meant a lot or portion. The Moirai, or Fates, determined the lot or portion in life that fell to every mortal and especially predetermined the inexorable moment and circumstances of a person's death. For the Greeks, the Moirai were more influential in human life than Zeus himself; they were the truly numinous realities no man or woman could avoid. The only choice one had was the choice to run from one's fate or to meet it with nobility.

One hears little or nothing in Christianity about fate. Thomas Aquinas specifically regarded fate as a pagan idea, although he did allow that we might give the name "fate" to the order impressed on life by God's Providence. The idea is not entirely lacking in the New Testament, however, as we can see from an examination of Galatians 6.

In Galatians 6:2 (RSV) we read: "Bear one another's burdens, and so fulfil the law of Christ." But in Galatians 6:5 we read: "For each man will have to bear his own load" (RSV). This sounds like a contradiction: first we are told to carry another's burden, and then we are told everyone must carry his own load. Again the Greek language comes to our rescue. In verse 6:2 the Greek word translated "load" is the word *baros*, which means a weight or pressure (our word barometer comes from it: a barometer measures the weight or pressure of air). But in verse 6:5 the Greek word is *phortion*, and a *phortion* was a burden that could not easily be shifted to someone else. For this reason it was the word for a woman's pregnancy, a soldier's pack, and the cargo of a ship, burdens that could not be easily transferred to someone else but that one must carry for oneself. Now, fate is a *phortion* and is therefore like the burden of the cross that we are told in Matthew's Gospel we must carry for ourselves: "If any man would come after me, let him deny himself and take up his cross and follow me" (Matt. 16:24, RSV). So also Matthew 10:38: "Anyone who does not take his cross and follow in my footsteps is not worthy of me" (cf. Luke 14:27).

The difference between the Greek idea and the Christian one, however, is that in the latter one's burden or cross in life can become one's destiny or spiritual goal. If it was the blind man's fate or burden to be selected by God to be born blind, it was also part of his destiny, a destiny that was fulfilled when Christ healed him. In such a way John's Gospel redeems human beings from the hopelessness of an inexorable fate that so weighed down the Greeks and offers a spiritual hope even in the midst of the most difficult circumstances.

After telling the story of how the blind man was healed, John goes on to the story of the conflict this engendered with the Pharisees and concludes with some powerful statements by Jesus. As with the story of the healing of the man by the pool of Bethzatha, so with this story, the historical material is used as a springboard for presenting the reader with spiritual truths.

The story begins with the curiosity of the neighbors and people who had known this blind man for many years and now saw that he had been cured. They ask him to tell them how this happened, and he does, explaining to them carefully the facts of the case: A man called Jesus made a paste, daubed his eyes, and sent him to the pool of Siloam, and then he gained his sight. The people then bring him to the Pharisees, who, being the authorities in such matters, should know about this. The Pharisees ask him to tell his story to them, which he does, again sticking carefully to the facts. As it happened, Jesus had healed the blind man on the sabbath, when no one was supposed to work. This upset some of the Pharisees who said, "This man cannot be from God; he does not keep the sabbath." But others, impressed by the healing, said, "But how could a sinner produce signs like this?" So they asked the healed man what he thought, and he, not caring about the negative judgments of the Pharisees who complained that the healing was done on the sabbath, declared forthrightly, "He is a prophet" (that is, a holy man from God).

We now have in the story a group of people who are identified with entrenched ideas, ideas on which rest their personal authority, and who are consequently disturbed by certain facts that would seem to contradict their belief system. They respond to this by trying to discredit the facts; they send for the man's parents. Evidently they hope they will say he never was blind, or at least provide some excuse for a rejection of the man's story.

However, the parents stick to the truth: he is our son, he was blind, now he sees. Then, afraid of the Pharisees, they urge them to talk to their son themselves.

Again they send for the man who had been healed, and say, "Give glory to God! For our part, we know that this man is a sinner." They are inviting the man to agree that Jesus must be a sinner and give him a "way out" by inviting him to give the glory to God. Now, the man by the pool of Bethzatha, angry that Jesus had cured him, tried his best to get Jesus into trouble, as we have seen earlier, but this man has courage: resolutely he repeats the facts: "I only know that I was blind and now I see."

When confronted by uncomfortable truths the human tendency is to deny the facts on which the truths rest, but this man will not deny the real facts in the case, not even to save himself from the consequences of making the Pharisees his enemies. Angered and frustrated, the Pharisees press him to repeat his story, no doubt hoping he will tell it somewhat differently this time and give them pretext for discrediting his testimony. But since the man has been telling the truth, it is not difficult for him to tell the same story again. Now he takes the offensive and challenges the Pharisees regarding their motives: "I have told you once and you wouldn't listen. Why do you want to hear it all again?" Then he adds, no doubt sarcastically, "Do you want to become his disciples too?"

Now the Pharisees become abusive, for when we cannot win an argument we tend to resort to a personal attack on our opponent (in logic this is called the argument *ad hominem* — to the man). As the Pharisees press the man still further it only leads him to draw his own conclusions about Jesus more deeply, finally concluding that Jesus must be from God, for otherwise he could not have performed the healing miracle. Angrily the Pharisees drive away a man whose experience they cannot deny and whose character they cannot destroy.

Then comes the story's great finale: Jesus appears again in the story and makes a pronouncement that is both enigmatic and profound.

> It is for judgment
> that I have come into this world,
> so those without sight may see
> and those with sight turn blind. (9:39)

It is precisely those who believe they see clearly and know everything and are in possession of the truth who are in fact spiritually blind. On the other hand, those who recognize their need and their blindness are the ones who are open to see the meaning of the Christ. It is the old demon ego again: when it believes it has all the answers, it is closed to the truth.

Some of the Pharisees heard Jesus say this and it makes them uncomfortable. Surely, they think, he can't be talking about us? Yet their suspicion is that perhaps he is. So they come to him for reassurance and say, "We are not blind, surely?" (1:40-41). Jesus then replies with another powerful statement:

> Blind? If you were,
> you would not be guilty.
> But since you say, "We see,"
> your guilt remains.

Psychologically, the great sin is not the fact that we do not possess all the truth. Who can say that he or she possesses all the truth? The great psychological blindness comes when we mistake our ignorance and error for truth. If only we can say, "Yes, I am blind ... in many respects I do not see the truth," then the way is open to us to be healed of our blindness. But when we persevere in the erroneous conviction that we see and understand all there is to be known about ourselves, life, and God, then we are truly blind.

~ 20 ~

SONS OF GOD
Parable of the Good Shepherd
John 10

THE TENTH CHAPTER OF JOHN'S GOSPEL is divided into two sections. The first is the Parable of the Good Shepherd. The second is another dispute between Jesus and his adversaries in which Jesus makes an important and unusual statement. We will look first at the text of the parable, and then to its symbolism, then we will examine the debate between Jesus and the Pharisees, and finally we will summarize a psychological-theological development in which one statement Jesus made to his adversaries played a central role.

The Parable of the Good Shepherd is based on images that were familiar to the people of Jesus' time: sheep, the sheepfold with its gate, the dangers to the sheep, and the role of the shepherd. In his parable Jesus turns this familiar setting into a powerful symbol for the passage of the soul through this life and for the importance of himself as the guide.

It begins with the matter of the legitimate and illegitimate ways of entering the sheepfold (v. 1). The gate is the proper way to enter and leave the sheepfold, but some people enter another way, and anyone who does this is a thief and a brigand. The expression "thief and a brigand" may sound redundant, but in Greek the word for thief, *kleptēs* (from which we derive our word "kleptomaniac"), refers to a person who steals by craft and fraud, while the word translated "brigand" is from the Greek *lēstēs* and refers to a person who robs by violent acts. The illegitimate people who would lead the sheep to their ruin do not enter by the gate because the gate is watched by a gatekeeper (v. 3), but the true shepherd enters through the gate because he is known to both the gatekeeper and the sheep, who recognize his voice and come to him when he calls. The sheep then follow the voice of the true shepherd as he leads them safely to pasture, but they will not follow the false stranger because they do not recognize his voice (v. 5).

The usual tendency with this parable is to see the sheep as allegorical symbols for Christians. Since sheep are placid, plodding animals that are not very bright this doesn't cast Christians in a very positive light. It is more in keeping with the parable, however, not to regard the sheep allegorically, but to understand them as symbols, a distinction that we made in the introduction. It will be remembered that something allegorical lets one known thing stand in the place of something else that is known; a symbol uses something known to refer to something largely or entirely unknown. In this case the sheep would not be the Christians, but our own instincts. Sheep may not be very bright, but they are bright enough on the instinctual level to know the voice of their shepherd and distinguish it from someone else's voice. The parable then is saying that within each of us there is an irrational, instinctual capacity to recognize the true from the false, and if we would only consult it we would follow the true guides of life. It will be remembered from the introduction that this was exactly the way Origen understood the parable. For him the sheep symbolized our own irrational and instinctual nature, which needs guidance but which also has a certain sense of direction and the capacity to distinguish the true guide and the true way from the false. All those persons who have within them, and follow, their instinctually knowing nature are the "sheep" referred to later in the parable in verses 14–16.

The thieves and brigands are usually identified with false leaders, specifically, people with the wrong or heretical teachings. It is certainly true that the world is full of egocentric people who are willing and anxious to be false guides to us and who will rob us not only of our worldly wealth but sometimes our very souls. Examples range all the way from Adolf Hitler to more subtle false leaders who like to play the role of guru to others and lead them down a false spiritual path. Unfortunately, even psychotherapists and clergy can be included among such false guides. Such false guides are never more dangerous, of course, than when they are unconscious of their true motives. They gain power over us not only because we have failed to consult our truest instincts (our "sheep"), but because our egocentricity plays into their egocentricity. We are often ready, as we have noted, to project the creative Center into someone else who then carries it for us so that we will not have to undertake the burden of our own conscious development. An unscrupulous spiritual "thief or brigand" will gladly do this for us since it plays into his hands. Kunkel called such people "idols" because others project the Center into them; he regarded all such arrangements as forms of idolatry. However, the thieves and robbers are not only people outside of us; they are also those egocentric propensities inside of us that lead us astray, the false and tempting urges and voices that call for us to deny the truth in order to fulfill egocentric desires. Origen saw this too and referred to the thieves and robbers as everything within us that is imperfect and defective because of our lack of consciousness.

Christ appears in the parable first in the symbol of the gate. It is not to be wondered at that Christ can be symbolized first in this parable as the gate and then as the shepherd, since we have already seen that it requires innumerable images to convey the meaning of Christ. A gate either opens to let someone in or out or closes to exclude people or confine them. Not only are gates important in our waking life; they also appear as important symbols in our dreams. For instance, people often dream of running to catch a train (which would take them symbolically further on the way to their spiritual destination). They arrive at the last moment at the railroad station but there is the gate, and by the gate the gatekeeper, who sees to it that only those who have tickets get through. That is, only those who have paid the price of consciousness are allowed to continue on the way. Christ as the gate not only is the opening through which the legitimate sheep find their way; he is also the power that bars the way to those who are not fit to find the way.

Later, in verse 11, the image for Christ changes from that of the gate to that of the good shepherd. The good shepherd plays here the archetypal role of the guide of the soul, another image that often appears in our dreams as well as a variety of myths and fairy tales. Christ as the good shepherd does not serve egocentric purposes, as do the false thieves and robbers; the sign and seal of this is his willingness to lay down his life for the sheep.

Just as a faithful shepherd might die in defense of his flock, so Christ is willing to die on behalf of his spiritual flock. This, of course, is a veiled reference to Jesus' forthcoming crucifixion, but it may also be understood more symbolically. As Jungian analyst Edward Edinger once pointed out, the Center consents to being broken and divided, as it were, in order that it can be assimilated by us, just as Christ in the Eucharist is broken and divided symbolically in the breaking of the host, so that his reality may be disseminated within and among the worshipers. All of this is part of the Christian *mystērion* (mystery) which is further described in verses 17 and 18: that reality we call Christ is available to us in very small portions, of which we partake inasmuch as we are able, and it is like a sacrifice made by God for our sakes that this can happen. And in fact in all psychological and spiritual advances in consciousness it works this way: the truth is assimilated only bit by bit.

In verse 14 we have another important nuance of meaning in the use of the word "know": "I know my own, and my own know me, just as the Father knows me and I know the Father." As might be suspected, the Greek word chosen here for the word "know" is *ginōskō*, which means intimate, experiential knowledge.

In verse 16 we read of "other sheep" who are not of this fold, but will also be taken in. The most obvious interpretation is that Jesus was referring to people who were not Jews but would also belong to him. Psychologically this is a way of saying that the Center is a reality in all humankind. Christ is within all of us, regardless of our color or religious persuasion. This is the basis for the archetype of Oneness that we will explore more deeply when we get to John 17.

These are powerful words that Jesus is saying, and they force his listeners to make a decision about which way they will go and what they will believe. Since the entrenched ego resists changes, many of the people who heard the Parable of the Good Shepherd were frightened. The quickest way to avoid the parable was to discredit the one who told it, which is why some of those listening to Jesus said of him: "He is possessed, he is raving: why bother to listen to him?" (v. 20). But others, while not yet fully persuaded, were at least willing to ponder the parable's meaning. They look at the facts of the situation and say, "These are not the words of a man possessed by a devil; could a devil open the eyes of the blind?" (v. 21).

John continues with a typical bit of historical reflection followed by a discourse. In verses 22 and 23 we are told not only that the feast of Dedication was being celebrated in Jerusalem, but John adds the detail that it was winter. Then comes the challenge that Jesus' adversaries put to him: "If you are the Christ, tell us plainly" (v. 25). This gives Jesus an opportunity to expand on the matter of his relationship to the Father and on the parable of the sheep. The statement on his relationship with the Father concludes with: "The Father and I are one" (v. 30). This is the strongest statement Jesus has yet made of his virtual identity with God, yet it stops short of the idea of absolute identification. It shows that Jesus' power and will are the same as the Father's and suggests a still more fundamental unity that implies a greater-than-human relationship.

His opponents do not miss the implication of Jesus' statement and pick up stones with which to stone him — the penalty for blasphemy. They believe him to be virtually equating himself with God and can understand this only as the greatest blasphemy against all that they hold to be sacred. This gives Jesus a chance to expand still further on his meaning. As he does so, he seems to have a certain sympathy with their inability to accept his statement of his proximity — if not identification — with the divine nature, for in verses 37–38, in which he appeals to his works for a testimony, he says almost tenderly, "If I am not doing my Father's work, there is no need to believe me; but if I am doing it, then even if you refuse to believe in me, at least believe in the work I do." He then adds a somewhat softer statement than "the Father and I are one": "then you will know for sure that the Father is in me and I am in the Father." One can sense an appeal in these words for friendship and understanding and can see in them an attempt to mitigate the polemical nature of these previous disputes. But to no avail. His adversaries want to arrest him, and Jesus is forced to elude them, since the time for his crucifixion has not yet come. He takes refuge on the far side of the Jordan River, and here, among the simple folk in the country, many people are persuaded by his personality and his words and come to believe in him.

In the midst of this discussion, however, Jesus makes a powerful statement: "Is it not written in your Law: *I said, you are gods?* So the Law uses the word gods of those to whom the word of God was addressed, and scripture cannot be rejected." The passage from the Old Testament Jesus has in mind is Psalm 82:6 in which

God is addressing the divine council of the "sons of the Most High" and declares to them, "I say, 'You are gods, children of the Most High, all of you; nevertheless, you shall die like mortals, and fall like any prince'" (NRSV).

This passage is of special interest because it brings us to the important idea in the early church of "deification" (*theōsis*) or, as it is sometimes called, "divinization" (*theōpoiēsis*). For reasons that we will examine shortly we hear little about this idea in the Western church, but in the first centuries of Christianity the idea of the deification of the soul through Christ was widespread, especially in the Greek-speaking East, and even today the idea of deification is central to the theology of the Eastern Orthodox Church. Deification means that the human soul is saved from its fallen state of mortality, corruption, and sin through a mystical union with Christ. This process, which is known as deification, is accomplished in the thinking of the Eastern Orthodox Church through the death and rebirth of baptism, the infusion of the life of Christ into the soul through the sacrament of the Eucharist, through a life of prayer that opens the soul up to God, through winning the battle against the egocentric sins of pride, envy, and malice, and through the increasing awareness of the soul that the temporal things of this world are pale reflections of the things that are eternal in the spiritual realm.[1]

The resulting process of transformation is energized and illuminated by the Holy Spirit, which, as another expression of God, shows the soul the path it is to follow and corrects the soul when it strays from this path. Thus the soul, which as we have noted always has the image of God within it, now moves into the likeness (archetype) of God. In this way a process continues that constitutes the highest human destiny and contains the meaning of life.

It is important to note that in the early church this was the work that Christ came to accomplish and this was the reason for the incarnation. For even as Christ became a human being, so human beings could now become like him; this was the Christian *mystērion* (mystery). The work of salvation therefore was accomplished not only on the cross but by virtue of the entire incarnation, life, death, and resurrection of Christ. For Eastern

---

1. Georgios I. Mantzaridis, *The Deification of Man* (Crestwood, N.Y.: St. Vladimir's Seminary Press, 1984), 33.

Christianity especially the incarnation did not simply point to the cross but was in itself a source of salvation for humankind since our fallen human nature had first to be restored to its essential nature by being commingled with Christ's divine nature before the salvation of the soul, conceived of as divination, could be possible.

Biblical references in support of the idea of deification include all those biblical passages (too many to enumerate here) that refer to the spiritual goal of life as the completion of the soul. The many Greek words in the New Testament that stem from the Greek word *telos* fall into this category. The *telos*, as we noted before, is the end, the goal toward which the soul moves and strives. When, for instance, Christ says, "You must therefore be perfect just as your heavenly Father is perfect" (Matt. 5:48), the word "perfect" is the Greek word *teleios*, one of the derivatives from *telos*. The word does not mean "perfect" as without blemish, but perfected as brought to one's completion or end state. Also undergirding the idea of deification are all those many biblical passages that dwell at length on personal transformation. Hebrews 4:12–16, 2 Peter 1:4, Luke 20:35–36, Romans 8:29, and Galatians 4:9 are examples, but it would take us beyond the scope of this work to cite all of this teaching about transformation in the New Testament. Most of all, the idea of deification rests upon the Fourth Gospel, which breathes the idea of it on virtually every page.

The idea of deification finds many representatives among the Fathers, beginning with Justin Martyr. For instance, Clement of Alexandria, speaking of the Gnostic, by which he meant the Christian who was "in the know," declared in a statement that embodied John 10:34, "In this way it is possible for the (Christian) Gnostic [i.e., a "Christian in-the-know"] already to have become God." I said, "You are gods, and the sons of the highest."[2] Clement's successor Origen, in discussing Christ as the divine Logos who leads people into all knowledge and truth, said that in so doing Christ imparted a new life, so that, in the words of historian Adolph Harnack, "humankind might now partake of his life and themselves become divine through being interwoven with the divine essence."[3]

In his great work *Contra Celsus* Origen wrote that the salva-

---

2. *The Stromata* 4.23.
3. Adolph Harnack, *History of Dogma* (New York: Dover Publications, 1961), 2:368. Cf. Origen, *Contra Celsus* 3:28.

tion of believers will begin "when they see that from Him there began the union of the divine with the human nature, in order that the human, by communion with the divine, might rise to be divine, not in Jesus alone, but in all those who not only believe but enter upon the life which Jesus taught, and which elevates to friendship with God and communion with Him every one who lives according to the precepts of Jesus."[4]

Even before Origen, Irenaeus said, "Jesus Christ became what we are in order that we might become what he himself is."[5] "It was for this reason," Irenaeus further argued, "that the Son of God, although he was perfect, passed through the state of infancy in common with the rest of mankind, partaking of it thus not for His own benefit, but for that of the infantile stage of man's existence, in order that man might be able to receive Him."[6] Indeed, elsewhere Irenaeus argues that Christ passed through *all* the stages of human life for this purpose — even that he lived to the age of fifty — in order that everywhere in life we human beings would be able to be transformed by partaking mystically of his reality.

Hippolytus took the idea even further, emphasizing that the transformative Christ lay within us and is available to anyone who comes to know his or her own soul:

> For thou hast become God; for whatever sufferings thou didst undergo while being a man, these He gave to thee, because thou wast of mortal mould, but whatever it is consistent with God to impart, these God has promised to bestow upon thee, because thou hast been deified, and begotten unto immortality. This constitutes the import of the proverb, "Know thyself," that is, discover God within thyself, for He has formed thee after His own image. For with the knowledge of self is conjoined the being an object of God's knowledge, for thou art called by the Deity Himself.[7]

The teaching about deification was especially prominent among the Christian thinkers of the Eastern church. Virtually all the major Fathers in the East spoke this language in explaining the mystery of Christ's redemption of humankind. So Athanasius

---

4. *Contra Celsus* 3.28.
5. Harnack, *History of Dogma*, 2:288. See Irenaeus *Against Heresies* v, preface.
6. *Against Heresies* 4.38.
7. *Elucidations* 10.30.

says, "For he was made man that we might be made God."[8] And in one of his letters, he writes, "For he has become man, that he might deify us in himself." And still again, "And we are deified not by partaking of the body of some man, but by receiving the Body of the Word Himself."[9]

Gregory of Nazianzen wrote similarly, "We become like Christ, since Christ also became like us: we become gods on his account, since he also became man for our sake."[10] Gregory of Nyssa also expounded the same idea in his great work *On the Soul and the Resurrection.*[11]

As we have noted the idea of deification was the cornerstone for the early church's idea of the Eucharist as a *mystērion* in which the worshiper was transformed into the likeness of Christ by partaking of Christ's mystical body and blood in the sacrament. For this reason Ignatius called the Eucharist the "medicine of immortality" (*pharmaokōn athanasias*).[12] This view became dominant through all of the Eastern church and much of the West until after Augustine. In the words of Adolph Harnack, "The whole transaction (i.e., the Eucharist), which is based on the Incarnation, is thus beyond a doubt itself the mystery of the deification (*theōsis*)."[13]

As mentioned, the idea of deification dwindled in the Western church after Augustine, though he himself was influenced by the idea. In the West the idea of Christian salvation became more rationalistic and legalistic, while in the East it seems more in tune with the early church and certainly with John's Gospel. With the advent of Protestantism the mystical element in Christianity, with some exceptions, retreated still further, and salvation theory was reduced virtually to the significance of the cross alone, where Christ paid a legalistic debt to God on behalf of sinful humanity. The more Christianity lost its mystical and psychological dimension the more extreme became its narrow legalistic thinking. In the East, while the saving benefits of the cross were recognized for their great importance, the idea of salvation was much broader, and, in the manner that we have seen, was expressed as a deification of the soul.

---

8. *Incarnation of the Word* 54. The word "we might be made God" is the Greek *theōpoiēthomen.*
9. *Letters* 60.4, 61.2.
10. *Orat* 1.5; also *Orat* 40.45.
11. See, e.g., *On the Soul and the Resurrection,* The Great Catechism 26.
12. Harnack, *History of Dogma,* 4:286.
13. Ibid.

To this day in the Greek Orthodox Church and other Eastern Orthodox Churches, the idea of deification is central, and the
Eucharist is still referred to in the ancient way as a *mystērion*,
expressing the ineffable mystery of the union of Christ with the
soul, with its consequential deification. Demetrios J. Constantelos, professor of history and religious studies at Stockton College,
writes:

> The Holy Spirit's power leads a human person to achieve
> the final aim of the Christian life, the *theōsis*, or deification,
> of human nature, a notion very dear to the Orthodox. *Theōsis*
> means life in God, the transformation of a human being into
> a little god within God. This notion is in perfect agreement
> with the Scriptures. As mentioned earlier, people picked up
> stones to cast at Christ. When Jesus asked why they were
> doing this, the people answered that it was because he was
> insulting God by calling himself God. And Jesus answered,
> "Is it not written in your Law, 'I said, you are gods'?" (John
> 10:34; Ps. 82:6).

Thus Jesus himself calls man a little god. This teaching has
been taken over by the Fathers and the tradition of the church. It
constitutes an important element of the eschatological teaching
of the Greek Orthodox Church.[14]

The similarities between the ancient doctrine of deification
and the modern idea of individuation as conceived by Jung and
Kunkel are striking. In both cases the soul of the individual yearns
to grow, and in both cases there is a source of energy for this
growth hidden away, as it were, in the unconscious. In the case
of the early Christians there was in the soul the image of God
that could transform the person into the likeness of God, and this
would be analogous to the image in the unconscious of the whole
person, or Self, which, according to Jung and Kunkel, is there
from the beginning and is the source of energy and guidance for
our transformation into a whole and completed personality. In
both cases the work of transformation does not lie within the capacities of the unaided human ego that must be aided by divine
power, symbolized by Jung and Kunkel as the energy of the Self,
in order to attain its goal. In both cases the egocentric faults of

---

14. Demetrios J. Constantelos, *Understanding the Greek Orthodox Church* (New York:
Seabury Press, 1982).

the ego must be overcome, and focus must be made on the dynamic inner Center. In both cases the darkness of ignorance must be lifted and a new consciousness must develop.

There are also, of course, many differences. Many of the ideas of modern psychology were unknown to the early Christians, and, in turn, their psychology sounds strange to our modern ear in many respects. Perhaps the most important difference, however, is that the early Christians believed the process of transformation was accomplished only through Christ, while Jung and Kunkel would say that it was a process open to all persons whether they openly confessed a belief in Christ or not, provided they fulfilled the necessary psychological and spiritual requirements. Kunkel, however, would say that named or unnamed the dynamic inner Center that furnished the energy for individuation was coincident with what the Christians would know as the Christ within. Thus when St. Paul said, "It is no longer I who live, but Christ who lives in me" (Gal. 2:20), he was referring to the shifting of the center of personality from the egocentric ego to the divine center within us all.

∼ 21 ∼

LIFE FROM DEATH
The Raising of Lazarus
John 11

IN THE INTRODUCTION we spoke of the various motifs that run through John's Gospel. One of the most important of these is that of life vis-à-vis death. The story of the raising of Lazarus from the dead, next only to the story of the resurrection of Christ, is the most important statement John makes on this vital theme. But already John has said a great deal about life and death. This is an appropriate place to summarize the comments on this motif that we have already made.

We have observed that the Greek language has two distinct words for life, *bios* and *zōē*, and that the former refers to the phenomenon of life in its outward manifestation while the latter refers to the living principle of life and is used in an inward, mystical sense with reference to the spiritual life. An entity that has *bios* will certainly die, but an entity that has *zōē* will have the capacity for immortal life because it partakes of an immortal, life-giving principle. Thus being infused with *zōē* is a necessary prelude to participation in eternal life, which is always contrasted in John with death. But eternal life is not to be identified solely with existence beyond the grave; rather, it is a spiritual state in which a person begins to participate here-and-now in this earthly existence. Death likewise is not reserved for the dissolution of the body, but in John's Gospel is a state into which a person can be moving in this present existence. In any given moment it can be said that we are moving either toward spiritual life or toward spiritual death, for this death relates to the death of the soul as well as to the death of the body.

The soul dies when it lives in darkness. This darkness is not natural darkness, but is the darkness brought upon the soul by ignorance and participation in evil. In contrast, the life lived through the Christ brings a spiritual enlightenment in which both consciousness and conscience[1] are strengthened. Thus the soul lives continually poised between the opposites of life-light-consciousness and death-darkness-sin. These are not the kind of opposites that can be conjoined together, for they involve choice and discrimination. They are not like two colors, say blue and red, that may be blended to produce a third color, purple, but are like two roads or ways that the traveler meets in his or her journey; only one can be taken, and the other must be put aside. The person who partakes of the living principle of life becomes alive, but the person who does evil becomes evil and that is death. In this way the traveler through this world is confronted all the time with the fact of judgment (*krisis*).

This motif is an old one in the Bible, although John has brought it to a new development. We meet it, for instance, in Deuteronomy 30:19, in which Yahweh says to the people of Israel:

> Today, I call heaven and earth to witness against you: I am offering you life or death, blessing or curse. Choose life, then, so that you and your descendants may live, in the love of Yahweh your God, obeying his voice, holding fast to him; for in this your life consists. (NJB)

We also meet with the idea in association with Sophia, the eternal Wisdom of God, whom, as we have seen, coexists with God and was believed to have incarnated as the Logos in Christ. Sophia says to us:

> For whoever finds me finds life,
>   and obtains the favour of Yahweh;
> but whoever misses me harms himself,
>   all who hate me are in love with death.
>   (Prov. 8:35–36 NJB)

We also find the idea in the synoptic Gospels. A man whom Jesus calls to follow him says that he will come but first he has

---

1. The biblical word *syneidēsis*, for instance, refers to both consciousness and conscience. One cannot exist without the other.

to bury his father. But Jesus says to him, "Leave the dead to bury their dead; your duty is to go and spread the news of the kingdom of God" (Luke 9:50, NJB). With regard to this passage Irenaeus says, "He says, 'Let the dead bury their dead,' because they do not have the spirit which quickens man."[2] This "spirit" is the *pneuma* we met in John 3, who is so closely associated with *zōē*, the living spirit of life.

We will now proceed to examine more closely the story of the raising of Lazarus, which is a centerpiece of John's presentation of the *mystērion* of life vis-à-vis death.

Verses 1–3: These verses set the stage for what follows. Note the historical details: the name of the village and of Mary and Martha, and the identification of Mary as the one who in a previous incident had anointed Jesus' feet with ointment and wiped them with her hair. Is Mary the same as the woman in Luke 7:37 who was a sinner? Scholars tell us that was unlikely, but it is not beyond the realm of possibility.

Verse 4: The Jerusalem Bible says that Jesus' statement "This sickness will end, not in death but in God's glory, and through it the Son of God will be glorified" has a double meaning. The miracle that Jesus will perform will glorify him, but that miracle will also bring about Jesus' death on the cross, which in turn will lead to a further glorification. We are in a position to see the double implication of what Jesus says, but at the time the disciples who were with Jesus must have been mystified. We are justified in assuming that one of them later told the author of our Gospel what Jesus had said. It is also noteworthy that the expression "the Son of God" has, in Greek, the article before "Son" and before "God." The emphasis is thus: *the* (unique) Son of *the* (one and only) God.

Verses 5–7: Jesus receives the message that Lazarus is critically ill, yet he lingers for two days before departing. During these two days Lazarus will die, but Jesus is not perturbed by his delay for he knows what he will do. All of this is still more setting of the stage for the miracle of resurrection that will follow.

Verses 8–10: The disciples caution Jesus about going back to Judaea for fear of his enemies who wish to stone him. Jesus' comment about the twelve hours in the day when it is safe to walk are often regarded as referring to the fact that since his ap-

---

2. Irenaeus, *Against Heresies* 5.9.11.

pointed time for death has not yet arrived it is still safe for him to return to Judaea. No doubt this is so, but the rather cryptic references to light suggest a more mystical meaning as well: the ordinary person, who has only the light of the world (*kosmos*), can walk safely in the day but not in the night. But, by implication, the one who has the light that is of God, and not of this world alone, will not stumble by day or night and so does not fear death.

Verses 11–16: The story stresses as strongly as possible that Lazarus is dead. At first Jesus uses a euphemism for being dead, saying that Lazarus is resting or asleep. When the disciples don't understand he uses plain language: "Lazarus is dead" (*thanatos*). The point of raising Lazarus from the dead is to confirm the faith of the disciples. Faith in what? Jesus' power? Yes, but more than that. It will be a confirmation of faith in resurrection. Just what this faith entails we will examine more closely when we come to the story of Jesus' resurrection. For now suffice it to say that the world of apparent appearances, that world in which you and I are mostly contained, a world in which death seems final and ultimate, is not the final reality. The final reality, which in the language of the early Christians is the resurrection, will break through in a lesser way in the miracle of Lazarus's resurrection, and in a much greater way in the story of Christ's resurrection.

Verses 17–25: The story continues with more convincing historical detail. The four days Lazarus had been in the tomb ensures that his body will be decayed. The statement that Bethany is only two miles from Jerusalem adds to the factuality of the story. The tension is heightened between the factual details of this world we perceive through our physical senses and the unseen spiritual world that will break through in the resurrection. Friends come to Mary and Martha from Jerusalem to console them in their grief, much as friends would come to one of us today for that purpose. It is a very human story and setting. When the word reaches the two sisters that Jesus is coming, Martha goes out to meet him, but Mary doesn't, perhaps because she is hurt that Jesus did not come earlier when he might have healed her brother and prevented his death. Martha also seems to reproach Jesus, for she says, "If you had been here, my brother would not have died." But she quickly adds a statement of faith, "but I know that, even now, whatever you ask of God, he will grant you." She can't quite say: "If you ask

it of God, my brother will be raised from the dead." Apparently
that remains for her too much of an impossibility. Jesus says to re-
assure her and prepare her for the coming miracle, "Your brother
will rise again." Martha replies, "I know he will rise again at
the resurrection on the last day." This comment by Martha (11:24)
shows that a general belief in life after death existed among many
of the Jews at the time of Jesus, the Sadducees, however, being
notable exceptions. This rather vague hope in an ultimate resurrection of the dead does not console Martha. Perhaps the whole
idea is too remote and too uncertain in her mind. In typical Johannine fashion, this statement by Martha provides the occasion
for a pronouncement by Jesus:

I am the resurrection.
If anyone believes in me, even though he dies he will live,
and whoever lives and believes in me
will never die.
Do you believe this?

The Fourth Gospel calls upon us not to believe simply in
Jesus' resurrection, but in *resurrection*. Resurrection, as we will
ultimately see before we reach the end of John's Gospel, is a certain state of being, much more than a single event, no matter how
startling that event. Note that the resurrection is conjoined with
"the life" — and here we are back at our word *zōē*, that is, the
living principle of life.

The statement "whoever lives and believes in me will never
die" is particularly important. The expression "in me" is put
strongly in the Greek (by the use of *eis eme*). It means "lives into
or within." The meaning is that if one is contained in the ineffable
reality of Christ, there is no death. This does not mean that the
physical body does not die, but it does mean that if we partake
of *zōē* the soul and the spiritual body do not die. We are called
upon to make a mystical entrance into Christ, to be spiritually
contained in an ineffable reality. The condition of this is "belief,"
or faith. As we already noted, this is not a matter of affirming
creeds, but is more like a "transference" to Christ. If one perseveres in the natural motion of the soul toward God, putting one's
energies into this, it constitutes faith. This is not a faith that is
opposed to knowledge, but is that quality of faith that leads to
knowledge. It is this faith that leads to the mystical identification
with Christ, to the *theōsis*, or deification, of which we spoke ear-

lier. It can be said that this is the goal of individuation, when seen from a Christian perspective.

Verses 27–44: Once again John uses many details as he continues his story: the words Martha used in speaking to her sister to tell her of Jesus' arrival; the way she spoke in a low voice; the presence of the friends; how Mary threw herself at Jesus' feet and reproached him for not coming earlier. Such details have the ring of historicity; they also draw the reader into the scene and make us feel as though we are immediate observers. As a storyteller, John is a master.

In verses 34 and 35, and again in verse 28, we are told that Jesus was deeply moved at Mary's anguish and at the demise of his friend Lazarus, so much so that his sigh of pain and sympathy came "straight from the heart." One wonders why, since Jesus knows what he is going to do and knows that this death is not the final negation that others think it to be. But this is no Docetic Christ,[3] but a real human being, with all the range of human emotions, although at the same time he is the Deity who is a God of heart and compassion for the sufferings of his/her children. The fact is that we do not comprehend the greater mysteries nor find the larger insights without passing through the pathos and suffering of life. A statement by the Greek playwright Aeschylus helps us understand the need for the pathos and the pain: "He who learns must suffer. And even in our sleep pain that will not forget falls drop by drop upon the heart. And in our despair, against our will, comes wisdom, by the awful grace of God."[4]

In verse 38 we are told that the place of burial was a cave. In the ancient world caves were special places where sacred and mystery-laden events took place. For instance, in Greece Zeus was said, according to one version of the story, to have been born and raised in a cave. Likewise the mystery rites of Eleusis, which were devoted to Demeter, the Mother Goddess, were celebrated in caves. As we have already noted, Christian tradition says that the stable in which Christ was born was in fact a cave. It also

---

3. The Gnostics taught that Christ was not really human, but only seemed to have a human body and appearance; therefore he never really experienced human emotions. This teaching is known as "Docetism."

4. Aeschylus, *Agamemnon*, Second Choral Ode. Many of the early Church Fathers regarded the Greek philosophers as inspired by the Logos, as we noted in a previous chapter, and Aeschylus was one of the most profound Greek commentators on the mysteries of life.

says that Christ taught the Lord's Prayer to the disciples in a cave, that Mary, the mother of Jesus, was buried in a cave, and that the Book of Revelation was revealed to John in a cave on the island of Patmos in the Aegean Sea (to this day Christians still make pilgrimages to a cave on this island where it is believed the revelation took place). As dark and mysterious caverns deep within the earth, caves are full of *yin*, that is, of feminine essence in the sense that we described in an earlier chapter. A return to the cave at death is symbolic of a return to God as the Mother, where life is born and to which life returns in order to be born again. So it is the place of the Christian *mystērion*.

In verse 42 we have the account of Jesus' prayer. Jesus prays as one who is in intimate communion with the object and source of his prayer. For the others, the Father is remote and unknown, for, as we have seen, the Father in John's Gospel is God as that which is ineffable and unknowable by the limited human senses and spiritual awareness. This, according to John, is the major reason why Christ came into the world: that through him the Father might become real and God's ultimate nature be revealed.

The final verse of the story describes in lurid fashion the appearance of the dead man — now raised to life — emerging from the depths of the cave still clothed in his burial shroud. It is a scene worthy of comparison with certain scenes from Shakespeare, or from the scene in the Old Testament in which the ghost of Samuel summoned up from Sheol for Saul's benefit, emerges from the shades of the underworld (see 1 Samuel 28). The whole event is deeply numinous. It must have affected deeply the consciousness of those who beheld the event and is intended to stir the imagination of the contemporary reader so that he or she is similarly affected by the numinosity of the power and reality of the unseen spiritual world that lies hidden just behind the veil of material reality. It is this world, ordinarily inaccessible to the consciousness of human beings because of the limitations of our senses and our minds, that is partially opened to Mary and Martha by the acts of the Lord. In such ways is faith quickened and true *gnōsis* stirred to life.

The story of the death and raising of Lazarus can also be placed in a broader setting: it is one of a type of stories that tell us that new life can only emerge when there has been the death of the old life. The Latin word for this death as the archetypal prelude to renewal is *mortificatio*, and it was an especially important word in later Christian mystical lore.[5] The *mortificatio* was an experience through which every soul had to pass if it was to eventually transcend its limited and broken state and become enlightened and completed. Looked at it in this way, Lazarus, who passed through death and burial and emerged to new life, is also the soul who must endure these same experiences. This is why Jesus weeps, for experiences of *mortificatio* are inevitably filled with a pain, grief, and suffering that cannot be bypassed. The way to all resurrection, all spiritual life, growth, and wholeness, must pass through the cave of the dark Mother who seems to take life away — only in the end to give it back to us renewed. John knows about this spiritual truth and, of course, will in time take us through the depths of the *mortificatio* experience in Christ's death on the cross and burial in the cave.

---

5. For an excellent account of the *mortificatio*, see Edward F. Edinger's *Anatomy of the Psyche* (La Salle, Ill.: Open Court Publishing Co., 1985), chap. 6.

∽ 22 ∽

THE ENIGMA OF JUDAS
The Anointing at Bethany
John 11:45–12:11

OUR PRINCIPAL FOCUS in this chapter will be on Judas, but some comments on the text in general are in order. Verses 11:24–54 inform the reader of the decision of the authorities to bring about Jesus' death. While some of the people believed in Jesus, others did not. The authorities, anxious and threatened by Jesus' popularity with a considerable portion of the people and afraid that belief in him may spread, call a meeting to decide what to do. The only answer seems to be to bring about his death, but this was a radical step to take. Caiaphas, the high priest in the year in which Jesus died, swings the balance in favor of the decision for Jesus' execution when he says "...it is better for one man to die for the people, than for the whole nation to be destroyed" (v. 49). Caiaphas means that if Jesus is allowed to live he might subvert the religious faith of all the nation, and to prevent that from happening it is better if he dies. However, the way Caiaphas words his statement amounts to an unconscious oracular prediction that Jesus' death will indeed be on behalf of all people, but not in the way Caiaphas supposes, for by dying, Jesus made the benefits of the Son of God available to people through the ages.

Chapter 12 begins with a heightening of tension: it is the Passover and many of the country people coming up for the feast are looking for Jesus. There is much talk: "Will he come, or will he not?" All of this, in addition to being historical detail, can be understood as part of John's artistry as a narrator; he has a keen sense of the dramatic, and the drama intensifies as we are told that the agents of Jesus' enemies are now looking for him. It is an interesting detail that those who come are mostly from the country. Are they more simple in their attitudes and so more open to faith?

Meanwhile Jesus has gone to Bethany — not more than a few miles from Jerusalem — to be with Mary and Martha and Lazarus. In verse 9 we learn that word spreads among the people that he is there, and many of them come to see this wonderworker and also Lazarus, the man who was dead but is alive again. When the Pharisees hear this they decide that Lazarus must also be killed. So when Caiaphas said "one man is to die" the ante is now raised from one person to two people. So it is when the bloodletting starts; it has its own energy, and many people may die before that destructive energy has finally consumed itself.

Now the spotlight of the story falls on Judas, who has already been briefly mentioned in 6:71, where Jesus referred to him as a devil. Mary, filled with her love for Jesus, brings some costly ointment and anoints the feet of Jesus, wiping them with her hair. It was not unusual for a hostess to provide a way for a traveler's feet to be washed since people mostly walked in those days and the roads were dusty; what was unusual was the use of the costly ointment. Judas criticizes this, complaining that the ointment could have been used better had it been sold and the money given to the poor. John adds as an aside for the benefit of his readers that Judas said this, not because he cared for the poor, but because he was the caretaker of the common purse and wanted to pilfer the funds. Jesus' statement, "Leave her alone; she had to keep this scent for the day of my burial," is thought by commentators to be his recognition that Mary is making an unwitting gesture of respect for his body, which will soon be dead and will require anointing. "You have the poor with you always, you will not always have me," is a recognition of the nature of eros. *Eros,* the Greek word for personal love, reaches out to particular people. It has a circle, and those who are included within that circle receive the warmth and bounty of eros. Jesus is in Mary's circle of eros, and the warmth of her love and affection is not to be denied because of the endless problems of the poor.

Of course, Jesus knows that Judas is a thief; with his extraordinary powers of intuition he certainly was not fooled by Judas's ploy that he wanted the money from the sale of the ointment to feed the poor. The questions that confront us are twofold: First, what leads people to lives and deeds of evil? Second, why did Jesus, knowing that Judas was a devil, have him as one of the twelve disciples?

In ancient times it was commonly supposed that people were influenced to do evil by a divine power. For instance, the Zoroastrians said there were two gods, Ahura-Mazda, god of light and beneficence, and Ahriman, god of darkness and evil. These two gods competed with each other for the souls of human beings, and if Ahriman won, that soul would be bound over to evil. In Greek mythology the goddess Atē roamed around the earth (which was called "the meadow of Atē") inciting human beings to lives and acts that led to ruin, folly, and sin. If a person did something rash, foolish, or evil, it was Atē who put the idea into that person's mind. And in early Christianity it was supposed that evil and criminal actions came from the devil or from evil demons, autonomous evil spiritual agencies who were ever present and ready to possess persons and incite them to evil.

In our modern era, however, since we have decided that the gods are dead and that there are no such things as spiritual agencies of evil, there is an effort to find a more rational explanation. Perhaps the most commonly held explanation among psychologists for the existence of moral evil is the theory that evil and criminal actions are the result of brutalizing childhood experiences. Children who are neglected, mistreated, and brutalized will grow up to be adults who are incapable of normal affection and who will mistreat others, passing along to other people the negative treatment they received during their impressionable and psychologically vulnerable years as children. A leading exponent of this point of view is Alice Miller, who, in her book *For Your Own Good*, argues that a child who is brutalized in his or her tender years will become an adult who in turn brutalizes others.[1]

The strength of this theory is its seeming simplicity and obviousness. It stands to reason that a child who is mistreated will be injured in some way, and what could be more reasonable than the idea that the evil the child receives will be passed on? It is also a theory that can be verified by many examples. There are, however, two weaknesses to the theory. One is that not all children who are brutalized turn out to be immoral, and, conversely, many children who were well treated when they were young turn out

1. New York: Farrar, Straus & Giroux, 1983.

to be criminals. This is a point that forensic psychologist Stanton Samenow makes in his book *Inside the Criminal Mind*.[2] His thesis is that adult criminal behavior cannot necessarily be predicted on the basis of childhood experiences, and that while there are many examples of brutalized children becoming adults who brutalize others, there are also many examples of children who were exposed to terrible experiences when they were young but grew up to be moral adults capable of making relationships. It would seem that although childhood experiences are an important factor in shaping the adult, there are other factors at work as well.

A second difficulty with this theory is that to a certain extent it begs the question. While the theory might explain why a particular person became an evil man or woman, it does not answer the question about why human nature as such had a propensity toward evil in the first place. Where did it all begin, this matter of our inhumane treatment of each other? Who was the first parent to abuse his or her child? What human being committed the "original sin" and why? It would appear that this theory, while a good explanation in certain particular cases, does not answer the broader issue of why the propensity toward evil seems to be so thoroughly ingrained in human nature.

Many Freudian psychoanalysts agree with Alice Miller with regard to the importance of childhood influences, but argue that the decisive influence on the child may not be outright abuse but more subtle psychological complexes such as the Oedipus complex. A case in point is that of Adolf Hitler. Hitler's biographers do not seem to agree on the kind of childhood he experienced. Alice Miller has argued that Hitler's father was a terrible man who subjected the child Adolf to frequent and severe beatings and forbade him to ever express his feelings and that this was the reason Hitler became such an evil man. Most biographers of Hitler, however, say that while Hitler's father was a heavy drinker, he was not worse than most German fathers of his era in history. Many psychoanalysts seem to agree with them and do not see Adolf's father as the main culprit, but rather his mother because her doting over her son involved him in a fatal Oedipus complex.

The argument from many psychoanalysts is that his mother's slavish devotion to her son bound him to her in an inescapable libidinal tie. When his mother became ill with cancer when Adolf

---

2. New York: Random House, 1984.

was an adolescent, we are told that he "agonized over her suffering, and nursed her tenderly day and night in her last weeks."[3] It seems that his mother's physician was a Dr. Eduard Bloch, who was Jewish. Dr. Bloch, acting largely under pressure from Hitler himself, took radical and painful steps to try to cure his patient of her illness, but the result was only prolonged and extremely painful suffering. Unconsciously, it is said, as a result of his unresolved Oedipus complex, Hitler was trying to save Germany (that is, his mother) from her enemies (that is, the Jews, who in his unconscious were all the evil Dr. Bloch). It was for this reason, we are solemnly assured, that Hitler murdered millions of Jews, and plunged Europe into a war that left thirty-two million people dead and a continent devastated.

While we are talking about Hitler, we might also mention Stalin, who was as evil a man as Hitler. Stalin was born into a poor family, as were most Russian children. His father appears to have been a drunkard, but he did work in a factory and supported the family to a certain extent; as far as I know he has never been accused of overt abuse of his children. His mother, however, was a paragon of motherly nurturing who strove mightily to see to it that her son received the best of opportunities, and she succeeded, for the young Joseph was admitted to schools run by the Russian Orthodox Church and received, gratis, a fine education and a warm and protective environment. But that didn't stop him from assassinating as many people — Jews included — as Hitler.

Modern psychiatry has a view of the origin of evil behavior that is more reasonable than that of the psychoanalysts and somewhat broader than that of those psychologists who lay all the blame at the door of childhood mistreatment. Referred to as a "field theory," it sees the social behavior of human beings as determined by a combination or network of biological (genetic), psychological (childhood), and social influences that determine not only the moral behavior of a person but the nature of personality itself. This view seems to be an advance over the strictly psychological viewpoint because it places the life of the individual in a broader context. However, it says nothing of the possibility of spiritual influences — either positive or negative —

---

3. See Helm Stierlin, *Adolf Hitler: A Family Perspective* (New York: The Psychohistory Press, 1976), 38ff.

also being a factor in producing what we call personality and in determining social or antisocial behavior.

Turning from the psychoanalytic and psychiatric viewpoints to Jungian theories, Jungian analyst Adolf Guggenbuhl-Craig in his thoughtful book *Eros on Crutches* suggests the hypothesis that psychopathic behavior comes from a deficiency of Eros, hence an inability to love, with a resultant lack of personal or social morality.[4] The lack of Eros means that the individual cannot stand in the shoes of another person, or even form an empathic connection to relatively impersonal realities, such as the environment. To a certain extent, he says, especially when it comes to our largely rapacious and unfeeling attitude toward nature, we are all psychopathic, but in certain individuals Eros seems to be totally deficient. As for why certain people become psychopaths, Guggenbuhl-Craig suggests that they may be that way because of a genetic predisposition. Just as some people have imposed on them a genetically originated physical disease (such as Huntington's disease or congenital diabetes, for instance) so psychopathology may be a genetically originated moral disease. And/or it may also be that the Self (the core of human personality) has a psychopathic element that becomes predominant in certain people.

Jungian psychology, while not entirely neglecting the importance of personal, historical psychological factors in shaping human personality, stresses the importance of the archetypes. The archetypes are those innate forms of the psyche that produce and give a distinctive shape to psychic energy. A grasp of the archetypal structure of the human psyche greatly enlarges our understanding of the sources of human behavior and of those patterns within us that shape our fantasies as well as our actions. Jungian psychology has shown that what we once thought of as the gods and goddesses are in fact personifications of archetypal powers in the psyche. So for every typical pattern in life there is a corresponding "deity," or archetype, which is its source.

One of the most important of the archetypes is the shadow. As the ego develops, it necessarily has a "companion ego," or an "alter ego" that develops along with it, and this is called the shadow. The shadow consists of all those qualities that could have become part of the ego but were rejected because they did not

---

4. Dallas: Spring Publications, 1980.

fit into the ego's ideal of itself or into its system of defenses. The shadow, inevitably feared by the conscious ego personality, is like the sinister Mr. Hyde in relationship to our seemingly personable Dr. Jekyll.

Could it be the shadow that is responsible for evil? Jung often suggested that this was the case, but Fritz Kunkel thought that the ego was more prone to evil than the shadow. It was the ego, Kunkel said, that because it was blindly living a lie was more sinister than the shadow. For this reason he once said that in a showdown between ego and shadow God is on the side of the shadow, while the secret is that the ego is the devil. The complex relationship that exists among ego, shadow, persona, and Self would take us beyond the scope of this present work, but suffice it to say that the egocentric ego is more to be feared than its dark companion the shadow.[5]

In places, however, Jung ascribed the origin of human evil not to the shadow per se but to the Self.[6] This amounts to asserting that the Self, the very core of human personality, is equally good and bad. We are back to Zoroastrianism except instead of there being two deities, one good and one evil, there is one divine image, that of the Self, which is equally good and bad. This dire psychological theory would seem to negate the possibility that there is any enduring and meaningful moral order to life and the universe, but in spite of this terrifying possibility some Jungians seem to be able to swallow it with remarkable ease.

A strong point of the archetypal theory of the psyche is that it opens the way for what might be called the irrational theory of the origin of human evil. If there is an archetype that lends itself to evil, then it may be that while all of us partake of the inclination toward evil that this archetype produces in us, some of us may have more inclination in that direction than others because in them the archetype may be a more important psychological constituent. The way the archetypes work can be compared to playing cards. When we play cards, all the players play with the same deck of fifty-two cards, but each player gets dealt his or her own particular hand with which to play the game. Thus, while

---

5. See John A. Sanford, *C. G. Jung and the Problem of Evil: The Strange Trial of Mr. Hyde* (Boston: Sigo Press, 1993). Also John A. Sanford, ed., *Fritz Kunkel: Selected Writings* (Mahwah, N.J.: Paulist Press, 1984).

6. See Jung's *Answer to Job* (Princeton: Princeton University Press, 1972), and my book *C. G. Jung and the Problem of Evil*.

the cards are the same for everybody, the hand we get to play is not the same. The archetypes may be like that. While on the one hand they are common to all people everywhere, on the other hand each individual has his or her own particular configuration of archetypes. This accounts for the fact that while we all partake of a common human nature there is at the same time a marvelous diversity of human beings. It may be that while no one is completely spared the archetype that inclines us to evil, some people find their "hand" contains the archetype of evil as an especially important card.

A family known to me from personal acquaintance is an example.[7] Of their three children two grew up well adjusted socially and were persons of good morals and character. But one boy at a very early age began a life of theft, which has characterized him ever since. Even when he was a small boy this lad would steal, even from his own parents, and no punishment, counseling, or influences deterred him from an immoral and self-destructive life. His parents were fine people and to ascribe their errant son's behavior to their mistreatment of him seems highly unconvincing. But the mother remembered when the trouble began. When her son was still a small boy he reported a terrifying nightmare. It was quite simple: In the dream he was in his room when a figure appeared at the window. It was a robber. The robber then flew in through the window and entered the boy. From that moment his behavior changed drastically and he began to steal. In Jungian language, the archetype of the thief made its preordained appearance and became a living psychic factor in his personality, shaping his very thought and inclining him toward a life of crime.

When we come to the biblical view of evil we find next to nothing of the idea that a person might be inclined toward evil because of destructive and alienated experiences in childhood. The idea of personal psychological development was virtually unknown not only to the early Christians but to the ancient world generally. But when it comes to the archetypal or irrational theory of the origin of evil the Bible has a great deal to offer.

There are several passages in the Bible that recognize the fact that there are some people who appear to be bound and determined to ignore God's will and lead immoral lives. The Old Testament, for instance, has an example of the way the Hebrew

---

7. I relate the story with their permission.

community was called upon to deal with what we might call today a nascent psychopathic personality. We read in the Book of
Deuteronomy:

> If a man has a stubborn and rebellious son who will not listen
> to the voice either of his father or of his mother and, even
> when they punish him, still will not pay attention to them,
> his father and mother must take hold of him and bring him
> out to the elders of his town at the gate of that place. To the
> elders of his town, they will say, "This son of ours is stubborn
> and rebellious and will not listen to us; he is a wastrel and
> a drunkard." All his fellow-citizens must then stone him to
> death. You must banish this evil from among you. All Israel,
> hearing of this, will be afraid. (Deut. 21:18–21, NJB)[8]

The ancient Hebrews apparently didn't waste much time putting up with a chronically antisocial personality: their way of
dealing with the evil was simply to eliminate the offender, but
sadly there is no evidence that this action rid the community
of the problem permanently. As for why this particular person
appeared to be incorrigible, we hear no explanation, but in the
New Testament we hear in several places of those who are "hard-
hearted." If the heart is hard, then it is blinded, and if the heart is
hardened, then a person cannot hear the word of God speaking
within.[9] Apparently it was recognized that certain people simply
did not respond to God's moral commandments and wishes as
other people did. Since the heart is the seat of feeling and emotion, as well as thought, we may surmise that persons lacking
in a sufficient capacity for eros or a personal, feeling connection
to others are rendered incapable of the moral life. Why certain
people were hard-hearted and others were not is not explained in
the Bible. Lacking our modern idea of a personal developmental
psychology, the Bible could not explain it on the basis of childhood experiences. There seems to have been a belief that people
could have avoided the hardening of their heart toward God and
God's moral commandments, but this is not well developed. As
with the existence of evil generally in the Bible, it is something
of a just-so story: it's just the way it is. However, to speak of the

---

8. Adolf Guggenbuhl-Craig called my attention to this passage in his book *Eros on
Crutches*, 47.

9. See for instance: Matthew 19:8; Mark 10:5; 16:14; 3:5; 6:52; Romans 2:5; Ephesians
4:18; Hebrews 3:8, 13; 4:7.

hardness-of-the-heart is certainly an accurate description of the
way evil operates once it gains possession of a person.

One thing the Bible is clear about is that to do evil is to become
evil. This was the reason for the fall of Adam and Eve from a state
of original perfection into the state known as original sin. They
were warned by God not to eat of the fruit of the tree of the knowledge of good and evil lest they come to "know" evil. The Hebrew
word for "know," as we have mentioned before, is similar to the
Greek word *ginōskō* (*gnōsis*), which means to know something by
having intimate experience with it; it is another way of saying
that to "know" evil by doing evil amounts to entering into an
intimate fellowship with evil. The former aids the conscience; the
latter destroys the conscience and, furthermore, darkens the soul
and obscures the capacity to know God. This is why the New
Testament repeatedly warns us against evil, for even small evils
can lead us to larger ones.[10]

The ultimate origin of evil in human beings, however, is ascribed by the Bible to the devil. The devil, as we have already
seen, is the "father of lies." He puts evil intentions in the hearts
of people and blinds them to the reality of what they are doing
by inspiring in them a lying spirit. When we tell lies to ourselves
about ourselves and about what we are doing, from the biblical
point of view we are falling under the power of the devil and
his principle of evil. The spirit of evil assumes the proportions
of a daemonic entity operating quite apart from the will of God.
From the point of an archetypal psychology such as Jungian psychology, it is a way of saying that there is an archetype of evil.
Therefore when we do evil it is not necessarily the result of our
previous life-conditioning (personal psychology), for at the core
of the impulse toward evil lies a daemonic archetypal power for
evil built into the psyche itself. But where Jung sometimes seemed
to believe that this archetypal energy for evil was a constituent
part of the Self, the Bible saw it as alien to and destructive of our
truest Self.

If our hearts have become hardened so that the normal feel-

10. A comment by Confucius on this subject is timely: "If good does not accumulate,
it is not enough to make a name for a man. If evil does not accumulate, it is not strong
enough to destroy a man. Therefore the inferior man thinks to himself, 'Goodness in small
things has no value,' and so neglects it. He thinks, 'Small sins do no harm,' and so does
not give them up. Thus his sins accumulate until they can no longer be covered up, and
his guilt becomes so great that it can no longer be wiped out" (from the *I Ching*, trans.
Richard Wilhelm [New York: Pantheon Books, 1950], 95).

ings of warmth and relatedness to our fellow human beings are obscured and a natural amount of conscience becomes inoperable, and if the ego falls under the spell of the devil and lies to itself about itself, then a human being is well on the way to becoming increasingly corrupted and finally becoming evil himself. But the Bible assumes that in spite of the fact that evil tendencies are inspired in us by the devil, the will is also involved. No matter how great the forces conspiring to bring us to evil, there is the element of choice. The Greeks would have said that even though Atē inclined a person to acts of sin and ruin, nevertheless the one who finally acted and lent his hand to the act was responsible and paid the consequences. The Christian would say much the same thing and therefore saw the human soul as constantly confronted with the necessity of choice. The very reason that allowed the devil to operate, in fact, appears to be that evil is necessary for the experience of choice to take place, without which experience true life and true love of God could not take place.

The story of Judas as brought to us in John's Gospel illustrates much of what we have been saying. As mentioned previously, in John 6:71 we are told that Judas is known by Jesus to be a devil. This might mean that Judas was already a person whose character was such that he was inclined toward evil, that is, one of the hard-hearted. In 12:4f we learn that Judas had become a thief, pilfering from the poor box. While not a heinous crime in itself, it nevertheless signified a serious slide in the direction of evil. That this slide toward evil took place in Judas is shown in John 13:2, where we learn that the devil put it into the mind of Judas to betray Jesus. In other words, Judas's mind is now open and vulnerable to the father of lies and his insinuations, insinuations that lead to the betrayal of his Lord, a much deeper evil than pilfering money meant for the poor. In 13:27 we are told that Satan actually entered into Judas. It is no longer a matter of the devil insinuating thoughts into Judas's mind; now the spirit of evil has actually possessed him. His will, once inclined toward evil, is now possessed by evil. Perhaps for this reason we read in John 17:12 that Judas is now one who chose to be lost, that is, no longer capable of salvation.

The story reaches its inexorable conclusion in Judas's betrayal of Jesus for the pittance of thirty pieces of silver. That is where the matter ends in John's Gospel, but in Matthew's Gospel we learn that when Judas saw the result of his betrayal of Jesus, that he was condemned to death, he felt such acute remorse that he committed suicide.[11] His remorse would constitute an emergence into some kind of consciousness. In our kindlier moments we can hope that this last minute stepping into a sort of consciousness, which brought with it enough decent feeling so that he experienced remorse, sufficed to make salvation possible for Judas after all.

The weaknesses of the biblical idea of the origin of evil are that it has no idea of a personal developmental psychology, and that it does not always explain itself. So, for instance, we are given no explanation for the fact that Judas was either fashioned by the devil into his instrument for evil or chose evil when the other disciples did not. Its strength is that it accurately describes the way life is and the way evil works. Even a cursory look at the way human beings act would seem to substantiate the idea that there is a malevolent power that works for evil in this world of ours. Whether we choose to think of the devil as a mythological entity or a psychological entity, some human beings certainly act as though they become possessed by such an evil power. The Bible also accurately describes the way a person becomes subject to this power: by consenting in small things to evil the will is increasingly corrupted until its doom is assured.

As for the ultimate fate of the inveterate sinner, the church could not agree. One strain of theology in the early church, for instance, said that the consequences of unredeemed sin in our once-and-only life on earth were permanent, and that at death we went either to eternal punishment or to eternal salvation. Another line of theological thought, however, believed that in the end all souls would be saved, those who had lived evil lives being eventually purged of their evil by the healing fire they would experience in the next life.[12] As for the reason evil existed at all, it is noteworthy that the church never developed an official theodicy (theory of the origin of evil in relationship to God), although the prevailing point of view, as noted, was the idea that the true love of God, the truly moral life, and the possibility of spiritual growth could be possible only in a framework in which moral

---

11. Another ancient tradition is that Judas's body became swollen to such an extent that he could not pass where a chariot could pass easily, so that a chariot crushed him and his bowels gushed out. See *Fragments of Papias* 3.

12. Tertullian can be taken as a typical representation of the first point of view, and Gregory of Nyssa a representative of the second.

choice was required. The one thing the Christian world agreed upon was that the power of God was such that no matter how great was the power of evil it could never extinguish the Light, and that God could use even evil for his greater purposes.[13]

Turning away from the question of why people do evil, we come now to the second question: Why was Judas allowed by Jesus to be one of the twelve disciples when he was known by him to be a thief? Various possible explanations have been suggested.

The most obvious answer seems to be that Judas was necessary in order that Jesus could be betrayed into the hands of his enemies, that he was needed in order to assist in the divine plan since Jesus' betrayal led to his arrest, which led to his crucifixion and then to the resurrection, with all of its saving benefits. The fact is, however, that Judas's betrayal by a kiss in the Garden of Gethsamene was hardly necessary; Jesus' arrest would certainly have taken place without it, for the soldiers would have had little difficulty in identifying Jesus even if Judas hadn't made their task a little easier by pointing him out to them with the kiss.

Jung, recognizing the inadequacy of this theory, has suggested that Judas had to be one of the twelve disciples in order to represent the shadow. The shadow, as we have seen, is the dark, repressed side of our personality that we prefer not to see, but it should be noted that groups have shadows as well as individuals. Jung's argument is that the disciples as a group were one-sidedly on the "light" side, and that there had to be someone to live out the dark shadow side for the group in order to create the necessary psychic balance. A comparison with modern family systems therapy would be a family situation in which all the members of the family are one-sidedly "good" and are unaware of their darkness so that inevitably, as a matter of psychological law, some particular member of the family has to become the wayward one, living out the family shadow. This person, usually a child, becomes the family scapegoat, and the unrecognized sins of the other members of the family are heaped upon him or her, as the case might be.[14] This theory has a good deal of merit to it since the disciples and Jesus did form a kind of spiritual family unit. The difficulty

---

13. So Joseph says to his brothers who planned his murder and sold him as a slave, "The evil you planned to do me has by God's design been turned to good, to bring about the present result: the survival of a numerous people" (Gen. 50:20, NJB).

14. As far as I know, the first psychologist to write about this phenomenon was Jungian analyst Frances Wickes in her still timely book on child psychology, *The Inner World of Childhood* (New York: Appleton-Crofts, 1927).

with the theory is that the shadow of the disciples was never denied. As we will see when we come to the story of Peter's denial of the Lord, the disciples were by no means perfect people, never thought of themselves as perfect people, and were never taught or trained by Jesus to deny their personal failings — quite to the contrary.

Elsewhere Jung points out that the story of Judas betraying Jesus is a typical story of the "mischievous betrayal of the hero." He points out that a similar betrayal occurs in the story of Baldur and Loki in Norse mythology.[15] In this story the beautiful and beloved god Baldur was betrayed by the evil Loki and destroyed by the treacherous mistletoe, which alone among the plants had not pledged itself not to harm the god. A similar story in Norse mythology can be found in the murder of the beautiful Siegfried by the malicious Hagen. In the realm of history, Caesar was betrayed in this way by his friend Brutus. Such stories suggest that there is an archetype of "the betrayal of the hero" and that the Christian story has elements of this archetype within it. The difference between the Christian version of this archetypal motif and the pagan is that in the Christian story the powers of darkness held no permanent power over the forces of Light. Christ, betrayed and murdered like Baldur, rises again in triumph, while Baldur was destroyed forever. Nevertheless, given the power of an archetype to shape both human imagination and outer events, Jung's thesis that the betrayal of Christ is an example of an archetypal theme merits careful consideration.

Jungian analyst Edward F. Edinger, in his insightful book *The Christian Archetype*, blends together the idea that Judas was necessary if the crucifixion was to take place with the idea that the element of betrayal was necessary in a story as archetypal as that of the death of the sinless Christ at the hands of evil. Edinger suggests that Judas had a certain destiny to perform and dutifully fulfilled it. He draws our attention to certain medieval pictures that depict Satan as a tiny demon entering the mouth of Judas as Christ gives Judas a morsel to eat. From this he infers that Christ "fed" Judas his assigned destiny and Judas faithfully carried it out. This, Edinger notes, is why the betrayal was accomplished with a kiss and why Jesus refers to Judas as "friend" (Matt. 26:50) as he receives the kiss.

---

15. C. G. Jung, *Symbols of Transformation, Collected Works 5*, paras. 41–42.

There are other possible explanations of the phenomenon of Judas as well — like the theory (unfortunately without any foundation that we know of in historical fact) that Judas was a zealot who was disappointed in Jesus' peaceful means of effecting change and wanted to precipitate a revolution, or Nikos Kazantzakis's explanation that Jesus and Judas were really kind of brothers in spirit, an interesting theory that is unfortunately without support except in Kazantzakis's fertile imagination.[16]

The fact is that both Judas and evil itself remain something of an enigma, a puzzle the mind cannot entirely resolve. This uncertainty of early Christian opinion and of the Bible with regard to the role of evil is both its weakness and its strength. The weakness of the biblical position is that there is no neat and tidy solution to the problem of evil, a fact the early church seemed to recognize since there never was an official theodicy in any of the Christian creeds. On the other hand, to admit a certain lack of knowledge where ultimate knowledge is not possible is not a sign of weakness but of strength.

16. Nikos Kazantzakis, *The Last Temptation of Christ* (New York: Simon and Schuster, 1960).

~ 23 ~

THE EMERGING SELF
The Messiah Enters Jerusalem
John 12:12–50

THE MOST IMPORTANT PART of chapter 12 is the story of Jesus' entry into Jerusalem, the well-known Palm Sunday story. The remainder of the chapter appears to be an amalgam of various sayings of Jesus. In this respect it is unlike the other chapters in John's Gospel in which we found well-organized discourses emerging from an opening story. Some sayings, especially verses 24–25, sound more like sayings from the synoptic Gospels than like Johannine sayings. For these reasons some commentators believe that much of the material in chapter 12 was not originally from John himself but was added by a later redactor (editor). On the other hand we need to keep in mind as we read chapter 12 that this is the last opportunity John has to tell his readers about Jesus' public ministry, for beginning with chapter 13 the focus is on Jesus' private ministry with his disciples, leading to the stories of the crucifixion and resurrection. It is possible that John was thinking something like, "I still have certain sayings of the Lord that I have not yet included, so I will put them in here because this is my last chance to do so." No matter how they found their way into the narrative, many of the sayings are important and worth our attention.

Verses 12–15 tell of the triumphal entry of Jesus into Jerusalem. Of course the crowds who greet him so enthusiastically do not know the true nature of that triumph. He does not come as the conqueror of earthly kingdoms but as the one who is spiritually

triumphant over the forces of darkness. The entry into Jerusalem
harkens back to prophecy from the Book of Zechariah:

> Rejoice heart and soul, daughter of Zion!
> Shout for joy, daughter of Jerusalem!
> Look, your king is approaching,
> he is vindicated and victorious,
> humble and riding on a donkey,
> on a colt, the foal of a donkey.
>   (Zech. 9:9, NJB)

The New Testament often relates events in the life of Christ to
prophecies from the Old Testament. This imparts a feeling of sacred history taking place within the unfolding of earthly history.
The earthly history is about the rise and fall of kings and kingdoms; the spiritual history is about the unfolding of a divine plan,
now being made manifest in the events of Christ and reaching the
consciousness of those individuals whose eyes are open to behold
it and whose ears are open to its message. From the psychological
point of view it is about the development of consciousness, the
emergence of the Self into human life. In fact, the whole Bible can
be seen as the saga of developing consciousness, first among the
Hebrews, later among the Christians.

The entrance by Jesus into Jerusalem on the back of a humble
donkey adds a touching aspect to the story. Kings and queens
may ride in chariots or in carriages, but the way of consciousness
is always a humble way. The donkey reminds us of the donkey
in the story of Balaam (Num. 22). It will be remembered that
the prophet Balaam was riding his donkey on the way to Moab
in order to prophesy against the Hebrews, but his donkey three
times darted off the path. Eventually Balaam saw why: the angel
of the Lord stood on the path barring the way; had Balaam continued, the angel would have killed him. The humble donkey saw
what Balaam could not see and thus saved his life. The animal
can thus represent that within us that can see God. Jung once said
that only the animals are truly pious for only the animals truly
do the will of God (the animals are all exactly what God wants
them to be; only human beings depart from God's will). Animals
often appear in our dreams where they typically represent our
guiding instincts and archetypal patterns. They play a positive
role in the psyche, and how we relate to them shows how related
we are to the Self. That Jesus was related to the animal kingdom

is shown in the Gospel of Mark, where we are told that after the temptations in the wilderness by Satan, Jesus was ministered to by the angels *and* the wild animals (Mark 1–13).

The enthusiasm of the crowd is exciting but short-lived. When the crucifixion comes the only crowd we hear about is the crowd that calls for the death of Jesus and the release of the robber Barrabas. Crowds, even those that appear to be kindly disposed, have a collective mentality that extinguishes individual awareness. The collective mind of a crowd has shallow roots and is easily swayed; for this reason crowds readily become destructive and even become the instruments of evil. This is especially likely to happen if the crowd projects the image of the Self onto a power-ridden individual who wants to use the crowd for his egocentric purposes. When this happens, as we have noted earlier, the leader poses as the Center and the crowd willingly gives up its freedom to him. Such a leader plays a quasi-divine role for the crowd, which rewards him with its mindless loyalty in return for relieving them of the burden of living consciously. In the case of the Palm Sunday crowd the projection was made onto Jesus and so the crowd was benign and no evil resulted from it, but if the projection falls on a destructive figure the results can be daemonic. Adolf Hitler's Germany is a good example of the destructiveness of crowd psychology when the masses project the Self onto an evil person.

Christianity was originally a religion rooted in the individual. Those who came into contact with Jesus, and those like Paul who knew Christ inwardly, had a religious faith grounded in their individual experience. While individual Christian experience still survives today, the crowd emphasis has often taken its place. This change took place quite early in Christian development. Certainly by the fourth century Christianity as an organized religion had changed markedly. In his book *Creation Continues,* which is a psychological commentary on the Gospel of Matthew, Fritz Kunkel looks at Jesus through the eyes and changing experience of the disciples. He shows how they were led through their interaction with Jesus and through their suffering to their own spiritual development. But later in Christian history, when the focus was on the crowd and not on the individual and when the church acquired temporal wealth and power, the danger arose that the ancient faith might become just one more collective movement. This is a danger that is alive and well today.

In the synoptic Gospels the contrast between the individual way and the collective way is shown in Jesus' saying in Matthew 7:13–14 (see also Luke 13:24):

> Enter by the narrow gate, since the road that leads to perdition is wide and spacious, and many take it; but it is a narrow gate and a hard road that leads to life, and only a few find it.

The contrast is clearly stated; on a wide highway many people can travel quickly and all at once, but on a narrow road or path people must go singly or in small groups. Clearly the wide road is the road most people are taking, and the narrow path is the individual path. This biblical image often appears in our dreams. For instance, people frequently dream of being on a freeway, a perfect symbol of the wide road that the collective takes, everybody going the same way mindlessly. But in other dreams the dreamer is on a narrow road or path, and this is the individual way. Sometimes in a dream the dreamer begins on a freeway but then turns off onto a road that quickly becomes quite narrow, or even a path on which the dreamer must walk, leaving the mechanical car behind. Then we know that a transition is possible from the collective way to the individual way.

In verses 20–22 we hear of certain Greeks (*Hellenes*) who also came to worship at the festival and told the disciples that they would like to see Jesus, of whom they apparently had heard. Modern commentators tell us that these Greeks were gentile proselytes to Judaism. Ancient commentators, however, tell us that they were not converts to Judaism but Greeks who, like the Jews, were monotheists, believing in one God; feeling their resemblance to the Jews they came to worship with them, but were not converted to the Jewish faith as such. At least, so says Cyril of Alexandria who writes with reference to John 12:20: "Such persons [that is, the Greeks], seeing that some of the Jews' customs did not greatly differ from their own, as far as related to the manner of sacrifice, and the belief in a One First Cause...came up with them to worship."[1] Whether the ancient commentator or the modern commentators are right is hard to say, but there is a good chance that the ancient commentator is correct because of the affinity between early Christianity and Greek philosophy. We have already noted that the early Chris-

---

1. Cyril of Alexandria, *Catena* 307.

tian thinkers found so much truth in Greek philosophy that they believed the Logos had taught the Greeks as well as the Christians. Many early Christian thinkers used Greek philosophy as a way of building Christianity into a complete worldview. Regardless of whether these people who wanted to see Jesus were Greek converts to Judaism or Greeks who wanted to worship with fellow monotheists (monotheism was rare in ancient times), John uses their request to see Jesus in order to introduce the statements from Jesus that make up the rest of the chapter.

Verses 23–24 contain the essence of John's mysticism. Jesus declares, "I tell you, most solemnly, unless a wheat grain falls on the ground and dies, it remains only a single grain; but if it dies, it yields a rich harvest." Lying hidden, as it were, within the grain of wheat is, *en potentia* (as a potential), the whole plant of wheat. As long as the grain remains, it is only one small reality, but if the grain dies, then in its dying there is released those forces that bring the plant to fruition, and from that plant comes a future multitude of seeds. Thus the death of the single grain brings about the emergence of a great abundance. Christ uses this image to reveal the mystery of his own death. By dying on the cross great forces are unleashed that spread throughout the spiritual world. One could say that with the death of the physical incarnation of Christ there emerges the Cosmic Christ, the new consciousness that spreads throughout the world and takes root in the souls of countless people.

John 12:23 is often compared with Paul's image in 1 Corinthians 15:35; in fact some scholars believe Paul derived his image from this Johannine verse. Paul is answering the question, With what sort of body are people raised at the resurrection? He answers:

> Whatever you sow in the ground has to die before it is given new life and the thing that you sow is not what is going to come; you sow a bare grain, say of wheat or something like that, and then God gives it the sort of body that he has chosen: each sort of seed gets its own sort of body.

At first glance it seems that the Johannine verse and the Pauline verse are saying the same thing, but there is a difference. With Paul the lifeless seed of wheat and the plant that succeeds it have little in common; so also the now dead earthly body has little in common with the glorious resurrection body. But with John, the death of the grain of wheat is part of a total process that leads in an integrated fashion to the emerging plant; so also with the death of the earthly ego there emerges a perfected soul. The individual who is rooted in the ground of Christ emerges, by dying, into a more beautiful existence expressive of a much greater reality than the ego.

The Johannine verse stresses the importance and the non-importance of the ego. The ego is an essential part of the plan of salvation, but is not the point of the plan. The point of the plan is the emergence of abundant new life, not the perpetual salvation of the ego. A good deal of later Christianity turned the mystery of the resurrection into a kind of cult of the perpetual glorification and salvation of the ego. But the ego, as we know it, is but a passing phenomenon; the true reality is the soul, or, in psychological language, the expression of the Self. The task of the ego is to accumulate consciousness and to be willing to die when its time comes; thus the ego is important, but not the most important thing. Anything less than this turns religion into another form of egocentricity.

Some of these mysteries are evident in the results of an individuation process. When a person has achieved a new consciousness, so that the center of personality has shifted from ego to Self, then that person has an invisible but profound effect on other people. Those in whom the seeds of new consciousness are taking root find their own consciousness expanding, and this creates an effect that spreads invisibly to others. These may be humble people, unknown to the writers of history. We may recall, perhaps, a grandmother who matured into a wise and aware old lady and who lives on in our memory as something of a spiritual guide. Or the person may have become famous, an Abraham Lincoln whose suffering produced a conscious development that affected a nation. The story told earlier of the German soldier who would not shoot the Jewish woman is an example; we do not know even the name of this soldier, but his act lived on in the minds of his family and was passed on to me and now lives on in the minds of the readers of this book. In such a way conscious development, known or unknown, never dies but bears its fruits forever in the spiritual world. Thus the ego, in dying, released its store of consciousness for the abundance of new life. For this reason Jung once said that the emergence of the Self is always the death of the ego, which may receive its life back but upon an entirely different ground of existence.

Verses 25–26, about those who love their life and therefore will lose it, have a strong resemblance to parallel sayings in the synoptic Gospels. There is a close parallel, for instance, between Matthew 16:24–25 (and its parallels Mark 8:35 and Luke 9:24): "For anyone who wants to save his life will lose it, but anyone who loses his life for my sake will find it" and John 12:25, "Anyone who loves his life loses it; anyone who hates his life in this world will keep it for the eternal life." Such a strong resemblance to synoptic sayings is so rare in John's Gospel that some commentators think this verse is one of those not from John, but from a later redactor. Just the same, verse 12:25 has a distinctly Johannine twist to it: the mention of "this world" and its contrast with "eternal life." Here again we see elements of John's mysticism. "This world" is a passing phenomenon. Though the unenlightened ego takes it for reality, it has only a provisional reality, as real, let us say, as a snowflake that will melt with the first warmth of spring. Therefore those who cling to the things of this world will be severely limited in consciousness. They will have the thinking of the "flesh," in the sense discussed earlier. In psychological language, they will never move beyond the narrow confines of their ego. Eternal life stands in sharp contrast to this. Eternal life here is not to be understood as "living forever." Rather, eternal life is an entirely new dimension of reality. It may be a dimension of reality in which time itself takes on an entirely new significance. For time, as commonly understood, is not an Absolute, but a special construction of the limited ego. What time is in and of itself escapes our comprehension. And in God as the Father there is no time.

Verse 26 also has comparisons with sayings from the synoptic Gospels. Compare the Johannine, "If a man serves me, he must follow me, wherever I am, my servant will be there too," with the synoptic saying, "If anyone wants to be a follower of mine, let him renounce himself and take up his cross and follow me" (Matt. 16:24; Mark 8:34; Luke 9:23). To follow Christ is equivalent to taking up the cross, and taking up the cross is equivalent to assuming the burden of the process of individuation. The process of becoming conscious requires that we carry the burden of our own being and our own psyche. Where others can project essential components of their personality onto other people — some carrying the projection of the shadow, others the projection

of the anima or animus, still others the projection of the Self —
the conscious life requires that we take back these projections and
assume responsibility for our own psyche. It also requires that we
carry the burden of our own particular lot or fate in life, that is,
of those inescapable conditions of our particular existence. This
is the psychological equivalent to carrying the cross. But note the
Johannine, "wherever I am, my servant will be there too." Here
again we have the enigmatic *egō eimi* — the "I am" that occurs
so often in John's Gospel. To be sure, this time the "I am" can
be taken as a casual grammatical construction, but in the spirit
of John's Gospel it speaks of the eternal presence of Christ as a
mystical reality abiding in the eternal "Now." This tells us that
we are not alone in this task of carrying our own burden. An essential element in the Christian standpoint, which differentiates
a Christian understanding from a secular one, is that the ego is
not alone in its efforts. We do not stand alone, but are supported
by an invisible Presence as soon as we turn our face toward our
task. This is a further extension of the teaching about deification.
We do not become changed in our nature to that which is incor-
ruptible through our own unaided efforts, but through mystical
participation in a much greater reality than ourselves.

It is as though there is a flow of life in us that instinctively
seeks to find its way to its goal. Our task is to follow this flow of
life, persevering in our efforts, aided by the force that lies behind
and within all life. An image from the *I Ching* is appropriate here:
"Water is something that out of necessity must flow. When the
spring gushes forth it does not know at first where it will go. But
the steady flow fills up the deep holes blocking its progress and
success is obtained at last."

The theme of deification is continued in verses 27–28. These
verses have been called the equivalent in John's Gospel of the
passion of Christ in the Garden of Gethsemane in the synoptic
Gospels. The same elements are in both: the anguish of Christ
("Now my soul is troubled"), the doubt about the forthcoming
crucifixion ("Shall I say, 'Save me from this hour?' "). From the
point of view of deification the pathos of Christ is essential. Even
as he was called upon to go through the darkness, to experience
the anxiety and discouragement, so must we also go through our
darkness, but we will not be alone, as he was not alone (for the
Father was with him).

In verses 28–29 we are told that a voice now came from heaven glorifying the death of Christ that is to come. We are also told that some of the people mistook the voice for a clap of thunder; others heard the voice but could not make out the words and they supposed it was an angel.

From our contemporary rationalistic point of view all of this is plain fancy. Many modern biblical scholars would dismiss such tales as part of the "mythology" of the Bible, by which they mean that the writers of the Bible had a mythic viewpoint that we are not to take seriously. In fact, what we call today the "mythic thinking" of the Bible is its way of expressing the conviction that just behind the visible, rational, and physical world is an invisible, spiritual, and meaningful world. The physical world of space and time and what we take to be causality and the spiritual and invisible world are so close together that they are interwoven with each other. The spiritual reality constantly permeates the physical, but our ordinary "fleshly" consciousness cannot see it. When we are encased in our rationalistic prejudices we believe material reality is the basis for what we suppose to be spiritual reality. Thus the brain is said to be the seat of and origin of what we call personality. But from the other point of view all of what we take to be physical reality is the expression of Mind. So for the early Christian, the physical world as we commonly understand it is the expression of the Mind of God (Logos), not the other way around.

In religious experience and in archetypal dreams the spiritual world breaks into our consciousness. This reality is in fact never far away, but our senses are dulled to it. Jesus knows of this other Reality but we do not, which is why he says in verse 30, "It was not for my sake that this voice came, but for yours."

In verses 31–32 we read again of the "sentence" that is passed on the world. The word translated here as "sentence" is the Greek word *krisis* (judgment) with which we are now familiar. As we have noted, once the opportunity for consciousness approaches we are all under crisis, or judgment, for how we respond to the call to consciousness will be crucial for us.

Now that the events of the crucifixion and resurrection are drawing near, the "prince of this world" can be overthrown. This is the *archōn*, the spiritual ruling power of this world.

Verse 32 — "I shall draw all men to myself" — is of special interest. The word translated "draw" is the Greek word *helkō*, which can mean variously: to hoist a sail, to draw one's sword, to drink in a long draught of water or wine, but also to draw something or someone to oneself. The image is that of a magnet that draws objects to itself by what appears to be an unseen influence. The magnet remains stationary; yet other objects are attracted to it. So Christ acts like a magnet drawing souls to himself. In Christian mysticism the cross was such a magnet, exerting its unseen but powerful influence on the souls of human beings. Various scholars rightfully point out that *this* is the answer given in John's Gospel to the quest of the Greeks, "We should like to see Jesus." Those who would see him should look to the cross and its mystical effects on the soul.

In verse 34 the question is posed "Who is this Son of Man?" This is a question we have already discussed, and in verses 35–36 John gives us at least part of the answer: He is the man of Light (consciousness). These verses embody one of the most beautiful and succinct statements about the meaning of Christ as the Light that can be found. They also show us the connection between Light and knowing versus walking in darkness and not knowing, for "he who walks in the dark does not know where he is going." We see stressed here once again the insistence in John's Gospel on both knowing and believing, knowledge and faith, each one reinforcing the other. The result of faithfully following the way of consciousness on the path to further self-knowledge and spiritual knowledge is the transformation of our state of being from the "flesh" to that of "sons [and daughters by implication] of Light."

Verses 37–40 tell us that even though Jesus had given many signs in evidence of his divine origin many did not believe him and that this was to fulfill a prophecy from the prophet Isaiah. Even some of those who thought they believed in him were half-hearted about it, and their frightened egos caused them to keep their belief to themselves out of fear of the Pharisees "for they put honor from men before the honor that comes from God." The main quotation from Isaiah that is cited in this passage is as follows:

> Go, and say to this people,
> "Listen and listen, but never understand!
> Look and look, but never perceive!"
> Make their ears dull, shut their eyes tight,
> or they will use their eyes to see,
> use their ears to hear,

> use their hearts to understand,
> and change their ways and be healed.
>
> (Isa. 6:9–10, NJB)

The theme of the hardening of the heart is a frequent one in the Bible. We find examples of it in the synoptic Gospels, the Book of Acts, and the epistles.[2] The biblical point of view is that spiritual and inner knowledge do not come to us through a purely intellectual process, but emerge as we emotionally experience the object and content of our knowledge. This understanding of knowledge is included, as we have seen, in the important New Testament word for knowledge, *gnōsis*.

Modern psychology would agree with this position, for if the ego becomes hardened so that feeling and the capacity for love are excluded, then psychological insight and moral awareness are dimmed to the point of extinction. When this happens to us it is as though a thick hard shell has encased us and nothing can penetrate our obstinate egocentricity. Then one of humankind's greatest gifts — free will — degenerates into a personalistic obstinacy. Kunkel puts it nicely when he says, "The enemy is the egocentric form of our own free will which has deteriorated into the will to power or the will to security."[3]

The antidote would be the arousal of the capacity to love and to feel, for not only does love enable us to identify with the plight of others and so free us from our egocentricity, it also opens us up to the capacity to feel the suffering of our soul. So important is the role of suffering in the process of becoming whole that the Christian mystic Meister Eckhardt once stated that "suffering is the swiftest steed that brings us to perfection."

In the quotation from Isaiah, it is the ears that are dulled and the eyes that are not open. These would be the spiritual senses, of course, not literally the physical ones. As we have noted earlier, the soul also has its senses. It "hears" the voice of God and "sees" spiritual reality; it even "smells" the presence of the divine,[4] and its powers of "taste" enable it to discriminate between good and evil. The puzzle is why God would (apparently) deliberately close up the hearts of certain people lest they "use their eyes to see

---

2. For example, see Exodus 4:21, 7:3; Matthew 13:14–15, 19:8; Mark 10:5, 16:14; Acts 28:26–27; Romans 2:5, and so forth.

3. Fritz Kunkel, *Creation Continues*, original edition (New York: Charles Scribner's Sons, 1952), 192.

4. See 2 Corinthians 2:15; Ephesians 5:2.

and use their ears to hear." Some commentators argue that it is not God's *desire* that a person's heart should be hardened, but that God *foresees* that this will be the case, and so incorporates this knowledge into the divine plan.[5] The psychologists, as we noted in our examination of the sources of evil, have more rational explanations, most of which prove unsatisfactory in one respect or another. We are left with a puzzle. The divine plan cannot always be made rational and is not always susceptible to our explanations. The answer to the question, "Why should things be as they are?" is not always clear to spiritual science, just as the study of natural science presents the natural scientist with questions that cannot always be answered.

The final verses of chapter 12 are introduced as a public statement ("Jesus now declared publicly"). This seems at variance with verse 36, which told us that Jesus withdrew into privacy after his final discussion of the Light ("Jesus left them and kept himself hidden"). It is reasonable to suppose, therefore, that verses 37–50 are out of place, perhaps a later addition to the text. Nevertheless, they make a suitable summary of the central teachings found in the Gospel thus far: the major themes of Light and Darkness, of this world and the other world, of Christ and the Father who sent him, of judgment and of eternal life; all find a place in this passage, which concludes the public ministry of Jesus as presented in the Fourth Gospel. From here, as we will see, there is a shift of emphasis as Jesus concentrates his energy on the inner circle of the disciples to prepare himself, and perhaps them as well, for the forthcoming events of the crucifixion and resurrection.

---

5. See the footnote to Isaiah 6:10 in the New Jerusalem Bible.

~ 24 ~

LOVING ONE ANOTHER
Jesus Washes the Disciples' Feet
John 13

As MENTIONED, this is the first of the teachings of Jesus in his inner circle. The main theme of this teaching is love, centered on the admonition that we are to love one another. We will therefore concentrate on the theme of love as viewed by John, but first we will make a brief textual analysis.

Verse 13:1 boldly introduces the theme. The Jerusalem Bible translation of the final words of this verse — "but now he showed how perfect his love was" — varies from other translations, such as the Revised Standard Version, the King James Version, and J. B. Phillips, which translate the verse "he loved them to the end," and the New English Bible, "now he was to show the full extent of his love." The literal meaning is "he loved them to the end" and is to be preferred to the Jerusalem Bible translation because it shows one of the most salient features of love: its perseverance, or, in biblical language, its "steadfast endurance" (*hypomonē*).

Verses 13:2, 18, and 21ff all relate to Judas, but we have already covered the meaning of Judas in a previous chapter. Verses 13:3–11 contain the well-known footwashing scene in which Jesus, contrary to all customs and expectations, since he was the leader of the group, performs the humble servant role and washes the disciples' feet. An interesting detail of this is the differentiation between the two Greek words for washing, *louō* and *niptō*. We met these words in the chapter in which we discussed the story of the man born blind. There we saw that *louō* means to wash the whole body, and *niptō* means to wash only a portion of the body. The word used in this passage is the word *niptō* since it is concerned with washing only the feet. However, there is a subtle play on the theme of washing in verses 10–11: "No one who has taken a bath needs washing, he is clean all over. You too are clean, though not all of you are." Here the "cleanness" is clearly spiritual cleanness. This suggests that the footwashing scene is not only the description of Jesus' act of love on behalf of the disciples, but also a symbolic reference to inward purity, which leads us to the psychological symbolism of the foot, which we will now consider.

Some ancient texts add to the end of verse 10 the words "except for his feet." The line would then read: "No one who has taken a bath needs washing, he is clean all over, except for his feet." For the traveler on the dusty roads of Israel, as we have already noted in the story of Mary who washed Jesus' feet, the feet need repeated cleaning. Symbolically, the story presents the importance of the soul remaining clean. Inevitably as we journey through life we accrue a certain amount of psychic contamination. Sometimes this occurs because we are doing things in life that go against the Self, but it can also occur because no one can go through life without picking up psychic contamination. Therefore, just as the body, especially the feet, needs repeated cleansing, so does the soul. The importance of this is often shown in our dreams. A frequent dream motif is that of bathing, or taking a shower, or swimming in some body of water. Such dreams usually refer to the importance of inner cleansing and renewal.[1]

The story of the washing of the feet takes on added significance when we consider the symbolism of the foot in our dreams. The feet are perhaps the most humble part of the body. In medical science the foot was evidently so neglected as an object of study that it fell by default to the lot of a separate profession, podiatry, to make it a specialty. As anyone knows, however, who has had a problem with his or her feet, it is far more essential than one might suppose. If we are able to go through life without much reflection on our feet, it is simply because they are doing their job so well. As many runners know, problems in the body often begin with the feet. Knee problems, for instance, often originate with how

---

1. If, however, the water in which we are bathing or swimming is itself contaminated, it is usually a sign that the dreamer is not paying enough attention to his or her shadow. By not noting our own darkness we allow it to fall into the unconscious, and thus contaminate our own inner waters.

the foot strikes the ground: if the foot "pronates" or otherwise is not performing its proper function, it sends a distortion through all the body that can result in problems in the knee or even in the upper torso. In dreams, feet are often said to represent sexual libido, but they can also represent our spiritual standpoint. Feet are what we stand on: so they are our standpoint in life, which needs to be firm, solid, and rooted to the earth of reality. To be barefoot in a dream is a rare but striking dream motif that may symbolize the possibility of acquiring a firm and natural psychological and spiritual standpoint that is uniquely our own.

There is also an ancient tradition that the spirit enters and leaves us not through the head but through the feet, for which reason we still speak of the "soles" (souls) of our feet.[2] Another old belief connects feet with the power to heal. One tradition is that a child who is born feet first is believed to have special healing powers; also that certain physical conditions could be cured by a person with healing powers trampling upon the afflicted person, for healing virtue lay in the feet.[3] The Sioux Indian shaman Black Elk is an example of the widespread belief that the feet were the way the spirit entered a person and were also therefore connected with healing. In this connection he tells us a story in which he was called upon to heal a little boy. After he drummed and chanted four times — in each of the four directions — to the Spirit of the World, he tells us that he "could feel the power coming through me from my feet up, and I knew that I could help the sick little boy."[4]

If the foot was the place where the spirit entered the body, it was also the place where a person was vulnerable to an enemy, especially if that person had engaged in a malicious activity. So according to ancient folklore there is the belief that if you can find the footprint of an enemy you can wound him by putting sharp stones or broken glass in the footprint, and if you take the earth that held the footprint and boil it in a kettle you can wound him for life. Still another belief is that if you take the dust of someone's

2. Joseph Campbell, e.g., notes that among some ancient people, the breath of life left the body from the soles of the feet, the "whorls" at the bottom of feet representing the path of the wind of life as it entered and left the body. See *Primitive Mythology* (New York: Viking Press, 1959), 235.

3. See, for example, C. A. Meier, *Ancient Incubation and Modern Psychotherapy* (Evanston, Ill.: Northwestern University Press, 1967), 101.

4. John G. Neihardt, *Black Elk Speaks* (Lincoln: University of Nebraska Press, 1961), 204.

footprint and bury it in a graveyard that person will become sick and die. For that reason it was at one time common for people who feared an enemy to obliterate their footprints.

This may seem at first glance to be far removed from the imagery of the Bible, but there is also a text from the Old Testament that uses the foot as a symbol for an area of unconsciousness that enables people to be caught for their misdeeds. Psalm 9 deals with the way God catches the wicked and succeeds in punishing them no matter how hard they try to evade him. In verse 15 we read, "The nations have sunk in the pit which they made; in the net which they hid has their own foot been caught" (RSV). Here the foot symbolizes something in the nations they have not dealt with that makes them vulnerable to the avenging powers of God.[5]

Interestingly enough, St. Augustine wrote a comment on this verse that connects together the idea of the foot as an area of vulnerability to the idea of the "foot of the soul," which is nothing other than the source of our capacity to love. Concerning Psalm 9:15 he says, "The foot of the soul is well understood to be its love: which, when depraved is called coveting or lust; but when upright, love or charity."[6] In the same passage he also reminds us of Paul's admonition in the Epistle to the Ephesians: "That being rooted and grounded in love, [you] may have power to comprehend with all the saints, what is the breadth and length and height and depth, and to know the love of Christ which surpasses knowledge, that you may be filled with all the fulness of God" (3:17–19 RSV). In this verse Paul uses earthy language. The Greek word translated "to be rooted" is the same word used in describing the rooting of a plant (*rizoō*, to take root), and the word translated "grounded" means "to ground, establish, render firm and unwavering" (*themelioō*).

It is not possible, of course, for us to know whether or not John was aware of the symbol of the foot for the source of our spiritual grounding, our powers of healing, and our love. He may have been more aware than we suppose, however, for presumably he knew the Jewish Scriptures well and must have been acquainted with Psalm 9:15 and the many other Old Testament passages that employ the foot as a spiritual symbol. In any event, the symbol of the foot as the source of psychological power and the entrance

5. For further symbolism of the foot akin to that of Psalm 9:15, see Psalm 17:5, 77:19, 89:51, 58:10; Proverbs 29:5; Song of Songs 7:1; Isaiah 37:25, and so forth.
6. Augustine, *On the Psalms*, Commentary on Psalm 9, v. 15.

to the soul was around for many centuries before John. It was "in the air" as it were, that is, a part of the collective symbolism in the unconscious, and it is safe to suppose that consciously or unconsciously John was influenced to emphasize the importance of the washing of the feet as preparation for his great discourse on love.

Continuing on, in verse 13:23 we meet the mysterious "disciple whom Jesus loved." It will be remembered from the introduction that one theory of the authorship of the Fourth Gospel is that it was written by this disciple, who may have been the owner of the upper room in which Jesus is now meeting with his disciples. In verse 13:33 the translation in the Jerusalem Bible "little children" is not a diminutive implying that the disciples were naive and childlike, but a term of endearment. The Greek word used here for child (*teknon*) comes from the Greek word *tiktō*, which meant to bear or to carry and was the word used for a woman who bore children. So the disciples are to Jesus as his spiritual children whom he has carried and given birth to and whom he loves dearly. Verse 13:38, which foretells of Peter's denial, ends a beautiful scene on a somber note. It is part of John's artistry that he does this. Beautiful and touching though the scene is, John does not let his reader forget that there are dark times ahead. But we will reserve a discussion of Peter's denial until later in our story and will also comment later on the mysterious significance in the Fourth Gospel of the number three.

We turn now to the core of chapter 13: the new commandment of love that we find in verses 34–35:

> I give you a new commandment:
> love one another;
> just as I have loved you,
> you also must love one another.
> By this love you have for one another,
> everyone will know that you are my disciples.

The difficulty from a psychological point of view with this command to love is that love cannot be willed. The person who tries to love by an act of will is likely to wind up with a persona that looks like he or she is loving, but with a shadow side hidden in the unconscious that negates it. Love must come from the heart if it is to be genuine; it cannot be feigned, not even with the best of intentions. The Jerusalem Bible reading above uses the English

imperative: "love one another" ... "you must love one another."
However, the Greek uses the subjunctive mood, not the imperative. The subjunctive in Greek can be used with the force of the
imperative, but it usually emphasizes conditionality and possibility. One could say in this context that the use of the subjunctive
admonishes us to love one another but also suggests that part
of our ability to fulfil the commandment is to become the kind
of persons who are capable of that love. From the psychological
point of view the person who is capable of love is the person who
has dealt with his or her egocentricity. We will look more closely
at how this works, using as a guide the insights of Fritz Kunkel.

Kunkel's idea is that love emanates naturally and creatively
from the Center, but the ego, as long as it is egocentric, blocks or
interferes with this outpouring of love. If the creative Center is
able to work through our personality, we do not have to will love
into existence; it will simply be there, creatively and effectively
and tempered with wisdom. The task is to enable this love that lies
within the Center to come through us, and this means working
through our egocentricity.

Egocentricity is hard to describe since there are as many ways
of being egocentric as there are people in the world. Still, major types of egocentricity can be classified in four ways. One of
these types, which Kunkel called the "Turtle," has already been
described in connection with the man by the pool of Bethzatha.
A second example is that of the "Clinging Vine." Let us imagine a small child of a tender or naturally nonassertive disposition
whose doting parents lavished upon him or her an undue amount
of affection and did all they could, for their own quasi-egocentric
reasons, to remove from him or her the natural hardships of life.
From such a matrix of influences there might well emerge the kind
of person who has discovered at an early age that the way to get
through life is to remain childlike and helpless, looking to other
people to furnish the necessary support and strength. Like a vine
that clings to a tree and cannot stand alone, so this personality
becomes a clinging vine who clings to others for strength.

What began as an undue reliance on parents who were over-
protective and indulgent develops into an egocentric means of
defense against a world outside of the home that is perceived as
hostile and forbidding. However, in order to find other people
who are willing to support and defend him, such a man must
qualify for their support. This means he must be very *needy* and

very *deserving*. A dedicated "Clinging Vine" personality can make a fine art out of achieving a posture of being needy and deserving; indeed he becomes so good at it that he himself believes in it firmly, which makes him all the more convincing to others. To his own mortification he discovers that he has been injured in some way that makes it impossible for him to carry his own weight in life. He believes none of this is his fault for he is the innocent victim of others' malice. Since his misfortunes are not his fault, he is deserving of the help of those who are more fortunate than he; indeed, if they will not help him they are surely selfish people.

Such is the succinct description of one of the many forms of egocentricity. How does this affect that person's capacity to love? Somewhere within that person is the creative Center, but it does not emerge into that person's life because the egocentric ego's distortions and defenses are too strong. In fact, the ego in such a case secretly resists and fears the creative Center, for the Center would call for him to stand on his own two feet and meet life head-on with courage and creativity. He has to repress and deny his very best qualities in order to maintain his egocentricity, and in this denial of the Center he is also cutting himself off from his capacity for love.

His inability to love, however, might not be always apparent to other people. Suppose, for instance, that you help such a person, that is, help him in the way he egocentrically wants to be helped, by offering to be the support for him in some way. He will seem to love you in return for it. He will sing your praises and may well adulate you in return for your beneficence, and both you and he may be persuaded that this is indeed love. But suppose one day you become fed up with supporting this clinging person. Perhaps he has pushed you too far and you rebel against the burden, or you just become bored with him, which happens easily because egocentric people are boring. To your surprise you are suddenly curt with him, and you cut him off and tell him to go out and help himself.

You will now find that his "love" has turned to hatred. He will complain bitterly about you and decry you as a treacherous and heartless person who abuses those less fortunate people who, through no fault of their own, cannot make their way in life. Clearly what passed for love was only egocentric desires fulfilled; the cause of his hatred is that you no longer go along with his egocentric desires. As long as we are egocentric, and to the extent that we are egocentric, all people and all relationships are distorted by it. We "love" those who fit in with our egocentricity and hate those who do not. Only as our egocentricity begins to be purged by life (if it ever is) can we begin to really love. If we achieve some insight into our egocentricity and if we begin to shoulder our proper burden of life's suffering, then our egocentricity can begin to diminish and with this the real Center emerges — and with this comes love.

Let us choose another example. Suppose you are a child with overly protective and doting parents who never made much of their own lives but have discovered that you are an amazingly talented little girl. And in fact you are talented. At an early age you show a marvelous capacity for music. You have a cheerful disposition, and as you develop, it becomes clear that you are going to be a beauty. When you get to school your teachers like you for your agreeable nature, your charm, and your talents. By the time you are a young lady you are well established as a gifted singer and a desirable date, you get the leading role in the school play, and you become the most popular girl on campus (at least with the boys). You are, in fact, one of life's "Stars," and you love to shine brightly on others, blessing their lives for them — as long as you receive their adulation in return. The fact is, however, that you so need to be the Star that unless you are the object of everyone's admiration you are wretchedly unhappy. The worst thing you can imagine would be to be scorned or laughed at, or, still worse, ignored or replaced by another Star greater than yourself.

Fortunately or unfortunately for the Stars of this world, there are many ways of achieving admiration. Some have talent, some beauty or strength, some scholastic abilities. If all else fails you can star at being good, for anyone can be "good" with just a modicum of effort. You can get all stars after your name for perfect attendance at Sunday school, or you can get all As in school, or you can win awards for good citizenship. You might even get to be a minister, and then you can achieve professional success by your goodness. If a Clinging Vine shows up he has you spotted a mile away. You spot him too for here is another way to star: by helping the needy. The two of you make an unholy alliance, though it appears to be forged in the name of God, for didn't God say that we should help one another? In fact, of course, we are not helping each other but are being what is called today "codependent" or "enablers," each enabling the other person to persevere in an egocentric state.

How the star's egocentricity affects her relationships is clear enough: those who admire her she "loves"; those who do not admire her or compete with her for admiration she dislikes. To the extent she is a star she doesn't really love anyone. Only if, through insight and suffering, her egocentric pretensions at being a star are purged from her can she begin to love, for only then can the real Center pour forth.

To take a different type of case, let us suppose that a boy has been raised in a harsh environment. Your parents are tyrannical and cruel and they abuse you as a child. You, however, are a fairly assertive boy and you don't knuckle under to them. What you do is protect yourself against the harshness of your early childhood experiences by building a hard shell around your more tender sensibilities. As you grow up your rule of life is that no one is going to get you again because you are going to get them first. In fact you have become a bully — or a worse tyrant than your parents were. Somewhere deeply inside is your heart, and here the real Center struggles for expression, but there is a hard wall around your ego and until it is cracked the real Center cannot show through. Thus your egocentricity dominates all your relationships. In your case it is not necessary to pretend to love anyone for you are not asking for favors from them, only obedience and subservience. Those who are subservient to you, you favor, and this is as close to love as you get; those who are not subservient are your enemies. In fact, you have become a tyrant, a "Nero"[7] of a personality whose egocentricity requires that you dominate others. If you should become a powerful dictator that would be the ideal situation. But what if there are other, more powerful tyrants around, perhaps at your place of work? Then you flip into the opposite and become the subservient follower, but when you get home you revert again and tyrannize your family. The greatest thing God could do for you would be to constellate a situation in which no one would let you bully them any longer (maybe your long-suffering clinging vine wife suddenly gets a modicum of courage from the real Center and leaves you!). Then comes a crisis as your egocentric adaptation to life collapses, and in this crisis you either die or begin to truly suf-

---

7. The Roman Emperor Nero was one of the world's worst tyrants.

fer so that the real Center can finally begin to emerge, bringing with it your own long-feared tender feelings and capacity to love.

The psychology of egocentricity and of the nature of the Center and the relationship of the two is too vast a subject to be discussed at more length here. Suffice it to say that Christ's commandment to love one another involves us in a long path of development in which we mature into our real Self, gradually leaving behind our egocentric defenses and pretensions.[8] Whether one calls this "the individuation process" or regards it as the process of Christian maturation, it is at the heart and soul of all love.

The fact that at the very end of John's chapter 13 there is the premonition of Peter's forthcoming denial of Christ shows that Jesus is aware that the disciples have not yet reached that point where their love is true. Peter, the leading disciple, is too caught in his own hidden egocentricity, and when the crisis of the crucifixion comes he will yield to his fear and deny his love for his Lord. But at this point none of this is known to Peter. He does not know himself that well yet, but God knows him, for "Not one of the things unknown to us escapes the knowledge of God."[9]

We have already explored in John's Gospel something of the meaning of faith and knowledge and have seen their interrelationship. Now we have examined some of the meaning of love. But even as faith and knowledge are related, so love is also related to faith, and knowledge to love. Both faith and love are categories of the soul; each one nourishes the other. And both faith and love lead to the knowledge of God. For the knowledge of God, as we have seen, is not an intellectual exercise but a soul exercise. It is an intimate knowing by experience, and it is love that leads us to such an experience. For this reason the knowledge of God is as available to the simplest and most humble among us as it is to the great and intellectually gifted. Irenaeus once stated the matter clearly when he wrote, "It is therefore better and more profitable to belong to the simple and unlettered class, and by means of love to attain to nearness of God, than, by imagining ourselves learned and skilful, to be found among those who are

---

8. For further reading on this topic see *Fritz Kunkel: Selected Writings* and *Creation Continues*, and my own books, *C. G. Jung and the Problem of Evil: The Strange Trial of Mr. Hyde* (Boston: Sigo Press, 1993), and, with George Lough, *What Men Are Like: The Psychology of Men for Men and the Women Who Live with Them* (New York: Paulist Press, 1988), chap. 3.

9. Gregory of Nyssa, *Answer to Eunomius's Second Book*.

blasphemous against their own God."[10] And from a contemporary source we are told, "For to love another person is to see the face of God."[11] But this, as we have seen, is possible only when the hard, egocentric shell around the heart has been cracked so that the genuine Center can pour forth.

---

10. *Against Heresies* 2.25.4.
11. From a song by Andrew Lloyd Webber in *Phantom of the Opera*.

~ 25 ~

BEYOND PSYCHOLOGY
Jesus' Farewell Discourse
John 14

THIS CHAPTER BRINGS UP FURTHER CONSIDERATIONS on the nature of the Father and how the Father can be known. We will consider this topic after we have first completed a textual analysis.

In verse 1 we have Jesus' recognition that the disciples are troubled, as the situation for Jesus becomes more threatening. Jesus reassures them and then in verse 2 tries to explain to them a great mystery: that in God there are many dimensions of reality. The Greek word *monē*, translated "many rooms" in the Jerusalem Bible, "mansions" in the King James Version, and "dwelling-places" in the New English Bible, is related to the Greek word *menō*, which means to dwell or sojourn. As long as our awareness is limited by that of our senses we cannot imagine any way that the soul could live except in this earthly existence and framework. Jesus points out that there are many possible abodes in which the soul can exist; he tells how he will go before the disciples into a spiritual realm unseen by them in order to prepare a place for them in a realm of reality that the ego in its fleshly state, limited as it is to sense impression and ego-awareness, cannot perceive. This spiritual realm of which Jesus speaks is, in fact, only apprehensible through inner experiences such as visions and ecstatic experiences, like the experience Paul describes in 2 Corinthians 12:1–4, in which he tells of being caught up into paradise and hearing things that cannot be put into any ordinary human language.

266

As long as our consciousness is limited to the information brought us by our physical senses and by our limited ego-consciousness, we tend to live in anxiety for we feel alone and unaided and therefore not able to cope with life's threats and problems. Jesus' prescription for this anxiety is faith in him, which also means faith in the reality of another world ordinarily unseen by us. Notice that the word "hope" is not used, for unless hope is rooted in a world apprehensible by faith it can be deceptive. Hopes founded on how things will turn out in this world may strengthen us for the time being, but in the long run if what we hope for does not come about, the soul may actually be weakened. For this reason hope has been called "the seducer of the soul." T. S. Eliot once wrote in his poem "East Coker," "I said to my soul, be still, and wait without hoping, lest you hope for the wrong things." And Nikos Kazantzakis once advised, "Don't be intoxicated into the taverns of hope or the cellars of fear. . . . I have neither hope nor fear, I am free." He is speaking of that point the soul may reach where it lives between hope and fear, resisting an identification with either side, living by a faith that there is more to reality than meets the eye. This is, it would seem, the basis for the peace Jesus refers to in verse 27, which is "a peace the world cannot give, this is my gift to you."

Christ also speaks in verse 3 of going away to prepare a place for the disciples, and then of returning again. This motif is repeated in verses 12, 18, and 28. The obvious reference is to Jesus' forthcoming death on the cross and then his return after his resurrection. Some further insights on why it was necessary for Jesus apparently to abandon the disciples are offered us in chapter 16, and we will consider further the matter of Jesus' departure and return at that time.

In verse 4 Jesus speaks of "the way." Thomas has difficulty with this idea of "the way" and asks, "How can we know the way?" Thomas in John's Gospel, as in the synoptic Gospels, is the literalist. In terms of Jung's typology, Thomas would appear to be a sensation type.[1] This means that his most developed psychological function is his sensation function. Thus he is keenly aware of immediate physical reality, but lacks a developed intuitive function and so has difficulty perceiving that which is possible but

1. Jung devised a typology that saw people as extroverts or introverts in their basic life orientation, and with four functions: thinking, feeling, sensation, and intuition. One of these functions is always the dominant one and its opposite is the inferior one.

not yet here, or that which is not visible to the physical senses. We live in an age that values the sensation function and the intellectual function and downplays the value of feeling and intuition. Therefore when Thomas asks "How can we know the way?" he is speaking for the prevailing point of view of our present time in history.

A further indication that Thomas is a sensation type is found in the Greek word for knowledge, which Thomas uses in verse 5 ("how can we *know* the way?"). The Greek word here is *oida*, which, as noted earlier, refers to knowing something because you have physically seen it, that is, to outer, objective knowledge. It is close in meaning to another Greek word, *horaō*, which means to see, behold, or look upon. When Jesus answers him in verse 7, "If you *know* me you know my Father too," he is using the now familiar word *ginōskō*, which is the word that refers to knowing through intimate experience of something, the word for all mystical knowledge. In verse 7 there is what appears to be a deliberate play on these Greek words by John. The first word in this verse for knowing is *ginōskō*, and the second is *oida*, so we have: "If you know me [*ginōskō*] you know [*oida*] my Father too. From this moment on you know [*ginōskō*] him and have seen [*oraō*] him." First comes the psychological or mystical knowing through intimate experience, then one's eyes are opened, as it were, and one can "see" God.

A similar play on words is found in the interchange with Philip in verses 8–9. Philip wants to "see" the Father (literally: "show us the Father") and Jesus answers with *ginōskō*: "Have I been with you all this time, and you still do not *know* me?"

In verse 6 Jesus makes the statement, "I am the way, the truth, and the life. No one can come to the Father except through me." The words "truth" and "life" are the now familiar words *alētheia* and *zōē*. The word translated as "way" is the Greek word *hodos*, which means a way, road, or means of access. Literalists interpret John 14:6 as meaning that the literal belief in Jesus is the way, and that those who do not make a "confession of faith" in the prescribed way cannot be saved. However, others see in verse 6 a statement that is essentially mystical. The word *hodos* as the "way" or "road" to some destination occurs in the New Testament over a hundred times. It is used in both a conventional sense and a mystical sense. Interestingly enough, like most of the New Testament words for salvation, *hodos* is a feminine word in Greek (though usually a word with this ending would be expected to be masculine in gender). It is used in Greek thought, as well as Christian thought, with reference to God's way. For instance, Aeschylus describes Zeus as "one who leads mortals in the *way* of understanding."[2] John's Gospel is the most unliteral document one could imagine. For John, Christ is the (mystical) way, the road that leads to the Light and to understanding. The way of salvation *is* the Way of following Christ. This involves far more than a verbal espousal of doctrine, for essentially this *way* is none other than the way of Sophia, who, we will remember, was regarded by the early church as embodied in Christ. It is the Way of Wisdom, of growing consciousness, of moral rectitude, and is the way that leads us (as any good road should) to our proper and intended spiritual destination.

There follow some tremendous promises. First, the disciples, who are ordinary mortals like ourselves, can live with tremendous power. In fact, whatever they ask for will be done, with one proviso, that it be asked for in Christ's name ("Whatever you ask for in my name I will do.") This means, of course, that our asking must be free of the taint of egocentricity; it must be an asking that comes from the true Center — otherwise we would not be asking in his name but in our name. Hence the glory rebounds not to the ego, but to God (v. 13).

Another important statement is found in verse 14: "If you love me you will keep my commandments." The expression "you will keep" could be construed to mean an imperative: "you *will* keep my commandments." Or it can be a simple statement of fact: "those who love Christ will also live in a certain way." The word translated "commandments" here is the Greek word *entolē*, a feminine word associated with moral precepts. The meaning seems to be therefore that those who love Christ will live consciously, following the Light, and therefore in a moral way.

The remainder of chapter 14 is largely concerned with the Father. It is to this topic that we now turn.

There are over one hundred references in John's Gospel to the Father, yet the Father himself never directly appears. He is also spoken of by Christ, who as the Son is in intimate relationship, even identity, with the Father, but yet is distinct from the Father in personality. This identity with, yet distinction from, the Father is

2. *Agamemnon*, First Choral Ode, Str. gamma.

a precursor of the Christian doctrine of the Trinity, as we will see when we examine John 16. While Christ is in direct relationship with the disciples, the disciples are not in direct relationship with the Father, but have their relationship with the Father through Christ. Many early Christian thinkers, pondering this mystery of the relationship of the Father to Christ and the lack of a direct relationship between the Father and his human children, concluded that the Father was unknowable. Christ himself said the same thing in John 14:46 when he declared, "Not that anybody has seen the Father, except the one who comes from God: he has seen the Father."

The picture we have of the Father in John's Gospel is that he is the utterly transcendent aspect of God, who can be known only through the Son. In Christian mystical thought, especially as developed among the early Greek theologians, the Father is God as the uncreated One, pure Being or Existence itself who cannot be known or described in any human categories. God as the Father brought into existence the created order, which the ancients divided into the intelligible and the sensible; the sensible order is the physical created order; the intelligible order is the spiritual order, which consists not only of the human soul, but of angels, principalities, powers, and all other manifestations of spiritual beings. God, while the author and sustainer of the created order, is not identical with the created order. There is no pantheism in Christian mystical thought, for while the Mind (Logos) of God may be seen in the created order, the created order as such is not God.

Since God is not identical with the created order, the Divine is also beyond the categories of space and time, for time is the measure of the flow of events, but in the Father there are no events and hence no time; hence time is a category of the created order as experienced by human beings, but is not a category descriptive of the author of the created order. The Divine might be thought of roughly as a vast ocean with no beginning and no end from which time flows, but for which, in itself, neither time nor space are relevant. In the words of Gregory of Nyssa,

All order and sequence of time in events can be perceived only in the ages of this creation, but the nature pre-existent to those ages (God as the Father) escapes all distinctions of before and after. . . . There is nothing (therefore) by which we can measure the divine and blessed Life. It is not in time, but time flows from it; whereas the creation, starting from a manifest beginning, journeys onward to its proper end through spaces of time.... But the supreme and blessed life has no time-extension accompanying its course, and therefore no span nor measure."[3]

It follows that God as the Father is beyond the powers of human comprehension or description. There are no adjectives with which to describe the Divine in its transcendental aspect. The Divine can therefore be described only in negatives: it is not created, it is outside of time, it has no limit, it cannot be measured by the unfolding of the ages.[4] Rather, "Within that transcendent and blessed Power all things are equally present as in an instant: past and future are within its all-encircling grasp and its comprehensive view."[5] The Divine as the transcendent is thus beyond any conceptual designation (*akatalēpton*), is without a name (*anōnymos*), and is uncreated and self-originated (*agennētos*). To quote Gregory again: "But if one asks for an interpretation or description or explanation of the divine nature [*tēs theias ousias*] we shall not decry that in such a science as this we are unlearned.... For there is no way of comprehending the indefinable as by a scheme of words. For the Divine is too noble and lofty to be indicated by a name: and we have learned to honour by silence that which transcends reason and thought."[6] And again he writes, "This is the Being [*ousia*] in which, to use the words of the Apostle (Acts 17:28; Col. 1:17), all things are formed; and we, with our individual share in existence, live and move, and have our being. It is above beginning, and presents no marks of its inmost nature: it is to be known of only in the impossibility of perceiving it. That indeed is its most special characteristic, that its nature is too high for any distinctive attribute."[7]

Rudolf Otto is helpful to us at this point. In his book *Mysticism East and West*, the distinction between the ordinary worshiper and the mystic is not that the mystic has a different relationship with God; rather, it consists in the fact that the mystic is contemplat-

---

3. Gregory of Nyssa, *Against Eunomius*, book 1.
4. This is known in the Eastern Orthodox Church as the "apophatic" mystical tradition, which means that God can be described only in negatives. In this respect the idea of the Father somewhat resembles the idea of Brahman in Hindu thought, who is to be described only negatively as "not this . . . not that."
5. Gregory of Nyssa, *Against Eunomius*, 10.
6. Ibid., book 1.
7. Ibid.

ing a different God than the ordinary worshiper or the systematic theologian. The ordinary worshiper relates to the God of "simple theism," that is, a God whom we describe in human terms and relate to as we might to a powerful and wonderful human being. The systematic theologian seeks by reason and logic to arrive at a certain knowledge of God, whom he then describes by the use of certain adjectives. A prime example of this would be medieval scholasticism, which attempted to plumb the depths of the divine by the use of reason and logic. The mystical theologian, however, recognizes that beyond the image of God that exists in our simple theistic viewpoint and beyond the rational categories of the theologian is the realm that John calls the "Father" and that Gregory describes as the Deity of whom nothing can be known and to whom no human categories apply. This is God as the "Wholly Other" than oneself, a Deity who can be known by the soul only in ecstatic mystical experience, but cannot be appropriated by the intellect. Writes Otto:

> It is characteristic of certain types of mysticism to seek the *Deus sine modis* (the God without modes) and to cherish Him in the soul. "God" is then experienced in an act of union. But man is a mystic as soon as he has this conception of God, even when the element of union recedes or remains unemphasized, which can easily happen in mysticism. It is the wholly non-rational character of this conception of God with its divergence from the intimate, personal, modified God of simple theism, which makes the mystic. Mysticism is not first of all an act of union, but predominantly the life lived in the "knowledge" of this "wholly other" God.... Mysticism enters into the religious experience in the measure that religious feeling surpasses its rational content, that is, as I have said elsewhere, to the extent to which its hidden, non-rational, numinous elements predominate and determine the emotional life.[8]

This way of thinking of the nature of God as the utterly transcendent is antithetical to the attitude toward the Divine that is common today and also to the rationalistic theology that dominates the theological thinking of most Western Christian churches. It is common today, instead of elevating human nature

---

8. Rudolf Otto, *Mysticism East and West* (New York: Collier Books, 1962), 158–59.

to its ultimate and perfect nature and so to closer intimacy with God, to bring God down to our human proportions and treat him as though he was our big brother or the kind of parent we always wished we had. In more formal Western theology it is to be supposed that the nature of God can be deduced by means of human reason (scholasticism), and that our theological treatises are truly descriptive of God's nature. For John, this knowledge of God as the transcendent is clearly impossible. Who are we, small creatures of God's enormous creative power, to know the One who is ineffable and beyond the powers of any human comprehension? This is the position taken by John, an attitude that existed in the early church and lives on even today among the Orthodox (Eastern) Churches and, indeed wherever the truly mystical spirit prevails.

This leads us to the matter of the religious epistemology (theory of knowledge) of the Fourth Gospel and of Christianity in general. If the Father is unknowable, inconceivable, and indescribable, then how can God be known? And as we saw in a previous chapter, the answer is clearly stated in John's Gospel: God is known through the Son, for while the Father cannot be known the Son can be known, and to know the Son is to know the Father ("If you know me, you know my Father too").

Now the Son, as we have seen, is the Logos of God, and from the Logos or Word of God comes the divine energy that created and is immanent in the world. To contemplate, therefore, the great expanse of the heavens is to contemplate the Logos of God. The scientist, as he or she studies the world of the atom or the movements of the heavenly bodies and begins to understand the laws and principles by which the creation lives and moves, is probing, as it were, the Mind of God expressed in the creation.

What is more, this expression of God through the Logos, or the Son, is also present within the human soul, which is also part of God's creation, and thus the divine energy at work in the Son, or Logos, is also at work within the very heart of a human being, which is why Christ says in John 14:23 that he will come to the one who loves God and will make his home with him. Indeed, the soul, as we have seen in our first chapter, is a dwelling place of the Logos par excellence. The Logos resides in the soul as an *imago dei*, and thus the soul bears a natural testimony to God; indeed the knowledge of God is the soul's natural inheritance. For this reason, Gregory of Nyssa once noted:

This truth [that God is in the soul] is taught in the Gospel, when our Lord says, to those who can hear what Wisdom speaks beneath a mystery, that "the Kingdom of God is within you" (Luke 17:21). Indeed that Word (i.e., the Logos) points out the fact that the Divine Word is not something apart from our nature, and is not removed far away from those who have the will to seek it; it is in fact within each of us, ignored indeed, and unnoticed while it is stifled beneath the cares and pleasures of life, but found again whenever we can turn our power of conscious thinking toward it.[9]

What Gregory and many other early Christian mystical theologians are describing is a psychological approach to a religious epistemology: one knows God because the image or imprint of God lives within the soul. This teaching has its roots in the New Testament in those passages that refer to the Christ within (such as Gal. 2:20), or the indwelling power of the Spirit (for example, Eph. 3:16; 1 Cor. 3:16). It is not, however, a psychology that is limited to the ego, but a psychology that assumes the existence of a "heart" or soul that amounts to what we would call today "the unconscious," a realm within us that has "secret thoughts" (1 Cor. 4:5), which often are unknown to consciousness but are always known to God (1 Thess. 2:4). Gregory points out that as long as our conscious attention, that is, the focus of our ego, is on the "cares and pleasures of this world" (in biblical language, on "the things of the flesh") we will be unaware of the inner life of the soul, but it is precisely in the soul that the reality of the Logos, or Word of God, dwells, through whom God can be known.

This ancient Christian epistemology is almost totally lacking in contemporary psychology. The kind of psychology a person holds depends to a great extent on the philosophical assumptions with which a person approaches the study of personality. The rationalist or materialist, who begins with the premise that nothing can exist that is not rational or material in nature, is bound to identify personality as an epiphenomenon of the body: "soul" then becomes nothing more than a functioning of the brain. Those who approach the psyche with the point of view of Freudian psychology would say that what we take to be God is nothing more than the projection of a father-like moral regularity function in the mind, a "superego" that has been instilled in us since childhood

9. Gregory of Nyssa, *On Virginity* 12.

by parental and other authoritative influences, or else would see belief in God as mere wish fulfillment. Only Fritz Kunkel, C. G. Jung, and certain of his followers, have been sufficiently free from rationalistic and materialistic biases to see that there are realities within the human soul that are not to be understood purely in terms of physiological functioning, nor as the residue of personal psychological experiences, but emerge from a universal mind or psyche that exists within all of us. Thus freed from materialistic biases, these psychologists were able to see that the soul is a quasi-divine reality in its own right.

Since Jung had this liberated point of view he was able to see and describe that process initiated in us from our very depths that seeks to bring us to a whole and completed state of being. We have already noted that Jung called this the individuation process, and that it is comparable to the ancient idea of deification (*theōsis*), or transformation of common unredeemed human personality into something akin to the likeness of God. What is more, Jung saw in the unconscious depths of the soul the greater center (the ego being the lesser center), which he likened to an *imago dei*. This idea of a second center to personality has its roots in the Bible (for example, Gal. 2:20) and was further elaborated in the psychologies of early Christian thinkers such as Tertullian and Gregory of Nyssa. But for them this second center was like the Logos of God functioning from within our very depths.

This is not to say, however, that we can exactly equate Jung's point of view with that of the early Christians. There is, for instance, the issue of the kind of God who is exemplified in the *imago dei* within the soul. Here the issue revolves around the matter of the relationship of evil to God (or the Self, to use psychological language). For the Christian, God was beyond evil, and even beyond good as we commonly think of it. God was the source of the call to a conscious and a holy life, but the urge in the human heart toward evil was originated from an adverse spirit of evil. Jung, on the other hand, seems in places, such as in his book *Answer to Job*, to argue that evil comes from the Self, that is, that the *imago dei* within the soul contains the urge to evil as well as toward good.[10]

A second issue revolves around the question of whether or not a knowledge of the *imago dei* within the soul can lead to a

---

10. For a more complete treatment of this topic see my book *C. G. Jung and the Problem of Evil: The Strange Trial of Mr. Hyde* (Boston: Sigo Press, 1993).

knowledge of a divine reality beyond the soul. Sometimes Jung argued this issue one way and sometimes another way. What could be called Jung's more official position was that while the *imago dei* in the soul gave rise in consciousness to the idea of God, one could not go beyond that to affirm the existence of a divine order or Being outside of the psyche. Epistemologically Jung was a Kantian who believed that the psyche had certain structures that shaped how it processed experience and also shaped the ideas by means of which the ego organized its experience. The idea of God, an important idea for optimum psychic functioning, was thus shaped by the *imago dei,* or image of the Self, within, but this did not mean that the resulting idea of God could be regarded as a metaphysical fact. "We are strictly limited," Jung once wrote, "by our innate structure and therefore bound by our whole being and thinking to this world of ours." To be sure, he added, "Mythic man . . . demands a 'going beyond all that,' but scientific man cannot permit this."[11] And elsewhere he stated categorically, "The structure of the mind is responsible for anything we may assert about metaphysical matters."[12] Jung therefore regarded the unconscious as the medium through which religious experience seemed to flow, but he also cautioned, "As to what the further cause of such an experience may be, the answer to this lies beyond the range of human knowledge. Knowledge of God is a transcendental problem."

For Jung, therefore, when he is speaking as a scientific man, the human psyche is, as it were, shut up in its own box, unable to arrive at a certain knowledge of any reality outside of those ideas that exist within its own consciousness. These ideas are shaped partly by sense impressions and partly by those innate categories or archetypes that are structural parts of the psyche and that give birth to and shape our most important ideas, such as the idea of God. But when Jung speaks as a "mythic man," that is, speaks from his heart and soul, he often talks of the Divine as though he believed in a God who existed outside of the psyche, the same God of whom theologians speak and whom the "common man" understands to be a reality perhaps within but certainly outside of himself. Sometimes he does this in a frustrating and irritating way.

---

11. C. G. Jung, *Memories, Dreams, Reflections,* ed. Aniela Jaffe (New York: Pantheon, 1963).

12. C. G. Jung, "On the Tibetan Book of Great Liberation," *Collected Works* 9, esp. paras. 766–67.

For instance, in his *Answer to Job* he first adamantly disclaims that anything he says in his book is to be understood as talking about God as an outer reality, but then proceeds to refer to God as though he is doing exactly that.[13] In his autobiography, *Memories, Dreams, Reflections,* Jung goes even further and discusses metaphysical issues in a way that leads us to believe that in his heart he believed in a Deity beyond the psyche.

There is one further element in any religious epistemology that must be taken into account, and this is the element of the numinous. As we noted earlier, when we are confronted by something numinous there is aroused in us wonder, awe, and the sense of something holy. That which is numinous, therefore, has the power to compel us to believe in realities that are beyond both ordinary experience and rational comprehension. Now, numinosity is an aspect of the Self, and therefore an experience with the Self of any depth produces effects in us that impel us toward beliefs that go beyond the rational. But this does not answer the question of whether or not the psyche is also effected by the numinous. Is there a numinous reality apart from the psyche? Is the numinous in the psyche an aspect of a greater reality outside of the psyche? The early Christians certainly thought so, for they believed in God within but also believed God transcended any merely human existence. Indeed, that is the question: if all human beings were to perish would God also cease to exist? Some would place such a high value on human consciousness that they would say the very existence of the universe depends on a human being to be conscious of it. Of course this seems to amount to a monumental *hybris* — a prideful human arrogance.

The awareness of the numinous may come not only from internal images, such as that of the Self, but from realities external to the psyche. Impress a hot coal on the body and we feel pain. Impress spiritual reality on the psyche and we feel numinosity. If this is so, then the sense of the numinous is not simply generated from the *imago dei* within but is also the result of impressions from spiritual reality outside of the psyche — however (strictly speaking) scientifically unknowable that reality might be. If we contemplate the expanse of the heavens on a glorious clear night, or if we marvel at the depths of love of a human being whom

---

13. If Jung had really wanted to be clear and scientific in his *Answer to Job* he would have substituted the term "Self" for God and thus avoided a great deal of confusion.

we know deeply, are not such numinous experiences capable of
arousing in us a wonder and awe that leads us to a belief in God
that is founded not on rational considerations but on an experience with a reality outside of ourselves that has moved the heart
to find its own way of knowing? How a person answers that question determines to a great extent his or her capacity for religious
knowledge.

Some light is thrown on this problem by the interesting grammatical construction in the Greek language called the "object
genitive" which we discussed previously. It will be remembered
that in this construction one noun in the nominative case is put
in a certain relationship to a second noun in the genitive case,
and this indicates that the energy or sentiment of the first noun
is both directed toward the second noun and is engendered by
the second noun. The biblical expression in Greek for the "love of
God" is an example of the object genitive. In this expression the
word *agapē,* or love, is in the nominative case and the word *Theos,*
or God, is in the genitive case. Thus the love we have toward God
is engendered by God's very own numinosity.

~ 26 ~

THE MYSTICAL UNION
The True Vine
John 15:1–16:5

JOHN 15 IS A STRIKING EXAMPLE of John's use of symbolic language. We can imagine that the image of Christ as the vine emerged into John's consciousness spontaneously as he was in a state of communion with its source: the Word of God within him. It is pure mysticism, concerned with the mystery of the transformation of the soul through union with God, and is one of the most important passages in the Bible for the idea of deification. Our approach will be first to note other places in the Bible where the symbol of the vine has been used with reference to God or God's actions. Then we will look more closely at this symbol and compare its imagery to the psychology of individuation. Finally we will note how the symbol of the vine has appeared in other religions in a way that is strikingly like the Christian imagery of the vine.

Two of the most important places in the Old Testament in which the vine is used as a symbol are found in Jeremiah and Isaiah. In Jeremiah 2:21, Israel is likened to a vine that God planted, but Israel turned away from its planter and produced fruit that was alien to God:

> Yet I had planted you, a red vine
> of completely sound stock.
> How is it that you have turned into seedlings
> of a vine that is alien to me? (NJB)

Isaiah 5:1ff has a similar image: God, like a good tiller of the soil, plants a vineyard on fertile ground with the just expectation that it will yield fine fruit, but all it produces are wild grapes of inferior quality. For that reason God will no longer protect it: he will let it go to waste, he will leave it unpruned and overgrown by brambles, and he will command the clouds no longer to send rain upon it. This vineyard, Isaiah tells us, is Israel, which God cherished and nourished but which turned from him and produced sickly fruit. Similar images occur in several other places in the Old Testament, with similar symbolic meanings.[1] These Old Testament images resemble the vine imagery of John 15 insofar as they contain the expectation, as does John's image, that the fruit that is produced will be sound. But they differ from John 15 because in the Old Testament images, God himself is not the vine, but only the planter of the vine, whereas in John 15 Christ does not plant the vine but *is* the vine.

Closer to the spirit of John's Gospel is the use of the image of the vineyard in the Song of Songs. In the eighth chapter of this beautiful love song, the lover likens his beloved to a vineyard, his very own, and she responds to him as the "one who dwells in the gardens," whose voice she yearns to hear. The erotic imagery of this love ballad of the Old Testament has long been viewed in mystical Christian literature as a portrayal of the love between Christ and the soul, whose union is as close as that of the loving gardener and his beloved vineyard.

Elsewhere in the New Testament we find the analogous imagery of the wild olive shoot used by Paul (Rom. 11:16ff). Here Paul compares the Christians to a new stock that has been grafted onto the root that once was Israel, whereas Israel has left its original source, though it may return. He warns his Christian disciples against what we would call an inflated attitude, reminding them that they are not the root (the source) and do not support the root; rather, the root supports them, for the source of their life lies in God. Here Paul's imagery is closer to that of John than is the imagery of the Old Testament, for in Paul, as with John, God is not merely the planter, but also the root of the tree, the source from which the life of his followers flows as long as they remain connected to it.

---

1. Other vine references in the Old Testament include Hosea 10:1; Jeremiah 5:10, 6:9, 12:10; Ezekiel 15:1–8, 17:3–10, 19:10–14; Psalm 80:8–18.

Turning now to the imagery of John's Gospel we see the striking image of Christ (v. 1) as the vine whose source is in the Father. All those branches that remain closely connected to the vine will grow strong and bear fruit, for Christ is the source of their life and strength (v. 5). However, those branches that do not bear fruit are cut off from the vine. They then wither and die and are cast into the fire (v. 7), for a branch cannot live without its connection to the vine. Those branches that do bear fruit are pruned by God, and this makes them stronger and their fruit more plentiful.

This imagery can be compared to the relationship of the ego to the Center. The ego has little vital life of its own. The source of its vitality and creativity lies in the Center, and as long as it has a connection to this Center it flourishes and brings forth the fruit of a life that is lived significantly. The task of psychotherapy, properly understood, as well as that of the spiritual life, is to establish the connection between the ego and the Center. As we have noted, this connection has been called the ego-Self axis and is the source of psychic health. At its best, the Christian sacramental and devotional life strengthens this connection of ego and Center. The recollection of dreams also helps forge this ego-Self axis or connection to our living Center. But if the ego is cut off from its Center it dies, just as a branch dies when cut off from its connection to the tree. Our egocentricity effectively cuts us off from the Center and brings about what amounts to a spiritual death. Depression is sometimes a symptom of this condition, and it may be that compulsive cravings are also expressions of the unconscious cravings of the soul for a connection to its deep inner source in the Center.

The fruit of the vine that is produced when the vine is healthy is analogous to the fruits of the life of individuation, that is, the life that is lived consciously, with a living connection between ego and the unconscious. The image of the vine can be understood as a portrayal of the positive, joyful side of the individuation process. We often hear about the difficulties of personal growth, of its painful side, of the dark times we must experience, and all of this is true. But there is also the positive and joyful side, for in the long run the fruits of individuation outweigh its difficulties, for from it emerge understanding, creativity, and the capacity to love. This does not mean that life will be easy for us, nor does it mean that the difficulties of life may not be great. A religious faith that believes that God will not let us suffer and that we will be immune to life's difficulties is an immature and egocentric faith.

What it does mean is that even if things are going badly we will have the strength to live through our experience creatively and grow in the process.

But there is also a warning in John's imagery of the vine: if a branch does not bear fruit it will be cut off and destroyed. This is similar to the Old Testament imagery in which God will destroy a vineyard he has planted that does not bear fruit. We also find similar imagery in Luke 3:9: " ... any tree which fails to produce good fruit will be cut down and thrown on the fire" (cf. Luke 3:17). This destruction of the worthless branches is represented in John's Gospel as the action of the Father. We can understand this to mean that there is a spiritual law that when some unit of life does not fulfill its intended purpose it is destroyed. As we have noted before, there is a ruthlessness in the spiritual world just as there is in the natural world. There is no room in a true religion for any sentimental ideas about God. God is not an overly tolerant parent who puts up with childishness and egocentricity on the part of his children, but is a Creator who expects creativity from us.

This aspect of the Deity is what can be called "the dark side of God." God's dark side destroys everything in us that is not fit to exist. It is as determined as is the husbandman who cuts off the sickly worthless branches and destroys them in the fire and is comparable to that capacity of the unconscious to ferret out and destroy all those elements of character, egocentricity, and unconsciousness that have thwarted the creative process within us. This dark side of God, however, is not evil, for it serves what is ultimately a creative purpose. The dark side of God destroys what is not fit to exist; evil, on the other hand, seeks to destroy what is sound and whole. Because of God's destructive side, God is called "the Destroyer"[2] by Paul (1 Cor. 10:10), and therefore God is to be feared with a holy fear. But God is not to be feared as we are to fear evil, for evil has the power to destroy the soul while God destroys only that which does not properly belong to the soul.[3]

For this reason we must care for the living process that goes on within us. Like a good gardener who tills the soil of the garden and cares for the plants, so we must till the soil of the soul and tend to the inner life. We are reminded of the three meanings of the word *therapeuō*, which we have noted before: to heal or cure,

---

2. The Greek word is *olothreutēs*, one who destroys; cf. Heb. 12:27.
3. For a further discussion of this distinction see chap. 9 of my book *C. G. Jung and the Problem of Evil: The Strange Trial of Mr. Hyde* (Boston: Sigo Press, 1993).

to render service to God, and to till the soil. We are called upon to undertake the therapy of the soul, and this involves caring for the soul as a gardener cares for the garden.

Many centuries ago Clement of Alexandria used this image of a gardener caring for the soul when he commented on this very passage that we are considering. Blind faith, he says, is not enough; the task also requires diligent inner work. He writes,

> Some, who think themselves naturally gifted, do not wish to touch either philosophy or logic; nay more, they do not wish to learn natural science. They demand bare faith alone, as if they wished, without bestowing any care on the vine, straightway to gather clusters from the first. Now the Lord is figuratively described as the vine, from which, with pains and the art of husbandry, according to the word, the fruit is to be gathered.
>
> We must lop, dig, bind, and perform the other operations. The pruning-knife, I should think, and the pick-axe, and the other agricultural implements, are necessary for the culture of the vine, so that it may produce eatable fruit. And as in husbandry, so also in medicine: he has learned to purpose, who has practiced the various lessons, so as to be able to cultivate and to heal. So also here, I call him truly learned, who brings everything to bear on the truth; so that, from geometry, and music, and grammar, and philosophy itself, culling what is useful, he guards the faith against assault.[4]

It remains to make a few comparisons between the symbolism of the vine in John 15 and the way the image of the vine appears in other psychological and religious traditions. First it is noteworthy that the vine occurs regularly as a symbol in our dreams. Here it plays much the same role as does the tree: it represents the process of individuation as a natural but also mystical process of growth leading to a flowering or consummation. The vine also occasionally occurs in fairy tales. The best known example is "Jack and the Beanstalk." The "beanstalk" is actually a giant vine that grows up into the sky where the giant and his wife live and where Jack ultimately finds the goose that lays the golden egg. Here the vine is a symbol for a connecting link between the conscious world on the one hand and the hidden treasures in the unconscious on

---

4. *The Stromata* 1.9.

the other hand. In the same way, in John's Gospel the vine is the link that connects and binds together the consciousness of those who follow Christ with Christ, who is the great source of their vital life.

In the symbolism of alchemy, which Jung has shown to be a storehouse of symbols for the individuation process, the vine (along with the tree) was said to appear frequently as an image in the alchemical retort. The alchemist was urged to meditate and pray upon this image of the vine that it might grow and flower because it symbolized the life of the vital process of transformation going on in the alchemical vessel. Jung believed that this alchemical image of the vine was influenced by the image of Christ as the vine in John 15, which in turn belongs to a widespread lore of the fruitful tree as a symbol for the success of the work of individuation.[5]

The most striking comparison, however, is to be found in the symbol of the vine as it appears in the ancient Greek religion of Dionysus. Dionysus was the Greek god of wine and ecstasy, and his worship eventually evolved into a mystery cult that offered the worshiper transformation and immortality. The vine was an important symbol in the cult of Dionysus because of the importance of the grape, and it soon achieved a mystical significance. Dionysus has a dubious reputation in the Christian world because of the association between Dionysus and drunkenness. However, the essence of Dionysus was not the vulgar (common) drunkenness, but ecstasy, in the original sense of that word. The word "ecstasy" is derived from the Greek word *extasis*, which means to stand apart from, or outside of, oneself. It is of great importance for the ego to know moments of ecstasy: otherwise the ego is confined to and shut up in an "ego box." This ego box is created by a purely rational attitude toward life and by a reliance totally on sense impression for information and stimulus. When this happens a person is rational, sensible, and factual, which has its advantages, but if this is the only experience open to the soul it leads to a psychic state that eventually becomes intolerable. Then the soul longs to burst out of what has become a prison and merge with the Divine. This "getting out of oneself" is *extasis*, or ecstasy, and to find healthy ways to accomplish this is vital to the vigor

---

5. See Jung's "The Philosophical Tree" in *Collected Works* 13.

and enlightenment of the soul. This the cult of Dionysus offered to its adherents.

At one time it was one of the main functions of religion to help people find the true ecstasy, that is, to offer ways in which a person could leave for the time being the usual boundaries and structures in which we are for the most part confined, so we could, through ecstasy, find a transforming and enlivening relationship with the creative powers within us. Today, however, many of our expressions of religion have so succumbed to the rational, mate- rial, and moralistic attitudes of our times that they have little to offer their adherents in the way of ecstatic release for the soul. The unrecognized need of the soul for spiritual ecstasy remains, however, and a considerable amount of alcoholism, drug addic- tion, and addiction to sexuality may be the result. Add to this the ingestion of so-called consciousness-transforming drugs and we can see that while the ego may achieve a temporary release through various methods such as these it does so at what may be a terrible price, for these methods of achieving ecstasy do not lead to the development of consciousness but to the reverse: the lowering of consciousness. The true ecstasy is to be found, as we have mentioned, through union with God, which is for the Christian made possible by union with Christ, and this union is the practical goal of all true mystical endeavor. Christ, as the "true Dionysus," enabled his followers to transcend the narrower "ethic of obedience" (to use Berdyayev's terminology) and step into the "ethic of creativity." In psychological language, in union with Christ one no longer lives only from the confines of the ego, but has a connection to the endless creativity of the Center within.

In original Christianity, which John's Gospel represents, Christ offered to the soul the way to a higher knowledge of God through ecstasy. For this reason the worship of Christ in the early church was through the celebration of the "Mysteries." Christ himself was a mystery in the sense of a *mystērion*, which, as we have already noted, is the way to a knowledge that can be acquired only through direct and personal experience. The worshiper, through participating mystically in Christ's death and resurrection and through being grafted onto Christ's life as the branches to the vine, achieved a knowledge of God via ecstasy. In this experience the old, tired, rigid ego was dissolved, and a new ego could be formed by the upsurge of creative powers from within.

While there is no direct connection between Christ and Dionysus, there is a certain similarity between the two with regard to what they symbolize. This similarity occurs in the New Testament in the use of a special word in Greek to refer to the triumphal procession of Christ when he has rid the world of the confining Archons and Powers of this world through his triumph on the cross. So we read in Colossians 2:15,

> He has overridden the Law, and cancelled every record of the debt that we had to pay; he has done away with it by nailing it to the cross, and so he got rid of the Sovereignties and the Powers, and paraded them in public, behind him in his triumphal procession.

And in 2 Corinthians 2:14 we read,

> Thanks be to God who, wherever he goes, makes us, in Christ, partners of his triumph, and through us is spreading the knowledge of himself, like a sweet smell, everywhere.

The key word in these two passages is the Greek word *thriambeuō*, which means "to celebrate a triumph." It was this word that was used with reference to a general who had defeated the enemy and now paraded triumphantly through the streets with his defeated opponents following abjectly behind in chains. It also was the word that was used by the Greeks to describe the triumphal procession of Dionysus as he led his followers in a festive procession because of his victory over death.

The following passage from Origen sums up a good deal of what we have noted about the powerful symbolism of the vine. In this passage, in which Origen compares the image of Christ as the bread to the image of Christ as the vine, he writes:

> To what men have said must be added how the Son is the true vine. Those will have no difficulty in apprehending this who understand, in a manner worthy of the prophetic grace, the saying: "Wine maketh glad the heart of man" (Ps. 104:15). For if the heart be the intellectual (that is, spiritual) part, and what rejoices it is the Word most pleasant of all to drink which takes us off human things, makes us feel ourselves inspired, and intoxicates us with an intoxication which is not irrational but divine, that, I conceive, with which Joseph made his brethren merry (Gen. 43:34), then it is very clear how He who brings wine thus to rejoice the heart of man

is the true vine. He is the true vine, because the grapes He bears are the truth, the disciples are His branches, and they also bring forth truth as their fruit. It is somewhat difficult to show the difference between the vine and bread, for He says, not only that He is the vine, but that He is the bread of life. May it be that as bread nourishes and makes strong, and is said to strengthen the heart of man, but wine, on the contrary, pleases and rejoices and melts him, so ethical studies, bringing life to him who learns them and reduces them to practice, are the bread of life, but cannot properly be called the fruit of the vine, while secret and mystical speculations, rejoicing the heart and causing those to feel inspired who take them in, delighting in the Lord, and who desire not only to be nourished but to be made happy, are called the juice of the true vine, because they flow from it.[6]

---

6. *Commentary on John* 33.

⌒ 27 ⌒

DEEPER MYSTERIES
The Coming of the Paraclete
John 16:5–33

JOHN 16:5 BEGINS WITH JESUS' DECLARATION that he is going to send the "Paraclete" to the disciples. He tells them that this was not necessary before because he was with them, but now that he is going away to the Father the Paraclete will come. However, this coming of the Paraclete is no mere substitute for Jesus because, as we discover in 16:7, it is good for the disciples that Jesus goes away precisely because it means the Paraclete will come. Why this is a positive step for the disciples we will consider shortly, but first we need to look at what this mysterious Paraclete is like.

In Greek the word "Paraclete" is *paraklētos*. The essential meaning of this word is "one called or sent for to assist another." From this derives the meaning of Advocate or Counselor. We are reminded of the story in Zechariah 3 in which Satan stands at the right hand of Joshua accusing him, but an angel of the Lord takes the side of Joshua, removes from Joshua his soiled garments and has him clothed in fresh ones, pronounces that his iniquity is taken away, and stands by him, nullifying the power of Satan. In such a way the Paraclete stands by us, helping us against the powers of evil and pleading our cause.

Elsewhere in John's Gospel the Paraclete is described as a teacher (John 14:26). A teacher stands on the side of our growing knowledge and awareness. A good teacher is a friend to all those who want to know and a helper who assists us in overcoming not only our ignorance but also our feelings of inadequacy and

288

discouragement. In 15:26 the Paraclete is also described as the spirit who will bear witness to Christ. Thus the Paraclete points the way to Christ. If Christ is the road to salvation (John 14:6), the Paraclete is the one who shows us the way to find that road and bears witness to its existence.

But most of all the Paraclete is the Spirit of Truth (John 14:16, 15:26, 16:7), and so is a counter to "this world," which lives in a kind of "mayanic unconsciousness" and so does not know the *real* world, (i.e., the spiritual world). As the Spirit of Truth the Paraclete will lead us to the "complete truth." Note that here it is not general truth to which the Bible refers but to *the* truth. The Paraclete is *the* Spirit of *the* Truth (*to pneuma tēs alētheias*). The reader will remember that *alētheia* means essential truth, and the presence of the article signifies that the truth involved is the essence of truth itself. It is also interesting that the word "will lead" is the Greek *hodēgeō,* which is compounded from *hodos* plus a Greek word meaning to lead or be chief (*hēgeomai*). (We encountered the word *hodos* already in John 14:6.) So the Paraclete is the Spirit who leads us to Christ as the Way and, as the guide to the complete truth, stands in an antithetical position to the devil who is the spirit of lies. Small wonder then that the Paraclete is not only *the* Spirit, but is the *Holy* Spirit.

The functions of the Holy Spirit are psychologically identifiable: wherever the truth prevails or is seeking to prevail, the Holy Spirit is there. There is a reality at work within us, even though we are often unaware of it, that seeks to bring us to the truth: the truth about our world, the truth about ourselves, the truth about God and life's purpose. It is indeed the opposite of that archetypal propensity toward evil that also seems to be an element in the human psyche: a tendency toward evil with which the ego, in its egocentricity, sides. This polarity of energies within our psyche is like the two masters of Matthew 6:24, both of whom we cannot serve.

It is therefore the Holy Spirit that brings unholy secrets to light. It is a psychological fact that it is extremely difficult for a person or a group to keep things of moral darkness hidden. Sooner or later the truth will come out, for unholy secrets are propelled into awareness by a powerful psychic force. Even if the unholy secret is never seen by others, it requires a great deal of psychic energy to keep it from being exposed. Holy secrets, on the other hand, can be kept, for the same Spirit of Truth who impels the unholy secrets into consciousness helps us in keeping the holy secrets.

An example of an unholy secret would be a crime, or perhaps an illicit love affair that damages the relationship with our wife or husband, or any kind of egocentric plot. But let us imagine that we lived in the era of World War II and we knew the identity of the freedom fighters. That too would be a secret, but it would be a holy secret and the Spirit of Truth would help us keep it rather than pushing it out into the general awareness.

The Holy Spirit is accordingly also that Spirit which brings to light matters of sin: "And when he comes, he will show the world how wrong it was, about sin, and about who was in the right, and about judgment..." (16:8). The Greek word for sin that is used here is *hamartia*, which we have already discussed, and we saw that its root meaning is "to miss the mark." In this context, sin thus denotes any failure of consciousness. It means to fail in our moral or psychological awareness when we are called upon to understand, or to live from our egocentricity when we are called upon to live from the Center. It is a function of the Spirit to bring to light all such failures and in this way to guide us in our individuation and moral growth. Thus the Holy Spirit is God operative in our relationships, our outer life, and especially in those inner depths that we call the unconscious.

The Holy Spirit can also be said to be the author of our dreams. The peculiar function of dreams is to show us our inner situation exactly as it is. Freud originally thought that dreams disguised the truth under a façade, but the reverse is actually the case. If we dream a frightening dream, for instance, a dream in which a dark power or dangerous person emerges, we must recognize that this is part of the truth about ourselves. Or if we dream a beautiful dream full of encouragement and power, we need to know that this is also part of our inner truth. This is one reason why the analysis of dreams, when properly undertaken, can be so valuable in both psychotherapy and spiritual direction.

The phenomenon of synchronicity can also be ascribed to the Holy Spirit. Synchronicity is the meaningful coincidence of seemingly disparate events. Event A and event B, which seem to have no direct connection with each other, can nevertheless be connected via the unconscious if they both participate in the same spiritual or archetypal meaning. So a meeting with someone who later proves to be vital in our life might appear on the surface to be accidental, but viewed in a deeper light the meeting of the two people who later prove of great value and importance to each other is guided by the Spirit operating through synchronicity.

We turn now to the important emphasis in John 16 on the departure and return of Christ. Jesus speaks to the disciples of his departure and return in verses 16:1–7 and again in 16:20–21, where he makes it clear that while at first his departure will be an occasion for grief on the part of the disciples, their sorrow will soon turn to joy. The depths of this experience are illustrated in the beautiful image of verse 21 of the woman giving birth to her child: at first the woman suffers, but when the time has come to give birth to the child and the child has been born into the world, there is great rejoicing. This is a psychologically important image, for the process of individuation can be likened to giving birth to an inner child. Indeed, it is often so described in dreams in which a mysterious woman is pregnant, or a dream in which a marvelous child is born at last.

Fritz Kunkel has an interesting perspective on this portion of John's Gospel. If Jesus had not left the disciples, he notes, they would have been left in a state of idolatry. You will recall that Kunkel regarded idolatry as occurring when the Center is projected onto another human being. As long as the disciples had Jesus with them they could project the Center onto him, but when Jesus left them they had to find the Center within themselves. Put in religious language, as long as the Christ was with them in the body the disciples would not discover the greater mystery: that the Holy Spirit within them would lead them to the Christ who dwells within the soul, from whom they could never be separated. The tribulation and distress the disciples had to endure when Christ did leave them at the time of the crucifixion was, Kunkel believed, an absolutely essential part of their growth into consciousness.

We might note in passing that something like this often occurs in psychotherapy or spiritual direction. When the client first comes to therapy he frequently projects the Center onto the therapist. This becomes part of the transference, as discussed earlier. Eventually, however, this projection must be withdrawn so the client can discover the Center in himself. The therapist usually assists in this transformation both wittingly and unwittingly. Consciously the therapist tries, at the right point in the therapy, to make it clear that she is not the Center. Unconsciously the therapist may also make blunders, or reveal painfully her own areas of unconsciousness. The client may then realize that this therapist is, after all, only human, and that the true Center lies within himself.

This loss of the physical presence of their Lord and his forth-coming crucifixion constitutes the second stage of initiation. In a previous chapter we mentioned the three stages of Christian initi-ation and described the first stage, which Dean Alan Jones called the crisis of meaning. The loss of Christ constellates the second stage, which Dean Jones called the crisis of betrayal. Of course it is not a true betrayal, only a seeming betrayal, but the disciples must undergo the experience as though the betrayal were real in order that they are thrown back upon themselves, thus with-drawing their projections from Jesus and finding the true Christ within. The fact that the disciples had not yet been initiated into the second stage of their development may be the reason Christ says "until now you have not asked for anything in my name" (16:24). The usual interpretation of this verse is that the disciples did not yet pray in Christ's name because he had not yet been glorified, but another possible meaning is that they had not yet prayed in Christ's name because their egocentricity was not yet eroded away. For this to happen the second stage of initiation is necessary: then the strength of their prayers can deepen.

It remains to comment on the relationship of John 16 to the Christian doctrine of the Trinity. The doctrine of the triune nature of God as such is not found in the New Testament, but the ele-ments of it are there, and John 16 is a good example, for here we find references to God as the Father, as the Son (Christ), and as the Holy Spirit. From such biblical texts and from Christian mysti-cal experience and speculations there arose that central Christian doctrine: the doctrine of the Trinity. In this doctrine the Father, Son, and Holy Spirit are regarded as three "Persons" (*prosōpon*), yet each one of these Persons is also the total Godhead. It is not that each one of the three Persons represents a certain portion or particular manifestation of the Godhead; rather each Person *is* the total Godhead. The relationship of the three Persons to each other and to the Godhead as a unity constituted the Christian *mystērion* of the three-in-one and was a theological puzzle that the greatest minds of the early church strived mightily to solve. How could these three "Persons" also constitute one "Being" (*ousia*)? It had to be shown that each Person was distinct, yet that they not only constituted a unity but that each expressed the fullness of God.

To be able to demonstrate the triune nature of God was to be able to distinguish between the Christian revelation and the more simple monotheism of Judaism. On the other hand the unity of God was to draw a distinction between Christianity and the polytheistic religions that abounded in the ancient world, and also between Christianity and Gnosticism, whose many "aeons" emanating from the Godhead sounded to the Christians like so many other "gods" in metaphysical disguise. But theological dangers lay on all sides: to make the distinction among the three Persons too great was to fall into the dangers of tri-theism or to necessitate the subordination of one Person of the Trinity to another. On the other hand, to fail to draw the distinctions carefully was to negate the mystery of the Trinity. If, for instance, it was said that the Father was uncreated and eternal, but the Son was created, then the Son became inferior to the Father. This led to the heresy of Arianism, which said that Christ was not of the same nature as the Father but was "elevated," as it were, to the Godhead.

It would take us beyond the scope of this work to go into details about the intricacies of the Christian doctrine of the Trinity or about the doctrinal disputes that arose from it. Suffice it to say that the theological mentality of the early Christian church, especially in the East, fascinated the ancient mind to a degree that seems almost incomprehensible to our modern mentality. Most people today regard the ancient arguments about the Trinity as antiquated theological hairsplitting and honor the idea of the Trinity only in "archaic" creeds (like the Nicene Creed), which embody defenses against ancient heresies that are largely unknown to Christian congregations today and that strike the modern mind as so many theological dinosaurs.[1]

The fact is, however, that for the early Christians, especially in the Eastern church, the nature of the Trinity was not only fascinating but had practical consequences. We have already spoken of the importance in early Christianity of the idea of the deification of the soul and have noted that this could not be accomplished except for the fact that the Logos of God incarnated as Christ in human nature, thus winning human nature back from its fallen and corrupted condition. Now, if this Logos were not wholly and truly God then this redemption of human nature could not have

---

1. A major exception is the mysticism of the Eastern Orthodox Church for which the Trinity is still a vital image of God and fundamental to its theory of deification.

taken place, and, as a consequence, deification would not be possible. Similarly, if the Holy Spirit was not also the Godhead itself
then the process of deification would be aborted; hence the importance for the thinking of the Eastern church that the Holy Spirit
proceed from the Father alone and not from the Father and the
Son. Behind the idea of the Trinity, therefore, lies a practical matter: how can human nature be changed, renewed, redeemed, and
brought to its ultimate destination? The Christian Trinity, moreover, was an object of mystical contemplation that drew the soul
ever onward toward its deification and ultimate union with God.
The full mystery of the Trinity was not arrived at by philosophical
speculation or rational thought, but was received as a revelation
in an ecstatic mystical and transforming experience. There was
also the idea in the early church that the archetype of the Trinity
was in the human psyche. Gregory of Nyssa, for instance, argued
that the human being also had a triune nature, embodied in the
soul (*psychē*), word (*logos*), and mind (*nous*). Gregory believed
that from this trinity within the human psyche the nature of the
triune God could be inferred.[2]

A difficulty with the doctrine of the Trinity is that it involves
such abstruse theological arguments that few people indeed are
able to understand them. There is even some reason to believe
that this is one major reason why Islam replaced Christianity in
north Africa and parts of the eastern Mediterranean world: the
simplicity of Islam vis-à-vis Christianity appealed to many people, and the theological divisions among the Christians weakened
the faith in the face of Islamic religious fervor.

By the nineteenth century most Christians honored the idea
of the Trinity by reciting the Nicene Creed but had little or no
understanding of its intricate theological meaning and had given
up trying to understand it, leaving that matter to trained theologians. As we saw earlier, this turned out to be a major reason that
C. G. Jung early in his life turned his back on the Christian church.
In his autobiography, *Memories, Dreams, Reflections,* Jung tells us
how he eagerly awaited the confirmation instruction he would
receive from his clergyman father because the young Carl was
intrigued by this mysterious doctrine of the Trinity and wanted
to understand it. But his father, no intellectual giant, dismissed
the matter quickly, saying it was all a mystery that could not be

---

2. See his treatise *On the Soul and Resurrection.*

understood and should be accepted on faith. That finished Jung off right there with the church because Jung believed that you either knew something or you didn't know it, and if you didn't know you shouldn't go around believing it "on faith."

Perhaps it was Jung's disappointment with his father and the church that gave him a certain bias against the number three, which was evident throughout much of his life. Jung seems to have regarded the number three, insofar as its symbolic value was concerned, as nothing more than a kind of mutilated number four. For Jung the number four was the number of the quaternity, therefore the number for wholeness. The four enclosed the whole of something, like the four corners of a square, but the number three was believed to be deficient. So when it came to the Trinity Jung believed it was deficient as a representation of the wholeness of God. What was missing in the Christian trinitarian God-image, Jung believed, was the feminine, or sometimes he said it was the principle of evil. In basing its image of God on the number three instead of the number four Jung believed Christianity left out a vital component and thus failed to present a complete symbol of the Self.

As far as the Gospel of John is concerned, however, the various Persons of God were neither masculine nor feminine, or, one could say, they included both masculine and feminine. The Holy Spirit, for instance, is neuter: the Greek *hagion pneuma* bears the neuter article. The Father, as we have seen earlier, is not a sexual designation but specified that which is uncreated and utterly transcendent, and there is no sexual distinction in the nature of God as the Transcendent. The Son, as we have seen, is the Logos of God, which is identical in the early Christian mind with Sophia, or divine Wisdom, which bears a feminine designation. Thus it is not quite correct to say that the Christian triune portrayal of the divine nature favors a purely masculine element and disregards the feminine. Moreover, as noted earlier, in Christian mystical theology God is beyond *all* human categories of thought. To describe the Godhead in terms of sexual identification would be to apply merely human categories to a reality beyond all comprehension, all description, and all conceptualization. As for evil, while John's Gospel is quite aware of the reality of evil John does not attribute *ousia* to evil, that is, evil has no being in itself. Evil is a contingent reality, not an ultimate reality; therefore while real as part of our human experience it is not real as part of the Godhead.

Of course this does not deny that God has a dark side, but, as we
have already observed, God's dark side destroys that which is
not fit to exist while evil seeks to destroy that which is fit to exist.

A better way to approach the meaning of the Trinity is to allow the number three to have its own symbolic integrity. It will
be remembered from the introduction that numerology — the
assigning of spiritual qualities and symbolic meanings to numbers — was of great significance in the early church, and that
virtually every number in the Bible was regarded as having a
mystical meaning as well as an arithmetical meaning. So for the
early Christians and for the Bible in general the number three was
not simply a mutilated four but had its own special meaning and
integrity: it symbolized either the completion of a revelation or
the completion of a process.

Regarding revelation, it can be said in general that the full manifestation of an archetype has a threefold aspect. In Greek mythology, for instance, the goddesses are almost always grouped in
threes (three Gorgons, three Fates, nine Muses, and so forth). Examples of this from the Bible include the following: In the Book of
Genesis we find that Abraham entertained three men, unaware at
first that these men were really angels. In Mark 9:5 the disciples at
the time of the transfiguration propose that three tabernacles be
erected as a commemoration. In Revelation 16:19 the great city of
Babylon is split by the angels into three parts. These experiences
all relate to the manifestation or revelation of some reality that
has a holy significance, a reality that can be known only through
revelation, that is, through an ecstatic mystical experience and
not through any philosophical or rational speculation.

The number three as a process number is even more frequent.
In fairy tales, for instance, one knocks on the door three times
and then it opens. In the game of baseball the batter gets three
strikes and then is out, and the team that is batting gets three
outs and then it relinquishes the batting to the other team. In the
Bible we see this use of the number three in Numbers 22, in which
Balaam's donkey bolts off the path three times before Balaam's
eyes are opened and he sees the angel with the flaming sword
standing in his path. In the Book of Jonah, the prophet is in the
belly of the whale for three days, and so also Christ is three days
in the realm of death after the crucifixion. In the Book of Samuel,
we learn that Yahweh called the boy Samuel's name three times,
and the old priest Eli bade Samuel to answer the Lord after the

completion of the third call. In the Book of Ecclesiastes we learn that the strongest cord is a threefold cord. In Acts 11:1ff Paul, in a trance, hears God's call to him three times. In the synoptic Gospels we are told that Christ in the wilderness was tempted by Satan three times, and that in the Garden of Gethsemane he admonished the disciples three times to stay awake and watch with him (after the third time he gave up on them). During the accounts of the trial and scourging of Jesus we learn that Peter denied the Lord three times and then broke down and wept bitterly. Christ, of course, rose from the dead on the third day, and in the final chapter of John's Gospel we find that Jesus spoke to Peter about love three times.

This is not to say, however, that the number four was neglected. The number four for the Bible and for the early Christians symbolized just what it did for Jung: totality. For this reason the prophet Ezekiel had a fourfold vision, which was then repeated in the Book of Revelation, and for this reason there were four Gospels, this number being required, Irenaeus said, because the number four represented completion.[3]

There was also an interesting connection between the numbers three and four. In the Book of Daniel, for instance, the three men in the fiery furnace are joined by a mysterious fourth presence. In the Book of Revelation the heavenly Jerusalem has four sides to it but each side has three gates. The four Gospels include three Gospels that are similar (the synoptic Gospels) and another (John's) that is called the Fourth Gospel. Theophilus of Antioch said that the first three days of creation were the Trinity: of God, God's Word, and God's Wisdom — but the fourth day was man, in whom the triune nature was embodied as body, soul, and spirit.[4]

Therefore, it is not that the number three was invalid, as Jung implied. Rather the two sacred numbers three and four had an affinity to each other, for added together they made the number seven, which was another holy number in Christian numerology, and multiplied together they made the number twelve, which was the "great round" and was perhaps the holiest number of all (the twelve tribes of Israel, for instance, and later the twelve disciples.

So it was that the early Christians were fascinated by the symbolic and spiritual qualities of the number three and believed that

---

3. Irenaeus, *Against Heresies* 3.11.8.
4. *Theophilus to Autolycus* 2.15.

the full revelation of God required a threefold expression of a divine unity, a unity that was, paradoxically, inherent completely in each member of the Trinity. The extent to which this belief was a dynamic mystical experience and not a mere theological abstraction is hinted at in the following comment on the Trinity from the early Christian theologian and mystic Gregory of Nazianzen:

> No sooner do I conceive of the One than I am illumined by the splendor of the Three, no sooner do I distinguish them than I am carried back to the One. When I think of any One of the Three, I think of Him as the whole, and my eyes are filled, and the greater part of what I am thinking of escapes me. I cannot grasp the greatness of that One so as to attribute a greater greatness to the rest. When I contemplate the Three together, I see but one torch, and cannot divide or measure out the undivided light.[5]

Times have changed today, however, and people are more practical and scientific than they are mystical. So the old metaphysical problems that fascinated the early Christians and that aroused such passions because they were believed to have practical consequences for the destiny of the soul no longer grip our imagination. Nevertheless, the ancient theology with its issues for the destiny of the soul are still alive in the psyche, and in our dreams the number three still carries its ancient and transformative meanings. These are meanings that, as perhaps Jung's father realized, can never be rationally explained, but can only be revealed to those persons who are in immediate contact with spiritual reality.

---

5. Gregory of Nazianzen, *Oratio* XL, 41; quoted from Vladimir Lossky, *The Mystical Theology of the Eastern Church* (Crestwood, N.Y.: St. Vladimir's Seminary Press, 1976). This book is highly recommended for the reader who wishes to explore further mystical traditions in the early Christian church, many of which are still alive in Eastern Orthodoxy.

~ 28 ~

THAT WE MAY BE ONE
The Priestly Prayer of Christ
John 17

JOHN'S CHAPTER 17 consists of a long soliloquy by Jesus known as the high priestly prayer. We will begin with a textual analysis.

Verse 1: The Greek word usually translated as "glorify" implies in this context "make radiant." We could say that the prayer begins with a reference to the numinosity of the Father, to be bestowed likewise on Christ as the Son.

Verse 2: The prayer is for eternal life to those who belong to God. This is not to be confused with a mere perpetuation of the existence of the ego, but in keeping with the totality of John's Gospel means participation in Eternal Life itself. If a person bathes in a river she is not the river but participates in the river. So the faithful participate in Eternal Life (*zōēn aiōnion*) becoming, as it were, one with it.

Verse 3: The essential quality of this life consists in the knowledge of God. The word for this knowledge, as we might suspect, is the now familiar *gnōsis* — the experiential, mystical knowledge. It is not exactly that we *have* this knowledge like a possession; rather, we participate in it. In this way our small awareness becomes one with *the* awareness of God. To *know* God is thus to acquire an entirely new consciousness.

Verse 4: Christ has "finished the work." The word translated "finished' (*teleioō*) is one of those words in the New Testament that stem from the Greek word *telos*, which, as we have noted, means a consummation, an end attained, a fulfillment or realization. It

299

is an important word, for the idea of Christianity is that God's work among us is a process, begun by Christ and completed in the deification of the human soul and the ultimate completion of the entire cosmos. It is also an important word for the psychology of individuation that sees the life of an individual human being as called toward a certain end or realization. The vision of John's Gospel is of one vast cosmic plan which has existed from the beginning in the Mind of God, which is played out in the drama of what we call history, and in which each individual plays his or her small part.

Verse 5: This verse is a reference to Christ's forthcoming crucifixion and resurrection. These events were highly numinous. In Matthew's Gospel this numinosity was marked by an earthquake that occurred at the precise moment of Christ's death on the cross (Matt. 28:2). Earthquakes in the Bible mark numinous events and signal the activity of God's power.[1] It is interesting in this connection to note that earthquakes in dreams signify a similar event on the level of individual psychology: the emergence of the numinous power of the Self, which will shake down everything that is not strong in the personality. While John does not mention the earthquake cited by Matthew, it is clear that for both evangelists the events surrounding Christ's death partook of a numinous quality.

Verse 6: Making the Father's name known entails a great expansion of consciousness in the minds and hearts of those who now know, through Christ, of the numinous and utterly transcendent Father. Naturally such an enlarged consciousness removes those who possess it from the collective mentality and limited awareness of those whose consciousness is shaped only by "this world."

Verses 7–8: Now at last the disciples know that the reality in Christ comes from the Father. We have here a mystical model of reality: the created, visible world is the expression of a Real world that is beyond the ordinary comprehension of human beings but can be known by a profound interior realization, a mystical insight that brings about a totally new consciousness. It is this comprehension that has been taught to the disciples by Christ; the disciples have partaken of a small portion of it and made

---

1. See for instance Matthew 27:51ff, 24:7; Mark 13:8; Luke 21:11; Acts 16:26; Revelation 6:12 (and many other places in Revelation); and Hebrews 12:26.

it their own, but not yet entirely as the events surrounding the crucifixion make clear.

Verses 9–10: It may seem strange that Christ is not praying for the world but only for the small circle of the disciples. Here "the world" may be understood once again as "this world of unconsciousness and ignorance." On the cross Christ died on behalf of the whole world, but here his prayers are intended especially for those few persons, his disciples, who are approaching a new consciousness. Regarding "this world" author Robert Johnson once commented, "The world isn't meant to work; but it does provide an arena for the advancement of individual consciousness."[2] The emphasis appears to be on quality. Unlike many contemporary religious leaders who count their success in the number of conversions, the importance in this chapter is not on numbers and quantity, but those changes in the quality of consciousness that take place only in individuals. And, of course, it is only from those changes of consciousness in individuals that the general consciousness of "this world" can be altered.

We also find in verse 9 a peculiarity in the use of a Greek word translated "pray" ("I am not praying for the world"). The Greek word used here and also in verses 9:15 and 9:20 is *erōtaō*; it is used in John's Gospel with reference to Christ's prayers to the Father. When the disciples' prayers are referred to, another Greek word (*aiteō*) is used. The usage of different words for the prayers of Christ and those of the disciples may be an expression of the qualitative difference between the relationship of Christ to the Father and that of the disciples to the Father.

Verse 11: "Holy Father" — the word *hagios* is used here which, as we have ready seen, means "separate from." So the Father is wholly separate from the "thinking of this world."

Verse 12: The reference to "except the one who chose to be lost" is literally in the Greek "except the son of perdition" (*ho huios tēs apōleias*) and is so translated in the King James Version and the Revised Standard Version. It is not clear why the Jerusalem Bible does not follow the Greek more closely in this instance. The reference is no doubt to Judas, as we have already suggested in our study of Judas. The image of the son of perdition is akin to the Greek image of the goddess Atē. As we have seen, Atē roamed

---

2. From a private conversation with Robert A. Johnson, author of *He: Understanding Masculine Psychology* (New York: HarperCollins, 1989), *She: Understanding Feminine Psychology* (New York: HarperCollins, 1989), and many other books.

around the earth inciting human beings to acts of sin, ruin, and folly. Those who allowed themselves to be influenced by Atē were led to moral, spiritual, and eventually worldly ruin. Even though Atē incited their acts, it was believed that in the final analysis the individual lent his or her will to Atē and so the individuals were morally responsible. In much the same way John believes the spirit of evil roams the earth seducing human beings to follow his promptings, and those who do so become themselves "sons of perdition."

Verses 13–19: These verses mark on the one hand the totally different reality to which Christ is now going, and on the other hand the darkness and unconsciousness of "this world," which rejects the enlightenment brought by the knowledge of God. Yet the prayer is not that the disciples be removed from the world. As noted, the world is like an arena in which consciousness can develop and like a great field in which spiritual work is to be done, but there is a prayer that their souls be protected from "the evil one," while in the world.

Here again we have the definite article in Greek before the word *ponēros*, which as we have seen can mean either "evil" or "the evil one" but always refers to evil as a spiritual power or agency. So Christ is not praying to God that the disciples be protected from evil in general, which might include protection from illnesses, difficulties, temptations, and so forth, but rather that they be protected from the pernicious spirit of evil that can destroy the soul. Similarly, the prayer is not that they be consecrated (literally "set aside") to truth in general, but to *the* truth, which is nothing other than the *logos*, or word of God.

Verse 20: This verse is a reference to the as yet unseen multitude who will believe in Christ through the words (*logos*) of the disciples. As the consciousness of the disciples increases, so does their influence on others. It is not the ordinary words of the disciples that will influence others but their *logos*, that is, their mind and comprehension. In our action-oriented culture it is hard to believe that what really changes the hearts and minds of others is not actions as such, but only those actions that proceed from people with an enlightened consciousness.

Verses 21–23: These verses center around the idea or image of being One. The language is thoroughly mystical. The disciples are to be One in the Father and the Son even as the Father and the Son interpenetrate and are One with each other. This mystical interpenetration also extends to the disciples themselves, who will be completely One, for even as the Father is in the Son, so the Son will be in them (v. 23). It is this Oneness that will move the ordinary consciousness of those in the world to belief. Clement of Alexandria employs the Pythagorean idea of the mystical quality of the One in order to explain this passage: "Accordingly that Pythagorean saying was mystically uttered respecting us, 'That man ought to become one'; for the high priest himself is one, God being one in the immutable state of the perpetual flow of good things ... and man, when deified purely into a passionless state, becomes a unit."[3]

This Oneness is a powerful image. We already have met the image of the One as a symbol for Christ. The goal of individuation is also expressed by the image of Oneness: the many elements that make up who we are, are united in a unity that is composed of a diversity. That early depth psychologist Gregory of Nyssa, as we noted earlier, saw the soul in a person as "a sort of populace of souls crowded together, each ... differing widely from the rest." This plurality of souls is reflected in our dreams by the multitude of people who appear in them. The marvel, Gregory went on to say, is that there is a Unity composed of them all, a Unity that "blends and harmonizes things (which are ordinarily) mutually opposed, so that many things become one."[4]

Christian representations of this Oneness are found in the rose windows of our churches and cathedrals. Rose windows are stained-glass windows made in a concentric design, usually with the figure of Christ or a symbol for Christ in the center, composed of many colors and symbols that are enclosed in the circle and grouped around the center. These mandalas, as Jung has shown, express the integration of the personality that is the result of the process of individuation. Indeed, Jung once said of the meaning of John 17:20ff that the secret of the passage "lies in the integration of all those disparate parts of yourself into a whole."[5]

In the mystical thought of John's Gospel, however, this Oneness refers not only to the wholeness of the individual but also to the wholeness of the community of all persons who belong to God. Jung's idea of individuation stresses the wholeness of the individual as over against the collective group. In fact, Jung

---

3. Clement of Alexandria, *The Stromata* 4.23.
4. Gregory of Nyssa, *Answer to Eunomius's Second Book*.
5. Jung, *Letters* 2, 145–46.

saw identity with a group not as wholeness but as a "participation mystique" in which the individual lost his or her uniqueness
and consciousness to the group so that a kind of corporate ego
was formed. Such a psychological condition usually results in
a diminution of consciousness and a surrender of individual
conscience to the collective will. Such a psychological condition
surely does exist — Nazi Germany is a classic example of it —
and is to be feared, but this is not what John's Gospel has in
mind. In John's Gospel the wholeness of the individual is not
found in a person as an isolated unit, but in a whole person who
lives in creative and conscious relationship with others. In fact,
our individual reality does not exist apart from our relationship
with others, for we are, in the final analysis, small units inter-
related with a creative Oneness that embraces eventually the
whole cosmos.

In this respect Kunkel is probably closer to John's Gospel than
Jung, for Kunkel believed that the Center not only was a reality within us but also a reality between us and another person
with whom we have come into relationship, and among us and
those who form a creative "We" group. Such a creative group
differs from the collective group Jung so justifiably feared, for in
the latter the awareness and conscience of the individual must
be surrendered to the group, whereas in the former the individual awareness and conscience of the individual is heightened
and nurtured by the larger group. Paradoxically, we become our
unique selves not only by discovering our inner identity but also
by discovering our communion with others, and ultimately with
all of nature and with God.

Verses 24–26: This is more of John's deeply mystical theology.
Consider the "glory" referred to in verse 24. The word "glory"
(*doxa*) signifies in this context, as it did in verse 1, the greatest
possible height of magnificence, the manifestation of a numinous
reality. And when Christ says that the Father loved him "before
the foundation of the world" it is no mere manner of speaking.
He is saying that before the world was created, before time even
began (since the Father is timeless) he, the Son, existed and was
loved by the Father. In verse 25 we are told again that the world
has not known the Father, for the Father is unknowable for the
reasons we have already given. He is known only by the Son, but
those who know the Son know (indirectly) the Father.

The Father is known in verse 26 "by name." "Name" in ancient times was no mere appellation but expressed the essence of the person or being who bore that name. Thus Christ has made known to the disciples something of the essence of the Father. The verse concludes with the final statement, "so that the love with which you loved me may be in them, and so that I may be in them." The word "love" here is *agapē*, a word that, as we have seen, expresses the most sublime of all forms of love. The implication is that at the Center of the Father is love. It asserts, in a way that totally escapes human comprehension, that at the very center of the deepest of reality there pours forth a love. It is not likely John could have received this revelation had he himself not experienced it.

~ 29 ~

CONFRONTATION
WITH THE SHADOW
Jesus Arrested
John 18:1–27

THE FIRST PART of John's chapter 18 is not only Christ's story but also Peter's story — and indirectly our story. In fact there are at least three elements to chapter 18: first, the historical element; second, the mystical element; and third, Peter's denial of the Lord.

As we have noted in the introduction, while John's Gospel is the most mystical of all the Gospels it also has the ring of history. Chapter 18 is a good example of this because it is filled with historical facts and details. There is the garden located just across the Kedron Valley where Christ was arrested and the fascinating detail that only John tells us: the name of the man, Malchus, whose ear the impetuous Peter cut off with his sword, a detail that adds little to the meaning of the story but that was evidently included by our evangelist because the man's name was known to him. Closely related to this historical detail is the mention in verse 26 that one of the people who asks Peter a difficult question about his relationship to Jesus is a relative of Malchus. What reason could there have been to include mention of this detail if it had not been an actual fact? Then after Jesus is arrested we are given details about Annas and Caiaphas. Annas, we learn, was the father-in-law of Caiaphas, and Caiaphas was the high priest that year and the same man who had said to Jesus' adversaries earlier in our narrative, "It is better for one man to die for the people."

The most fascinating historical detail, however, is the mention in verse 15 of the "other disciple" who accompanied Peter as they followed Jesus on the way to Jesus' trial. We are told that this other disciple was known to the high priest and that it was this disciple who was able to get Peter admitted to the inner chamber by speaking to the woman who was tending the door. Clearly this other disciple was familiar with the inner workings of Jerusalem and was known to important people. It seems almost certain that this other disciple mentioned in chapter 18 is the same person who is mentioned in John 20:2 as the disciple whom Jesus loved. As we saw in our introduction, one theory is that it is this disciple, who was not one of the twelve but was perhaps the owner of the upper room, who either wrote John's Gospel or was the basic source of information for it.

The mystical element in chapter 18 begins with the matter of the garden in which Jesus was arrested. No doubt it is a historical fact that the arrest took place in the garden across from the Kedron Valley, but gardens are also special places in religious lore. A garden is a contained place in which people have worked closely with nature to produce special results. We already noted in our study of the Greek word for healing that in the ancient mind the idea of service to God, of healing, and of the cultivation of a garden were all closely associated, the word *therapeuō* being used to denote all of these activities. In Greek mythology gardens were sacred to the goddess of love, Aphrodite. In Christian lore, gardens were places of meditation and conversion. St. Augustine, for instance, tells us that his conversion experience took place in a garden. In the symbolism of the unconscious, dreams of gardens occur when the dreamer has begun to undertake the work of the care of the soul, for the soul, like a garden, flourishes when it receives deliberate and loving care and attention. Given the sacredness of gardens, it is no surprise that we read in John 19:41 that Jesus was buried in a garden.

The most important mystical element in this chapter, however, is the use in verses 5, 6, and 8 of the Greek expression *egō eimi*. Earlier we discussed the grammatical meaning of the expression *egō eimi* and noted that it has three uses: first it is used with a predicate, just as it is in English where we say, for example, "I am a man" or "I am a doctor" or "I am a woman." This is the common usage of the expression and it has no special religious significance. A second usage occurs when the *egō eimi* has no expressed predicate but does have an implied predicate. An example of this we noted in our study of John 4:26. Here the woman of Samaria says that she knows that the Messiah will come and Jesus says, *egō eimi*, which, with the implied but not stated predicate, would mean "I am *he*" (the one whom you are expecting). But some scholars believe there is also a third use of the *egō eimi* in which it occurs without any predicate stated or implied. This usage is called the "absolute *egō eimi*" and would have to be translated simply: "I am."

John's Gospel makes frequent use of this expression, while it rarely occurs in the synoptic Gospels. For John, therefore, we can assume that the expression *egō eimi* has special importance. Only in one or two instances does John use the expression with a stated or clearly implied predicate. In all the other usages John uses the *egō eimi* standing alone. The question is whether or not in all of these instances there is a predicate that is implied or whether John is using the absolute *egō eimi*. The answer to this question is important, for if John is using the absolute *egō eimi*, then he is using it in a mystical way.

It would appear that many, if not most, modern scholars prefer to believe that the expression *egō eimi*, whenever it occurs in John's Gospel, always is used with an implied predicate. Philip Harner, for instance, observes that Rudolf Bultmann, who is probably the most influential biblical scholar of the modern era, regards all of the *egō eimi* expressions as variations of the *egō eimi* with a stated or implied predicate.[1] This interpretation, of course, removes from the expression the mystical or mythological element that Bultmann found so abhorrent and strenuously sought to delete from biblical interpretations generally.

There are a number of passages, however, where no predicate is stated and in which it is difficult to come up with an implied predicate. These passages include 8:24, 28, and 58, 13:19, and the three verses already cited in John 18.[2] The modern tendency to

---

1. See Philip Harner, *The "I Am" of the Fourth Gospel* (Philadelphia: Fortress Press, 1946), 58. I am indebted to Dr. Harner for many of the insights in this chapter into the meaning of the *egō eimi* in John's Gospel.

2. There is also John 9:9, in which the man who was born blind and had been healed, in reply to his neighbors about whether or not he was really the man who was born blind, says, "*egō eimi*." As Harner points out, this is the only occurrence in John of the expression *egō eimi* that is not from Jesus. It seems clearly to be an example of the usage of *egō eimi* with an implied predicate. The man who was healed means: "I am (he whom you once knew as the man who was blind)." See Harner, *The "I Am" of the Fourth Gospel*, 2.

translate the *egō eimi* in a conventional rather than a mystical way is clear when one reads modern translations of the *egō eimi* in John 18:5, 6, 8. In the Revised Standard Version, Phillips, the New English Bible, the New Jerusalem Bible, and the New Revised Standard Version the expression is translated "I am he." So, for instance, in John 18:5 when the officers come to arrest him, Jesus says to them, "Whom are you looking for?" When they answer, "Jesus the Nazarene," Jesus replies, *egō eimi.* In the above Bibles, this is translated, "I am he" (that is, the one for whom you are looking). Only the King James Version qualifies this translation by putting the "he" in italics (which means the word is supplied by the translator and not found in the original text). The reader of translations other than the King James Version, however, would not realize the deliberate ambiguity of the Greek as used by John, but would suppose that the Greek text says nothing more than the mundane, "Yes, I am the man you are looking for."

If the *egō eimi* of John 18 is the absolute *egō eimi*, then the consequences for biblical interpretation are considerable. For as we noted in chapter 9, the *egō eimi* standing alone is the equivalent of the great "I am" statement in Exodus 3:14. The people have asked Moses for the name of this new God whom they are to follow. When Moses asks what he is to tell the people God's name is, God says to him: "I am he who is" (NJB). God is therefore the great "I am." Much the same thing is reiterated in Isaiah 44:6, where Yahweh proclaims, "I am the first and I am the last" (NJB). The God who is "I am" is the God with no beginning and no end, the God for whom time is not a category, the One who is beyond time, the God in whom what we call past, present, and future are all included at once, the God whom Plato said "includes the beginning, and end, and middle of all things."[3] This is the God whom John calls the "Father," the Deity of all mystical contemplation, unnameable, and knowable only fragmentarily in times of mystic contemplation, revelation, or divine inspiration.

Could it be that when Jesus used this expression *egō eimi* he meant to equate himself with the "I am" of the God known to the Hebrews and to Plato? Or at least that he used the expression in a deliberately ambivalent way, letting the reader assume for him or herself whether he meant "I am he" or "I am"? That John did

---

3. As quoted by Justin Martyr in his *Hortatory Address to the Greeks* 25. All of this section by Justin is most illuminating with regard to the understanding of the biblical expression "I am."

intend the expression to be understood as equivalent to "I am" is strongly suggested by two facts. First, when the expression is used in John 8:58, as we noted before, the Jews angrily took up stones to throw at him. This shows that they recognized Jesus was using the expression in its absolute sense. In John 18:5 and 6 the same usage seems implied, for when the soldiers hear Jesus say *egō eimi* they promptly fall to the ground! There would be no need for them to fall to the ground if they assumed that Jesus was simply saying, "I am the one for whom you are looking," but if they recognized the numinosity of the statement "I am!" then they would certainly be struck with awe and fear.

The ancient writers noticed this point. So Gregory of Nyssa says with reference to John 8:5, "When those who were armed with swords and staves drew near to Him on the night before His passion, He caused them all to go backward by saying, 'I am He'" (with a capital *H* denoting the Deity). Similar statements were made by Augustine, who says that the fact the soldiers fell to the ground shows that there was "supreme power."[4]

From the psychological point of view, Jesus' use of the *egō eimi* is what the New Testament calls a *skandalon* (from which we get our word "scandalous"). A *skandalon* confronts and confounds the ego; it turns the ego's usual expectations and beliefs upside down; it is outrageous, a divine trick played on all our conventional expectations. Yet without such scandalous insights taking place the mysterious process we call individuation does not occur. As long as the ego remains caught in its conventionality, its worldview and its view of itself being wholly contained in the collective mentality, psychological development cannot take place. At its inception Christianity was a *skandalon,* an offense to the Jews and foolishness to the Greeks (1 Cor. 1:23; Gal. 5:11). Now Christianity as a religious movement is in danger of losing its vitality, as it becomes ensnared in the conventional, and as the powerful and numinous impact of the Gospels is emasculated by the rationalistic and materialistic mentality of our times.

The third element in John 18 is the story of Peter's denial. John tells the story with great skill. First he throws the "spotlight" on Jesus (vv. 12–14) and then shines it on Peter (vv. 16–18). Then it returns to Jesus (vv. 19–24), and then once again it falls

4. Gregory of Nyssa, *Against Eunomius* 2.11. Augustine, *On the Gospel of John* 31.8; cf. 28.2; 37.9.

on Peter (vv. 25–27). By means of this artistic literary device suspense builds up, and we, the readers, see all the more clearly the difference between Peter and Christ. Christ knows what he is doing. In full consciousness of his purpose and destiny he faces his adversaries with steadfast endurance and calm courage. Peter, in contrast, is thrown into his areas of darkness. Those parts of himself of which he is not aware catch up to him and throw him into confusion and fear. Out of this dark matrix comes his denial, which leads to his bitter anguish. On this cross of his own individuation, which forces him to become conscious of all the darkness within him, Peter is psychologically crucified.

From the psychological point of view, Peter's struggle is between his egocentric ego and his real Self. In his deepest heart he loves his Lord and is devoted to him. When in John 13:36 he said he would lay down his life for Jesus, he spoke from this deepest Center, and in fact, according to tradition, Peter did eventually die for his faith in Christ. But when he made his declaration of his love for Christ he failed to recognize his shadow. His old ego had not yet died. It lived on with its desire to protect itself and its fear to give up its life, and in this crisis of Jesus' arrest it reasserted itself. Peter thought his old ego had been changed, or, more likely, he had never become aware of the depths of his egocentricity, and so it continued to cast a dark shadow over him. As a result, Peter betrayed not only Jesus, but also his deepest Self, the Christ within.

We, of course, are like Peter. As Kunkel has pointed out in his book *Creation Continues*, the story of Jesus is also the story of the disciples, and in the disciples we see ourselves reflected back to us. Only when we are put to the test, as Peter was, is the most firmly entrenched part of our shadow brought to the light of consciousness. Given the painfulness of this experience, it is no wonder that in the Lord's Prayer we pray, "Do not put us to the test." What person in his or her right mind would ask for such a dark and dreadful experience? Yet in this experience lie the seeds of our salvation, for without confrontation with the shadow, consciousness cannot develop, nor can the Real Self emerge.

It was the maid at the door whose challenging question ("Aren't you another of that man's disciples?") evoked Peter's first denial. God used her as an unwitting instrument of the divine purpose, for her question began a process that eventually forced into consciousness everything in Peter that had hitherto languished in the darkness of psychological ignorance. When another person asks Peter a similar question ("Aren't you another of his disciples?") Peter denies his Lord a second time. Then a relative of the man whose ear Peter cut off asks Peter, "Didn't I see you in the garden with him?" And for the third time Peter denies the Lord. The number three, as we have seen earlier, is the number for the completion of a process. The third denial does it; Peter has "struck out" and he knows it. Shamed and bitterly disappointed in himself, Peter, according to Luke's Gospel, and we cannot doubt that it was so, goes outside and weeps bitterly.

We will remember from our previous study of Judas that Judas also experienced shame when he realized the despicable nature of his betrayal of Jesus. Judas's response was to commit suicide. Peter might have been tempted to commit suicide also, we do not know, but he did not do so. Peter was able to endure the shame as part of the cross of individuation to which he was affixed and from which he could not escape. Eventually Peter's pain cleansed his soul. The shame was burned away by his suffering, and the old egocentricity was melted down and dissolved by his tears.

Why Peter could survive his ordeal and be saved and Judas was destroyed can be explained by the contrast between their lives. Judas had indulged in thievery; he had taken money for his betrayal of Jesus. He had gone too far in the direction of evil and unconsciousness. There are certain "lines" in life, and if we cross over a line, then we have gone too far and may not be able to return. One can go only so far in the direction of evil before our evil, like a fatal disease, lays hold of us and destroys the soul. When this happens we can be helped only by the extraordinary grace of God, from which Judas had separated himself. But Peter has not yet gone over that line, and he is able to be saved by his own courageous facing of his darkness, his heartfelt tears, and God's love for him, which never wavered. There was always hope for Peter, and this helps us know that there is also hope for us.

~ 30 ~

"WHAT IS TRUTH?"
The Crucifixion and
the Dilemma of Pontius Pilate
John 18:28–19:42

THE END OF JOHN'S CHAPTER 18 and the first half of chapter 19 focus on Jesus' encounter with Pontius Pilate. We have seen that in John's Gospel the spotlight frequently shifts from Jesus to one of the other characters in the Gospel narrative. It has fallen on the disciples, on Jesus' adversaries, on the man born blind, on the woman of Samaria, on the man by the pool of Bethzatha, on Judas, and on Peter, and now it falls on Pontius Pilate. It is part of John's artistry to portray Jesus all the more clearly by showing the impact the Christ had on others. The human situation in which the message of the Gospel is relevant is thrown into sharp relief by John's portrayals of the human beings who encounter him. So important for John is the interaction of people with Christ that even now, at the climax of his story when the major focus is on the crucifixion, he nevertheless allows the spotlight first to shine on Pilate. In so doing John demonstrates once more that he is a keen psychologist, for he succeeds in showing us not only the psychology of a man caught in a dilemma but also what it means to be a person whose consciousness is limited to the collective thinking of this world. But John also uses the dialogue between Jesus and Pilate to show us, the readers, once more the living confrontation between the world of concrete historical reality on

313

the one hand, and the world of spiritual or archetypal reality on
the other hand.

John does not portray Pilate as a completely bad man. Rather,
he is a matter-of-fact man who has been appointed to enforce
Roman law and to keep the peace. We are given the impression
that overall Pilate tries to do this in a blunt but fair way. From
the beginning of the story of Jesus before Pilate we are given the
impression that Pilate saw Jesus as an innocent man and that he
tried to find a way to free him. He even tries to "coach" Jesus to
say the right words so he would have a reason for acquitting him.
Toward the end of the encounter, motivated by an increasing fear
of the strange powers of this man whom he is urged to condemn,
Pilate almost begs Jesus to deny the charges against him in such
a way that he can free him. The artistry with which John tells this
story leaves the reader with the realization that the person who
is *really* on trial is not Jesus but Pilate himself — and, indirectly,
all of us who now read the tale.

Pilate's dilemma reaches its climax in verses 19:1–11. Here Pilate is depicted as generally a fair person who has nothing against
Jesus. But for Pilate as with all the other characters in the Gospel
who meet him, a meeting with Jesus is also a confrontation with
himself, and Pilate is forced to face his own truth in this situation.
Shall he send to death a man whom he believes to be innocent
in order to satisfy the crowd and fulfill the technicalities of Roman law? He would gladly let Jesus go, but to do this he needs
something from Jesus that would give him a basis for refusing
to send him to his death. Seeking to find some excuse for not
sending Jesus to the cross, Pilate asks him, "Where do you come
from? . . . Are you refusing to speak to me?" But Jesus does not
answer, because he knows that where he comes from (the Father)
would not be intelligible to Pilate.

Note that in this passage we are told by John, "When Pilate
heard these things his fears increased." What fears? Fears for
Jesus? No, rather, fears for himself. Pilate has heard the crowd
say that this Jesus claimed to be the son of God. Now, Pilate may
have thought he did not believe in spiritual reality, and yet, somewhere in himself, he had enough of a sense of God to be frightened
at the implication that maybe this man whom he is called upon
to sentence *is* a son of God. Pilate has deep inside himself a small
voice that says, "Yes, this man in front of you just may be a son of
God. What then?" It looks like Jesus is on trial but really Pilate is

on trial, and in this trial he just might begin to become conscious. But this remains only a small voice in him, and Pilate has not yet learned the importance of listening to his inner voices. His "old self" wins, the old Pilate with whom he has associated himself for so many years that he thinks this is his only self, and in the end Pilate condemns Jesus to death.

In so doing did Pilate also condemn himself to death? There is, as we have seen, a spiritual death of the soul that is far worse than the death of the body. Has Pilate incurred this spiritual death? John does not tell us with certainty one way or the other. With Judas, it was clear that he had incurred his spiritual death; with Pilate the matter is different. So when Pilate says to Jesus, "Are you refusing to speak to me? Surely you know I have power to release you and I have power to crucify you?" Jesus replies, "You would have no power over me if it had not been given you from above; that is why the one who handed me over to you has the greater guilt." Pilate's guilt is there because he would not confront the spiritual truth of the situation and would not face his own inner conflict, but we are left with the feeling that his guilt is not so great that in the end his soul might still be saved.

The climax of Jesus' encounter with Pilate is reached over the issue of truth. Jesus says, "I came into the world for this: to bear witness to the truth." And Pilate answers, "Truth? What is that?" In what tone of voice did Pilate say, "Truth? What is that?" Did he speak with skepticism, with derision, or perhaps from despair? The fact that Pilate said what he did suggests that on some level of his being Pilate has perhaps for a long time been asking himself if there is any ultimate truth and has been unable to come up with an answer. Perhaps he has become infected with his own despair over ever finding an answer to this question. Most probably, he has kept this deeply important question that is very alive in his unconscious from becoming fully conscious. It is as though the question, "What *is* truth, Pilate?" has been asking itself in his own inner being, but Pilate has pushed it aside with his defensive veneer of skepticism or despair rather than plunging into a search for it. But now his spiritual lethargy catches up with him. No longer is the issue one of whether or not there is truth; rather it is an issue of what does one do when one is *confronted* with truth.

Pilate's problem is not that he lacks a certain sense of morality, but that his consciousness is entirely limited to the things of this world. For Pilate the world is as it appears to be to a person whose idea of reality is limited to the information brought by the physical senses and by the prevailing collective ideas of his time. Pilate belongs to "this world." "This world," however, as John has shown us so often, is not the real world but verges on being an illusion. On the other hand, Jesus speaks from and for the real world — the spiritual or archetypal world — a world perceivable and knowable to those with inner vision and enlarged consciousness. The contrast between the two is shown clearly when Jesus says to Pilate, "My kingdom is not of this world." But Pilate can only take him concretely and reply, "So you are a king then?"

The scene with Pilate comes to a swift conclusion in verses 19:12–16. Pilate is now anxious to free Jesus. He is motivated not only by a sense of justice but also by his own uneasiness over what it will mean for him if he condemns Jesus to death. The fact that this anxiety is not entirely conscious to him does not keep it from filling him with a feeling of ill-defined but disquieting dread. But the more conscious fear is his fear of the Roman authorities. Pilate is here for two reasons: to enforce justice and the law, and to keep the peace. If there is a showdown between these two goals, the Roman authorities will opt for keeping the peace. The crowd knows this. Their final way of persuading Pilate to send Jesus to the cross is not to argue Jesus' guilt, but to point out to Pilate the danger he is in if the Roman authorities over him should become involved. So they shout to him, "If you set him free you are no friend of Caesar's; anyone who makes himself king is denying Caesar." This does it for Pilate, for he wants no trouble from Caesar, and he recognizes that this hostile crowd will bring that trouble upon him if they have to. At this point Pilate may have begun to fear for his own life, and if it is a choice between Jesus' life and his, he knows what to do. So his final act is to send Jesus to his death. Yet, Pilate had his limit, for when we read in verse 21, after Christ is on the cross, that the chief priests said to Pilate he should not write "King of the Jews" on the placard over the cross but that "This man said, 'I am the King of the Jews,'" Pilate declared defiantly, "What I have written, I have written."

The narrative now shifts to the cross. We know that death by crucifixion was the common method of executing criminals in the Roman empire at that time. It was a prolonged death marked by pain and disgrace; death was ultimately produced by suffocation, if it had not already been brought about by loss of blood. The fact that Christ died the death of a common criminal, accentuated by the fact that he was crucified between two thieves, represented for the early Christians that Christ consented to live in a world of evil, that is, to take upon himself the whole reality with which we ordinary human beings must also live.

This common cross, which was originally a means of execution, became for the Christian world a mystical symbol. The early Christians saw the cross everywhere around them: in the birds in flight, in the sails of a ship, in the figure of a human being with arms outstretched, in constellations of heavenly bodies. For them the cross pointed to an ineffable reality manifested everywhere in the created order for those with the eyes to see it.

The cross is in Christian imagery a mandala — a fourfold, concentric shape. The arms of Christ outstretched on it symbolize the whole of creation being embraced by Christ while the place where the four arms of the cross join is the Center. There are, of course, many mandalas found in religions all over the world, suggesting, as Jung has shown, that everywhere life strives for wholeness and completion. There are also many other religions in which the symbol of the cross plays an important role, as Jung has also shown in his many writings.[1] But the Christian cross is a little different, because it is fixed into the ground. The reason that one of the extensions of the cross is longer than the others is because it is grounded. This fixedness in the ground of the Christian cross relates to its rootedness in human life. Mystically speaking, *we* are the ground in which the mystery of the cross is to be grounded. Then and then only does the mystery become realized. When a person goes through the *mystērion*, the mystical initiation into the hidden significance of the cross, then the cross has become real, that is, has been grounded in actual human existence. As Gregory of Nyssa has put it:

> It is the property of the Godhead to pervade all things, and to extend itself through the length and breadth of the substance of existence in every part...and that which is this existent, properly and primarily is the Divine Being...and which is the very thing we learn from the figure of the cross; it is divided into four parts, so that there are the projections, four in number, from the central point where the whole converges upon itself; because He Who at the hour

---

1. See, for instance, Jung's *Dream Analysis*, 340ff.

of His pre-arranged death was stretched upon it is He Who binds together all things into Himself, and by Himself brings to one harmonious agreement the diverse natures of actual existences.[2]

In verses 25–27 we have once again the prominence of the feminine in John's Gospel, and also of the number three, for by the cross John tells us are the three women: Mary of Magdala; Jesus' mother, whom we met in John 3; and Mary, wife of Clopas, who was Jesus' mother's sister. Where were the disciples? We must assume that they were afraid to be there, or perhaps they could not bear the pain of watching him die. The women alone were not afraid, or perhaps we should say that their love was strong enough that it overcame their fear, and strong enough so that they could endure the pain of watching the one they loved suffer. So in the end Christ died attended only by the three women and by the unknown disciple whom Jesus loved, whom we have reason to believe is also the narrator of the Gospel story, "John" himself.

In verses 28–30 we have more emphasis on the completion of a process: "Jesus, knowing everything had now been completed, ... said, 'It is accomplished.'" Once again we have the emphasis in John's Gospel on the work of God seeking to bring to a *telos* — an end state — a longstanding divine plan. But the work continues in the human soul, which must now, through the power of Christ with whom the soul has mystical participation, also be brought to the intended *telos*.

After Jesus' statement, "It is accomplished," he dies. The text says, "He gave up his spirit." It is interesting that the Gospel does not say, "He gave up his soul." Ordinarily the soul was regarded as the principle or entity that enlivened the body, and when death came the soul was believed to leave the body with the last breath, or, to put it the other way around, when the soul left the body, the body died. But here it is the spirit (*pneuma*) not the soul (*psychē*) that was said to leave Christ's body. As we noted earlier, the spirit in biblical thought is more generic than the soul. Souls are individual. Count the number of people in a room and you know how many souls are there. But spirit is more like a principle of life that moves among and within many people. Thus we are souls, but not spirits, although we can be souls enlivened by the spirit. For Christ at his death to let go his *spirit* suggests that now

---

2. *The Great Catechism* 32.

the spirit of Christ has become universal. With his death it moves throughout the world and can enliven the soul of any of us.

Christ having died, the soldiers come to take his body away. They intend to break the legs of Christ, which scholars tell us was a customary way of being sure that the person really had died or to hasten death if it was imminent but not quite final. In the case of Jesus, his legs are not broken for two reasons, one ordinary, one spiritual. The ordinary reason John gives was that the soldiers perceived that he was already dead. The spiritual reason for this is given us in verse 36: "All this happened to fulfil the words of Scripture, 'Not one bone of his will be broken'" (see Wisd. 2:18–20; Isa. 53).

If the soldiers did not break the legs of Christ because they realized he was already dead, it makes all the more enigmatic the fact that one of them pierced his side with a spear. Why the soldier did this when it was evident that Jesus was already dead is not clear. Perhaps one soldier was not entirely satisfied, or perhaps, like many a soldier before him and since, he simply wanted to use his weapon. From the point of view of our Gospel, however, the piercing of Christ's side with the spear is artistically and spiritually important, for out of his side poured forth both blood (which was to be expected) and water (which was not to be expected). Now, water symbolizes that which cleanses. So water from Christ's side symbolizes the living water, which was discussed in John 4 in the story of the woman by the well of Samaria, and which cleanses us from the primal sin of unconsciousness.

A new character now emerges in the Johannine Gospel: Joseph of Arimathea. We are told in Matthew 27:57 that Joseph of Arimathea was a rich man. He must have been in order to have had the tomb that he now made available for Christ's body, for only a wealthy person could afford such an elaborate burial sepulcher. His importance in the Jerusalem community is also suggested by the fact that he was able to get access to Pontius Pilate and receive his permission to take Jesus' body. Thus wealth, which is so often a great enemy to spiritual development, can, in the hands of those few people who have sufficient consciousness and integrity to use their wealth creatively, be a boon to humankind, enabling certain things to be accomplished that otherwise would not be accomplished. While Joseph of Arimathea was an important enough figure to be mentioned in all four of the Gospels, his role appears to be a relatively minor one: the provider of the tomb.

Later Christian tradition, however, made Joseph of Arimathea a central figure in the famous legend of the Holy Grail. According to this story, Joseph of Arimathea had come into possession of the cup used by Christ at the Last Supper, and it was this cup that he now used to catch some of the blood of Christ. Later it was said that Joseph took the chalice to Britain, where, because of the unbelief of the populace, it disappeared, to become the object of a sacred quest by many knights in later centuries. For our purposes we can see the symbolism of the cup in these terms: for a psychic or spiritual content to be retained by consciousness and not, as it were, poured out on the ground and lost, it is necessary to "catch" it. This can be done if we have a way of grasping the symbolic or spiritual meaning of something. This network of symbols and ideas that enables us to understand and hold on to matters of spiritual importance is like a cup that catches and retains a liquid. This is one reason why religious images and psychological ideas can be so important; they enable us to retain meanings that otherwise would be lost.

We are also told that Nicodemus came and assisted in the burial of Jesus. This is the same Nicodemus whom we met in John 3, who came by night and asked Jesus how a man might be born again. This is clear evidence that what Jesus said to him that night was like a seed that took root in him and grew, so that Nicodemus, like Joseph of Arimathea, became one of Jesus' secret disciples.

So Jesus is buried in the tomb. The death and burial of Jesus is part of the general symbolism of *mortificatio:* before anything new can be born, something first must die; out of the death of the old there emerges that which is new. It is a universal bit of symbolism that is found in alchemical lore and that C. G. Jung and Edward Edinger have shown to have profound psychological meaning for the process of individuation.[3] We also found it earlier in the twelfth chapter of John's Gospel in the image of the grain of wheat that must fall into the earth and die in order that it may then yield a rich harvest. So it was that Christ died and was buried, but three days later the resurrected Christ brought forth a tremendous outpouring of new consciousness and of God's grace.

---

3. See Edward F. Edinger, *Anatomy of the Psyche* (La Salle, Ill.: Open Court Publishing Co., 1985), chap. 6.

∼ 31 ∼

THE MYSTERY
OF CHRISTIAN SALVATION
The Cross and Resurrection
John 20

WE WILL BEGIN with a brief textual analysis of John 20, and then consider in more depth the meaning of the central Christian event and symbol: the death and resurrection of Christ.

In verse 1 we learn that the resurrection of Christ took place on the first day of the week. This is symbolic of the dawn of a new day in the life of humanity, for with the resurrection of Christ a new consciousness comes into the world. The first day of the week was also reckoned in the early church as the eighth day: the seven days of the old week plus the first day of the new week equaling eight. Eight thus became one of the sacred numbers among the Christians, symbolizing the resurrection of Christ and the wholeness of humanity.

As we have noted before, one indication of the importance of the feminine in John's Gospel is the fact that Mary of Magdala was the first person to arrive at the tomb of Christ as well as the first person to see the Risen Christ. Astonished to see that the tomb is empty she runs back to Peter and the other disciple (that is, the author of our Gospel) and tells them what she has seen. Peter and the other disciple run to the tomb, but the other disciple runs faster, reaches the tomb first, and sees the linen shrouds that had covered Jesus' body lying on the ground. Apparently acting out of deference to the prominence of Peter, he waits for Peter to come and allows him to enter the tomb first. After Peter entered, the other disciple also entered, saw the empty tomb, and believed. This may well be an autobiographical statement. The comment that hitherto the disciples had failed to understand the Scripture is, so scholars tell us, a reference to such Old Testament passages as Psalm 16:8–11 and Psalm 2:7.

The disciples return to their home, but Mary of Magdala stays by the tomb weeping, kept there by the strength of her love. She is the one, therefore, who sees the two angels sitting where Jesus' body had been, but she evidently supposed they were men.[1] When she turns from speaking with the angels she sees Jesus standing there and thinks that he is the gardener, but when Jesus calls to her, "Mary," she recognizes him. Mary exclaims in Hebrew, "Rabbuni," which scholars tell us was a Hebrew expression, a more solemn mode of address than "Rabbi" and often used with reference to God. This being so, Mary's exclamation can be understood, along with that of Peter (Matt. 16:16) as the first declaration of the Christian faith that Christ was indeed God. The Lord then forbids her to touch him: "Do not cling to me," for as we will see, there is something remarkable about the body of the risen Christ. Following his bidding, she now runs to tell the disciples that she has seen the risen Lord.

Jesus now makes his first wonderful and mysterious appearance to the disciples. The disciples are gathered together on the evening of that same first day of the week. John makes special mention of the fact that the doors to the room in which they were meeting were closed. Jesus then came and stood among them, passing right through the closed door! The disciples are filled with wonder and joy and receive from Jesus the Holy Spirit, that is, their personal empowerment by Christ. This empowerment of the disciples, however, does not rest on their earthly office, but on their personal consciousness. They have spiritual authority because they have become conscious; it is not an authority that can be conveyed through ecclesiastical channels or political position.

Thomas, however, was not with the others when Jesus came to them. The other ten disciples (Judas had defected) tell Thomas what has happened, but Thomas has to see the holes the nails made in Jesus' hands and put his fingers in the holes and put his

---

1. It often happened in the Bible that angels were at first mistaken for ordinary men. See Abraham's encounter with the angels in Genesis 18.

hand in the wound in his side.[2] Eight days later the disciples are again gathered in the room, and this time Thomas is with them. Once more John specifically states that the doors of the room were closed, yet Jesus is suddenly there with them. Because he wants Thomas to believe, he invites him to put his finger in the wounds in his hands and to feel the wound in his side. Thomas does so and believes. This gives Jesus a chance to utter the words that seem to end John's Gospel and that John clearly intends for our benefit:

> You believe because you can see me.
> Happy are those who have not seen and yet believe.

Before we leave the text of John 20, we need to ponder the meaning of Jesus' body after his resurrection. As we have seen, John made it quite clear that Jesus' body entered the room where the disciples were even though the doors were closed. Evidently, then, his body after the resurrection had unique qualities enabling him to pass through what we think of as solid matter. John also carefully explained that Thomas touched Jesus' body and felt his wounds, so Jesus' body after his resurrection was no phantom, but a tangible and somehow physical reality.

From the point of view of many people today, these physical appearances are products of John's imagination, and the stories of Jesus' body after his resurrection are not to be taken seriously, but are to be seen as illustrative of an unscientific magical or mythological thinking with which we must now dispense in order to arrive at a mature faith. From the point of view of the early church, however, they were evidences of the reality of the spiritual, or subtle, body. References to such a spiritual body occur in the epistles, and such a belief clearly belonged to John. The idea was that a soul without a body was a disembodied soul, like a ghost; a complete or true human being had to have a body, so the Christian belief was that after a person died that person lived in a spiritual body. It was spiritual, but not ethereal; it was real and tangible, but did not have the same qualities as our earthly physical body.

---

2. Thomas appears to be what is called in Jungian psychology a sensation type. According to Jung's typology, certain people are strongly oriented to outer, physical reality and facts, and so are called "sensation types." They are to be contrasted with intuitive types, who perceive what is real through an intuitive process. John himself was almost certainly an intuitive type. Thomas became an important apostle in the early church. Tradition says that he went to India and China and founded Christian communities in those distant countries. To this day there are Christian churches in India that claim their origin from him. For an imaginative account of the adventures of Thomas in India see the apocryphal work *Acts of the Holy Apostle Thomas*, in *The Ante-Nicene Fathers*, 8:535ff.

This way of thinking, which might appear fanciful to many of us today, may literally be true. For instance, accounts of persons who have been clinically dead but returned to this life to tell their stories (so-called out-of-the-body experiences, meaning out of the physical body) leave the distinct impression that in that time when they lived outside of their earthly body they lived in another kind of body, for they experienced themselves not as "pure spirits," but as embodied souls having form and extension.

The crucifixion and resurrection of Christ are the grand finale to the Gospel story. Everything that has come before in John's Gospel has been pointing to this great event. It is the *telos* — the goal or end — toward which the whole narrative has been moving. To understand the meaning of Christ's incarnation and his crucifixion and resurrection is to understand the heart of Christianity. It may be, however, that there is not one single meaning to the event of the cross, but many meanings that yet complete one whole. We will examine some of the many interpretations of the saving benefits of the cross of Christ and contrast the more literal interpretations with the more mystical interpretation that is suggested by John's Gospel.

The first interpretation of the cross is that it was the payment by Christ of a debt owed by humanity to God, so that we human beings could be freed from our guilt, Christ having paid the penalty for us, and therefore be saved from the punishment that awaits those who die with their sins unredeemed. This interpretation, which is known in theology as the penal-substitutionary theory, regards the cross as a necessary payment for our sins without which salvation would be impossible. This doctrine is widespread among fundamentalists and evangelical churches and is also prominent in Roman Catholic theology. It is at least given lip service by "mainline" Protestant churches. On the other hand, many people today find the reasoning behind this theory difficult to understand, and the implications of this theory are for some even repellant. I think it can be said that this theory of the atoning efficacy of the cross, in its extreme forms, turns away about as many people from Christianity as it attracts. We will now look more closely at the reasoning behind this idea of the atonement offered by Christ on the cross, at its strengths and weaknesses.

Perhaps more than any other religion, Christianity and its parent Judaism are concerned with sin, that is, with the propensity of human beings to commit evil acts and live evil lives. While the problem of human evil and sin was of concern to the ancient Greeks, it was not the overriding feature of Greek religion as a whole, and while it plays a role in Eastern religions, such as Buddhism and Hinduism, it is not the central religious problem for the religious systems of the East.

The early Jews and Christians saw that the human race was filled with evil. They were keenly conscious of the wrongdoing around them and aware of the depths of evil that human beings could display. At the same time they believed in a God who was just and who called for a just life from those men and women whom he had created. Thus there was a great disparity between the lives people led and the lives it was believed God wanted them to lead. This gap between the two was the occasion of guilt. It was also the occasion for God's possible rejection of those human sinners who had gone against his wishes and laws.

This tendency of human beings to lie, cheat, steal, murder, and practice self-deception was not believed to have originated from God; consequently as long as people practiced evil the relationship with God was broken. The ancient Jews were acutely conscious of this tendency toward sin as well as acutely conscious that the one and only God rejected human sin and those who practiced it.

The Jews and the Christians believed God had created the first human beings good. Their fall from their original goodness was called "original sin." The first human beings, it was argued, must have done something wrong to turn away from God as they had done. The story of Adam and Eve in the Garden of Eden, disobeying God's commandment not to eat of the fruit of the tree of the knowledge of good and evil, was regarded as the original sin that brought into the human race its well-nigh fatal attraction to evil. Because of this original sin a way had to be provided for human beings to re-establish their broken relationship with God and thereby be able to live their lives correctly and with divine favor.

Today many people may imagine they are too sophisticated to indulge in such mythological thinking, but the fact is that the story of the Fall in the Garden of Eden accurately describes in its own way the human condition. Clearly there is in the human race a marked tendency toward evil. When people give themselves over to evil, the relationship with the creative Center is broken (psychologically speaking), and a relationship with God is destroyed (theologically speaking). Thus the idea of human sin and a need for restoration to wholeness has a psychological validity to it, and even though the biblical language of the Fall may sound strange to modern ears it is not to be dismissed so quickly. I believe it was G. K. Chesterton who once quipped that the only doctrine of Christianity that is empirically verifiable is that of original sin, and that is the one people are always trying to get rid of.

So far the Jewish and Christian points of view agree, but a disagreement takes place on how the restitution with God can be made. For the ancient Hebrews, atonement (reunion with God) was effected by the right sacrifices. An example of right sacrifice is found in Exodus 92:5, in which the people of Israel are instructed by Moses and Aaron to sacrifice a young animal "without blemish, a male one year old, you may take it from either sheep or goats." This pure unblemished animal would be the animal that Yahweh would find an acceptable offering, and its sacrifice would restore a broken relationship between God and his people. With the coming of the Law, the relationship with God became more individual, for then it was not only the nation of Israel that was obliged to make restitution to God for sin, but also the individual had to do so as well.

Those Jews who became the first Christians, however, Paul being the most important example, found that this solution was not possible for them because none could be so perfect that they could keep the Law. Rather than feeling saved by the Law, sensitive souls like Paul felt all the more condemned because of it. Here the atonement of Christ came into the picture: the expiation of sin required the payment of a debt. Human beings were incapable of paying the debt by fulfilling the Law, so Christ paid the debt for humanity on the cross. He was the pure sacrificial lamb whose sacrifice God required, and through his blood[3] penitent human beings could once more establish a relationship with God.

As with the story of the Garden of Eden so with the story of the saving act of Christ on the cross, many people find it hard to take literally. The essence of this teaching, however, is that the grace of God saves us from a psychological moral condition from which we cannot extricate ourselves. The idea that Christ died on the

---

3. There is an ancient belief that the soul, which animated the body, resided in the blood, which carried it throughout the whole body. This may be part of the origin of the idea that Christ's blood saved, for it represented the life-essence of Christ given to us on our behalf to renew our lives.

cross for our sins is a powerful statement about the grace of God. It says that there operates in the spiritual realm a freely given power that restores us to ourselves and restores our relationship with God, a power that heals the soul, one that we do not have to earn by works but comes as a gift. Such a gift of the grace of God is visible to the psychotherapist, who, if she has not succumbed to inflation, knows full well how little she can do to heal the client, but also knows that there is a power — a grace — that comes from a Higher Power that can heal what no human being can heal.

On the other hand, if the Christian teaching is taken too rigidly and literally it can become destructive. If, for instance, there is said to be a certain condition for receiving the otherwise free grace of God, such as the public confession of sin and acceptance of Jesus according to a certain verbal formula, then the freedom and grace of healing and forgiveness may be curtailed. Driven to extremes, this approach would deny salvation to all persons who for whatever reasons do not verbally and literally, using a certain explicit verbal formula, accept Christ's saving action on the cross. Many people find it repellant that certain persons may be damned forever because they have not met these conditions for salvation and might refuse to worship a Deity who condemns young children to hell because they have not confessed the Lord or had the proper baptismal ceremony. When the saving grace of Christianity is turned by literalism into another form of the Law, then the God of grace is lost once again, and a new form of spiritual rigidity comes that is like the one it sought to cure.

It is interesting, therefore, to note that in John's Gospel there is scarcely a word that relates to this particular theory of the atonement. For John, the meaning of the cross is different. Certainly God's grace is there in John's Gospel, but there is no legalism in his Gospel, no "you must do this or pay the penalty." For John's Gospel breathes a different kind of spirit.

From the point of view of John's Gospel, the cross can best be understood as a *mystērion*, a "mystery" to be grasped and understood as one passes through a process of change and a renewal of consciousness that amounts to something like a transformation into the likeness of God. This is the deification that we have noted in many passages in John's Gospel. It is a mystical teaching that says that we are mysteriously transformed by a profound union with Christ. The Eucharist, in which we partake mystically of the body and blood of Christ, is seen as an example of the *mystērion* of the cross experienced sacramentally in ritual. To be transformed via a "mystery" is highly experiential. It does not revolve around the correct verbal profession of faith but occurs through the life-giving change of one's being and consciousness. It is far more difficult and subtle to describe than the legalistic theology we have discussed because essentially each individual passes through the transforming *mystērion* of Christ in his or her own way. The best way to describe this process of transformation is through a mystical or psychological language, and, as we have seen, this is the language of John's Gospel. But what does the cross have to do with such a *mystērion*? The answer is, a great deal.

The cross points to the central Christian mystery, which is like a developmental progression into the fullness of our humanity and toward a union with God, these two processes being inseparable. As we have seen, the cross in its fourfoldness is a mandala, a symbol for wholeness. Its four extensions embrace and unite above and below, earth and heaven, left and right, and thus make a unity out of diversity. Its rootedness in the ground means that this process of transformation is not an ethereal idea but is a process rooted in the reality of the lives of actual human beings. Christ nailed to the cross shows us the way we must go: nailed to our own process of creative change, which is something from which we cannot escape and from which we must not try to escape. Indeed, so vital is the image of the cross as a symbol of our own individuation that Jesus declared, "Anyone who does not take his cross and follow in my footsteps is not worthy of me. Anyone who finds his life will lose it; anyone who loses his life for my sake will find it" (Matt. 10:38; cf. Mark 8:34; Luke 9:23).

The pain and torture of the crucifixion express the difficulty and painfulness of the process of psychological and spiritual transformation. The need to endure or carry the cross expresses the reality that this is a process no one can complete for us: each one must carry his or her own psychological burden, the burden of his or her own suffering. No other person, no institution, no religious "system of salvation" can do this for us; we must carry our own process and shoulder our own psychological burden of becoming conscious.

It is also of the nature of the cross that love must suffer. Christ suffered because he loved. The women at the foot of the cross suffered because they loved. This consciousness and growth for which we strive is not achieved intellectually but passionately.

It is not brought about simply by learning or psychologizing, but through loving as well, for it is love that is both beautiful and painful, that opens us up to a larger consciousness, and that finally merges with divine love to ennoble the soul.

Regarding the resurrection, it must be noted that the Greek word for resurrection, *anastasis*, is to be understood not only in the narrower sense of a restoration from death to life, but also in the broader sense of a general spiritual awakening and renewal of life in all of its dimensions. If psychologically the death of Christ on the cross, which we are bidden to emulate by carrying our own cross, is the death of our old egocentric personality, then the resurrection is the emergence in us of a new consciousness, rooted in the creative Center within us. Part of the great Christian *mystērion* is about this mystery of deep inner transformation in which the old person dies and the new person lives through participation in a personality much larger than the ego.

The cross can thus be understood as a symbol for this process of transformation, but it is more than a symbol; it is also that process itself. It is not only a historical event that took place on that first Good Friday but is a continual event going on all the time in the lives of human beings in the here and now whenever their consciousness is transformed as they bear their own process of suffering, and thus find the deeper Center within themselves.

It would be a mistake, however, to identify the crucifixion and resurrection with a purely psychological process, for the crucifixion and resurrection are also a cosmic process. As far as John's Gospel is concerned, the Gospel concludes with the statement with which it began. In John 1:14 we read of the coming of Christ: "All that came to be had life in him and that life was the light of men, a light that shines in the dark, *a light that darkness could not overpower*" (John 1:4–5; emphasis mine). On the cross the powers of darkness did all they could to destroy the light of God, but the light rose again indestructible. This I take to be a central message of John's Gospel and a fundamental meaning to Christianity, which makes it a most hopeful faith, not because all will be well in this world, but because nothing can separate us from the love and light of God. Evil, which did all it could to destroy the light of Christ on the cross, could not destroy that Light, for the power of the Light rose again.

The powers of evil are represented in the New Testament as the "rulers" (*archontes*), "powers" (*dynameis*), and "authorities" (*exousiai*) of this world, which we discussed briefly in chapter 17. As Gerd Theissen and Walter Wink have pointed out in their excellent works, Christian thinkers from the beginning recognized that not all the evil in the world could be laid at the door of the first sin of Adam and Eve in the Garden of Eden. While this "original sin" may have left humanity open to the influence of evil, it did not account for all of its existence in the world. Instead, there were invisible spiritual powers at work in the world so strong that unaided human efforts were not enough to overcome them. The most ancient view of the cross is that on the cross Christ won a cosmic victory over these powers. They did their worst but could not destroy him because he rose again. "The light shines in the darkness and the darkness has not overcome it" (John 1:5). Neither can the powers of evil destroy any individual soul that unites itself with the power of Christ and the cross via that process of deification that we have described.

At the very least, this Christian statement of the meaning of the cross is the most hopeful statement in the spiritual lore of humankind. It makes of Christianity an ultimately hopeful religious faith: no matter how great the darkness, no matter how powerful are the forces of senseless destruction, there is an essential divinity at the core of life that no power on heaven or earth can destroy.

On the cross hung the most conscious person the world had ever known. In him the mind of God was exemplified and revealed. When the consciousness of a single person is increased, it affects the general consciousness of humanity. Mystically and psychologically Christ's sacrifice was his death on the cross in order that the new consciousness might be disseminated throughout the world and the powers of Light over spiritual darkness be manifested and made complete. This would be the mystical meaning of Christ's statement in John 12:24, "I tell you most solemnly, unless a grain of wheat falls on the ground and dies, it remains only a single grain; but if it dies, it yields a rich harvest." By dying on the cross the grain of consciousness in Christ was sown in the psyche of humankind. With this a new order began and a new development became possible for human life everywhere.

A rough analogy might be made with the idea of a "sacrifice" in the game of baseball. If there is a runner on first base, and the batter bunts the ball, the batter is easily thrown out at first base but the runner on first advances to second base, from which position he can more readily score a run. This play is known as a "sacrifice" because the batter deliberately hits the ball in such a way that he will very likely be thrown out but his teammate will advance; in such a way did Christ's death on the cross advance the consciousness of humanity.

All of this is more than theological speculation. There is evidence that is mounting that if a single member of a species achieves a new awareness or adaptation, this new awareness becomes readily available to other members of the species even though they have no direct contact with the first individual to achieve it. Known as the "M" effect, this remarkable fact has been shown to exist on many levels of life, ranging from the microscopic to the human.[4] In some such way the consciousness of Christ may have spread throughout the spiritual world, thus advancing the possibility of our own growth in consciousness and increased relationship with God.

---

4. See Michael Talbot, *Beyond the Quantum* (New York: Bantam Books, 1987).

~ 32 ~

JESUS' FINAL APPEARANCE
Wait While I Am Coming
John 21

JOHN 21 IS A MYSTERIOUS CHAPTER; we wonder why it is here at all for it looks like the final verses of chapter 20 were a definite conclusion to John's Gospel. Scholars therefore understandably conclude that chapter 21 is a later addition to the original Gospel, an appendix added probably by someone other than John himself. A common explanation for this addition is that a question arose in the early church concerning the authority of Peter and that this chapter was added to reinforce Peter's authority in matters of church discipline and doctrine. This explanation no doubt has merit, but it fails to take into account the subtle but highly significant symbolism in the story. It is this symbolic content — which sounds typically Johannine — that we will now consider.

John begins by telling about the disciples' fishing expedition. He is surprisingly explicit about this. Five of the disciples are named and two more are mentioned, one of whom turns out to be the disciple whom Jesus loved (v. 7). The total number of the disciples is thus seven. The specific naming of the disciples has the ring of historicity about it. So does the fact that Peter is said to have been almost naked (v. 7). As we have come to expect in reading John's Gospel, while his Gospel is the most symbolic and mystical of all the Gospels it is also filled with explicit historical details. The inclusion of these details suggests that chapter 21 may be written by the same author as the rest of the Gospel, though it might have been a later addition. It is also worth noting that it was this disciple whom Jesus loved who was the first in this story to recognize Jesus.

Regarding the story's symbolic content we can note first that we have here again the mysterious number three, which reappears in the conversation between Jesus and Peter (vv. 15–17) in which Jesus asks Peter a question three times. As we have seen, the number three in the Bible is usually the number for the completion of a dynamic process.[1]

Second is the fact that the story centers around fish. The fish has been called the New Testament animal because it appears so frequently in the Gospels, and in fact Christ was called the fish in the early church. Fish appear frequently in our dreams, where they usually symbolize contents of the unconscious that are, like fish, swimming around as it were in the depths of the psyche but which can be "caught" and lifted up to consciousness where they may be "eaten," or integrated. Fish, however, must be fished for. So the fisherman must fish in the depths of the lake for the fish, just as the person who follows his or her dreams must fish for them in the unconscious. So the symbol of fishing in John 21 aptly symbolizes the bringing up of unconscious spiritual or psychological contents into consciousness.

In this connection there is an interesting Greek word, *kalchainō*, which means two things: (1) to search for the purple-fish, (2) to search in the depths of one's mind, or to ponder deeply. The story behind this curious word is that there existed in ancient Greece a mollusk from which the Greeks made a special purple dye. Divers would descend to the bottom of the ocean floor in search of this shellfish, which was highly prized. This became a metaphorical expression for plumbing the depths of one's own mind. Thus searching for the fish, exploring the depths of the sea, finding unconscious contents in oneself, and exploring the inner mind are all related images and ideas.

What is more, when the disciples reach the shore they find Jesus cooking a fish. Now, as we saw in the story of the feeding of the multitude, in the language of the unconscious when something is to be eaten it means that there is an unconscious content that is ready to be assimilated. This, of course, is part of the eucharistic symbolism that we have noted before: by eating of the bread and wine we symbolically integrate into ourselves the

---

1. See the *Classic Greek Dictionary* (New York: Hinds and Noble Publishers, 1901), 346.

essence of Christ. Perhaps the fish in this story, which is almost ready to eat, is the meaning of Christ himself, which is now ready to be assimilated into human consciousness.

However, we do not have here just an indiscriminate number of fish; to the contrary, there are exactly 153 fish. We are back again to our number symbolism. The number seven, according to St. Augustine, signified the Holy Spirit, as well as the consummation of time, "For there is a revolution of all time in seven days." He also said of the number 153 that "This is a great mystery in the great Gospel of John."[2] Following an elaborate numerical process, Augustine reached the conclusion that the 153 mystically signified the abundant number of people who would be saved. We could say that looked at outwardly the number may signify the abundant salvation of God, and inwardly it may signify the integration of unconscious contents into the conscious personality. What must be recognized is that the number 153 is no accident, as Augustine pointed out; it appears in the Gospel story for a purpose.

The story now shifts to the conversation between Jesus and Peter (vv. 15–20). Three times Jesus asks Peter if he loves him, and three times Peter claims that he does. The repetition of the questions and answers is explained partly by the need for a threefold repetition in order to make something final. However, there is also a play on words in the Greek. When Jesus asks Peter if he loves him, the first two times he uses the Greek word *agapaō;* the third time he uses the word *phileō. Agapē* is the word used for the love of friendship. Does John mean to use these words interchangeably, or does he use *agapaō* first and then *phileō* to make a point? The point might be that Peter does not meet Jesus on the level of his question. For when Jesus asks Peter if he loves him — *agapaō* — Peter replies with the lesser word — *phileō.*

We now come to the mysterious "second" conclusion to John's Gospel, the discussion between Peter and Jesus about the unknown disciple (John 21:19–23).[3] The discussion in which we will now engage about this passage may seem to the reader to become excessively technical, but the person who perseveres in following

---

2. *On the Gospel of St. John,* Tractate 122.

3. The first, of course, being John 20:30–31. I am greatly indebted to Allan Anderson, professor emeritus of philosophy and religion at San Diego State University, for the insights that follow. Professor Anderson first pointed out to me the mistranslation of John 21:22, 23 and suggested the major points of the argument that follows. However, if there are any errors, they are entirely my responsibility.

the argument may discover a valuable insight into early Christian thinking. The question is, why are Jesus and Peter discussing the future of the unknown disciple? A prevailing belief among scholars goes like this: In Mark 9:1 Jesus says to his disciples, "I tell you solemnly, there are some standing here who will not taste death before they see the kingdom of God come with power." That is, they would not die before the Second Advent of Christ. The point of view we are now considering says that the disciple whom Jesus especially had in mind in Mark 9:1 was John the son of Zebedee (one of the twelve). It is thought by many scholars that the writer of John 21 is a redactor and not the author of the first twenty chapters of the Gospel and that this man has identified John the son of Zebedee with the disciple whom Jesus loved. When this disciple did die after all, it seemed to nullify Jesus' words in John 9:1: "Truly I say to you there are some standing here who will not taste death before they see the kingdom of God come with power" (RSV). The point of the passage we are now considering is that Jesus did not say this disciple would never die by way of an absolute promise; the promise Jesus made in 9:1 was conditional, not absolute, and depended on the continuing will of Christ. This emerges in verse 20, in which the redactor points out, "Yet Jesus had not said to Peter, 'He will not die,' but, 'if I want him to stay behind till I come.' "

An alternative explanation for this concluding passage is that Jesus speaks differently about the disciple whom he loved than he does about Peter because the two disciples have a different way of following their Lord. The important verses are 22 and 23, which are translated in the Jerusalem Bible, "If I want him to stay behind *till I come,* what does it matter to you?" I have emphasized "till I come" because this is the key expression. "Till I come" translates the Greek *heōs erchomai.* The translation "till I come" is found in virtually all the modern translations. However, the Greek expression does not mean "till I come" but "while I am coming." The technical aspects are as follows: In Greek grammatical construction the conjunction *heōs* means "until" when it is combined with the particle *an* and with the verb in the subjunctive. When *eōs* occurs without *an* and with the verb in the indicative it is translated "while."[4] The grammatical distinction would appear to be quite

---

4. See H. W. Smyth, *Greek Grammar* (Cambridge, Mass.: Harvard University Press, 1920), paragraphs 2422, 2423, 2425, 2426. According to Smyth, *heōs* without *an* and with

clear, and in fact, in John 9:4, which has a construction similar to that of 21:22 (*heōs* without *an* and with the indicative) it is translated "while it is still day." It would seem, then, that the Greek does not have Jesus say, "If I want him to stay behind till I come" but "If I want him to stay behind *while I am coming.*"

Given the fact that the proper translation for 21:22, 23 (or at the very least the preferred translation) would be "while I am coming," it is surprising that we do not find it translated that way. The reason may be that "while I am coming" implies a mystical view of the Second Coming of Christ. Christ is not coming at some definite point in the future but *is* coming all the time. It also implies a different mode of discipleship for the beloved disciple than for Peter. Peter is the activist. He is the one who is told to watch over and feed the flock of Christ. The beloved disciple is the one who is simply to wait while Christ is coming. He is to abide (*menō*), doing "nothing" but being in a highly developed state of consciousness while Christ returns in a mystical way by returning to the hearts and souls of people.

There are some people who change the world by their correctly motivated activity. And there are some people who change the world by achieving a certain quality of consciousness and holding to it. As Allan Anderson once put it, "such a person does nothing, yet everything gets done."[5] In our Western world, which is activistically oriented, all change is thought to come from direct actions even if those who act are themselves egocentric. But in more spiritual, mystical, or psychological traditions, effective changes are made via the unconscious, that is, the superior consciousness of one person invisibly affects and changes others even though no direct action is taken. This appears to be John's way.

Then comes the final stroke in John 21:25: "There were many other things which Jesus did; if all were written down, the world itself, I suppose, would not hold all the books that would have to be written." Is this a mere flourish on John's part with which to end his Gospel? Gregory of Nyssa thought not. This ending verse is there, he argued, because in fact the Divine Mind is so vast that our world and our worldly consciousness could not possibly hold the knowledge of it. The Logos so far surpasses human understanding that if the whole world as we know it was

---

the indicative may mean "until" only with reference to a definite present or past action (John 21:22 involves a future action).

5. From a private conversation.

filled with books about God's mind, there would still be an infinity of meaning not yet touched upon. With Gregory's words we will conclude our commentary:

> Embrace with your mind the whole world, and when you have come to the knowledge of supramundane (divine) nature, learn that these are the true works of Him Who sojourned for thee in the flesh, which "if each were written" ... the world itself could not contain the fulness of Christ's teaching about the world itself. For since God hath made all things in wisdom, and to His wisdom there is no limit ... the world, that is bounded by limits of its own, cannot contain within itself the account of infinite wisdom.[6]

---

6. *Answer to Eunomius's Second Book.*

GLOSSARY OF GREEK TERMS

Note: Each Greek word is followed by the approximate English meaning. Numbers refer to the page on which each Greek word is first explained.

agapē: love, 103
agennētos: uncreated, 271
agnoēma: a sin of ignorance, 196
aiteō: to pray, ask, 301
akatalēpton: incomprehensible, 271
aletheia: truth, 105
angelos: messenger, angel, 189
anōthen: from above, 79, 81
anthrōpos: a man, human being, 102
archōn: ruler, 188

baptein: to dip, baptize, 39
baros: a weight or pressure, 205
blepō: to see, 28

diabolos: adversary, devil, 195
doxa: glory, 304
dynameis: powers, 189

egō eimi: I am, 117
ek: out from, 88
entolē: commandment, 269
erōtaō: to pray, 301
exousia: authority, 188
extasis: ecstasy, 284

gnōsis, ginōskō: knowledge, to know, 16

hagios: holy, set apart, 161
hamartanō: to miss the mark, to sin, 134–35
helkō: to draw, drag, 158

heōs: while, until, 335
hodos: the way, road, 268
horaō: to see, 28
hybris: wanton arrogance, 150
hygiēs: sound, health, 134
hypakouō: to obey, 62
hypomonē: steadfast endurance, 255
hypotassō: to be subordinate to, 62

iaomai: to cure, 126

kainos: new (in quality), 88
kalchainō: to search in the depths of one's mind, 333
kephalē: head, 62
kleptēs: thief, 209
kosmos: world, 92
krisis: judgment, 181
kryptos: secret, hidden, 81

lēstēs: brigand, 209
logos: word, 18
louō: to wash (whole body), 39, 204

menō: to abide, 336
moira: lot, portion, 205
monē: dwelling place, 266
mystērion: mystery, 33

niptō: to wash (a part of the body), 204

oida: to see, know, 83
olothreutēs: the destroyer, 282n

INDEX

Above and below, 77
Active imagination, John's use of, 9
Adam and Eve, and origin of evil, 237
Advocate. *See* Holy Spirit; Spirit
Aeschylus, 269
  illness and health, 202
  on suffering, 225
Alchemy, 41
American Indian lore
  Above and Below in, 79
  See also: Black Elk
Anderson, Allan, 334n, 336
Anger, 85
Animals
  Jesus and, 244
  role in dreams, 244
Archetypal world, 188
  Jung on, 233–34
  according to Theissen, 188
  and threefold manifestation, 296
Archetypes
  definition, 98
  of the Greek Gods, 69
Articles (Greek grammar), 85, 101,
  115, 156, 222, 302
  importance of, 85
Asklepius, 94, 110
Atē (Greek goddess of folly), 230, 302
Athanasius, 217
Atonement, theories of, 324–25
Augustine
  enigmas, 155
  on faith, 129
  on foot symbolism, 256–57
  on the light that cannot be
    overcome, 102
  on number symbolism, 334

  on symbolism, 2n
  on women, 66
Author of Fourth Gospel. *See* Fourth
  Gospel (author of)

Baptism, 39
  See also: John the Baptist; Water
Berdyayev, Nicholas, 285
Black Elk, 81, 257
  See also: American Indian lore
Blood of Christ, 326
Body of Christ
  and the center within, 17
  psychological meaning of, 148–49
  and the resurrection body, 323
  symbolic meaning of the eating of,
    159
Borsch, Frederick H., 97–98
Bread, symbolism of, 153
Bristow, John, 60, 168–69
Brown, Raymond E., 63

Caves
  birthplace of Christ, 25, 80
  as places of secret teachings, 80
  symbolic meaning of, 225
Center, 16, 127, 134, 148, 205, 261, 285
  Christ as, 219
  and creativity, ego, and freedom,
    82, 105
  Eucharist as a service of, 158
  in healing, illness, and sin, 132–33
  individual morality and, 161
  Kunkel on creativity of, 137
  love from, 260
  projection of, 211, 299
  See also: Ego; Kunkel, Fritz; Self

Evil (*continued*)
  and the soul, 221
  and spirit of truth, 289
  and the Trinity, 296
  and will, 158
  See also: Atē; Cross; Dark side of
    God; Devil; Principalities and
    powers; Shadow

Faith
  Clement of Alexandria on, 123
  Jung on, 123
  and knowledge and light, 184,
    264
  and the soul, 123
  and transference, 123
Fate, Greek idea of, 205
Father, God as; Father/Son
    relationship, 48
  and the "I am" (*egō eimi*), 209
  and oneness, 214
  psychological meaning of, 138
  and the transcendent Deity, 183–84,
    270, 300, 304
  See also: Son; Trinity
Feet, symbolism of, 256
Femininity, 44–70
  Adam and Eve and, 66
  in American Indian lore, 66
  and cave symbolism, 226
  Christ on, 284
  at the Cross and Resurrection, 318
  and Dionysus, 384
  and early church, 68
  in God, 22
  Greek attitude toward, 59
  and individuation, 69
  Jesus' attitude toward, 46, 168–69
  and Jesus and women in adultery,
    168–69
  and metaphors for God in the Bible,
    47
  status of during Jesus' time, 52
  in story of Mary and Martha, 54
  symbolized as water (yin), 50
  in the Trinity, 295
  See also: Wisdom (Sophia); Women

Fish
  Christ symbolized by, 25
  importance of in New Testament,
    332
Flesh, 249, 251–52
  five meanings of, 14, 160
  to spirit transformation, 87
Food
  in John's Gospel, 116, 153, 162–63
  See also: Eating; Eucharist; Fish
Foot. *See:* Feet
Four
  the Cross and, 328
  Irenaeus on, 297
  symbolic meaning of, 295
  See also: Number symbolism; Three
Four functions, the
  and Jung, 267
  and Thomas, 267
Fourth Gospel (author of), 6–7, 29, 177
  as disciple Jesus loved, 332, 334–35
  as observer of Jesus' trial, 307
Freedom
  Christ and, 170
  meaning of, 170
  and truth, 193
  See also: Center; Choice; Ego; Love

Gardening, 307
  soul and, 282
Gate, symbolism of, 211
Gnosticism, 112
  definition, 16n
  and Docetism, 225n
  and femininity, 59
  and John's Gospel, 6
  negative attitude of, 81
God, 197, 269–70
  dark side of, 282
  in John's Gospel, 327
  and psychotherapy, 327
  and sexual connotations, 45
  triune nature of, 292
  See also: Dark side of God; Evil;
    Father; Holy Spirit; Knowledge;
    Son; Soul; Spirit; Trinity
Gordimer, Nadine, 35

Irenaeus
  on death for lack of spirit, 222
  on deification, 216
  on the Four Gospels, 297
  on Gnostic devaluation of faith, 122

Jesus
  and femininity, 46
  and illness, 200
  See also: Center; Christ; Femininity;
    Self; Son of Man/God
Jews
  attitudes toward, 115
  understood symbolically, 92
  See also: Pharisees
John. *See:* Fourth Gospel (author of)
John the Baptist, in Fourth Gospel, 37
Johnson, Robert, 301
Jones, The Very Reverend Alan, 33
Joseph of Arimathea, and the Holy
    Grail, 319
Joy
  as product of individuation, 45
  and Sophia, 22
Judas, 228–42, 315
  contrasted with Peter, 310
  and Jesus, 162
  and problem of evil, 229
Judgment, 207, 221, 251
  Greek word for, 181
  See also: Choice; Individuation
Jung, Carl
  on animals, 244
  on Christ as God of freedom, 170
  and evil, 146, 193
  and faith, 123
  on the four functions, 267
  on making the darkness conscious,
    102
  on nature and meaning of oneness,
    140
  on the numinous, 151
  on the problem of evil, 234, 275
  on science seeking the truth, 34, 186
  on the Self/Center, 82

Kazantzakis, Nikos, 267
Kirsch, James, on Jesus, 99

Knowledge of God, 270, 272–73
  and dowry soul, 24
  Greek word for, 16
  John's Gospel and, 24, 112
  and meaning of sin, 24
  and truth, 193, 264
  See also: Faith; Father; Gnosticism;
    Knowledge; Sin
Kunkel, Fritz, 167, 218
  on the Center and Christ, 82, 218
  and Christian theology, 40
  on the creative ego response, 169
  on creativity of the Center, 169
  on evil as the devil, 187
  on evolution consciousness, 31–32
  on four egocentric types, 133, 260
  on the Gospels, 246
  on idols of people, 211, 291
  on Jesus leaving disciples, 291
  on the psychology of love, 260
  See also: Center; Ego; Egocentricity

L'Heureux, Conrad, and illness in the
    Old Testament, 201n
Life after death, 220
  See also: Life/eternal life;
    Resurrection
Life/eternal life
  in the Fourth Gospel, 137
  as a goal, 157
  and the Kingdom of God, 164
  and living bread and the soul, 164
  as "living water," 108
  as a new dimension of reality, 249
  See also: Life after death
Light/darkness, 13, 91, 100, 180, 187
  Christ and, 252
  and the conscious, 102
  Jung on, 101
  and Resurrection, 101, 328
  See also: Truth
Literal interpretation of the Scripture
  Christian salvation and, 327
  narrowness of, 145, 166, 177
  Samaritan woman and, 108
  symbolic language of, 1
  See also: Symbols/symbolic
    language